THE CLASSICAL DOCTRINE OF CIVIL WAR IN INTERNATIONAL LAW

In the classical law of nations there was a doctrine of civil war. This book sets out to recover the forgotten legal tradition that shaped the modern world from 1575 to 1975. The result is an autonomous reassessment of four hundred years of the law of insurgencies and revolutions, both in state practice and in legal scholarship. Its journey through centuries of rebellion and the rule of law touches some of the most basic questions of international law across ages. What does it mean to stand among the nations of the world? Who should be welcomed among the subjects of international law, who should not, and who should decide? Its findings not only help make the classical doctrine understandable again, but also offer potential new insights for present-day lawyers about the origins, aspirations, and vulnerabilities of the legal tradition with which they work today.

VILLE KARI is an Assistant Professor of the History of International Law at Tilburg University, as well as an affiliated research fellow at the Erik Castrén Institute of International Law and Human Rights. He is a Doctor of laws, a trained judge, and a Rapporteur for the Antarctic Treaty Consultative Meeting. He has held visiting fellowships at the University of Melbourne, Paris 1 Panthéon-Sorbonne, Sciences Po Paris, and the University of Cambridge.

CAMBRIDGE STUDIES IN INTERNATIONAL AND COMPARATIVE LAW: 196

Established in 1946, this series produces high quality, reflective and innovative scholarship in the field of public international law. It publishes works on international law that are of a theoretical, historical, cross-disciplinary or doctrinal nature. The series also welcomes books providing insights from private international law, comparative law and transnational studies which inform international legal thought and practice more generally.

The series seeks to publish views from diverse legal traditions and perspectives, and of any geographical origin. In this respect it invites studies offering regional perspectives on core *problématiques* of international law, and in the same vein, it appreciates contrasts and debates between diverging approaches. Accordingly, books offering new or less orthodox perspectives are very much welcome. Works of a generalist character are greatly valued and the series is also open to studies on specific areas, institutions or problems. Translations of the most outstanding works published in other languages are also considered.

After seventy years, Cambridge Studies in International and Comparative Law sets the standard for international legal scholarship and will continue to define the discipline as it evolves in the years to come.

Series Editors

A list of books in the series can be found at the end of this volume.

THE CLASSICAL DOCTRINE OF CIVIL WAR IN INTERNATIONAL LAW

VILLE KARI
Tilburg University

CAMBRIDGE
UNIVERSITY PRESS

CAMBRIDGE
UNIVERSITY PRESS

Shaftesbury Road, Cambridge CB2 8EA, United Kingdom

One Liberty Plaza, 20th Floor, New York, NY 10006, USA

477 Williamstown Road, Port Melbourne, VIC 3207, Australia

314–321, 3rd Floor, Plot 3, Splendor Forum, Jasola District Centre, New Delhi – 110025, India

Cambridge University Press is part of Cambridge University Press & Assessment, a department of the University of Cambridge.

We share the University's mission to contribute to society through the pursuit of education, learning and research at the highest international levels of excellence.

www.cambridge.org
Information on this title: www.cambridge.org/9781009218689

DOI: 10.1017/9781009218665

When citing this work, please include a reference to the DOI 10.1017/9781009218665

First published 2026

Cover image: La Rochelle harbour *(Bassin des Chalutiers)*, historic port in western France with Hermione Fregate / Sebastien Gaborit / Collection: Moment / Getty Images

A catalogue record for this publication is available from the British Library

A Cataloging-in-Publication data record for this book is available from the Library of Congress

ISBN 978-1-009-21868-9 Hardback

To Susanna Kari, Tove Kari, and Saima Kari.

To Susanna Kan, Lyle Kan, and Sanna Kan

CONTENTS

ACKNOWLEDGEMENTS

This book originated as a doctoral thesis for the University of Helsinki in 2020. Although the text now at hand has been thoroughly rewritten and shortened, the research at its core is still the same, as are its key findings. I therefore take this opportunity to renew my thanks to all the scholars and institutions whom I acknowledged in some detail in that original incarnation of this book. Thank you all once again, with my deepest gratitude.

This work has been made possible by Tilburg University and its Department of Public Law and Governance, which has provided me with an academic home and the privilege of teaching the history and theory of international law to a new generation of lawyers. In Paris, the Cujas, Sorbonne, and Sainte-Geneviève inter-university libraries and the Bibliothèque nationale de France have afforded me many precious hours of peace and quiet, and I remain greatly indebted to them for this as well as for their invaluable collections. Over the years, my research has benefited from the generous support of the Emil Aaltonen, Ella and Georg Ehrnrooth, and Niilo Helander foundations, the March 25 fund, the Academy of Finland, the Association of Finnish Lawyers, and the Tilburg University starting grant project 'A Legal History of the Global Commons'. I extend my thanks to all my funders and benefactors.

Throughout the editing of this book, I have benefited from the invaluable expertise, guidance, and patience of the staff at Cambridge University Press. Finola O'Sullivan, Marianne Nield, Natasha Burton, and Edgar Mendez graciously allowed me to properly finish the manuscript and then carried the book to its publication with great care and attention. Sri Hari Sugumaran from Integra managed the editing process, and Diana Witt composed the index with great expertise and insight. Above all, I am indebted to my unparalleled copyeditor, Virginia Hamilton, whose diligence and devotion transformed this manuscript into its best possible form. I present my sincere thanks to each of them.

In Tilburg, I have been fortunate to have the assistance of Maria Hanswijk and Amit Dolev, who proofread the manuscript, helped revise its bibliography, and kept the book on my agenda amidst the regular cacophony of competing academic responsibilities. Warm thanks also to my many academic friends, including Margareta Brummer in Helsinki and Maurits den Hollander, Hanna Lukkari, Richard Clements, Emily Sipiorski, Deepak Mawar, and all the others in my cohort of frontline teachers in Tilburg. Likewise, Professors Randall Lesaffer, Heikki Pihlajamäki (in Helsinki) and Dave de Ruysscher have always ensured that I am welcome in the company of legal historians, for which I also express my appreciation.

As always, I remain profoundly grateful to my alma mater, the University of Helsinki, to the Erik Castrén Institute of International Law and Human Rights, and to the brilliant scholars of the Helsinki school of international law – it has been an immense privilege to share in their intellectual adventure. As a scholar, I owe everything to my teachers and mentors Martti Koskenniemi and Jan Klabbers, who always believed in this work and who gently but firmly held me accountable for bringing it to its conclusion. Thanks also to Anne Orford, Eyal Benvenisti, and Emily Crawford, whose merciful but perceptive assessments of my thesis allowed me to better understand the overall nature of my work. Despite my debt to these scholars, none of them probably would have written this book the way I have, and none of them should be held responsible for any errors, omissions, and mistakes on these pages. For these, I alone bear responsibility.

I thank Kyösti Kelhä and Osman Nalbantoglu for providing me with enduring models of a man. I also thank my Mum and my Dad and my dear brother Anssi. Above all, my deepest gratitude goes to my wife and lifelong companion, Susanna Kari, and to our two wonderful daughters, Tove and Saima. Their affection and support give true meaning to everything I do. As always, behind every achievement stands a courageous and remarkable woman.

TABLE OF CASES

The Alexandra (1863) 176 Eng Rep 295
The Ambrose Light (30 September 1885) 25 Fed Cas 408
The Amy Warwick (1862) 1 Fed Cas 799
The Anna Christiana (27 November 1778) 165 Eng Rep 37
The Arantzazu Mendi (1938) P 233
The Arantzazu Mendi (1939) AC 256
Banco de Bilbao *v.* Sancha and Rey (1938) 2 KB 176
The Bee (11 December 1778) 165 Eng Rep 50
The Bello Corrunes (1821) 19 US 152
The Bermuda (1865) 70 US 514
The Circassian (1865) 69 US 135
The Commerce (4 September 1777) 165 Eng Rep 19.
La Conception (1821) 19 US 235
The Crenshaw (29 August 1861) 12 Fed Cas 95
The Dickenson (1776) 165 Eng Rep 1
The Divina Pastora (1819) 17 US 52
Dole et al. *v.* New England Mutual Marine Ins Co (1864) 7 Fed Cas 837
The Estrella (1819) 17 US 298
The Fourth-of-July Privateer (6 November 1818) 1 Op Atty Gen 24
The Friendship (4 September 1777) 165 Eng Rep 19
Hanna's case (13 December 1871) 29 RIAA 143
The Hendrick and Alida (2 October 1777) 165 Eng Rep 22
Henfield's Case, Case No. 6360 (1793), 11 Fed Cas 1099
The Hiawatha (29 August 1861) 12 Fed Cas 95
The Hornet (1870) 12 Fed Cas 529
The Immanuel (1799) 165 Eng Rep 284
Lawrence *v.* Dana et al. (1869) 15 Fed Cas 26
The Louisa (13 November 1778) 165 Eng Rep 33
Lindo *v.* Rodney (1782) 99 Eng Rep 385
Mauran *v.* Insurance Company (1867) 73 US 1
The Montijo (United States *v.* Colombia) (1875) 2 Moore's *Arbitrations* 1421
The Nuestra Señora de la Caridad (1819) 17 US 497
The Nueva Anna and the Liebre (1821) 19 US 193
The Parkhill (23 July 1861) 18 Fed Cas 1187
The Peterhoff (1867) 72 US 28

Salvador Prats *v.* United States (1868) III Moore's *Arbitrations* 2886
The Prize Cases: The Brig Amy Warwick; The Schooner Crenshaw; The Barque Hiawatha; The Schooner Brilliante (1863) 67 US 635
Prosecutor *v.* Tadić, Case No. IT-94–1, Decision on Jurisdiction (ICTY, 2 October 1995)
The Rebecca (5 December 1778) 165 Eng Rep 46
Republic of Peru *v.* Peruvian Guano Co (1887) 35 Ch D 489
Rose *v.* Himely (1808) 8 US 241
The Sally (2 October 1777) 165 Eng Rep 20
The Santissima Trinidad and the St Ander (1822) 20 US 283
Shortridge *v.* Macon (1867) 22 Fed Cas 20
Talbot qui tam (1784) 1 US 95
Texas *v.* White et al. (1869) 74 US 700
Thorington *v.* Smith (1869) 75 US 1
The Three Friends (1897) 166 US 1
The Tropic Wind (13 June 1861) 28 Fed Cas 218
Underhill *v.* Hernandez (1897) 168 US 250
US *v.* Klintock (1820) 18 US 144
US *v.* Baker et al. (30 October 1861) 24 Fed Cas 962
US *v.* Klein (1871) 80 US 128
US *v.* Palmer et al. (1818) 16 US 610
US *v.* Peters (1809) 9 US 115
US *v.* Smith (25 October 1861) 27 Fed Cas 1134
The Venezuelan Preferential Case (22 February 1904) 9 RIAA 99

BIBLIOGRAPHICAL ABBREVIATIONS

Acts and Ordinances of the Interregnum	C. H. Firth and R. S. Rait (eds), *Acts and Ordinances of the Interregnum, 1624–1660* (3 vols, HMSO 1911).
Am Stat Pap For Rel	*American State Papers: Foreign Relations* (6 vols, Gales and Seaton 1832–1861).
BFSP	*British and Foreign State Papers* (170 vols, Public Records Office/Ridgway and Sons 1814–1977).
CSP	*Calendar of State Papers* (Public Records Office 1856–1969).
CTS	Clive Parry (ed), *Consolidated Treaty Series* (Oxford University Press c. 1969–1981).
Dana's *Wheaton*	Henry Wheaton, *Elements of International Law* (8th edn, Richard Dana ed, 1866; Carnegie Endowment reprint by G. G. Wilson, Clarendon Press 1936).
Davenport	Frances Gardiner Davenport (ed), *European Treaties Bearing on the History of the United States and Its Dependencies* (4 vols, Carnegie Institution 1917–1937).
Dig	*The Digest of Justinian* ([c. 530–533] 4 vols, Alan Watson ed, University of Pennsylvania Press 1985, revised edn 1998).
DJBP	Hugo Grotius, *De jure belli ac pacis libri tres* ([1625] Francis Kelsey tr, Carnegie Institution 1913).
Doniol	Henri Doniol, *Histoire de la participation de la France à l'établissement des États-Unis d'Amérique* (5 vols, Imprimerie nationale 1886).
FRUS	*Foreign Relations of the United States* (US Government Printing Office 1861–).
General Collection of Treatys	Samuel Whatley (ed), *A General Collection of Treatys of Peace and Commerce, Renunciations, Manifestos, and Other Publick Papers, from the Year 1642, to the End of the Reign of Queen Anne* (4 vols, Knapp 1732).

Hackworth	Green Haywood Hackworth, *Digest of International Law* (8 vols, US Government Printing Office 1940–1944).
JCC	*Journals of the Continental Congress, 1774–1789* (34 vols, US Government Printing Office 1904–1937).
Lawrence's *Wheaton*	Henry Wheaton, *Elements of International Law* (William Beach Lawrence ed, Little, Brown 1863).
Manning's *Dipl Corr*	William Manning (ed), *Diplomatic Correspondence of the United States Concerning the Independence of the Latin-American Nations* (3 vols, Oxford University Press 1925).
Marsden	Reginald G. Marsden, *Documents Relating to Law and Custom of the Sea* (2 vols, Navy Records Society 1915–1916).
Martens, *Causes célèbres*	Charles de Martens, *Causes célèbres du droit des gens* (5 vols, 2nd edn, F. A. Brockhaus 1858–1861).
McNair, *Opinions*	Arnold McNair, *International Law Opinions* (3 vols, Cambridge University Press 1956).
Moore's *Arbitrations*	John Bassett Moore, *History and Digest of the International Arbitrations to Which the United States Has Been a Party* (6 vols, US Government Printing Office 1898).
Moore's *Digest*	John Bassett Moore, *A Digest of International Law* (8 vols, US Government Printing Office 1906).
Moore's *Adjudications*	John Bassett Moore, *International Adjudications, Ancient and Modern, History and Documents* (6 vols, US Government Printing Office 1933).
NDAR	William Bell Clark and others (eds), *Naval Documents of the American Revolution* (13 vols, US Government Printing Office 1964–2019).
OR Armies	*The War of the Rebellion: A Compilation of the Official Records of the Union and Confederate Armies* (128 vols, US Government Printing Office 1880–1902).
OR Naval	*Official Records of the Union and Confederate Navies in the War of the Rebellion* (US Government Printing Office 1894–1922).
Perry, *Sources*	Richard Perry (ed), *Sources of Our Liberties: Documentary Origins of Individual Liberties in the United States Constitution and Bill of Rights* (American Bar Foundation 1952).

PFAA	Peter Force, *American Archives. Fourth Series* (6 vols, M. St Clair Clarke and P. Force 1837–1846) and *Fifth Series* (3 vols, M. St Clair Clarke and P. Force 1848–1853).
Pickering's *Statutes at Large*	Danby Pickering (ed), *The Statutes at Large from the Magna Charta, to the End of the Eleventh Parliament of Great Britain, Anno 1761 [Continued to 1806]* (46 vols, J. Bentham 1762–1807).
Rep	*The Republic of Plato* (Benjamin Jowett ed, 3rd edn, Clarendon Press 1888).
Rev Dipl Corr	Francis Wharton (ed), *The Revolutionary Diplomatic Correspondence of the United States* (6 vols, US Government Printing Office 1889).
RIAA	*Reports of International Arbitral Awards/Recueil des sentences arbitrales* (34 vols, United Nations 1948–).
Rymer's *Fœdera*	Thomas Rymer, *Fœdera, conventiones, litteræ, et cujuscunque generis acta publica, inter reges Angliæ et alios quosvis impeatores, reges, pontifices, principes, vel communitates* (20 vols, 2nd edn, J. Tonson 1727–).
Smith	Herbert A. Smith, *Great Britain and the Law of Nations* (2 vols, P. S. King & Son 1932, 1935).
Stuyt	A. M. Stuyt, *Survey of International Arbitrations 1794–1938* (Springer 1939).
State Trials	Thomas Bayly Howell (ed), *Cobbett's Complete Collection of State Trials* (34 vols, Hansard 1809–1826).
US Stat	*The Statutes at Large of the United States* (Little Brown 1845–1874, US Government Printing Office 1874–1950, National Archives and Records Administration 1950–).
Vattel	Emer de Vattel, *The Law of Nations, Or the Principles of Natural Law Applied to the Conduct and to the Affairs of Nations and of Sovereigns* ([1758] Charles G. Fenwick tr, Carnegie Institution of Washington 1916).

Introduction

A Classical Doctrine

All international law presumes a doctrine of civil war. The subjects and participants of the law of nations have always had to determine whom to welcome among them and whom to refuse. In situations where the lawful order within an individual state is under serious contestation, myriad legal questions emerge between the parties, foreign countries, and the world at large. Is there a point at which an insurgency ceases to be an internal affair and becomes a matter of international law? Who represents the state or nation during a civil war? Should the world recognise one, two, many lawful authorities in a civil war, or none at all? Should the laws, administrative acts, and judgments of insurgent governments and rebel courts be considered valid? Who should be responsible for the harm a civil war causes to foreign nationals or their property? How should the world deal with a manifestly illegitimate or putative government, a government in exile, or a pretender to the throne? Are foreign states permitted – or even obliged – to lend assistance or to intervene? When several warring factions seek the floor in the international institutions of the world, whom should the world listen to, and why?

If international law is understood to have a finite sphere of subjects, then its integrity depends on some implicit or explicit distinction between those who qualify as its participants and those who do not. Accepted legal theory suggests that the recognition of legal subjects is a matter of both *fact* and *law*, and that statehood is often evaluated and debated in terms of the criteria of effectiveness and legitimacy.[1] A civil war, then, would be an internal conflict in which these criteria are being

[1] James Crawford, *The Creation of States in International Law* (2nd edn, Oxford University Press 2007) 4–6; Martti Koskenniemi, *From Apology to Utopia: The Structure of International Legal Argument* ([1989] Cambridge University Press 2005) 272–282.

contested and redefined, possibly leading to a transformation in the sphere of subjects of international law. Who is to distinguish those deemed to be within the sphere from those who are not, and on what basis? Here, the potentialities inherent in the indeterminacies and disagreements of international law give the law both a transformative and a conservative character: the language of the law can be deployed both for and against a revolution, to articulate the differences between the parties, and to persuade the world to adopt a particular framing of the dispute or a particular interpretation of justice.

A brief look at the long history of the questions of recognition and civil war in international law suffices to show that the potential for disagreement is infinite and that law on the matter has never been settled. It is a familiar fact that opposing political sides seldom agree on the legal characterisation of insurgents. But also, more impartial legal observers who might nominally share a similar political perspective, professional attitude, or cosmopolitan ethos have time and again failed to find common answers to the problem. History knows countless labels assigned to those who have been considered legitimate actors or denied a legal standing among nations: privateers and pirates, militias and terrorists, revolutionaries and rebels. More often than not, insurgents have carried multiple such monikers simultaneously, so that one person's 'pirate' has indeed been another person's 'freedom fighter'. The legal history of civil wars thus binds together international law with the histories of revolution, empire, decolonisation, and the creation of states in general, raising the fundamental questions that lawyers, statesmen, and judges have for centuries debated about what it means to be a subject of international law, and about who is to be included and who excluded from the family of nations, or even from humanity at large.

This book examines the story of the classical doctrine of civil war in international law, a particular normative vocabulary through which jurists and statesmen debated matters concerning rebellion and revolution from early modern times until the early twentieth century. The expression 'classical doctrine of civil war' was coined in 1958 by Jean Siotis, who used it when distinguishing the modern terminology of non-international armed conflicts (which we still know and use) from the language and tradition of the law of civil wars in the preceding centuries.[2] In this usage, the word 'classical' refers broadly to the old 'Westphalian'

[2] Jean Siotis, *Le droit de la guerre et les conflits armés d'un caractère non-international* (LGDJ 1958).

law of nations, which facilitated the co-existence of states from the early modern period until the early twentieth century. It was characterised by the legality of war as a final means of dispute settlement, in contrast to the (post-)modern era, in which the use of force is meant to be restricted under an international structure of collective security.[3] This periodisation is retrospective, of course; the jurists and scholars who wrote within the classical tradition saw themselves as modern and forward-looking authors, even when their work largely involved interpreting and categorising historical precedents. The 'classical doctrine of civil war' is therefore a theoretical construct, a useful passage of professional lore, one that offers a sketch of a past against which present-day lawyers may also contemplate the modern law of internal conflicts so as to better understand where it comes from and why it reads the way it does.

The underlying principles of the classical doctrine of civil war – such as the notion of public war, the prohibition of self-help, and the concept of the pirate – originated from Roman law and, as such, were among the oldest in the law of nations. Practically, however, the classical doctrine of civil war was largely a product of the age of sail and steam. It rose and fell with the needs and necessities of European empires, and later the United States, as they dealt with various overseas colonies and when those overseas colonies then began to assert their independence. The problem that the doctrine of civil war commonly sought to address was essentially this: how should states deal with foreign subjects, colonists, and indigenous populations that rose to resist their lawful governments and demanded international recognition? The issue was particularly pertinent in the age of sail, because insurgents would often expand their struggle to the high seas by flying their own flags, commissioning their own privateers, and establishing their own prize courts. Whenever this happened, imperial metropolises and foreign governments found themselves negotiating the difficult question of the legal status of the insurgents – that is, whether and when the insurgents might indeed have standing under the law of nations, as opposed to being dismissed as common pirates and rebels.

Over the centuries, a certain, recurrent pattern of legal milestones emerged in such classical civil wars. An internal conflict would inevitably

[3] See e.g. Randall Lesaffer, 'The Classical Law of Nations' in Alexander Orakhelashvili (ed), *Research Handbook on the Theory and History of International Law* (2nd edn, Edward Elgar 2020) 326–358; Hans Kelsen, *Principles of International Law* (Rinehart 1952) 3–89; Wolfgang Friedmann, *The Changing Structure of International Law* (Stevens & Sons 1964) 4–5; Georges Scelle, 'La guerre civile espagnole et le droit des gens' 45 *Revue générale de droit international public* (1938) 265, 271.

become a concern in the international domain when an insurgent faction declared its own prize jurisdiction to the world and began to commission warships and privateers to enforce its cause on the high seas. A prize jurisdiction implied valid legal standing before the law of nations; it could thus be claimed that, for the purposes of waging their civil war, the insurgents had authority *de jure belli* to transfer to the captors ownership of property captured from the enemy.[4] This was typically the first mark of sovereignty that insurgents claimed, and it simultaneously brought before the world their demand to be acknowledged not as pirates but rather as lawful belligerents. In response, governments acting to subdue insurgents in their colonies and overseas possessions typically resorted to the use of belligerent rights at sea, in particular by declaring blockades or by demanding to visit and search foreign vessels for contraband cargo. Under the law of nations, the legality of such belligerent acts was limited to formal states of war only, which in turn raised the question of whether something more than internal policing was at play in such circumstances. Further problems of legal characterisation arose in connection with the treatment of captives (whether held as prisoners of war under the law of nations or awaiting individual criminal trials for treason or piracy), the treatment of foreigners and their property in areas affected by the conflict, questions of public debt, and other aspects of the conflict. Although such issues could be of great legal and practical significance, they nevertheless often remained within the territorial jurisdiction of a state and were thus a degree less intractable than the problem of belligerent rights in the truly international space formed by the high seas.

In response to these legal concerns, domestic and foreign governments, diplomats, scholars, and courts sought to establish a degree of legal certainty by determining the status of the conflict and the parties involved, as well as the legal obligations that would flow therefrom. At the heart of the classical law of civil war was the question of whether or not foreign states could, would, or should declare themselves neutrals, and whether the parties in a civil war could lawfully exercise belligerent rights against their nationals. What was at stake for foreign states was their neutral rights and the protection of their subjects against unlawful

[4] For example, Hugo Grotius, *De Jure Belli ac Pacis*, III.1 and III.6; Report of the law officers of the crown (18 January 1753), II Marsden 348, 350–351; René-Josue Valin, *Traité des prises* (Jérôme Légier 1763) 176; *Lindo* v. *Rodney* [1782] 99 Eng Rep 385; J. H. W. Verzijl, W. P. Heere, and J. P. S. Offerhaus, *International Law in Historical Perspective*, pt IX-C: *The Law of Maritime Prize* (Martinus Nijhoff 1992) 571–576 ; David J. Bederman, 'The Feigned Demise of Prize' 9 *Emory International Law Review* (1995) 31, 33.

depredations, expropriations, and damages. Armed interventions were not out of the question either. Consequently, the question of state responsibility became another common element in classical civil wars, arising from damages caused to foreigners, on the one hand, and from the breaches of neutral duties, on the other. Events arising from a classical civil war were regularly debated before judges in domestic and foreign courts and in its aftermath referred to international arbitration before mixed claims commissions tasked with resolving any remaining international property claims. That said, it should be stressed that even in the contemporary legal imagination the classical law of civil war could have only limited global applicability; its history was dominated by that of transatlantic revolutions. Although nominally presented as universal law, in practice the classical law of civil war was clearly contingent on the imperial priorities of Europeans, and later the United States, in the non-Western world. When dealing with what they called 'the Orient', international lawyers maintained the colonial dynamic of difference, which gave little hope to indigenous aspirations of sovereign equality with the so-called civilized nations.[5] In these encounters the classical law could still play a role, but that role was mostly to justify its non-applicability, to the disadvantage of rebelling natives and colonial subjects.

The eventual decline of the classical doctrine of civil war was brought about by the reduction of these insurrectionary encounters on the high seas. This began with the abolition of privateers in the 1856 Declaration of Paris, which made maritime war the monopoly of sovereign states and thus deprived most insurgents of a chance to establish a legitimate presence at sea. Although diplomats and jurists continued to use the legal language of civil war to apprehend and argue internal legal conflicts well into the twentieth century, by the time of the Spanish Civil War their classical concepts and principles had undeniably become obsolete. Despite the efforts of many lawyers to modify and reinvent the classical doctrine to make it better fit the new age characterised by aerial bombings and guerrilla warfare, the conceptual language underlying the classical doctrine was eventually superseded by the modern language of the law of non-international armed conflicts. This replacement took place particularly in the drafting of the Common Article 3 of the 1949 Geneva

[5] See generally Anthony Anghie, *Imperialism, Sovereignty and the Making of International Law* (Cambridge University Press 2005) 32–114; Arnulf Becker Lorca, *Mestizo International Law: A Global Intellectual History 1842–1933* (Cambridge University Press 2014) 41–75; Martti Koskenniemi, *The Gentle Civilizer of Nations* (Cambridge University Press 2001) 127–136.

Conventions, although it took until 1975 for the academic community of legal scholars and publicists working at the Institut de droit international to bury the classical doctrine.

The classical doctrine of civil war is not entirely foreign to present-day legal scholarship. Studies in the law of non-international armed conflicts often note the distinction between the 'classical' times of war and peace, on the one hand, and the 'modern' post-World War era of collective security, on the other, with introductions to the classical principles serving as a contrast to or precursor of the modern law.[6] Recent scholarship has also produced critical reassessments of the nineteenth-century roots of the modern laws of war,[7] as well as the role of insurgencies in the rise of state responsibility.[8] Civil wars also appear in the general history of international law[9] and in the field of intellectual history.[10] But over the last sixty years there have been few, if any, studies devoted to the classical doctrine of civil war per se.[11] The present book seeks to make up for this want of attention by offering a narrative on the doctrine's rise and fall in international law. It places the classical doctrine front and centre and explores the emergence, change, and decline of that body of law in a way that aims to make it understandable and accessible to readers. In doing

[6] Eliav Lieblich, *International Law and Civil Wars: Intervention and Consent* (Routledge 2013) 71–121; Sandesh Sivakumaran, *The Law of Non-international Armed Conflict* (Oxford University Press 2012) 9–29; Anthony Cullen, *The Concept of Non-international Armed Conflict in International Humanitarian Law* (Cambridge University Press 2010) 7–21; Lindsay Moir, *The Law of Internal Armed Conflict* (Cambridge University Press 2002) 3–29.

[7] Eyal Benvenisti and Doreen Lustig, 'Monopolizing War: Codifying the Laws of War to Reassert Governmental Authority, 1856–1874' 31 *European Journal of International Law* (EJIL) (2020) 127–169; Rotem Giladi, 'The Enactment of Irony: Reflections on the Origins of the Martens Clause' 25 EJIL (2014) 847–869; Rotem Giladi, 'Francis Lieber on Public War' 4 *Göttingen Journal of International law* (2012) 447–477. See also John Fabian Witt, *Lincoln's Code: The Laws of War in American History* (Free Press 2013); Oona A. Hathaway and Scott J. Shapiro, *The Internationalists: How a Radical Plan to Outlaw War Remade the World* (Allen Lane 2017).

[8] Kathryn Greenman, *State Responsibility and Rebels: The History and Legacy of Protecting Investment Against Revolution* (Cambridge University Press 2021); Alan Tzvika Nissel, *Merchants of Legalism: A History of State Responsibility (1870–1960)* (Cambridge University Press 2024). See also Andrea Leiter, *Making the World Safe for Investment: The Protection of Foreign Property 1922–1959* (Cambridge University Press 2023).

[9] Stephen C. Neff, *War and the Law of Nations: A General History* (Cambridge University Press 2005) 250–275; Stephen C. Neff, *Justice in Blue and Gray: A Legal History of the Civil War* (Harvard University Press 2010).

[10] David Armitage, *Civil Wars: A History in Ideas* (Yale University Press 2017).

[11] Compare David Kennedy and Martti Koskenniemi, *Of Law and the World* (Harvard University Press 2023) 206.

so, the book takes a new, retrospective look at an old conversation that last took place in the works of Jean Siotis, Erik Castrén, and Roscoe Oglesby some five decades ago.[12] Their books are still available in academic libraries, but their relative obscurity, when read from today's perspective, justifies this revisit of that tradition.

In this book, the classical doctrine of civil war is understood first and foremost as a professional language or a vocabulary of international law.[13] The argument, therefore, is that there used to be a classical language with which international lawyers debated civil wars before the establishment of the vernacular found in international law today. 'Civil war' used to be a formal legal concept. The legal principles and concepts of the classical doctrine formed the frame of reference within which statesmen and jurists could express the positions of governments, insurgent factions, or other parties whose perspectives they sought to explain or examine. This is therefore ultimately a story about the rise and fall of a certain way of speaking and writing about internal conflicts in a persuasive way among and across the legal profession. Of course, civil wars as actual historical and political events did not arise or disappear with the classical law concerning them. Insurrection remains a dominant form of warfare in the world today; while the number of inter-state conflicts may have fallen since 1945, the number of intra-state conflicts has at the same time increased.[14] International lawyers today study and debate non-international armed conflicts as intensely as ever. But the arguments and principles deployed for this purpose no longer hinge on the legal concept of 'civil war' as such, and certainly not in the sense inherited from the days of Pomponius, Grotius, Vattel, Jefferson, Bolívar, Wiesse, Rougier, and Olivart. The difference between the present-day

[12] Jean Siotis, *Le droit de la guerre et les conflits armés d'un caractère non-international* (LGDJ 1958); Erik Castrén, *Civil War* (Suomalainen Tiedeakatemia 1966); Roscoe R. Oglesby, *Internal War and the Search for Normative Order* (Martinus Nijhoff 1971).

[13] Here I am influenced by Martti Koskenniemi's notions of law as language, sensibilities, and legal imaginations, which both vary in time and remain surprisingly (or uncannily) recognisable. See e.g. Koskenniemi, 'Style as Method' in *The Politics of International Law* (Hart 2011) 294–306; Koskenniemi, *Gentle Civilizer*, 1–10; Koskenniemi, *To the Uttermost Parts of the Earth* (Cambridge University Press 2021) 1–15. Compare Kennedy and Koskenniemi, *Of Law and the World*, 43–55.

[14] Christine Bell, *On the Law of Peace: Peace Agreements and the* Lex Pacificatoria (Oxford University Press 2008) 28–30; Kalevi J. Holsti, *Peace and War: Armed Conflicts and International Order 1648–1989* (Cambridge University Press 1991) 272; Hathaway and Shapiro, *The Internationalists*, xix, 352–353, 366–369; Meredith Reid Sarkees and Frank Wheylon Wayman, *Resort to War: A Data Guide to Inter-State, Extra-State, Intra-State, and Non-state Wars, 1816–2007* (CQ Press 2010) 337–340.

vernacular and the professional language of the classical authors is pronounced, and during the research and writing of this book it has become evident that the classical doctrine has in many ways become inaccessible or even incomprehensible from within today's legal vocabularies. This book therefore seeks to expand the knowledge available to present-day international lawyers in the hope of making the language of the classical doctrine accessible and understandable once again.

The book has been written at a time of growing geopolitical uncertainty, with the world's predominant powers beginning to reconsider the illegality of the annexation of territory by force and, by way of consequence, the general renunciation of war as an instrument of national policy in their relations with one another.[15] In this light, it should be made clear that this book is not, and never was meant to be, a revivalist history, nor does it seek to glorify the classical law of civil war. It aims to offer a modestly critical post-mortem of the subject, exploring how the doctrine once came to be and then faded away. What will hopefully be proven is that past lawyers do not seem to have escaped the inevitable politics of domination, revolution, and recognition that are the inevitable companion of any legal arguments concerning insurgencies and the making of states in the world at all times. The familiar theoretical message here is that in this field of law there is no escape from the politics of international law, which permeates our understanding of internal conflicts as much today as in the past. No particular set of legal rules, concepts, or principles in history has managed to circumvent the political and ethical burdens that weigh heavily on all legal decision-making concerning war and peace, freedom and union, or the killing of the innocent.[16] If the world of international law and the use of force is today exposed to criticism for false universalism, then the classical law of war and peace was exposed to criticism as an apology for naked power between states. There were good reasons for abandoning the classical principles of war and peace in the twentieth century. If today all histories

[15] Compare General Treaty for Renunciation of War as an Instrument of National Policy, Paris, 27 August 1928, 94 LNTS 57, art I.

[16] For example, Jan Klabbers, 'Intervention, Armed Intervention, Armed Attack, Threat to Peace, Act of Aggression, and Threat or Use of Force: What's the Difference?' in Marc Weller (ed), *The Oxford Handbook of the Use of Force in International Law* (Oxford University Press 2015) 488–506; Martti Koskenniemi, 'The Lady Doth Protest Too Much: Kosovo, and the Turn to Ethics in International Law' 65 *Modern Law Review* (2002) 159–175.

of international law are an implicit expression of politics,[17] then perhaps here lies the politics of this book: to avoid any illusions about a past in which things were purportedly better with respect to international law and civil war. One would do well to avoid spurious nostalgia for a past law, whereby it might be possible to somehow 'bracket' or 'civilise' wars, including even internal ones.[18]

The classical doctrine of civil war never really worked as a legal 'system'. Never was there a set of clear, mutually agreed international rules of conduct and responsibility regarding civil wars supposedly agreed upon by states voluntarily and then dutifully adhered to even if they had reason to dispute the potential outcomes. The idea of such a system was implicitly an ideal advocated by nineteenth-century international lawyers writing on civil war, and it forms a thread that runs consistently through the whole narrative – but the successes of this ideal were always very limited. In the age of sail, as in the present day, civil wars represented extreme and exceptional circumstances, in which the shortcomings of international law surface, often because of the lack of an authoritative, objective perspective that could identify the relevant rules and connect them with the pertinent facts in a manner that would leave no room for disagreement. Lacking access to an objective and universal interpretation of the law, jurists and statesmen in the past, as in the present, were often guided more by what they thought was right or just or expedient or advantageous than by the logical application of technical legal rules and principles.

Of Old Men and the Sea

The theoretical problem of civil war was, in a way, a question of jurisdiction and whether the applicable law in an armed conflict should be domestic law or the law of nations. War waged in due form as public war was permissible under the classical law of nations. It was a lawful prerogative of sovereigns, a method of resolving international legal

[17] See Anne Orford, *International Law and the Politics of History* (Cambridge University Press 2021) 310–320.

[18] See Carl Schmitt *The Nomos of the Earth* ([1950] Telos 2006) 140–151; James Q. Whitman, *The Verdict of Battle: The Law of Victory and the Making of Modern War* (Harvard University Press 2012) 12–19; Compare Martti Koskenniemi, 'Carl Schmitt and International Law' in Jens Meierhenrich and Oliver Simons (eds), *The Oxford Handbook of Carl Schmitt* (Oxford University Press 2013) 600–608. See also Joseph Weiler, 'Cancelling Carl Schmitt?' (*EJIL: Talk!*, 13 August 2021).

disputes in a binding manner, in contrast to diplomacy, arbitration, and adjudication, whose purpose was precisely to help settle disputes without recourse to that method of last resort.[19] War was thus a normal, albeit regrettable, state of affairs. Hugo Grotius stated calmly that war was 'the condition of those contending by force, viewed simply as such'.[20] According to Emer de Vattel, war was 'that state' in which a nation prosecutes its right by force.[21] Francis Lieber studied the laws of war that were 'established in a state of violence'[22] and had himself 'no morbid feeling about war'.[23] Such thinking has sometimes been referred to as a legal procedure, 'war in due form', a 'war-prerogative', a 'duel', or a 'princely trial by combat'.[24] The lawfulness and normalcy of war continued to be the paradigm up until the twentieth century, even finding an echo in Oppenheim at the time the League of Nations was beginning to operate.[25]

Few internal conflicts were 'wars' in the sense meant by the law of nations. The inviolable authority of states in their internal affairs was a cornerstone of sovereignty. As Jean Bodin put it, 'the subject is never to be suffered to attempt any thing against his soveraign prince, how naughty & cruel soever he be'.[26] Authorities of the law of nations agreed. Grotius, for example, concluded that, unlike sovereigns waging public war, any pirates and brigands who did not constitute a state could not avail themselves of the law of nations.[27] Similarly, Gentili stressed how pirates could not wage war in a proper sense and noted how the Romans had never applied the term 'civil war' to their contests with Spartacus or other insurgents.[28] Throughout the classical law of nations, internal conflicts were regularly accompanied by some measure of legal

19 *DJBP* II.1. and III.3; Compare Hans Kelsen, *Law and Peace in International Relations* (Harvard University Press 1942) 27–55.

20 *DJBP* I.1.2

21 Vattel III.I.1.

22 'Lecture by Dr. Francis Lieber on the Laws and Usages of War – No. 1' *New York Times* (27 October 1861).

23 Lieber to Sumner, 27 December 1861, in Thomas Perry (ed), *The Life and Letters of Francis Lieber* (Osgood 1882) 323–325, 325.

24 Neff, *War and the Law of Nations*, 131–158; Whitman, *Verdict of Battle*, 8–24; Lieblich, *International Law and Civil Wars*, 73–76.

25 Lassa Oppenheim, *International Law* (3rd edn, Longmans, Green 1921) II.1.1, § 54.

26 Jean Bodin, *The Six Bookes of a Commonweale* ([1576] Richard Knolles tr, G. Bishop 1606) II.5, 225.

27 *DJBP* II.18.2.

28 Alberico Gentili, *De iure belli libri tres* ([1612] John C. Rolfe tr, Clarendon Press 1933) I.4.40–I.4.41.

contestation between the incumbent governments and the insurgents over this question. The rulers and governments, being well in charge of the situations most of the time, sternly maintained their sovereignty and rejected any insinuation that the insurgents were more than rebels and pirates. The insurgents, for their part, did their utmost to challenge the status quo and convince the world that they were more than domestic rebels, more than pirates or brigands, but indeed belligerents: subjects of the law of nations, or at least the laws of war.

In most cases, lawful governments had little difficulty denying domestic rebels any legal standing. Governments were, after all, voices of the sovereign and had the final say on their internal affairs. But there were, broadly speaking, three (or four) categories of legal confrontations where the internal sovereignty of states would come under serious challenge. The first category involved the direct relationship between the incumbent government and an insurgent faction. If an insurgent faction could extend its campaign far and wide enough to force a government to enter into something we might call a state of exception, declaring legal measures that extended the regular limits of a peacetime constitutional legal order, then this would lead to questions about the legal nature of the ongoing conflict. The famous English common lawyer Edward Coke illustrated this very well when he defined a state of war as the moment 'when by invasion, insurrection, rebellions, or such like, the peaceable course of justice is disturbed and stopped so as the courts of justice be as it were shut up'.[29] For the most part, governments could still claim to pursue counter-insurrectionary campaigns through domestic law, putting down riots and treasonous uprisings in the name of law enforcement, public order, and criminal justice. But a particular complication was the question of whether captured insurgents were criminals or could be treated as prisoners of war. Widespread insurgencies could produce such numbers of captured individuals that dealing with them as individual criminals – entitled to full procedural and legal rights guaranteed in constitutions or the common laws of the land – exceeded the readiness of governments to accommodate and deal with them by due process.[30] Conversely, governmental troops could be captured by insurgents, and these captured individuals stood a chance of being returned as part of prisoner swaps or, in a worst case scenario, might be subjected to reprisals for any harsh

29 Edward Coke, *Institutes of the Lawes of England* (Societie of Stationers 1628) I.412.

30 For example, suspensions of habeas corpus: 1 Will & Mar c 2 (1688); 9 Geo 2 c 1 (1745); 17 Geo 3 c 9 (1776); 34 Geo 3 c 54 (1794); 38 Geo 3 c 36 (1798); 39 Geo 3 c 15 (1799); 57 Geo 3 c 3 (1817); 12 US Stat 755 (1863).

treatment inflicted on captured rebels. Practices between governments and insurgents might in such cases take forms that resembled the treatment of prisoners of war – a domain under the law of nations. Again, questions would arise as to whether a state of war – a civil war – existed.

A second category of potentially belligerent relations were those where there was international pressure for a government to admit that a state of war existed between itself and a faction of its citizens. These cases involved recourse to de facto belligerent measures against foreign nationals in areas beyond national jurisdiction – that is, on the high seas. Under the general law of nations, the principal effect of a state of war was that its existence brought about binding legal effects and relationships between nations. The rights and duties of belligerents had their counterpart in the rights and duties of neutrals. From the perspective of third states, the problem was how to distinguish between lawful belligerent actions taken by warring parties and unlawful hostilities, unfriendly deeds, and sheer piracy. It was overwhelmingly (though not exclusively) maritime issues that were involved here, because the most tangible international effects of a state of war in the age of sail and steam stemmed from belligerent measures like blockades and visits and searches of ships. Contraband cargoes and even entire neutral vessels might be captured by the belligerents and condemned in their prize courts.

The prize courts of individual nations were at the heart of these events. As already mentioned, prize jurisdiction implied an extraordinary claim of authority, one sovereign's assumption of power to adjudicate the ownership of property taken at sea from the subjects of another sovereign. Failure to show due regard for the rights of innocent parties, neutrals, or anyone otherwise protected by treaties or international law could lead to diplomatic scandals, confrontations, legal claims, reprisals, and even unwanted wars.[31] Insurgencies and civil wars were fought at sea in this manner, just as international wars were. Whenever a group of insurgents established a prize court and commissioned its privateers, this gave rise to a legal conundrum: what gave these insurgents the right to do so? What distinguished them from ordinary pirates? How could anyone tell the difference? If the conflict was a war, foreign nations were obliged to respect the adjudication of prize tribunals. If it was not war, no such tribunal could be opened, and any insurgent captures were acts of piracy.[32] Thus, when foreign merchantmen and cargoes began to find

[31] *DJBP* III. 2, especially §§ 4–5; Gentili, *De iure belli libri tres*, I.21.
[32] Compare Dana's *Wheaton* fn 15, § 23.

themselves in trouble with belligerent actors, internal conflicts and unrest had a habit of turning into matters of international law due to very circumstance. As a consequence, foreign powers would engage in tense discussions with the incumbent governments, and from time to time they would declare themselves neutrals, acknowledging that a war existed between a government and a part of its population.

A third category of potentially belligerent relations arose from violations of foreign property rights within the territorial jurisdiction of the state in conflict. Sometimes these did not differ much from disputes arising from captures at sea, as both could give grounds for property claims, reprisals, and the application of diplomatic protection. Reprisals are known to have been issued in response to maritime captures by 'pirates' of a certain nationality as well as expropriations of property rights on land,[33] and by the age of revolutions the principle of diplomatic protection was acknowledged by the classics of the law of nations.[34] When foreign nationals – as residents, investors, creditors, merchants, or otherwise – suffered losses or expropriations due to insurgencies, they would need to seek redress from the state undergoing the civil war or through diplomatic protection from the foreigner's own government. If at this point the incumbent governments refused to acknowledge the existence of a civil war, they could be deemed responsible for any resultant violations of the law of nations protecting foreign interests. When the practice of privateering was prohibited in the nineteenth century and most civil wars stopped reaching the high seas, state responsibility became an even more prominent question connecting civil wars with the law of nations.

The classical doctrine of civil war was inseparably linked with the problem of recognition, whether it be recognition of states or governments, belligerencies or insurgencies. The two standard theories of recognition – a constitutive theory suggesting that subjects of international law become such through recognition in law, and a declarative theory suggesting that we recognise things because they already exist in fact – were mostly formulated by lawyers in the late nineteenth and early twentieth centuries, though the long history of the law of civil war illustrates how the essence of the problem had been very present in legal arguments for centuries before.[35] Recognition has been referred to

[33] I Marsden 39, 119, 121, 126.

[34] *DJBP* II.25.1–2; Vattel II.VI.71 and 77.

[35] Crawford, *Creation of States*, 1–28.

as the most 'political' of all questions in the discipline, and for good reason.[36] Centuries of futile debates suggest that it is impossible to exhaustively determine a priori under what conditions the relevant facts in the world meet the legal requirements of sovereignty, or even what the relevant facts and precise legal requirements (and exceptions thereto) are. The story told in this book corroborates the intractable nature of recognition. While it does not seek to find a solution to the problem, one noteworthy finding emerges from the historical record in this regard: when faced with the question of recognition, courts of law have tended to turn to the official view of their governments in pursuit of an answer. This position – which I shall informally call the 'Gazette principle' in reference to William Scott's decision in *The Immanuel*[37] – has offered adjudicators a way to remove the critical question of recognition from their own courts and into the political or constitutional domain. Determining whether an actor is a subject of international law is not a matter for the courts but rather for the state from which the court's jurisdiction flows, so the argument goes. Modern jurisprudence still largely conforms to this view.[38] But as will be seen, there have also been exceptions to this principle in practice.

The classical doctrine of civil war became obsolete with the early twentieth century's renunciation of war. By this time, new theories about collective security and the peaceful settlement of disputes began to take the place of lawful war in international legal thought. This transition led to a crisis (if one may call it such) for the law of neutrality, which still played a key role in the legal vocabulary of civil wars. The transition was not straightforward, and many writers expressed considerable reservations about its feasibility and consequences. But in the end, the concept of civil war and much of the accompanying historical and argumentative language faded away almost imperceptibly, along with many other remnants of classical nineteenth-century law. For many lawyers this posed little problem, as they reinvented the law of civil war as the law of non-international armed conflicts to take its place.

This book tells the story of the law of civil war from the early modern times up to those years. It seeks to explain the way in which the old legal vernacular of civil wars rose and fell in ever-changing state practice, and how the doctrine had a second coming in the literature at the turn of the

36 Hersch Lauterpacht, *Recognition in International Law* (Oxford University Press 1947) 1.
37 *The Immanuel* (1799) 165 Eng Rep 284, 286.
38 Crawford, *Creation of States*, 17.

nineteenth to the twentieth century. The book spotlights a self-evident but often opaque storyline in the history of the law of nations, providing a roadmap (or at least breadcrumbs) for scholars interested in exploring the matter further. For readers' convenience, a summary of the story can be found in the book's concluding chapter.[39]

[39] The many sources cited in the course of this book were written in various languages. Where translations into English were available (as indicated in the Bibliography), I have relied on these and gratefully acknowledge the importance of their contribution to the literature. Otherwise, translations into English are my own.

1

The Origins of the Classical Doctrine of Civil War

> Petrarch asked if there was anything more to history than the praise of Rome. And we ask . . . 'Is there anything more to history than the call for revolution, and the fear of revolution?' And let me simply add this question: 'And what if Rome once more conquered the revolution?'
>
> Michel Foucault, *'Society Must Be Defended': Lectures at the Collège de France, 1975–76*

The doctrine of civil war emerged as part of the 'classical' law of nations, as early modern scholars in Europe sought to respond to the breakdown of the medieval legal order by adapting old Roman concepts and elements of the *ius commune* to their contemporary needs.[1] By the seventeenth century and the Peace of Westphalia, they had reconceived the law of nations as a matter of sovereign equals who dealt with one another through war, diplomacy, and legal claims that were less dependent on papal or other religious authority. In the absence of a universal authority to determine the justice or injustice of the use of force between sovereign nations, legal scholars eventually accepted that, in the event of hostilities between sovereign Europeans, the causes of all sovereigns might have to be accepted as legitimate for the time being, while the legality of individual hostile actions could be assessed under the law of nations that was emerging from long-standing practice and custom. The result was the modern laws of war, peace, and neutrality, which the jurists and courts of various nations continued to debate throughout the age of sail.

This new European order of states came coupled with the rise of overseas empires and increasingly organised technologies of maritime trade and warfare, which led to the development of the first global principles of international law and placed the rest of the world apart from the self-defined civilisation of Europe. Over time, much of the story of the classical doctrine of civil war would revolve around questions of

[1] Randall Lesaffer, 'The Classical Law of Nations' in Alexander Orakhelashvili (ed), *Research Handbook on the Theory and History of International Law* (2nd edn, Edward Elgar 2020) 326–358.

whether and how subjects could constitute sovereign entities in the remote lands divided from Europe by vast oceans.

The concept of war as a legal institution – separated from peacetime law through the declaration that marks its beginning and the peace treaty that marks its conclusion – had already existed in classical antiquity. The concepts of public war and distinguishing lawful enemies (*hostes*) from brigands and pirates (*latrones* or *prædones*) were of ancient Greek and Roman origin.[2] This distinction was essential for the law of nations. Public enemies might be protected by principles of *ius gentium*; for example, they would regain their personal status and property when ransomed and repatriated after captivity. Brigands and pirates, on the other hand, were outlaws under the law of nations and subject to domestic criminal laws enacted by their rulers.[3] The notion of public war was a foundational concept, part of the medieval just war doctrine of St Augustine and St Thomas Aquinas.[4] Vitoria, in the sixteenth century, acknowledged the distinction,[5] and in 1625 Hugo Grotius concurred with the learned Gentili that 'pirates and brigands [*piratæ et latrones* in the original Latin] who do not constitute a state, cannot avail themselves of the law of nations'.[6]

The basic legal problem posed by civil wars was whether armed insurgents could qualify as public enemies or whether they should be treated as mere pirates and brigands. Civil wars might be fought as public wars of the highest calibre (think of Sulla, Caesar, or Octavian),[7] but lesser rebellions repressed under criminal law, as when the Romans crucified Spartacus and his men or Pompey Magnus subordinated the Mediterranean 'pirates' to Rome.[8] The *Digest* provides legal grounds for punishing treason (*maiestas*), public disorder, and the unauthorised possession of arms. In Ulpian's words, treason was a crime committed

[2] Ulpian and Pomponius in *Dig* 49.15.24 and *Dig* 50.16.118; David J. Bederman, *International Law in Antiquity* (Cambridge University Press 2001) 208–209. Likewise, Plato distinguished between 'discord' (*stasis*) among Hellenes and 'wars' (*polemos*) waged against Barbarians; see *Rep* § 470.

[3] Alberico Gentili, *De iure belli libri tres* ([1612] John C. Rolfe tr, Clarendon Press 1933) I.4.

[4] St Thomas Aquinas, *The 'Summa Theologica' of Thomas Aquinas* (R. & T. Washbourne 1917) II-II.40.1.

[5] Francisco de Vitoria, *De indis et de ivre belli relectiones* (Ernest Nys ed, John Pawley Bate tr, Carnegie Institution 1917) I.VI.2–6, 167–169.

[6] Hugo Grotius, *De jure belli ac pacis libri tres* ([1625] Francis Kelsey tr, Carnegie Institution 1913) II.18.12. See also III.3.11.

[7] David Armitage, *Civil Wars: A History in Ideas* (Yale University Press 2017) 51–58.

[8] The Cilician pirates were sometimes compared to public enemies. See Manuel Tröster, 'Roman Hegemony and Non-state Violence: A Fresh Look at Pompey's Campaign against the Pirates' 56 *Greece & Rome* (2009) 14–33. Also Gentili, *De iure belli*, I.4.40–41.

against the Roman people or against their safety, not just against the person of an emperor.[9] The civil war problematic touched the very foundations of law, throwing into question the validity of legal systems, the prohibition of self-help, and the public monopoly on violence. In the old *ius civile* access to centralised justice defined the state of peace, while private vendettas and retaliation indicated a state of war or anarchy.[10] At the same time, the capacity to provide legal protection was a prerequisite for sovereign authority, and the question of to whom such capacity and authority rightfully belonged might be open to dispute; in a classical anecdote Alexander the Great asked a pirate what entitled the man to prowl the seas in search of plunder, to which the man replied the same right as that which entitled Alexander to go conquering the world.[11]

Early modern scholars and jurists recognised this inheritance.[12] Yet, their era brought new challenges at a practical level, which forced them to find novel ways of turning theory into practice. In the age of sail, colonial insurgencies were commonly fought on the high seas. The appearance of insurgent privateers and filibusters made internal wars international affairs, not simply because they operated beyond state borders but particularly because the law of nations increasingly expected all maritime captures to be adjudicated in prize courts.[13] This raised one of the most crucial practical questions in the classical law of civil war: were the decisions of the rebel prize courts valid? As fate would have it, later in the age of sail new states came to exist as international entities first of all through their prize jurisdictions and privateer commissions. To be meaningful, insurgent prize jurisdiction and letters of marque rested on international recognition: the rebel privateers demanded to be distinguished from *piratæ et latrones*, while the retaliating governments

[9] For example, *Dig* 48.4.1, 3 and *Dig* 48.6.1–5, 11.

[10] Callistratus in *Dig* 4.2.13 and *Dig* 43.16.1–2, 27–28. Aeschylus' *Eumenides* deals with this as well.

[11] Marcus Tullius Cicero, 'De res publica' in Francis Barham (ed), *The Political Works of Marcus Tullius Cicero*, vol I ([c. 51 BCE] Edmund Spettigue 1841) III.263; St Augustine of Hippo, *The City of God* ([426 CE] Catholic University of America Press 1949) IV.4; Gentili, *De iure belli*, I.4.

[12] Gentili, *De iure belli*, I.iii; Edward Coke, *Institutes of the Lawes of England* (4 vols, Societie of Stationers 1628) I.412.

[13] For example, Report of the law officers of the crown (18 January 1753) II Marsden 348; Georges Feron, *Des tribunaux de prises (organisation, compétence, procédure)* (Pedone 1896) 25–30; Paul Reuter, *Étude de la règle: 'Toute prise doit être jugée'* (Les éditions internationales 1933); Stephen C. Neff, *Rights and Duties of Neutrals* (Manchester University Press 2000) 25–26; Richard Pares, *Colonial Blockade and Neutral Rights, 1739–1763* (Clarendon Press 1938) 59–64.

demanded the opposite. The question of civil war therefore became acute not so much when civil unrest broke out in a state as when foreign powers – now increasingly 'neutral' powers – had to address belligerent measures taken against their flags by governments putting down insurrections, or when their own nationals had taken up privateer commissions from foreign insurgents. In the age of sail, the legal rubicon was crossed with insurgent prize courts.

When reacting to a colonial rebellion, European empires often resorted to blockading the insurgent ports. Their actions often extended to the high seas (which at the time started three miles from the coast), where parties in a public war could stop neutral vessels, search them for contraband, and even seize them. The problem was this: if a sovereign state claimed to exercise its belligerent rights and demanded that foreigners observe their neutral duties, then there necessarily existed a state of war in the legal sense. A mere internal police action gave no right or authority to interfere with foreign vessels; even less would it permit the extreme measure of instituting a maritime blockade. But if a state of war was present, there had to be two or more international legal subjects engaging with one another as belligerent parties (for otherwise there was no telling whether a state was arbitrarily misusing its belligerent rights). Governments rarely admitted that their insurgents might constitute independent subjects under the law of nations; to do so would have been to essentially relinquish sovereignty over them. This often led to a contradiction between their legal positions (that there was no war) and their actions (waging war at sea). From such situations developed the state practice that led into the conceptualisation of the classical law of civil war.

1.1 Early Modern Civil Wars

1.1.1 The Dutch Revolt

It took eighty years for the inhabitants of the Netherlands to reject the Spanish crown and establish their independent republic. Closely tied to the religious wars caused by the Reformation in Europe, the Dutch Revolt began to brew after a wave of Protestant iconoclasms erupted in 1566, to which King Philip responded by instructing the notorious Duke of Alba to suppress the Low Countries. Insurgencies began to break out on land and at sea, and in 1572 the Dutch 'sea-beggars' captured the town of Brill, marking a general insurrection. By 1609 the Dutch had established de facto independence, though it was not until the Treaty of Münster in 1648 that they received recognition from Spain.[14]

The legal position of the Spanish crown towards the revolt was predictably strict: it considered the Netherlands as its lawful possession and any Dutch insurgents as criminals punishable in accordance with domestic laws. The crown jurist Balthazar Ayala maintained that 'rebels ought not to be classed as enemies, the two being quite distinct, and so it is more correct to term the armed contention with rebel subjects execution of legal process, or prosecution, and not war'.[15] Rebels had no recourse whatsoever to the law of nations, as they had neither the right nor just cause to wage war, whereas any war against them was by definition just.[16] Alberico Gentili agreed. Brigands did not have access to the laws of war, 'because that law is derived from the law of nations, and malefactors do not enjoy the privileges of a law to which they are foes'.[17] Dutch statesmen and jurists, among them Hugo Grotius, challenged this view by asserting that revolutionary facts against a ruler might effectively delegitimise a formal overlord, in particular if that lord had turned into a tyrant.[18] Accordingly, the Dutch claimed that the prince of a country was appointed by God to protect his subjects, and that if he instead chose to molest them, then he 'must be regarded not as a prince but as a tyrant'.[19] But in addition to arguing the illegitimacy of Spanish rule over the Netherlands, the States General built their case on a claim about their own ancient legitimacy, which they founded upon a historical claim of past autonomy and dormant sovereignty. They held that in the past the Netherlands – and Holland in particular – had constituted a legal subject in its own right, and that Spanish rule had been contractual in nature and

[14] Treaty of Münster, 30 January 1648, 1 CTS 1, art I.

[15] Balthazar Ayala, *De jure et officiis bellicis et disciplina militari libri III* ([1582] John Westlake tr, Carnegie Institution 1912) I.2.14.

[16] Ibid I.2.15.

[17] Alberico Gentili, *De iure belli*, I.4.35. He directly referred to Ulpian and Pomponius and, with authority from Cicero, famously characterised pirates as 'common enemies of all mankind'. Grotius agreed with this principle. See *DJBP* III.3.2 and II.18.2. See also *DJBP* III.3.11.

[18] A 'tyrant' is a ruler who has lost legitimacy to the extent that resistance against the tyrant might be just. At the time, the classical concept had been resuscitated in clandestine Huguenot monarchomach publications such as the *Vindiciae contra tyrannos* (1579). See Walter Rech, *Enemies of Mankind: Vattel's Theory of Collective Security* (Martinus Nijhoff 2013) 193–209, 218–220; Stefanos Junius Brutus (pseud), *Vindiciae contra tyrannos* ([1579] George Garnett tr, Cambridge University Press 1994) eg folio 115 (p 97).

[19] Dutch Act of Abjuration, 26 July 1581, in Oliver J. Thatcher (ed), *The Library of Original Sources*, vol V (University Research Extension Co, 1915) 189–197.

subject to constitutional conditions. The Dutch therefore claimed to have a distinct international personality derived from the past, which they would now legitimately revive. Their revolt was not simply a rebellion of inferiors against a superior; rather, it was a public international war fought by a union of free provinces to sever a particular foreign allegiance.[20]

The Dutch Revolt was fought at sea from its outset. The provinces asserted their subjecthood under the law of nations in 1568, when William of Orange and Louis of Nassau invoked the right of reprisal against the Duke of Alba and proceeded to commission filibusters against his regime. William's title as the sovereign of Orange mattered here – for example, by making it possible for Queen Elizabeth of England to gradually consider William as a lawful belligerent against Alba.[21] Since the capture of Brill, Dutch admiralty courts[22] had begun to examine captures made by sea-beggars (although in practice many prizes were doubtless sold without adjudication). In 1597, Prince Maurice established the Dutch Admiralty Colleges and instructed them to carry out prize proceedings.[23] After Philip III of Spain imposed major trade restrictions on Dutch commerce in 1598, establishing something of an embargo or a blockade, the States General stepped up its efforts to commission privateers.[24] In 1599, it announced general reprisals against Spain, declaring 'for good and lawfull prize, all persons and goods, under the dominion of the Spanish king, in all places where they shall or may be got'.[25]

[20] Peter Borschberg, *Hugo Grotius 'Commentarius in Theses XI'* (Peter Lang 1994); Ville Kari, 'Hugo Grotius and the Classical Law of Civil War' 41 *Grotiana* (2020) 412–427.

[21] J. B. Black, 'Queen Elizabeth, the Sea Beggars, and the Capture of Brille, 1572' 46 *English Historical Review* (1931) 38–39; Hugo Grotius, *De rebus belgicis, Or, The Annals and History of the Low-Countrey-Warrs* ([1657] Middle Temple 1665) 60; Jonathan I. Israel, *The Dutch Republic: Its Rise, Greatness and Fall, 1477–1806* (Oxford University Press 1995) 170–171. Also, Alex Ritsema, *Pirates and Privateers from the Low Countries, c.1500–c.1810* (Alex Ritsema 2008) 15.

[22] J. H. W. Verzijl, W. P. Heere, and J. P. S. Offerhaus, *International Law in Historical Perspective*, pt IX-C: *The Law of Maritime Prize* (Martinus Nijhoff 1992) 581–582.

[23] Instructions to the Admiralty College, 13 August 1597, *Groot Placaeat-boek* (1664) II.5.8.1. Also *Recueil van alle de Placaten, Ordonnantion, Resolutien, Instriuctien, Lysten en Waarschouwingen, betreffende de Admiraliteyten, Convoyen, Licenten, en verdere Zee-Saaken*, pt 1 (Jacobus Scheltus 1730) 1–26.

[24] Marjolein't Hart, *The Dutch Wars of Independence: Warfare and Commerce in the Netherlands 1570–1680* (Routledge 2014) 136.

[25] Edict of the Estates General of the United Provinces, 2 April 1599, in Hugo Grotius, *Commentary on the Law of Prize and Booty* (Martine Julia van Ittersum ed, Liberty Fund 2006) 503–510, at 506–507.

This is the context in which the affair of the *Santa Catarina* took place and in which Hugo Grotius became directly involved in legitimating the Dutch maritime struggle. Since 1578 the crown of Portugal had belonged to the king of Spain, leading to a connection between the Dutch Revolt against Spain and the encroachments on Portugal's empire in the East by the Dutch East India Company (Vereenigde Oost-Indische Compagnie, or VOC). The Amsterdam admiralty board, which was adjudicating the case in 1604, had to consider not only the legitimacy of the actions taken by the Dutch but also the validity of their prize jurisdiction. In its verdict the admiralty college, by all appearances, seemed unconcerned about the fact that the Portuguese had completely refused to acknowledge the Dutch prize jurisdiction. 'Nobody has come forward for the protection of carrack and cargo', it noted and issued a default judgment in favour of the captors. The legal meaning of this non-appearance – a challenge about whether or not the States General *could* validly grant such reprisals – was thus suppressed, and the owners of the carrack were summarily dismissed for 'contumacy'.[26] In substance, the board then agreed with the principal position of the captors: from among the many justifications for self-defence and reprisal, it retained that a just war had been waged by the Dutch against the Portuguese. The general reprisals declared in 1599 had been valid and had authorised the capture of Portuguese vessels, even if there could be doubt over whether that authorisation extended to the Straits of Malacca.[27]

So far, we have observed how hostilities at sea raised questions relating to the law of nations between the warring parties. But increasingly complex problems emerged also from the relations between the belligerents and foreign flags. Rebel captures of Spanish goods led inevitably to difficulties with neutrals, because Spanish ships would often also carry neutral cargo, or Spanish cargo might be taken from onboard neutral ships. Martine Julia van Ittersum recounts in detail one such incident, the capture of the wealthy East Indiaman *St Jago*, which turned out to be laden with goods partly belonging to an influential Florentine merchant, Francisco Carletti.[28] Like the matter of the *Santa Catarina*, the *St Jago*

26 Verdict of the Amsterdam Admiralty Board, 9 September 1604, in Grotius, *Commentary*, 510–514.

27 Ibid 513–514. A key passage reads: 'in the kingdoms of *Spaine*, *Portugall*, or other places of *Europe*, under the dominion, subjection, or command of the new king of *Spaine*'. For more analysis, see Martine Julia van Ittersum, *Profit and Principle: Hugo Grotius, Natural Rights theories and the Rise of Dutch Power in the East Indies (1595–1615)* (Brill 2006) 22–24.

28 Van Ittersum, *Profit and Principle*, 123–151, esp 139; see also Grotius' footnote at *DJBP* III.1.5.4.

affair was dealt with as though it were a wartime capture done in a public international war. The claim dealt expressly with the rights of neutrals – and where there were neutrals, there were international belligerents at war as well. In subsequent centuries, the doctrine of civil war would revolve around the same questions.

Queen Elizabeth initially refused to recognise the sea-beggars in 1571 or to admit England's involvement, ostensibly prioritising the interests of neutral shipping near the British Isles.[29] At the same time, English privateers were taking letters of marque from the Prince of Orange or his associates, and the British naval records show an extensive anti-piracy campaign taking place at sea.[30] In 1575, Elizabeth still sent her representatives to the Netherlands to demand again that the Dutch insurgents leave neutral trade unmolested.[31] Ten years later, after Francis Drake's successful voyage of circumnavigation, her policy towards Spain had shifted considerably. In 1585, Elizabeth authorised an expeditionary force to the Low Countries and agreed to the Treaty of Nonsuch, which recognised the Dutch republic, provided for shared prize jurisdiction and procedure, and arguably transformed the Dutch Revolt into an international war.[32] Ultimately, the intervention led to claims and complaints from neutrals against England, and in 1588 a special commission of civilians from the Doctors' Commons was constituted to deal with these matters.[33]

The problems of neutrality and civil war were therefore very much present in the Dutch Revolt, and they arose from the maritime theatre of the war. It was in these circumstances that admiralty colleges were established in 1597, general reprisals declared in 1599, and the Dutch East India Company established in 1602. By this time, the United Provinces were well on the way to de facto international statehood. The war culminated in the signing of the Twelve Years' Truce in 1609, after which most European powers granted the Dutch republic their recognition.[34] The insurgents' privateer warfare between 1568 and 1609

29 *Calendar of State Papers, Spain (Simancas)*, vol 2: *1568–1579* (HMSO 1894) xxxviii.

30 1 Marsden 211–236.

31 *DJBP* III.1.5.4.

32 Treaty of Nonsuch, 10 August 1585, in *A General Collection of Treatys, Manifesto's etc*, vol II (2nd edn, Knapton et co 1732) 83–88, esp arts VI, XXV, XXVI; Placaat of the States General, 6 February 1586, ibid 89; Patent and Commission of the Captain-General (1585) in 15 Rymer's *Fœdera*, 799–801.

33 Alain Wijffels, 'Sir Julius Caesar' in *Oxford Dictionary of National Biography* (Oxford University Press 2008).

34 Israel, *Dutch Republic*, 405–406.

had brought to the surface the legal questions that forced jurists to transform the abstract legal concepts of the law of nations into political practice. The events were not exceptional, as similar events took place also in the English Civil War, which broke out soon after the Dutch Revolt concluded.

1.1.2 The English Civil War

The trial and execution of Charles I fundamentally challenged early modern understandings about the legitimacy of revolutions and what the law of nations would permit peoples to do when oppressed by a tyrant. In the English common law, the king could in principle do no wrong, and royal statutes defined treason as a crime against the king rather than a crime by the king. But the Parliamentarians found a way forward through Bodin's marks of sovereignty and the Roman law of *maiestas*, which helped them split the king's two bodies and characterise the king's treason as a crime by Charles Stuart against the fundamental law of the land.[35] According to the articles of impeachment, Charles had been trusted with a limited power to govern for the benefit of the people and for the preservation of their rights and liberties. To overthrow those rights, he had sought 'tyrannical power to rule according to his Will' and had then 'traitorously and maliciously' gone to war against Parliament. Being responsible for the civil war, he was also guilty of all damages and suffering caused by it.[36] In response, Charles refused to acknowledge the legitimacy of the ad hoc high court. 'Remember, I am your King – your lawful King', he noted and reminded the court that England had never been an elective kingdom but rather a hereditary one. Reciting his own title as a trust from God 'by old and lawful descent', he claimed to himself represent the people better than his judges and refused to submit to the court's jurisdiction.[37]

But the court was not alone in addressing the question of the legal status of the king and Parliament. Privateers, prize judges, and foreign crowns had to deal with the issue throughout the Interregnum and the Restoration. After the capture of Charles I, the civil war was carried on at sea by Charles II, together with his brother James, Duke of York, and his cousins Rupert and Maurice, who led a large naval detachment that had

35 Alan Orr, 'The Juristic Foundation of Regicide' in Jason Peacey (ed), *The Regicides and the Execution of Charles I* (Palgrave 2001) 117–137. See also *Dig* 48.4.1.

36 4 *State Trials* 1070–1002.

37 4 *State Trials* 1073–1076. The Act constituting the court is in 1 *Interregnum* 1253–1255.

mutinied against Parliament in 1648. They continued their war under royal commissions and privateer instructions from the exiled heir to the throne,[38] and within weeks of the regicide the fleet, under Prince Rupert, was taking prizes off the coast of England. With great haste, the Parliamentarians appointed three 'sea generals' to defend their shores. Among them was the famous Robert Blake, who pursued Rupert for a good two years on the high seas.[39]

The duel between Rupert and Blake brought the English Civil War to the doorsteps of foreign crowns. In 1649, Rupert's fleet took shelter in the port of Lisbon, where he was welcomed by the king of Portugal, John IV, who, like the other Catholic monarchs of Europe, refused to recognise the Commonwealth. The king promised Rupert and Maurice all the protection in his power and the free use of his ports, gave them supplies and provisions, and purchased their prizes.[40] In response, Parliament sent Blake to Lisbon and instructed him to destroy the rebel fleet and other vessels joining or supporting them. He was specifically instructed to designate the royalist fleet itself as *piratæ et latrones*, but to spare any foreigners involved as prisoners of war.[41] Blake was to assert the legitimacy of the Commonwealth, to state the piratical nature of the former monarchy, and to maintain a certain observance of the law of nations with respect to third powers. What therefore occurred in Lisbon was a clash between two claims to sovereignty, with John of Portugal caught in the middle.

When Blake reached Lisbon, he sent an ultimatum to John, demanding that the Portuguese hand over the princes, failing which he would interpret their refusal as an unfriendly act and blockade the port. This, he argued, was for 'the common advantage of nations, which is disregarded, unless pains are taken to exterminate pirates, that most nefarious tribe, the enemies of the world'.[42] In effect, he was demanding that John recognise

38 For example, 1 Marsden 533 and 2 Marsden 1.

39 J. R. Powell (ed), *The Letters of Robert Blake Together with Supplementary Documents* (Navy Records Society 1937); R. C. Anderson, 'Royalists at Sea' pts 1–4, *Mariner's Mirror* 9(2) (1923), 14(4) (1928), 17(2) (1931), 21(1) (1935).

40 Eva Scott, *Rupert, Prince Palatine* (Putnam's Sons 1899) 241.

41 Powell, *The Letters of Blake*, 11; Anderson, 'Royalists at Sea' pt 3 (1931) 139. The instructions are calendared in CSP Dom 1649–1650, 483–485. Additional instructions to Blake, 20 April 1650, 20 Rymer's *Fœdera* 580, 581, instructing '*Quod Piratæ & Latrones qui Civitatem faciunt* [sic], *jure Gentium uti non possunt*, and being as they are *hostis humani generis*'. Compare *DJBP* II.18.2. The mis-citation is as printed in the *Fœdera* and may or may not come from the original letter (it should be 'non faciunt'). See also Popham's parallel instructions printed after Blake's.

42 Blake to king of Portugal, 20 March 1650, in Powell, *Letters of Blake*, 54; A paper to the king of Portugal, 5 April 1650, 20 Rymer's *Fœdera* 579.

the Commonwealth and declare Rupert a fugitive pirate.[43] Prince Rupert, on the other hand, presented his commission from Charles II, heir to the English throne, arguing that Cromwell was but a pretender and villain – and 'how shameful a thing it was for a Christian King to treat with rebels'.[44] The two opposing admirals now confronted each other in a legal stalemate. They were both essentially relying on the same arguments – namely, legitimacy and recognition. Each asserted their own lord's legitimacy and dismissed the opposing faction as pirates and rebels. Blake's position was that the tyrannical king Charles Stuart had been lawfully tried, found guilty, and executed by a high court of the land, and that consequently it was Rupert's putative commission from Charles II that was invalid. Rupert could in turn respond that the so-called court that had condemned its king had been illegitimate and godless, or not even a court, and that in fact England was now not ruled by a stable government but occupied by a temporary cabal of 'tumultuous, factious, seditious soldiers and other disorderly and refractory persons',[45] which brought with it nothing but robbery, chaos, and anarchy.

What would King John of Portugal do? His different options all entailed an interpretation of both the law and the facts. At first, he refused to yield before Blake's armada and tried to act as neutral broker vis-à-vis the two warring parties.[46] After his request that Blake give Rupert a three days' head start was refused, John affirmed his support for Charles II, refused to recognise Cromwell, and braced for the coming blockade.[47] In the end, Rupert's fleet broke the blockade with the help of French and Portuguese vessels, suffering significant losses. The chase continued, first into the Mediterranean and then to the West Indies, where, since the beginning of the privateering campaign, the colonists had found themselves infested by filibusters, who even began to attack and seize ships in harbours.[48] In 1651, Parliament's first Navigation Act established an

[43] See also A second paper to the king of Portugal, 15 April 1650, 20 Rymer's *Fœdera* 580.

[44] Scott, *Rupert*, 242.

[45] Scott, *Rupert*, 243.

[46] Agreement between Vane and Mendes de Vasconcellas, 28 March 1650, in Powell, *Letters of Blake*, 76; Litteræ directæ Principi Ruperto per Lusitanicum, 27 December 1650, 20 Rymer's *Fœdera* 573; for Prince Rupert, 18 March 1650, 20 Rymer's *Fœdera* 578.

[47] On the encounter, see Scott, *Rupert*, 241–244; Ward and others (eds), *The Cambridge Modern History*, vol IV (Macmillan 1907) 463–464. For documents, see Blake's correspondence in Powell, *Letters of Blake*, 54–96; Additional instructions to Blake, 20 April 1650, II Marsden 5; Report of the admiralty judges, 24 March 1651, II Marsden 11.

[48] Helen J. Crump, *Colonial Admiralty Jurisdiction in the Seventeenth Century* (Longmans Green 1931) 41.

English trade monopoly in the overseas colonies, where shipping was dominated by free-trading Dutch fluyts.[49] The Act prohibited all trade with the loyalist colonies and declared all trespassing ships lawful prize. Despite initial resistance from the colonists, the West Indies were eventually brought back under Commonwealth control, and by the time Prince Rupert appeared there in 1652 he found there was no longer much support.[50]

The persistence of the legal issues raised in such maritime encounters both in Europe and in overseas colonial waters eventually forced foreign governments to choose between recognising Cromwell's government or continuing to support the king in exile. While most of them opposed the Commonwealth as fundamentally illegitimate, there were various instances of accommodation and recognition of the Interregnum, brought on by mercantile competition and continuing religious strife coupled with the rising English sea power. Back in Portugal, Robert Blake turned on John IV and forced him to sign articles providing for the return of all English persons and ships captured by Rupert and Maurice, the punishment or extradition of loyalists, compensation for private claims made by the English, and reparation of 50,000 pounds in addition to the seized Portuguese property amounting to over 100,000 ducats.[51] The First Anglo-Dutch War, which was sparked by crackdowns on Dutch merchants in the West Indies under the Navigation Act in 1652, likewise turned in favour of Blake's navy: in the peace treaty of Westminster in 1654, the Netherlands recognised the republic of England as its counterpart and agreed not to harbour its 'rebels'.[52] The kingdoms of Denmark and Sweden soon followed suit,[53] as did Portugal, which, in its definitive treaty of peace with Cromwell, reaffirmed that 'neither side shall receive or protect the rebels or fugitives of each other'.[54]

By contrast, Catholic Spain, the Holy Roman Empire, and the Papacy opposed Cromwell's interregnum throughout its existence. When in

49 An Act for Prohibiting Trade with the Barbadoes, Virginia, Bermuda, and Antego, 3 October 1650, 2 *Acts and Ordinances of the Interregnum* 425–429.

50 Carla Gardina Pestana, *The English Atlantic in an Age of Revolution, 1640–1661* (Harvard University Press 2004) 86–107. See also CSP Colonial, America and West Indies vol 1 (1574–1660) 1 February 1651 onwards.

51 Preliminary Articles of Peace, 29 December 1652, 2 CTS 463, art IV.

52 Anglo-Dutch Treaty of Westminster, 5 April 1654, 3 CTS 225, arts VI–VII. See also 3 CTS 271.

53 See 3 CTS 257, 3 CTS 355, 4 CTS 127. Also, Russia invited the Protectorate's trade representative in Archangel to Moscow (3 CTS 315).

54 Treaty between England and Portugal, 10 July 1654, 3 CTS 281, art I.

1650 Anthony Ascham was named Commonwealth ambassador to Madrid and charged with obtaining recognition from Spain, a group of armed English loyalists murdered him and his translator at a dinner table shortly after their arrival.[55] Following the outbreak of the Anglo-Spanish war, ignited by Cromwell's 'Western design', Spain signed an alliance with Charles II, with the exiled king pledging to end the suppression of Catholicism in England and to support a Spanish reconquest of Portugal and its overseas territories.[56] The English peace treaty with the Netherlands and the convergence of England's and France's interests in the West Indies resulted in Mazarin and Louis XIV agreeing to an alliance with Cromwell after extensive negotiations.[57] The first treaty of 1655 mostly concerned proper prize procedures and adjudication, expressly providing for the restoration of all ships or goods 'taken by rebels, under colour of any commissions whatsoever'.[58] This alliance between the Catholic Sun King and the Protestant regicides (which marked a significant repudiation of Spanish monopoly in the New World and had long-lasting repercussions on colonial geography there) illustrates how the traditional crowns could at the time still allow themselves to consider republican aspirations in England and the Netherlands as posing little threat to their own legitimacy. Conversely, after Charles II's restoration to the throne, France and the other Continental monarchies quickly established new treaty relations with England, effectively removing the English Commonwealth and Protectorate from the European public order.

One final, noteworthy feature of the legal disputes surrounding the English Civil War was the use of international arbitration to settle large quantities of private property claims and disputed prize matters in bulk. The most prominent were the Anglo-Dutch arbitrations provided for in the peace treaty of 1654.[59] The first concerned wartime detention of English ships in Danish ports at the request of the United Provinces, for which the Dutch now agreed to compensate the English shipowners; on 31 July 1654, a commission of four arbitrators awarded them

[55] The documents are in 20 Rymer's *Fœdera* 586–590.

[56] Secret Treaty between Spain and Charles II, 12 April 1656, 4 CTS 71.

[57] Anglo-French Treaty of Westminster, 3 November 1655, 4 CTS 1; Treaty of Paris, 9 May 1657, 4 CTS 347. Compare David L. Smith, 'Diplomacy and the Religious Question: Mazarin, Cromwell and the Treaties of 1655 and 1657', *e-Rea, Revue électronique d'études sur le monde anglophone* (2014) 4–6.

[58] Anglo-French Treaty of Westminster, art XX.

[59] Anglo-Dutch Treaty of Westminster, arts XXVIII and XXX.

compensation amounting to some 93,000 pounds.[60] A second commission, sitting in London, addressed the causes of the Anglo-Dutch war directly: its four arbitrators were instructed to examine the total claims between the English and Dutch East India Companies arising from the treatment of their merchants anywhere from Greenland and Russia to the East and West Indies since 1611. The British merchants filed claims amounting to some 2.7 million pounds for excessive charges and taxes beyond those agreed in summits between the English and Dutch East India Companies before 1619, the expulsion of the English East India Company from the spice islands, maltreatment of British persons, and other grounds. The Dutch countered with over two million pounds' worth of claims over unpaid British expenses according to the same cost-sharing agreements, costs for providing maritime security in the East Indies, unlawful wartime seizures of Dutch East India Company property, and more. In the end, the tribunal awarded the English East India Company the sum of 85,000 pounds and proceeded to 'make void, extinguish, obliterate, and altogether wipe out and commit to oblivion (so as never to be revived at any time, and upon any pretence by any person whatsoever) all complaints, pretensions and controversies mentioned more at large above'.[61]

The Anglo-Dutch arbitrations were not isolated incidents; there are references to the settlement of claims through arbitral proceedings in the Protectorate's treaties with Portugal in 1654[62] and France in 1655[63], as well as acknowledgement of the provision for Anglo-Dutch arbitration in the Anglo-Danish peace treaty of 1654.[64] As a method of dispute resolution, arbitration was readily available to Cromwell and the United Provinces thanks to established arbitral practices within the Dutch and English East India Companies.[65] It was thus set to emerge onto the world stage and take the place left vacant by the demise of papal

[60] Arbitral award of 31 July 1654, III *General Collection of Treatys* 112, 3 CTS 303. According to the arbitration rules, the following day they would have been 'shut up in a Room ... without Fire, Candle, Drink, [Food] or other Support, till they have agreed'.

[61] Règlement pursuant to the Treaty of Peace, 30 August 1654, 3 CTS 319; Andrew Ruoss, 'Between Companies: The Arbitration of 1654 and the Evolution of Corporate Strategy in the East Indies Trade' 31 *Journal of World History* (2020) 519, 527–531. A further claims convention from 1655 refers to one more batch of claims to be arbitrated in Amsterdam (3 CTS 431).

[62] Treaty between England and Portugal, art XXV.

[63] Anglo-French Treaty of Westminster, art XXIV.

[64] Treaty between England and Denmark, 15 September 1654, 3 CTS 355, art IV.

[65] Ruoss, 'Between Companies', 523–524.

arbitrations after the Reformation and the Peace of Westphalia. To some extent, the constitution of several arbitral tribunals to concurrently settle the outstanding disputes between the English republic and the various European crowns can be seen as a precedent for the widespread rise of post-revolutionary arbitrations in the nineteenth century, where dealing with international state responsibility became a regular initiation rite for newly independent states. By contrast, Cromwell's arbitrations were not imposed on the English interregnum but rather established mostly to its benefit. They were designed to address outstanding commercial claims or alleged breaches of belligerent and neutral duties as ordinary international disputes. An example is the London Arbitration of 1654, which dealt with matters reaching back to the recognition of the Dutch republic. In this respect, the Anglo-French arbitration provided for in 1655 can be considered an exception as it addressed foreign prize complaints arising directly from the Civil War.

***

Overall, the naval and privateer warfare associated with the English Civil War raised similar questions about belligerency and neutrality as the Dutch Revolt had. Such common problems involved insurgent prize jurisdictions, the legitimacy of belligerent interference against neutrals on the high seas, the treatment of insurgent flags in foreign ports and domains, and the legal status of captives as lawful prisoners of war or criminal pirates. They emerged from the particular circumstances of the age of sail, they were well established in case law by the late seventeenth century,[66] and they would persist in conditions of insurgency and revolution into the late nineteenth century. Similar disputes over maritime warfare and jurisdiction would arise in more or less every classical civil war, whether they were about the prizes of John Paul Jones in Texel and Bergen,[67] the Baltimore privateers in the service of the Spanish American republics,[68] the Confederate mariners trying to access European ports after the abolition of privateering,[69] or other similar incidents.

It is therefore not a surprise that a common legal doctrine of civil war began to emerge in the writings of learned publicists during these conflicts, as the Dutch revolutionaries sought to justify their cause in terms of the law of nations and the English jurists sought to confirm the validity of

66 Golding's Case, 12 *State Trials* 1269.
67 See Chapter 2.
68 See Chapter 3.
69 See Chapter 4.

their Commonwealth in the aftermath of the king's execution. Though the process would take several generations of scholarship, by the eve of the American and French revolutions the core principles of the classical doctrine of civil war would be available in the common textbooks of the law of nations.

1.2 Doctrinal Origins

The question of civil war was very much present in the writings of the early modern publicists of the law of nations, from the Spanish scholastics to the Enlightenment. The classics pondered the lawfulness of war conducted by subjects against their sovereigns, and each in their own way sought a balance between affirming the authority of lawful governments to put down rebellions and allowing for subjects to rise against their rulers in extreme circumstances. They typically found themselves in some sort of middle ground, and there was little else that they could do. To reject a ruler's right to establish order in their territory would have been unacceptable for any sovereign state, and to categorically deny the legitimacy of revolutions would have run contrary to historical evidence. But there was a second way in which the legal principles of civil war appeared in the classics: the emerging laws of legation and embassies – that is, the question of who could have a voice under the law of nations and in what circumstances. In this way, the practical questions arising from insurrections fought at sea forced European scholars and justices to greatly exert their legal imaginations in pursuit of appropriate legal distinctions that could help answer the question of who was a pirate and who a privateer. While the question about the right of a people to arise against their ruler was often discussed in the abstract terms of natural law and universal order, the issue of representation and subjecthood was understood as a more practical matter, belonging in the human-made, volitional law of nations.

Although one cannot speak of any particular linear development or advancement in the theory of the classical doctrine of civil war, the scholars of the law of nations did gradually proceed from general principles of legitimacy and revolution to a detailed taxonomy of degrees of insurgency, distinguishable from each other by rules of recognition established in the law of nations. In the seventeenth century we see the emergence of this mindset, when Alberico Gentili and his contemporaries begin to elaborate the principles of legation and representation in situations of disputed sovereignty. Gentili's work on the laws of war demonstrates early modern jurists' clear awareness of the perpetual problem of civil war since antiquity, as well as their strong commitment to the old Roman law principles that considered the notion of public authority and an unconditional prohibition of self-help as being bound together with a denunciation of rebels and pirates under the law of nations.[70] Yet, as we have seen, in Gentili's period experiences of rebel legations and questions of their standing under the law of nations led scholars to rethink the boundaries between those dichotomic principles. Later, Enlightenment scholars such as Christian Wolff and especially Emer de Vattel put into words these emerging concepts of the classical doctrine of civil war in the law of nations in an attempt to distinguish between riots, insurrections, and civil wars and the legal effects befitting each. That Vattelian theory of civil war became the legal framework through which contemporary lawyers perceived the events of the American revolution of 1775–1783.

1.2.1 The Right to Resist

When Jean Bodin sketched his unitarian theory of absolute sovereignty, according to which a ruler was responsible only to God and subjects were not permitted to arise against their sovereign,[71] he was reflecting the anxieties of European elites in the wake of events such as the St Bartholomew's Day massacre in Paris in 1572. Bodin decried civil war as barbarism and the Machiavellian tyranny of rulers as a violation of higher laws;[72] he sought a middle-ground solution based on the suggestion that a ruler was immune from earthly laws but not from natural law and divine judgment.[73] During the Dutch Revolt, jurists in the Netherlands took their legal positions with these stakes in mind, but insisted on earthly constitutional constraints for rulers. Hugo Grotius argued for Dutch independence under both natural law and the law of nations in a number of publications through his career.[74] In his manuscript *Commentarius in Theses XI*, he argued the Dutch case by reference to Bodin's theory. Like Bodin, he divided the

70 Gentili, *De iure belli*, I.4.

71 Jean Bodin, *Six Books of the Commonwealth* [1576] eg I.8, II.5.

72 Bodin, preface to the French original (du Puy 1576) ii–iii.

73 Jean Bodin, *On Sovereignty* ([1576] Julian H. Franklin ed, Cambridge University Press 1992) xxiv–xxvi.

74 Hugo Grotius, *De iure praedae commentarius* (Gwladys L. Williams tr, Clarendon Press 1950); Grotius, *The Antiquity of the Batavian Republic* ([1610] Jan Waszink tr, van Gorcum 2000); Grotius, *De Rebus Belgicis*.

monolithic concept of sovereignty into a number of functional competences or 'marks of sovereignty',[75] but rejected Bodin's insistence on the unity of sovereignty. He argued instead that the different marks could belong to several institutions or be shared among them.[76] Whoever possessed any one of these particular marks of sovereignty – say, the right to decide on taxes – also had a natural right to defend that function by whatever means were necessary.[77] Whoever undertook such a just war in defence of a mark of sovereignty also acquired the other marks for the duration of that war and, if successful, perpetually in full independence.[78] When applied to the case of the Dutch republic, Bodin's theory could found the argument that the Estates of Holland since time immemorial had enjoyed a right to veto any new taxes proposed by Philip, and that therefore, under natural law, they could fight back against Spain.[79] Though the *Commentarius in Theses XI* remained unpublished in Grotius' lifetime, a similar stance was reflected in *De jure belli ac pacis* and its chapter on the war of subjects against superiors. The question of whether insurgents were pirates and brigands boiled down to an assessment of necessity, which was an implicit acknowledgement that royal prerogatives were subject to limits.[80] While private persons could not take it upon themselves to pass judgment on the legality of a ruler's claim (instead they 'should accept the fact of possession'[81]), there were important exceptions to this rule. These included situations of 'extreme and imminent peril', such as when a ruler had manifestly abandoned a kingdom or set out to destroy its people, and, most importantly for the Dutch, circumstances in which a 'free people' fought to regain its freedom from a ruler who had violated its rights.[82]

Grotius' implicit notion of a social contract as a basis for sovereignty was not unique. It had been explored by the Spanish scholastic Vazquez de Menchaca[83] and was developed further in England and France during the

75 Borschberg, *Commentarius in Theses XI*, 118–120, 205.

76 Thesis 4 in Borschberg, *Commentarius in Theses XI*, 225–235, esp 227. Borschberg notes the influence of Vázquez de Menchaca, ibid 85–88.

77 Thesis 5 in Borschberg, *Commentarius in Theses XI*, 237–251.

78 Thesis 8 in Borschberg, *Commentarius in Theses XI*, 259–267.

79 Theses 9–11 in Borschberg, *Commentarius in Theses XI*, 269–283.

80 *DJBP* I.4.2.

81 *DJBP* I.4.6 and I.4.19–I.4.20.

82 *DJBP* I.4.7. Grotius was borrowing the list of a Scottish-born Catholic jurist called William Barclay, from c. 1600. See *DJBP* I.4.8–I.4.18; also *DJBP*, student edn by Stephen Neff (Cambridge University Press 2013) 71, fn.

83 Annabel Brett, *Liberty, Right and Nature: Individual Rights in Later Scholastic Thought* (Cambridge University Press 1997) 165–204, esp 173 and 204; Borschberg, *Commentarius in Theses XI*, 85–88; *DJBP*, Neff's edn, xxxi.

following century. In *Leviathan* (1651), Thomas Hobbes explored the secular origins of sovereign power in order to anchor the authority of monarchs to natural first principles that would be independent of religious denominations. While doing so, he distinguished between instituted and acquired sovereignty: a commonwealth by acquisition came to exist through forceful conquest (that is, by fact), which led to the vanquished submitting to the conqueror; yet once submitted, the subjects were no longer permitted to dissolve their bonds to the ruler.[84] Though Hobbes regularly rejected any right of subjects to rebel against their sovereign, *Leviathan* still could not avoid noting extreme circumstances in which subjects might still have recourse to their natural and inalienable right to self-preservation.[85]

Authors after Hobbes increasingly emphasised the revolutionary argument that a ruler who ceased to perform the protective functions of a sovereign became a tyrant and could lose sovereign status. Samuel Pufendorf, for one, agreed that the conquered could be understood to have given their consent to the conqueror at least tacitly, and therefore it was 'reasonable that the power of any possessor should be binding, *provided he rule like a lawful prince*'.[86] His contemporary John Locke reversed the Hobbesian logic of the social contract by arguing that society was not based on mutual fear, but rather on a sociable need to create a lawful order to safeguard everyone's life, health, liberty, and possessions and to enable everyone's pursuit of their lives in a spirit of mutual trust and tolerance.[87] In this context a ruler had a defined function and therefore a duty to ensure the protection of private property, which made the ruler in fact the servant of the people instead of their master. Whensoever a ruler then violated this fundamental rule of society and sought absolute power, they forfeited the power entrusted in them, and the people had 'a right to resume their original liberty' and to establish a new legislative authority.[88] In such a situation, if the ruler's courts and institutions provided no remedy, a war against the ruler would be imminent because (and here Locke borrowed from Coke's definition of war and peace) 'where there is no judge on earth, the appeal lies to God in heaven'.[89] The *Two Treatises of*

[84] Thomas Hobbes, *Leviathan* (Andrew Crooke 1651) 119, 139–142.

[85] Ibid 87–88, 89–90, 153–156, *et passim*; Patricia Sheridan, 'Resisting the Scaffold: Self-Preservation and Limits of Obligation in Hobbes's *Leviathan*' 24 *Hobbes Studies* (2011) 137–157.

[86] Samuel Pufendorf, *De jure naturae et gentium libri octo* ([1688] C. H. Oldfather tr, Clarendon Press 1934) VII.8.9–10. Emphasis added.

[87] John Locke, *Two Treatises of Government* ([1690] Yale University Press 2003) II.II.6–8.

[88] Ibid II.XIX.222.

[89] Ibid II.III.21.

Government was no longer on the middle ground between the right of the sovereign and the needs of the people; it was a work openly asserting a right of resistance to unjust authority. Locke's influence on the later American revolutionaries is well known; this principle was adopted by Thomas Jefferson in 1776 in the Declaration of Independence, and likewise by George Washington's first naval captains who inscribed on their flag the words 'An Appeal to Heaven'.[90]

The theory of a people's right to resist a ruler who violates their societal compact or the constitution provided a foundation for the rise and consolidation of the principles of the classical law of civil war in the Enlightenment era, as it repeatedly called into question the traditional legal preconception of revolutionaries as mere *piratæ et latrones*. In the law of nations, the legal fate of insurgents and their privateers turned the essence of these philosophical debates into reality. The problem of internal strife was not limited to whether or not there could exist a revolutionary right against a sovereign right; problems also arose especially when revolutionary facts confronted sovereign counter-claims. In the face of the wider world, the recurring question of the justice of insurrections took the shape of a diplomatic problem: the international legal standing of insurgents and possible recognition thereof. Practical experience tended to support Bynkershoek's candid answer that '[i]n political matters, at any rate, it is expedient that possession be nine points of the law'.[91]

1.2.2 The Law of Legation

In *De Jure Belli ac Pacis*, Hugo Grotius first dwells on the natural law pertaining to nations and rulers. When he finally moves on to the volitional law of nations – the *ius gentium* proper – his first topic is the law of legation – that is, the right to engage in diplomatic exchanges by sending and receiving emissaries or making treaties. The starting point of the law of nations is thus the question of international legal subjecthood. It is no coincidence that the question of who does or does not have legal standing was (and is) the crux of the international law of recognition as well as the classical doctrine of civil war. Although the main rule remained that the law of legation belonged only to sovereigns, Grotius

90 Reed to Glover, 20 October 1775, 2 NDAR 538; Resolution of the Massachusetts General Court, 29 April 1776, 4 NDAR 1302–1303.

91 Cornelius van Bynkershoek, *Quaestionum juris publici libri duo* ([1737] T. Frank tr, Carnegie Endowment 1930) II.III.158–159.

expressed something of an exception in the case of a 'true' civil war (*bellum vero civilibus*):

> In civil wars, however, necessity sometimes opens the way for the exercise of this right [of legation], though in an irregular fashion. Such a case will arise when a people has been divided into parts so nearly equal that it is doubtful which of the two sides possesses sovereignty; and again, when two persons with practically equal rights are contending for the succession to the throne. Under such circumstances, a single people is considered for the time being as two peoples. . . . Pirates and brigands, who do not constitute a state, cannot avail themselves of the law of nations.[92]

This brief passage encapsulates the core issue of the classical doctrine of civil war, which is that the distinction between pirates and revolutionaries might be determined on the basis of effective control rather than natural right. Grotius was not the first to summarise the principle; Alberico Gentili, in particular, had already thoroughly explored the matter in his 1585 treatise on the law of embassies. While Gentili also considered that rebels and pirates were to be denied embassies,[93] the opposite was true in civil wars: 'When in the strife each faction lays claim by word and deed to the whole organization of the state or to half of it, the right of embassy will certainly hold between the combatants.'[94] In 1598, Gentili confirmed these principles in his *De iure belli*, in the very same chapter as where he defines the pirate as the common enemy of mankind.[95] Again, crossing the threshold from an insurgency to a genuine civil war in the world of facts could transform a rebelling domestic subject into a lawful public enemy.

The topic of civil war also linked the law of recognition with that of neutrality at the time both were emerging.[96] In public wars, Grotius wrote, 'those at peace should show themselves impartial to either side in permitting transit, in furnishing supplies to troops, and in not assisting those under siege'.[97] At the same time, he affirmed the continuing right of exiled kings to maintain their thrones and enter

[92] *DJBP* II.18.2.

[93] Alberico Gentili, *De legationibus libri tres* ([1585] G. J. Laing tr, Oxford University Press 1924) II, 76–81 and 84.

[94] Ibid II, 82–83.

[95] Gentili, *De iure belli*, I.4.

[96] Philip C. Jessup and Francis Deák, *Neutrality: Its History, Economics and Law*, vol I (Columbia University Press 1935) 4; Neff, *Rights and Duties of Neutrals*, 27–28; Jochen A. Frowein, 'Recognition' in *Max Planck Encyclopedia of Public International Law* (Oxford Public International Law 2010). Compare footnote under *DJBP* III.1.5.

[97] *DJBP* III.17.3. See also III.17.1.

into valid treaties, and he considered it permissible for foreign thrones to assist them against usurpers.[98]

Grotius' influence was not confined to tribunes of academics. Charles II, for one, benefited directly from such provisions, which enabled him to issue valid commissions to his supporters. But they were utilised by Cromwell's regime as well in its search for legal justifications for its transition from insurrectionary government to new legitimacy. Casting the king as a tyrant was one thing, but casting Parliament as legitimate and having magistrates take oaths of engagement was quite another.[99] At the heart of the engagement controversy was Anthony Ascham, who sought to systematically apply Grotian thinking to the situation of civil war and conquest within England.[100] In his book *Of the Confusions and Revolutions of Governments*, Ascham wrote: 'To assure our consciences of a Justifiable obedience during the confusions or revolutions of Warre, it is best and enough for us to consider, *Whether the invading party (just or unjust) have us or the meanes of our subsistence in their possession or no*.'[101] He reviewed the recent practice of essentially *uti possidetis* peacemaking in the French wars of religion – although he did not mention that the same principle was also being applied in the Peace of Westphalia – and recommended that a similar rationale based on de facto power and possession be applied within a kingdom in the wake of a civil war. On this, he expressly referred to Grotius' grant of the right of embassy to insurgents during a war, adding that 'in regno diviso, gens una pro tempore quasi duæ gentes habentur'.[102] Ascham's advice implied that the outcome of civil war in England should be considered legitimate under the general law of nations applicable to all public wars.

1.2.3 *The Doctrine of Civil War: Wolff and Vattel*

In the eighteenth century, Christian Wolff and Emer de Vattel gave the classical doctrine of civil war a more definitive form. Building on the

[98] *DJBP* II.16.17–18, III.20.3.

[99] Quentin Skinner, 'Conquest and Consent: Hobbes and the Engagement Controversy' in Skinner, *Visions of Politics*, vol 3: *Hobbes and Civil Science* (Cambridge University Press 2002) 287–307.

[100] Annabel Brett, 'Protection as a Political Concept', 102–103.

[101] Anthony Ascham, *Of the Confusions and Revolutions of Governments* (W. Wilson 1649) I.VIII.34 (italics in the original).

[102] Ascham, *Confusions*, I.VIII.37–38. As Annabel Brett correctly points out (Brett, 'Protection as a Political Concept', fn 44), the principle was in reality first articulated not by Grotius but by Alberico Gentili in his *De legationibus* and *De iure belli* in 1585 and 1598.

principles of Gentili and Grotius, they identified discrete categories of internal conflicts, which followed a progression from riots and rebellions to broader insurgencies and finally to genuine civil wars.[103] They also presented the doctrine of civil war as a distinct branch of international law, unlike their predecessors, who saw it as related to legation or the legitimacy of rulers.

The German polymath Christian Wolff included in his 1749 treatise on the law of nations a scientific terminology and taxonomical progression of different categories of internal strife, from local tumults and riots to broader rebellions and, finally, civil wars. Wolff's propensity for systematisation reflects his lifelong project of developing the foundations that would establish German as the rigorous scientific language, using a 'scientific method' that emulated Carl von Linné's paradigmatic *Systema naturae* (1735). Wolff defined 'rebellion' ('ein Aufruhr') as a situation in which subjects took up arms without just cause against the ruler of the state, and 'civil war' as a conflict in which subjects took up arms for a just cause.[104] If there was uncertainty as to whether a conflict was a rebellion or a civil war, its participants could be called the disaffected ('die Misvergnügten') or the malcontents ('die Malcontanten').[105] A situation in which a crowd congregated and used force against magistrates or private persons and their property was a 'riot' ('ein Aufstand'), and the participants were to be punished under criminal law.[106] Even though Wolff's German terminology was never adopted abroad, the idea of a rational taxonomy of internal conflicts was taken up by later writers. Although the distinctions were never very clear-cut, they did become a characteristic of later theories of the law of civil war, if not for their utility then at least because they lent the doctrine some scientific and positivist gravitas.

Other aspects of Wolff's views on civil war were less groundbreaking. Wolff placed his examination of rebellion and civil war in a section of his book that dealt with peace as opposed to war, and civil wars are not mentioned at all in his discussion of the laws of war. Also, situations in

[103] See Vattel III.18.293–294. Lauterpacht notes that Grotius 'is speaking of the right of legation of the parties to the civil war *inter se*' but that the passage may have been 'indirectly' influential beyond that limit. See Hersch Lauterpacht, *Recognition in International Law* (Cambridge University Press 1947) 100.

[104] Christian Wolff, *Jus gentium methodo scientifica pertractatum* ([1749] J. H. Drake tr, Clarendon Press 1934) §§ 1010–1011.

[105] Ibid § 1011.

[106] Ibid §§ 1013–1014.

which the ruler of a state waged war with their rebellious subjects were classified under the outdated concept of 'mixed wars'.[107] And, perhaps most importantly, even though Wolff separated civil war from rebellion as distinct concepts, his test for civil war remained its having natural justice as its cause. On the right of resistance, Wolff was relatively conventional (and somewhat circular): since it was prohibited for subjects to resist their ruler, most internal conflicts would not be civil wars – 'except when it is allowable'.[108] Under the law of nations, the distinction between a rebellion and civil war hinged on a just cause, so that resisting the wrongs of a ruler without a just cause was 'not civil war, but rebellion'.[109] Foreign powers, 'inasmuch as they ought not to intrude themselves in the affairs of others', were instructed to consider all insurgencies as 'innerliche Unruhe' (internal unrest) – assuming they chose to take note of them at all.[110] At the end of the day, the criteria of a just cause fell into indeterminacy, it being ultimately conditional upon the constitutional relationship between the people and their ruler. In his earlier work on natural law, Wolff had leaned on the logical conclusion that any exceptional right to resist supreme authority would in and of itself nullify that supreme authority; he had therefore maintained that subjects and magistrates could do no more than voice complaints or ultimately disobey (and then flee) their sovereign. But à la Grotius, he had at the same time conceded a just cause for resistance in situations where the ruler was bound by constitutional limits and sought to overstep them.[111]

This changed with Emer de Vattel's *Droit des gens* (1758), where the test between civil wars and domestic insurgencies was primarily one of tangible facts, not natural rights. To overcome the tension between the right to resist and the duty to obey, Vattel turned his attention to a formalist understanding of civil war – that is, away from the law of nature and towards the volitional law of nations proper.[112] Even before Vattel, authors had sometimes admitted that as there was no superior earthly interpreter of whether in war a cause was just or unjust, then it might be expedient – for third parties especially – to treat the war on both

[107] Ibid § 609.
[108] Ibid § 1012.
[109] Ibid § 1012.
[110] Ibid § 1011.
[111] Wolff, *Jus naturae, methodo scientifica pertractatum Pars Octava, sive ultima* (Magdeburg 1748) §§ 1044–1054, esp 1047.
[112] Walter Rech, *Enemies of Mankind: Vattel's Theory of Collective Security* (Martinus Nijhoff 2013) 209, 216–217.

sides as just and thus equal in terms of belligerent rights and duties. Vattel abandoned the concepts of private and 'mixed' wars and maintained that the law of nations applied solely to public wars.[113] Instead of excluding civil wars from this category, he extended the notion of public war – and therefore the law of nations – to also cover civil wars on an equal footing with international wars:

> Civil war breaks the bonds of society and of government, or at least suspends the force and effect of them; it gives rise, within the Nation, to two independent parties, who regard each other as enemies and acknowledge no common judge. Of necessity, therefore, these two parties must be regarded as forming thenceforth, for a time at least, two separate bodies politic, two distinct Nations. That being so, it is perfectly clear that the established laws of war, those principles of humanity, forbearance, truthfulness, and honour, which we have earlier laid down, should be observed on both sides in a civil war.[114]

Civil war having now become a war under the law of nations, all parties were obliged to observe the customary laws of war and neutrality as in public, inter-state wars.[115] This meant a categorical acceptance of the belligerent status of the rebel side. In a proper civil war, just as in all international wars, both sides would enjoy equal rights in full, and what was permissible to one belligerent was permissible to the other as well.[116] When international lawyers debated the question of belligerent recognition a century later, they were still accepting this monolithic nature of the concept of civil war.

Not all internal conflicts were civil wars. Like Wolff nine years before him, Vattel also classified internal conflicts based on their factual scale and severity, accepting a distinction between small, local commotions and large, political uprisings that would endure in time, scope, and impact on a scale sufficient to become wars of international relevance. Like Wolff, he maintained the term 'rebel' as a general reference to all subjects who unjustly take up arms against the ruler of their society.[117] Rebellious events of a smaller scale were divided into local 'popular tumults' and movements of 'sedition' directed at official magistrates that might have to be put down by force. And, wrote Vattel, 'when the evil extends and wins over the majority of the citizens in a town or

[113] Vattel III.1.2.
[114] Vattel III.18.293–294. He reaffirms the protection of insurgents in III.18.287.
[115] Vattel III.18.295.
[116] Vattel III.12.191.
[117] Vattel III.18.288.

province, and gains such strength that the sovereign is no longer obeyed', then a state of 'insurrection' was at hand.[118] A ruler was free to deploy any sovereign means within the state when dealing with uprisings from all these non-civil war categories, although in practice mercy was recommended whenever the popular discontent rested on some justified basis.[119]

Vattel also linked the law of civil war to the question of neutrality. In civil wars, the role of foreign nations was considered to be one of impartiality. Since they ought not to interfere in the domestic affairs of an independent state, and both sides in the conflict therefore remained 'equally alien' to them, Vattel suggested that 'it only remains for them to interpose their good offices for the re-establishment of peace, and this they are called upon to do by the natural law'.[120] In the event that peace could not be made, third parties might 'decide for themselves the merits of the case, and assist the party which seems to have justice on its side'.[121] If a people had a just cause to resist their ruler, foreign powers might be permitted to assist them, and if the war had attained the level of civil war, they might take sides with one or other of the belligerents as in an inter-state war.[122] This acknowledgement of a right of intervention, which may sound surprising, aligned with the general lawfulness of war in Vattel's law of nations, which never fully prohibited even offensive wars. To decide when a ruler was a 'manifest' tyrant and when not, Vattel relied on a contractualist view that emphasised both constitutional restraints and the Lockean idea that all authority was derived from the people. He even suggested that if a manifest tyrant infringed the rights of 'humanity', then foreign powers had the right to intervene against the tyrant.[123]

The teachings of Wolff and Vattel certainly had their limitations, as they were based on Enlightenment principles reflecting a rather utopian belief in the capacity of objective reason to tame the world of states. They spoke to a Europe that was finding its footing after the War of the Spanish Succession and Newton's discovery of the falling apple, a continent heading towards the profound political and industrial revolutions that were to come. In the spirit of the times, their work was inspired by the power of persuasive ideas over raw nature. Only from such

118 Vattel III.18.289.
119 Vattel III.18.290–291.
120 Vattel III.18.296.
121 Ibid.
122 Vattel II.4.56.
123 Ibid.

denominational rationalism could the idea emerge that internal conflicts were naturally occurring phenomena fitting a taxonomy of factual circumstances, and that they might be controlled and tamed through the power of logic and persuasive norms. State practice in the long nineteenth century would provide many reasons to question and to condition such expectations. But despite everything, Vattel's chapter on the law of civil war, in particular, became the basic doctrine for a century to come. Even though the political world did not consistently follow its tenets, its enlightened rationalist framework provided a common conceptual language and legal ideals to underpin subsequent diplomatic debates and case law.

***

The final step in the emergence of the classical law of civil war was the amalgamation of the Lockean revolutionary ideology and the Vattelian law of civil war with the emerging laws of war and neutrality in the first major transatlantic civil war. The American Revolution of 1775–1783 would bring together these elements in a grand, historical *cause célèbre* marking the true starting point of the classical doctrine of civil war in state practice.

2

The American Revolution

The path to the American Revolution of 1775–1783 was paved with disputes about colonial trade and taxation. As a result of the Seven Years' War (1756–1763), the British Empire had gained vast new possessions in the New World, but its control over colonial commerce remained relaxed at best. During the war, colonists and colonial officials had frequently neglected or circumvented imperial trade restrictions and blockades – for example, by trading with the enemy under contrived flags of truce.[1] In 1763, the Privy Council sought to implement a new structure of imperial oversight in the New World that would bring the colonies under closer control by London.[2] To address the problem of insubordination in the administration of admiralty justice, a new regional vice-admiralty court was established in Halifax, Nova Scotia, charged with exercising admiralty jurisdiction over the entire New World.[3] It also repurposed the colonial navigation laws to provide tax revenue from the colonies. The empire was deeply in debt following the war, and London considered it only reasonable that the colonies make a bigger contribution to financing their defence.[4]

As is well known, the imposition of taxes to cover the rising costs of imperialism was not well received in America. Instead of complying, the colonists began to claim that, by virtue of the constitutional rights enjoyed by all free Englishmen since the revolution of 1688, they should be entitled either to set their own taxes or to be represented in the British

1 Richard Pares, *War and Trade in the West Indies, 1739–1763* ([1936] Frank Cass 1963) 395–468; Carl Ubbelohde, *The Vice-Admiralty Courts and the American Revolution* (University of North Carolina Press 1960) 23–40.

2 Granville's Report of the Treasury Commissioners, 5 October 1763, in *Acts of the Privy Council of England*, Colonial series, vol IV (1745–1766) 569–572.

3 Ubbelohde, *Vice-Admiralty Courts*, 4, 44–54.

4 Granville's Report. For levies introduced to this end, see e.g. Sugar Act, 4 Geo III c 15; Stamp Act, 5 Geo III c 12.

parliament.[5] There is an obvious parallel here with the Dutch Revolt. Despite colonial protests, the British colonial revenue model expanded, while the Halifax vice-admiralty was reinforced by three similar, but short-lived, courts in Boston, Philadelphia, and Charleston.[6] Colonial boycotts and expropriations of regulated imperial trade goods in the early 1770s led to the strict imposition of imperial oversight and the stationing of troops in the colonies,[7] which in turn caused the first Continental Congress to be convened in 1774. Gradually, London lost its grip on the administration of the colonial economy in the New World. To restore control, it would have to resort to new and increasingly warlike measures. The more warlike the measures, the more evident became the existence of a state of war between the empire and its colonies. The resulting wave of revolution and civil war would resonate throughout the New World for half a century.

2.1 Insurgent Prize Jurisdiction

Throughout the age of sail, rebel factions forced their claims to sovereignty upon the world stage by commissioning privateers and insurgent navies. In the American Revolution, the conflict spread to the seas and coastal waters within weeks. In July 1775, the Continental Congress encouraged each colony to provide vessels to protect its harbours and waters 'against all unlawful invasions' and depredations.[8] After the naval bombardment of Falmouth in October, it ordered George Washington to fit a small number of cruisers at continental expense.[9] In late 1775, it began to grant letters of marque against British shipping and foreign

[5] Resolutions of the Stamp Act Congress, 19 October 1765, in Richard Perry (ed), *Sources of our Liberties: Documentary Origins of Individual Liberties in the United States Constitution and Bill of Rights* (American Bar Foundation 1952) 261–271; James Otis, *The Rights of the British Colonies Asserted and Proved* (J. Almon 1764) 47–58.

[6] For example, 6 Geo III c 12; 7 Geo III c 41; 7 Geo III c 46. *See also* Ubbelohde, *Vice-Admiralty Courts*, 128–147, 190–194.

[7] Diary of John Adams, 17 December 1773, in Gordon S. Wood (ed), *John Adams: Revolutionary Writings 1775–1775* (Library of America 2011) 286–289, at 287. The four 'coercive acts' are at 14 Geo III 19, 14 Geo III c 45, 14 Geo III c 54, and 14 Geo III c. 39.

[8] 2 JCC 189 (18 July 1775); Henry J. Bourguignon, *The First Federal Court* (American Philosophical Society 1977) 43.

[9] Washington to Congress, 5 October 1775 and 12 October 1775, in John C. Fitzpatrick (ed), *The Writings of George Washington from the Original Manuscript Sources*, vol 4 (US Government Printing Office 1931) 9–13, 22–25; Resolution in 3 JCC 293 (13 October 1775). Instructions to Broughton and Manly in Jared Sparks (ed), *The Writings of George Washington*, vol III (Harper & Brothers 1847) app X, 516–520.

vessels trading with the British. Insurgent prize proceedings were consequently established soon after the first captures had been made, and Washington requested a place to libel them for prize.[10] These were serious ambitions in 1775; the Declaration of Independence was still seven months away. Until this point, the confrontation between the continental army and the British expeditionary force had remained a matter of colonial resistance against imperial efforts to restore order around New England. The Congress was still vacillating between pursuit of the colonies' constitutional rights as imperial subjects and assertion of full sovereignty by declaring independence. By granting letters of marque and claiming prize jurisdiction, the thirteen colonies would be exercising belligerent rights reserved to sovereign powers.[11] Not only did this mark the establishment of the first federal jurisdiction – a notable innovation in the domestic realm – but it also signified that the Congress was claiming for itself under the law of nations jurisdiction to condemn property seized from the British crown and its subjects.

In November 1775, the Continental Congress recommended the establishment of prize courts in each of the United Colonies and itself assumed appellate prize jurisdiction.[12] Initially, it reserved the right to appoint a committee for each prize appeal as necessary, but a permanent committee of appeals was established in 1777, and finally the task of prize adjudication was assigned to dedicated professionals at a new Court of Appeals in Cases of Capture.[13] By then, the colonies were acting on the presumption that they were a belligerent power[14] waging a public war under the law of nations against their former colonial overlords – although how to secure recognition from the existing members of the family of sovereign nations was quite another matter.

[10] Washington to Congress, 8 November 1775 and 11 November 1775, in Fitzpatrick, *Writings of Washington*, vol 4, 71–75, 81–84. The Massachusetts Privateering Act of 13 November 1775 is in James Austin, *The Life of Elbridge Gerry* (Wells and Lilly 1828) app A, 505–512.

[11] Austin, *Life of Elbridge Gerry*, 93.

[12] 3 JCC 371–376 (25 November 1775) and 3 JCC 378–387 (28 November 1775). See also Bourguignon, *First Federal Court*, 45–48.

[13] J. C. Bancroft Davis, *The Committees of the Continental Congress Chosen to Hear and Determine Appeals from Courts of Admiralty and the Court of Appeals in Cases of Capture Established by That Body* (Banks & Brothers 1888) 3–15, followed by 110 brief case notes.

[14] The establishment of prize courts also raised the question of whether the United States was one or thirteen entities. A landmark case in this regard was the complicated affair of *The Active*. *See* 13 JCC 281, 283–284; *US* v. *Peters* (1809) 9 US 115; Hampton L. Carson, 'The Case of the Sloop "Active"' 7 *Green Bag* (1895) 17–26; Bourguignon, *First Federal Court*, 101–134. Also *Talbot qui tam* (1784), 1 US 95.

The establishment of American prize courts was therefore a pragmatic response to the legal necessities arising from the actions of the first insurgent warships. Its coterminous legal side effects – the assertion of belligerent rights by rebel colonies whose sovereignty remained unclear, and the subsequent diplomacy of recognition – spread like ripples in the international arena as the conflict between the thirteen colonies and the British Empire escalated into a prolonged naval war. The enactment of Prize Acts put these questions to the table, not just for Great Britain but for the whole community of nations the Americans eventually wished to join as equals. The colonists were well aware of the import of their decisions at the time; for them, resistance on the high seas was a formidable wager against the full might of the British Empire – and, in a way, against the European system of colonisation itself. It was 'the most wild, visionary mad project that ever had been imagined . . . an infant, taking a mad Bull by his horns'.[15]

2.2 Response from the British Empire

2.2.1 *Colonial Blockade*

Negotiations between Philadelphia and London were pursued during the insurrection. The colonists continued to petition the king for constitutional guarantees, still portraying themselves as loyal subjects willing to stand down once their demands were properly addressed,[16] while the crown sternly rejected them as rebels, traitors, and criminals.[17] The official British policy dictated that the war be treated as a domestic rebellion with no standing under the law of nations, and London imposed further restrictions on colonial trade and fishing.[18] At the end of 1775, a royal Prize Act prohibited all trade and intercourse with the thirteen colonies 'during the continuance of the present rebellion'.[19] Like Cromwell's Navigation Act in 1650, the measure sought to regain control over insubordinate colonies through a total closure of their ports and assigned the task of curbing the rebellion to admiralty courts.[20] From

[15] Diary of John Adams, 5 October 1775, in Charles Francis Adams (ed), *The Works of John Adams*, vol 3 (Little Brown 1851) 7.

[16] Declaration of Congress, 6 July 1775, 4(2) PFAA 1865; Petition to king, 8 July 1775, 4(2) PFAA 1870.

[17] Royal proclamation, 23 August 1775, 4(3) PFAA 240.

[18] 15 Geo III c 10, 18.

[19] 16 Geo III c 5 (22 December 1775).

[20] See Cobbett's *Parliamentary History of England*, vol XVIII (1774–1777) 1057.

1776 onwards, all captures in America were systematically referred to the Halifax vice-admiralty, which adjudicated hundreds of matters during the war.[21]

Was the closure of all colonial ports by a Prize Act a blockade? Establishing and maintaining a maritime blockade was a belligerent measure of warfare that presupposed the existence of a public war under the law of nations. During the course of the war, as France increasingly intervened in, and then openly joined, the conflict, the British measures developed into a full-scale blockade directed against its international adversaries.[22] But measures such as the Prohibitory Act of 1776 kept raising the question of whether Great Britain had implicitly acknowledged the existence of a civil war well before the French intervention in 1778.[23] In early 1777, the British parliament had passed two landmark bills that noted the escalation of the American rebellion into something resembling a civil war. These included another new Prize Act[24] and a so-called treason Act,[25] the first of which permitted the issuance of privateer commissions against the rebels and the second the detention of colonial rebels without habeas corpus rights. While the first bill seems to have passed in Parliament largely as a technicality,[26] the bill that suspended American colonists' habeas corpus rights provoked vehement debate over the status of the rebels and the insurrection. This was because it characterised the American resistance as 'a rebellion and war' waged 'openly and traiterously' against the crown and provided that anyone seized, taken, or even suspected of high treason or piracy in the colonies or on the high seas could be confined 'without bail or mainprize'.[27] For the British, the problem was that while the Act sought both to relieve the empire of the burden of ensuring due process for each

[21] George F. Dow, *American Vessels Captured by the British during the Revolution and War of 1812: The Records of the Vice-Admiralty Court at Halifax, Nova Scotia* (Essex Institute 1911) 1–95 (listing more than three hundred).

[22] Lance E. Davis and Stanley L. Engerman, *Naval Blockades in Peace and War: An Economic History Since 1750* (Cambridge University Press 2006) 59–65.

[23] *See* Jean Siotis, *Le droit de la guerre et les conflits armés d'un caractère non-international* (LGDJ 1958) 59–60. See also *Ware* v. *Hylton* (1796), 3 US 199, at 228.

[24] 17 Geo III c 7.

[25] 17 Geo III c 9.

[26] The House of Lords removed the term 'letter of marque' from the bill and replaced it with 'commission'. One may wonder whether this was because the former was an instrument under the law of nations, whereas the latter would have been considered a more general term. House of Lords, 14 February 1777, *Journal of the House of Lords*, vol 35 (1776–1777) 51.

[27] 17 Geo III c 9.

individual 'traitor', it could be interpreted as transforming the status of the colonists, changing them from pirates and brigands into lawful enemies. Critics insisted that because the British 'were neither involved in a rebellion at home, nor engaged in a war without', there could be no legitimate reason to invest the crown with 'so dangerous a power'.[28]

The British government refused to recognise the American revolutionaries until the very end and the peace of Paris in 1783. Throughout the war it maintained that it was dealing with an internal rebellion waged by traitors against the lawful constitutional order. The British government came closest to recognition in April 1778, when it dispatched the Carlisle Commission to treat with the rebels for peace. Its instructions included authority to enter into ceasefires, agree to a system of self-rule, and, importantly, to 'admit of any claim or title to independency in any description of men, during the time of treaty, and for the purpose of treaty'.[29] This was to be construed as having no binding effect beyond the actual negotiation; the commission was advised to give greatest attention to ensuring that 'the sovereignty of the mother country should not be infringed, nor any powers given or ascribed to [the colonies] that should be capable of being construed into an impeachment of the sovereign rights of His Majesty, and the constitutional control of this country'.[30] The commission failed to persuade the colonists to accept a truce.

2.2.2 *Prisoner Exchanges*

On the battlefield, the war was savage, often fought with guerrilla and frontier tactics that involved terror and scorched earth. In particular, the British naval bombardments of coastal towns caused the insurgents to clamour for determined and sustained retaliations.[31] John Fabian Witt's acclaimed study mentions a situation in which Thomas Jefferson held the

[28] *The Annual Register*, 1777 (J. Dodsley 1778) 53–66, esp 55, 62. Edmund Burke made no mistake about this: 'Whenever a rebellion really and truly exists, which is as easily known in fact as it is difficult to define in words, government has not entered into such military conventions, but has ever declined all intermediate treaty which should put rebels in possession of the law of nations with regard to war.' Burke to Farr and Harris, 3 April 1777, in *The Works of the Right Honourable Edmund Burke, Collected in Three Volumes* (J. Dodsley 1792) vol II, 103–155, at 109.

[29] 'Royal Instructions to the Peace Commission of 1778' in Samuel Eliot Morison, *Sources and Documents Illustrating the American Revolution 1764–1788* (2nd edn, Oxford University Press 1965) 186–203, at 188.

[30] Ibid 200.

[31] For example, 21 JCC 1017–1018, 1029–1030.

royal governor of Detroit and his officers as 'fit subjects to begin on with the work of retaliation'.[32] One of Martens' *causes célèbres* recounts a moment when George Washington considered executing a randomly chosen officer as a belligerent reprisal.[33] In correspondence, however, commanders on both sides sought mutual engagements to promote the humane treatment of the sick, wounded, and civilians; for the rebels, this was not only a matter of enlightened consideration but also part of their efforts to convince the world of their worthiness among the civilised nations.[34]

The question of the legal status of captives posed a very tangible legal problem in the field. Were they criminals, each deserving a jury trial for treason, or prisoners of war? The insurgents, of course, demanded recognition of their captured fighters as lawful prisoners of war who could be spared from hanging and repatriated through prisoner exchanges. The British government was reluctant to engage in cartels with the crown's subjects. The reason was obvious: cartels had standing under the customary law of nations, and Britain saw the colonial rebellion as an internal matter under its own sovereign imperial jurisdiction. With habeas corpus suspended, it sought simply to lock up the rebels in jail for the duration of the conflict, pending trial for treason. But as the conflict extended over years, both on land and at sea, commanders began to negotiate prisoner exchanges. On both sides, tensions emerged between the military commanders and their governments, and both London and the Continental Congress continued to stumble over the question of international recognition. Eventually, both land armies having accumulated significant numbers of captives, their generals began to arrange ad hoc cartels with no clear legal status.[35] Even the capture of Lord Cornwallis seems not to have led to a general agreement. When Cornwallis surrendered at Yorktown, he sought to characterise himself as capitulating 'to the combined forces of America and France'.[36] When the moment of formal capitulation arrived, he feigned illness and remained

[32] John Fabian Witt, *Lincoln's Code: The Laws of War in American History* (Free Press 2013) 33–35.

[33] Charles de Martens, *Causes célèbres du droit des gens* (2nd edn, F. A. Brockhaus 1859) vol III, 311–321. See also Washington's letters 19 and 20 April 1782 in Fitzpatrick, *Writings of George Washington*, vol 24, at 136, 144; 22 JCC 217–218; 23 JCC 716–720, 847–848.

[34] Witt, *Lincoln's Code*, 19–27.

[35] Betsy Knight, 'Prisoner Exchange and Parole in the American Revolution' 48 *William and Mary Quarterly* (1991) 208–213.

[36] Quoted in Barbara Tuchman, *The First Salute: A View of the American Revolution* (Ballantine Books 1988) 285.

absent, while his adjutant attempted to surrender his sword not to Washington but to the French commander Rochambeau.[37]

As time passed, rebel naval authorities reached bespoke arrangements with their British counterparts in New York and Halifax.[38] Captured insurgent mariners could be tried in Britain and faced the additional threats of British impressment or being hanged for treason. In Paris, Benjamin Franklin was determined to direct the American privateering efforts towards bringing about prisoner exchanges. He eventually initiated an entire theatre of war near the British Isles to secure the release of American mariners in return for English captives across the Channel. Before the French intervention in 1778, his privateers were not permitted to place their captives in French jails. Franklin therefore tried to obtain letters of sea parole – that is, release at sea against a letter that could be used to free an American in exchange. The British called his bluff and bluntly refused. But once France had joined the war, Franklin managed to bring about exchanges in fact, if not in law.[39] The British authorities persisted in considering the exchanges as falling within royal prerogative rather than the laws of war, with many captives being accorded royal pardons (as convicted subjects, not as lawful enemies) before being shipped out for the swap.[40]

2.2.3 Prize Courts

The British courts had found themselves dealing with the revolutionary war from the very beginning. In 1776, the Admiralty and the King's Exchequer confronted each other in the high court of admiralty over whether Britain was engaging in acts of war or taking police action.[41] The matter concerned a rebel ship that had left Philadelphia for Nantes to trade American goods for arms and supplies in France. En route, the crew had mutinied against the master and voluntarily surrendered the ship in Bristol. The controversy began in the court of admiralty as a prize case, with the Admiralty claiming its traditional droits. But then the king's

37 Ibid 284–290; also Harlow Giles Unger, *Lafayette* (Wiley 2003) 158–159.

38 William M. Fowler Jr, *Rebels under Sail: The American Navy during the Revolution* (Charles Scribner's Sons 1976) 115, 257–260.

39 William Bell Clark, *Ben Franklin's Privateers: A Naval Epic of the American Revolution* (Greenwood Press 1956) 9–22; Catherine M. Prelinger, 'Benjamin Franklin and the American Prisoners of War in England during the American Revolution' 32 *William and Mary Quarterly* (1975) 261–294.

40 Clark, *Franklin's Privateers*, 18.

41 *The Dickenson* (1776) 165 Eng Rep 1.

advocate James Marriott intervened and argued that the vessel and its cargo should belong to the crown as a confiscation in which the Admiralty had no share. Marriott argued that the case 'must be understood to be prize of forfeiture, for cause of rebellion, not war'.[42] The Admiralty replied that the Act of Parliament 'plainly considers the present case as a case of war'. To Marriott's surprise, Justice Hay then condemned the ship, affirming that 'this act is a declaration of war, and the Courts of Admiralty are to proceed to confiscation under it'.[43] The decision – which had openly admitted war – was immediately disputed as erroneous because the power to declare wars was at the time the king's prerogative and did not belong to Parliament in the first place.[44] When Lord Mansfield decided a similar question in 1782 in connection with property seized during the capture of St Eustatius, he had less difficulty in affirming admiralty jurisdiction over the matter because it concerned a formally declared international war between Britain and the Netherlands.[45]

A second problem that came before the British courts was how to distinguish between individual rebels and loyal subjects in America. The details of prize rules and navigation laws attracted the interest of potential smugglers and profiteers, and many prize cases in the admiralty courts involved straightforward smuggling, forgeries, and counterfeit papers.[46] More sophisticated entrepreneurs might pretend to be neutral subjects themselves or join in a common venture with foreign merchants to benefit from the latters' neutral rights. Disputes soon arose about the status of the thousands of loyalist refugees who were migrating back to Europe and trying to bring with them to Britain some of their possessions or their produce.[47] On paper, the Prohibition Act and the de facto blockade seemed to consider all those domiciled in the colonies as insurgents. But both the alleged rebels and the loyalists spoke the familiar English language and sailed out from the same colonial ports, and their ships could plausibly have been designed and built on either side of the Atlantic. Many Americans might also quite reasonably have dealings

42 Ibid 5.
43 Ibid 11.
44 Ibid 11–12, fns.
45 *Lindo* v. *Rodney* [1782] 99 Eng Rep 385 (fn 1).
46 For example, *The Louisa* (13 November 1778) 165 Eng Rep 33; *The Anna Christiana* (27 November 1778) 165 Eng Rep 37; note also *The Bee* (11 December 1778) 165 Eng Rep 50.
47 For example, *The Friendship* and *The Commerce* (4 September 1777), both at 165 Eng Rep 19.

both in Britain and America. Ship commanders and prize courts therefore sought better ways to distinguish between friend and foe than their domicile or 'natural allegiance', which mariners had traditionally determined from a crew's language and manners and from the ship's design and ports of origin.[48] Eventually, the high court of admiralty saw itself with no alternative but to try to determine the character of individual colonists on a case-by-case basis, relying on what little evidence there was of their politically relevant actions. Thus, in the case of the *Sally*, Justice Hay restored the property captured from a former judge who had refused to give an oath and fled America, but condemned other parts of the same cargo because these had been insured in America and with the intention that the owner would yet return to the colonies.[49] James Marriott, who succeeded Hay in 1778, cited Hay's precedent and interpreted it as a test for distinguishing between rebels and loyal subjects based on whether or not the alleged refugee would still be welcome to return to America.[50] By now, the admiralty courts were helped by the several of Acts of allegiance that had been passed by the colonies and which required civil servants, professionals, and craftsmen to take personal oaths of abjuration and allegiance.[51] The somewhat sudden upshot of these deliberations was that the age of revolution began to profoundly transform the way nationality and citizenship were understood both in law and ordinary parlance; with the spreading of popular revolutions, the old assumptions about lifelong allegiances by birth began to transform into a political concept of personal allegiance.

2.3 Foreign Reactions: Neutrality, Recognition, and Intervention

Long before the French intervention, Britain had found itself at odds with foreign powers over seizures of rebel cargoes in foreign vessels and captures of neutral ships suspected of rebel activity. As the British government denied the existence of a state of war, its jurists had to contrive legal arguments that would enable them to pursue belligerent actions on the high seas while avoiding any reference to the laws of war that might suggest the existence of a state of war. The colonies, on the

[48] Nathan Perl-Rosenthal, *Citizen Sailors: Becoming American in the Age of Revolution* (Harvard University Press 2015) 30–44, 53–59.

[49] *The Sally* (2 October 1777) 165 Eng Rep 20.

[50] *The Rebecca* (5 December 1778) 165 Eng Rep 46.

[51] The Act cited by Marriott is in Thomas Cooper, *The Statutes at Large of South Carolina*, vol I (1836) 147–151.

other hand, saw themselves as fully valid belligerents, emphatically insisting on the applicability of those laws. Foreign officials and merchants found themselves asking to what extent they could deal with the colonists without risking reaction or retaliation from Britain. In addition to prize cases involving the capture of neutral vessels, there were two common situations in which the actions of the 'belligerents' clashed with foreign interests – first, when insurgent merchantmen and privateers docked at foreign ports, And second, when, eager to seize the new opportunities of wartime commerce, the subjects of those foreign countries engaged in trade with the rebel colonies.

2.3.1 Pirates or Privateers?

Europe was still the home of hereditary monarchies, and there was initially little public support for the colonial rebels, other than in certain academic and intellectual circles in Scandinavia, Germany, and France.[52] The rulers of Portugal, Denmark and Norway, Sweden, the Netherlands, and the Holy Roman Empire all strongly disapproved of the revolution. Catherine II of Russia remained somewhat distant, while Prussia's Frederick the Great refused to receive the American representatives and even turned a blind eye when the British raided their offices. Portugal, Denmark, the Netherlands, and Austria all prohibited their subjects from supplying any contraband to the revolted colonies, though only Portugal closed its ports entirely to the Americans.[53] But not all of Europe rallied to the cause of the old regime. Since the very beginning of the troubles, France and its ally Spain displayed an interest in taking advantage of British colonial unrest to deliver a long-desired *revanche* after the Seven Years' War. By 1776, both France and Spain had in practice opened their ports to American privateers and allowed volunteers to join the insurgents.[54] With France's intervention in 1778, the American Revolution escalated beyond the stage of 'civil war' in any Vattelian sense and at the same time became an international war proper. Foreign governments began to increasingly treat the American rebels as de facto belligerents, and the governments of Prussia, the Netherlands, Sweden, and Russia began to welcome insurgent vessels in their ports on

[52] Samuel Flagg Bemis, *The Diplomacy of the American Revolution* (Indiana University Press 1957) 113–114; Harlow Giles Unger, *Lafayette* (Wiley 2003) 17–30.

[53] Bemis, *Diplomacy*, 114–115; 1 Moore § 60, at 169; Paul Leland Haworth, 'Frederick the Great and the American Revolution' 9 *American Historical Review* (1904) 460–478.

[54] *The Annual Register*, 1776 (J. Dodsley 1777) 182–183.

the basis of a policy of neutrality.[55] The emphasis of the maritime war also shifted. The British prize cases from 1778 onwards focus increasingly on French property and neutral commerce with France rather than the thirteen colonies.

From the start, Britain demanded that all friendly powers in Europe detain rebellious American vessels or their prizes.[56] Their complaints elicited the (very British) reply from France that a king could not interfere with the due course of the law in courts.[57] In a legal opinion in May 1776, James Marriott argued that under the law of nations a sovereign had a right to claim the property of its own citizens regardless of conditions of war and peace.[58] No foreign state or judicature could decide who was a rebel and who was not, and any foreign state refusing to hand over any requested subjects would create a right, under the law of nations, 'not only to take them by force [but also] make reprisals, as well as establish a like treatment in reciprocity'.[59] Any effort by Britain's allies to grant protection to insurgents would lead to a cessation of the alliance, because insurgents 'can only be protected on the ground of their being avowed to belong to some other independent body' in direct violation of the sovereign's rights.[60]

The American counter-position is illustrated by the cases of the Bergen and Texel prizes. In 1778, three British vessels captured by John Paul Jones' squadron were brought to the port of Bergen, then part of Denmark. While the prizes were there, the British ambassador demanded that they be seized and handed over to the crown.[61] The Danish government complied on the grounds that the king of Denmark had not 'as yet' acknowledged the independence of the colonies, as a consequence of which the vessels could not be considered as lawful prizes.[62] Benjamin Franklin protested that legitimate American privateers had unjustly been 'stripped of their property' and demanded that Denmark either repeal the

55 For example, III Rev Dipl Corr 346–349; IV Rev Dipl Corr 218–222. See also Jean Siotis, *Le droit de la guerre*, 63.

56 Committee of Secret Correspondence to Deane, 1 October 1776, II *Rev Dip Corr* 157–161, at 161.

57 Vergennes to Stormont, 15 July 1777, in Martens *Causes célèbres*, vol III, Cause II, No III.

58 Excerpt from Marriott's report, 6 May 1776, in II McNair *Opinions* 326.

59 Ibid.

60 Ibid.

61 On the Bergen prizes, see Roscoe R. Oglesby, *Internal War and the Search for Normative Order* (Martinus Nijhoff 1971) 1–5; 2 Moore's *Digest* § 329, at 1076–1077; 1 Moore's *Digest* § 60, at 169; 5 Moore's *Arbitrations* 4572.

62 Franklin to Bernstorf, 22 December 1779, III Rev Dipl Corr 433–435, at 434.

order of restoration or, if it was too late, accept state responsibility for the expropriation and award due compensation.[63] The affair led to a long diplomatic dispute between Denmark and the United States, which would far outlast the revolution.[64] By contrast, in October 1779 Paul Jones landed in the Netherlands with his famous prizes the *Serapis* and *Countess Scarborough*, on board which were 504 prisoners. Again, the local British ambassador protested that the ships had been 'seized by the pirate Paul Jones, a Scotchman, a rebellious subject and state criminal'.[65] But unlike the Danes in Bergen, the Dutch did not seize the prizes or the crews as the British had requested. In their past treaties, Britain and the United Provinces had agreed to prohibit their subjects from aiding, receiving, or supplying the enemies of either party 'of any rank or condition whatever'.[66] Accordingly, the Dutch claimed to be adhering to a position of neutrality, according to which they would avoid rendering decisions on the legality (or illegality) of foreign prizes and instead instruct them to put to sea as soon as possible.[67] This did not satisfy the British; a year later, the dispute dissolved into the broader matter of Britain's declaration of war on the Netherlands.

Pressure from Britain to detain the rebel privateers and their prizes had less impact on France and Spain than on Norway and in the Netherlands, both of which had supplied secret aid and armaments to the insurgent colonies back in 1776.[68] Relations between Britain and continental Europe deteriorated as the US commissioners managed to secure a succession of loans for their cause and then began fitting privateers from French ports. The commissioners also identified friendly ports in which their prizes would be received and adjudicated. These privateer operations were well under way by 1777,[69] but prior to concluding

63 Ibid.

64 Oglesby, *Internal War*, 4; Wheaton to Upshur, 23 August 1843, in *Executive Documents of the House of Representatives*, 28th Cong, 1st sess, Doc No 264, at 6.

65 Yorke to States-General, 29 October 1779, III Rev Dipl Corr 396–397.

66 Treaty of Westminster, 9 February 1674, 13 CTS 123.

67 Resolution of the States-General, 19 November 1779, III Rev Dip. Corr 420–421. The correspondence is also in Martens' *Causes célèbres*, vol II, Cause X, where this resolution is No XVI.

68 Bemis, *Diplomacy*, 41; Marquis de Olivart, *Del reconocimiento de beligerancia y sus efectos inmediatos* (L. Péant 1895) 11–12; Vergennes to the king, 2 May 1776, and to Stormont, 15 July 1777, in Martens' *Causes célèbres*, vol III, Cause II, Nos II and III; Floridablanca's memorial, 17 August 1777, II Doniol 570, 598. On Deane's arrangements with Lafayette and others, see II Rev Dipl Corr 218–221, II Doniol 379.

69 Franklin and Deane to Committee of Secret Correspondence, 12 March 1777, II Rev Dipl Corr 283, esp 286–287.

a formal alliance with the United States in 1778, France tried to remain within the limits of its treaties with Britain. Thus, upon British protestations, some American privateers were momentarily imprisoned by the French and their prizes restored.[70] In reality, these chastisements did not prevent the Americans from disposing of their prizes through less official channels.[71] In time, talks spread about foreign powers adopting a 'neutral' stance towards the American rebellion. When Captain Lee was detained in Bilbao, the Spanish officials received orders from the court to set him free, accompanied by 'a general declaration, that his catholic majesty was neuter in the dispute between England and America'.[72] By late 1777, the rebels were already having warships built for them at various docks in Europe, and their naval operations were already wide enough to cause minor disputes with what they themselves called the 'neutral nations'.[73]

But the situation never went far enough to require a clear position to be taken on whether or not 'neutrality' was possible in a civil war. After 1778, the war that had begun as a colonial insurrection now took on the quality of an international conflict, in which neutral policies could be adopted with respect to the Anglo-French conflict and the Americans could be considered as French proxies (if they were considered at all). At this point, there was also no longer any reason for France to prohibit American prize adjudication on its territory. Accordingly, the French naval ministry and the American commissioners drafted new prize regulations on judicial co-operation between their prize officials. The regulations provided that each of the two states would allow the other's vessels to bring prizes into port, where the local prize officials would deal with the investigations and forward the relevant findings and documents to the other's judicial prize officials for adjudication. The Americans would forward French prize matters to the Conseil des prises, while the French would refer American prize decisions to the commissioners in Paris, which for a time meant Benjamin Franklin alone.[74] Eventually, the

70 See II Rev Dipl Corr 322, 364, 376–377.

71 Deane to Morris, 23 August 1777, II Rev Dipl Corr 378, esp 381.

72 Ibid 379. Also II Doniol 37–40.

73 Commissioners to Committee of Foreign Affairs, 30 November 1777, II Rev Dipl Corr 433–436.

74 Prize regulations of 16 August 1778, II Rev Dipl Corr 685–687; Clark, *Ben Franklin's Privateers*, 75–80. One such judgment is in *Works of Benjamin Franklin*, vol V (William Duane 1809) 301–302.

French relieved Franklin of the responsibility of prize adjudication and assigned it in full to the more competent Conseil des prises.[75]

2.3.2 *Neutral Trade and Smuggling*

Before the revolution, trade between the thirteen colonies and foreign nations had been severely restricted by British navigation regulations. When colonial unrest grew into a gradual rebellion in 1774 and 1775, the empire responded with further limitations, which culminated in the completely suspending trade into the colonies at the end of 1775. At the same time, standing together against their mother country, the thirteen colonies responded in a diametrically opposite way, opening up their ports for trade to any foreigners willing to take their chances against the royal navy.[76] The rebel demand for war materiel soon found a supply in the small islands of the Caribbean basin, such as Dutch St Eustatius and the Danish St Croix.

Tiny St Eustatius, in particular, became a thriving supply port for the insurgents, their main source for gunpowder, and a channel for correspondence between the Continental Congress and its agents in Europe.[77] St Eustatius had been declared a 'free port' by the Dutch in 1756 and was not bound by Dutch duties or trade restrictions. In addition, the Dutch still held the precious 'Free Ships make Free Goods' concession from Britain.[78] The role of Dutch traders during the Seven Years' War was something of a legend: thanks to the free ships clause, their merchants had been able to take over the bulk of trade between France and its colonies in the New World. Once the French had essentially outsourced their colonial *grand cabotage* to the Dutch, British admiralty courts intervened with a new Rule of the War of 1756, according to which the free ships clause enabled the neutrals to trade 'with' the enemy (in their own interest) but not 'for' them (taking over their trade).[79] However, in 1776, because Britain denied the existence of an official state of war

75 Clark, *Ben Franklin's Privateers* 21–22, 137–143, 169–172, *et passim*.

76 Davis and Engerman, *Naval Blockades*, 56–59.

77 Barbara Tuchman, *The First Salute: A View of the American Revolution* (Ballantine Books, 1988); J. Franklin Jameson, 'St. Eustatius in the American Revolution' 8 *American Historical Review* (1903) 683–708; *Authentic Rebel Papers Seized at St. Eustatius, 1781* (L. Lambert 1781).

78 For example, Treaty of The Hague, 17 February 1668, 10 CTS 441, arts X–XI; Treaty of Westminster, 6 February 1716, 4 Davenport 1–3, 29 CTS 413.

79 Richard Pares, *Colonial Blockade and Neutral Rights, 1739–1763* (Clarendon Press 1938) 180–224. See also *Berens* v. *Rucker* [1760] 95 Eng Rep 175, at 176 (Mansfield *obiter*

between itself and its rebelling colonies, it could not point to any 'enemy' ports in America where the Dutch would be trading as 'neutrals'. In the absence of a state of war, Britain had to limit itself to its own navigation Acts and to diplomatic pressure, which explains the strict prohibition of trade to the colonies and all export of arms that it imposed in 1775. This invited some apparent compliance, as the States-General issued a proclamation prohibiting any unlicensed export of arms (as did Denmark).[80] But the practical result was more smuggling and contraband trade in and through the neutral ports in the West Indies.[81]

On 16 November 1776, a diplomatic incident flared up between Britain and the Netherlands when Fort Orange at St Eustatius saluted the American rebel brigantine *Andrew Doria*, which was flying the new thirteen-striped Continental flag.[82] At the same time, reports from the colony began to speak of open trade with American rebels and the fitting of rebel privateers.[83] The British government demanded a public disavowal of the salute by the Netherlands, the curbing of Caribbean smuggling, and the disciplining of the local governor. In a manner not entirely explicable under the law of nations without the admission of a state of war, the Admiralty also instructed its West India fleet to visit and search outbound Dutch vessels for contraband and armaments.

But however much the clandestine trade disturbed Anglo-Dutch relations, admiralty courts were keen to maintain the impression that the British naval vessels were operating within the rule of law. In individual cases they often interpreted the treaties in force to the benefit of the neutrals, even in the face of facts patently to the contrary. In 1777, a Dutch ship *Hendrick and Alida*, laden with powder, guns, and foreign officers allegedly on their way to the Dutch provincial army on St Eustatius, was captured by the royal navy.[84] Although the ship was built in Boston and its cargo was quite probably heading for the American rebels, and although there were omissions in the ship's papers, Judge Hay refused to condemn the ship or its cargo. Marriott, who was representing the captors, pleaded that the Prohibitory Act was simply

dictum). The case for the rule was laid out by James Marriott in the pamphlet *The Case of the Dutch Ships, Considered* (R. and J. Dodsley 1758) esp 11–15.

80 Proclamations of the States-General, 20 March 1775 and 18 August 1775, 4(2) PFAA 277, 4(3) PFAA 156; Edict by the king of Denmark, 4 October 1775, 4(3) PFAA 942.

81 Jameson, 'St. Eustatius', 690.

82 See Tuchman, *The First* Salute; Jameson, 'St. Eustatius'; *Authentic Rebel Papers.* On the Danish St Croix, see Jameson, 'St. Eustatius', 691.

83 Tuchman, *First Salute*, 52–59.

84 *Hendrick and Alida* (2 October 1777) 165 Eng Rep 22.

failing, unless 'a less gentle doctrine' should be adopted as a matter of necessity. But Hay maintained a firm stance and protected the neutral commercial adventure, saying that it would be 'too high for any such Court of Justice as this to assert, that the Dutch may not carry in their own ships to their own colonies and settlements every thing they please'.[85] If there was a problem, it belonged to the government and not the judiciary.

The situation of St Eustatius remained precarious until 1780 and the British declaration of war on the Netherlands, after which Admiral Rodney overran and plundered the island.[86] The rocky port was soon retaken by the French, and for the rest of the war it became a supply base in an international conflict, not only for the American rebels but also for their allies.

2.3.3 *Intervention and Armed Neutrality*

France's diplomatic and armed intervention marked a decisive moment in the American Revolution. On 6 February 1778, the French minister plenipotentiary Gérard signed two treaties on behalf of France with the commissioners of the United States. The first of these, a treaty of friendship and commerce, marked the recognition of the union of the thirteen former colonies as a sovereign state.[87] The second was a treaty of alliance in preparation for the international war that would surely follow when Britain reacted against France in defence of its sovereignty.[88] That war would follow from the recognition was never in much doubt, especially after the French crown informed the British court that it was willing to protect by force the inviolability of its friendly trade with the independent United States.[89] However, this was not too problematic under the law of nations, because in the late eighteenth century there was no prohibition on the sovereign right to wage war or even engage in what we might today consider an act of aggression. In fact, the initiation of formal belligerent relations helped to clarify the situation, marking the outbreak of an international war like any other – even if the immediate *casus belli*

85 Ibid 32.
86 This was the action that led to *Lindo* v. *Rodney* (1782) 99 Eng Rep 385.
87 Treaty of Amity and Commerce between France and the United States, 6 February 1778, 46 CTS 417.
88 Treaty of Alliance between France and the United States, 6 February 1778, 46 CTS 447.
89 Declaration by the Marquis de Noailles to Lord Weymouth, 13 March 1778, 2 Doniol 823.

involved the discourteous act of recognising the revolting British colonies as independent and sending an expeditionary force to support them.

In terms of the law of civil war, the intervention was of significance for at least two reasons. First, it meant that a European power was unilaterally, formally, and positively recognising the emergence of a new sovereign nation out of the rebellious colony of another power. While it was not the first time an insurgent province achieved international recognition under the law of nations (the Dutch Republic being an obvious example), the fact that recognition was given in such an open and definitive form, and punctuated by armed intervention, led later generations of scholars to closely associate the genesis of the doctrine of civil war with the American Revolution. Second, the French intervention transformed the American Revolution from a civil war into an international conflict between European powers. Now, the Americans could be understood both as insurgents and as French proxies. Similarly, the European foreign powers could now adopt general policies of neutrality vis-à-vis the international conflict between France and Britain, as distinct from a British civil war. This meant that jurists who enquired to what extent a 'civil war' existed in America never really received a proper answer; now, the legally predominant relationship in the conflict was the war between Britain and its Continental adversaries. The principal legal disputes arising from the conflict – such as the question of the status of free ships and free goods – touched British and Continental maritime interests at large, and the culmination of the conflict in the League of Armed Neutrality of 1780 is better understood as part of the main storyline of belligerent and neutral rights in international law rather than the particular law of civil war.

But although the character of the conflict changed in the history books, the intervention did not imply any immediate change in the status of the rebels. Indeed, most of the difficulties of neutrality mentioned earlier, such as the affair of the Bergen prizes and John Paul Jones' expulsion from Texel, occurred during the 'international' phase of the conflict. So, while the European powers were now choosing their alignments primarily with regard to the conflict between the two major powers, when it came to the rebels the legal difficulties and disputes remained. With the exception of France and the Dutch Republic, all foreign powers (including Spain) did not recognise the independence of the thirteen colonies until they had been recognised by Britain in the Treaty of Paris in 1783.[90]

[90] The US was recognised by France in 1778, by the Dutch Republic in 1782, by Great Britain in 1783, by Spain in 1783, by Sweden in 1783, by Prussia in 1785, by Portugal in 1791, by

Spain's involvement in the American Revolution began as gradual diplomatic intervention and remained indirect throughout the conflict. Spain was much less eager than France to support the British colonists through armed support for the obvious reason that it was still running its own American empire, as it had since the Treaty of Tordesillas. It was nonetheless subjected to pressure and persuasion by France, while its foreign minister, Floridablanca, tried to barter with Britain, proposing non-intervention by Spain in exchange for the acquisition of Gibraltar.[91] When Britain would have none of such propositions, and when France sealed its American alliance, Spain engaged in a project of mediation, presenting the Catholic king as a grand peacemaker between France, Britain, and the thirteen colonies. In the spring of 1779, after a few months of fruitless attempts, Madrid presented its final proposal for a roadmap to peace negotiations between the French and British courts.[92] A familiar problem arose from the ultimatum's insistence that 'during this interval the Colonies shall be treated as independent in fact', which the British found totally repugnant. In return, the Spanish pointed out that the British armies had entered into prisoner exchanges with the rebels; it would thus be 'extraordinary' or 'even ridiculous' if the British government, after treating the Americans as belligerents, were not to consider them internationally independent, at least de facto.[93] Britain's refusal to negotiate opened the way for Spanish involvement in the war alongside France. Within days, Spain signed an alliance with France – but not the American insurgents – and declared war.[94] In the Treaty of Aranjuez, Spain and France listed several key objectives they pursued through the war. These included, for Spain, the restitution of Gibraltar and Minorca and, for France, the expulsion of the British from fisheries in Newfoundland. They pointed out, however, that the treaty did not entail any recognition of the Americans by the king of Spain.[95] Although Spain's efforts in the New World were primarily focused on defending its own colonial waters and possessions 'beyond the Line', its troops gave

Denmark in 1792, by Austria in 1797, and by Russia in 1803. Source: US Office of the Historian website, country files, https://history.state.gov/countries.

91 See Bemis, *Diplomacy*, 77–78.

92 Ultimatum from Madrid to France and Britain, 3 April 1779, III Rev Dip. Corr 466–467, III Doniol 832ff.

93 III Rev Dipl Corr 467.

94 Treaty of Aranjuez, 12 April 1779, 47 CTS 115, 4 Davenport 145.

95 Ibid art 4. The Americans had preliminarily consented to the possibility of such an arrangement; see Separate and Secret Act between France and the United States, signed in Paris, 6 February 1778, 46 CTS 457.

direct assistance to colonial insurgents from its territories in Spanish Louisiana and the Mississippi River.

The American revolutionary war ultimately drew forth a collective intervention by neutral powers, which decided to actively defend their commercial interests together. The revolution took place halfway through a century of legal disputes between the British Empire and Continental powers over the freedom of neutral commerce. The question here was the familiar tension between the old *Consolato* rule observed by the British (according to which enemy cargo could be captured from onboard neutral ships) and the Continental views demanding freedom of the seas and general adoption of the flag principle (according to which neutral flags protected all cargoes).[96] British interference in neutral shipping led Continental scholars and jurists to look back to Martin Hübner's advocacy of neutral rights as universal customary law.[97] The British view – as restated in a lengthy legal opinion by James Marriott – was that free ships make free goods only when expressly agreed by treaty and not by virtue of a general principle.[98] The disagreement escalated in 1780, when several neutral powers in continental Europe joined with each other in the League of Armed Neutrality.[99] The initiative came from Catherine II of Russia, whose commercial treaty with Britain permitted neutral trade except as regards a relatively restricted list of contraband goods.[100] Russian vessels nonetheless found themselves in British prize courts or were harassed by rebel privateers. This led Catherine to declare that she was prepared to protect her neutral flag and subjects by force, and she circulated a project for an armed neutrality in the courts of Europe.[101] The resulting League was initially formed via mutual treaties

[96] Stephen C. Neff, *Rights and Duties of Neutrals* (Juris 2000) 29–32, 38–40, 50.

[97] Martin Hübner, *De la saisie des batimens neutres, ou Du droit qu'ont les nations belligérantes d'arrêter les navires des peuples* (2 vols, 1759). Compare Marriott, Case of the Dutch Ships.

[98] James Marriott, *Mémoire justificatif de la conduite de la Grande Bretagne en arrêtant les navires étrangers et les munitions de guerre destinées aux insurgens de l'Amérique* ([1778] B. Rickerstaff 1801).

[99] On the politics of the League generally, see Bemis, *Diplomacy*, 149–163; Francis Piggott, *The Freedom of the Seas Historically Treated* (HMSO 1920) 39–60; William S. Carpenter, 'United States and the League of Neutrals of 1780' 15 *American Journal of International Law* (1921) 511, 515–522.

[100] Treaty of Amity and Commerce between Britain and Russia, 20 June 1766, 43 CTS 365, arts X–XI.

[101] Declaration Regarding the Principles of Armed Neutrality, 28 February 1780, in James Brown Scott, *The Armed Neutralities of 1780 and 1800* (Oxford University Press 1918) 273.

involving Russia, Sweden, and Denmark. The next three years saw the accession of the Netherlands, Prussia, the Holy Roman Empire, Portugal, Austria, and the Two Sicilies.[102] In practice, the league constituted its own protected convoy system and closed off the Baltic Sea (through which Britain obtained much of its naval stores) from all belligerent activities. The members of the league agreed 'to observe the most scrupulous neutrality', pledged unity in diplomatic demands and reprisals in respect of belligerents if their ships were molested, and agreed to 'act in concert for their mutual and reciprocal defense' in the event they were attacked. They also determined what they would accept as being contraband and declared all other commerce free under four principles derived from Catherine's original declaration: freedom of neutral navigation; 'free ships make free goods'; the requirement for blockades to be kept effective; and uniform, prompt, and legal prize proceedings in the event of capture.[103]

In retrospect, scholars have not agreed on whether or not the league was 'successful'.[104] On the one hand, it led to British acquiescence to some of the neutral demands, especially with respect to the pacification of the Baltic.[105] Likewise, the American rebels assured they would comply with the declaration and sought the additional advantage of international recognition by empowering their ministers to accede to the league's regulations 'if invited thereto' (no such invitation came).[106] On the other hand, the constitution of the league led almost immediately to the outbreak of war between Great Britain and the Netherlands, which sowed confusion among its members. Reneging on their guarantees of

[102] The treaties and documents are in Scott, *Armed Neutralities*, 290–436, and in Francis Piggott and G. W. T. Omond, *Documentary History of the Armed Neutralities 1780 and 1800* (University of London Press 1919) 206ff.

[103] Convention for an Armed Neutrality between Russia and Denmark and Norway, 9 July 1780, in Scott, *Armed Neutralities*, 299. The other treaties follow, including the Dutch resolution of accession at 325, followed by British reprisals and privateer instructions.

[104] Translated excerpts from Alvarez, Bergbohm, Bluntschli, de Boeck, Boye, Calvo, von Dohm, Geffcken, Hall, Heffter, Katchenovsky, Kleen, Louter, Manning, Martens, Matzen, Nys, Perels, Phillimore, Pradier-Fodéré, Prittwitz, Rivier, Trescot, Twiss, Walker, Wehberg, Westlake, Wharton, Wehaton, and Woolsey are collected in Scott, *Armed Neutralities*, 1–273.

[105] 'British Additional Instructions to the Commanders of Merchant Ships and Vessels Having Letters of Marque and Reprisals', 15 February 1781, in Scott, *Armed Neutralities*, 365; 'British Additional Instructions to Privateers and Warships', 20 April 1781, in Scott, *Armed Neutralities*, 391.

[106] Resolution of the Continental Congress 5 October 1780, in Scott, *Armed Neutralities*, 323–324; Carpenter, 'United States and the League', 520.

mutual security, they failed to rally to the aid of the Netherlands and instead, after nervy correspondence, merely offered their good offices and mediation between the parties.[107] The Netherlands abandoned its neutrality, recognised the United States of America, and concluded treaties recognising prize proceedings and recaptures between the states.[108]

Regardless of its successes and failures, the 1780 armed neutrality episode represented an early attempt at a coordinated international response to a major colonial civil war, with third states staking their positions without reference to the formal sovereignty of the metropolitan empire involved. The league linked the political and economic interest in collective intervention and collective self-defence to the problem of decolonial revolutions in the law of nations. As such, it was a rather liberal example, contrasting with the anti-revolutionary cooperation in Europe that would follow in the decades after the French Revolution. Over the next century, the problem of revolutionary civil wars would continue to trouble the world's maritime powers as they sought to balance their legal positions between respect for the formal sovereignty of their equals and the inevitable revolutionary changes taking place overseas during the first wave of decolonisation.

2.4 Conclusion: The Aftermath

In the classical law of nations, war was a legitimate method of dispute resolution – 'that state in which we prosecute our right by force'.[109] A duly conducted war enabled sovereigns to resolve a legal claim in situations where all pacific means had failed and where victory on the battlefield could still determine the legitimacy of the competing causes – or at least allow one side to force the other to submit to its terms.[110] In principle, much hinged on attaining military objectives or on the outcome of 'decisive' battles,[111] but in practice any results emanating from the wager of war would still have to be implemented through rather mundane legal work. It was a general purpose of peace settlements to address the

[107] Scott, *Armed Neutralities*, 325–380; Piggott and Omond, *Documentary History*, 321–333.

[108] Treaty of Amity between the Netherlands and the United States, 8 October 1782, 48 CTS 137; Convention on recaptured vessels, 8 October 1782, 48 CTS 169.

[109] Vattel III.1.1.

[110] For example, *DJBP* II.1.1–6; Gentili, *De iure belli libri tres*, I.3; Vattel III.1.3–4; Oppenheim, *International Law* (3rd edn, Longmans Green 1921) 65–67.

[111] James Q. Whitman, *The Verdict of Battle: The Law of Victory and the Making of Modern War* (Harvard University Press 2012) 50–55, 76–94.

underlying causes that had led to war, as well as to deal with the legal claims that had arisen both before the hostilities and during them. These were by no means confined to the public realm. Experience had taught jurists and governments that during hostilities, as in adventurous peacetime commerce, troublesome private claims had a tendency to proliferate over time.[112] Ancient maxims taught that whoever had been forcibly deprived of their possessions must be allowed to recover whatever damage they had sustained, and to be returned to the state they were in originally, prior to the hostilities.[113] In the absence of a higher authority, it was left for sovereign states themselves to determine what outcomes such principles should, and could, produce in reality. As a consequence, peace treaties typically dealt not only with public questions of territory and sovereign jurisdiction but also private claims dealing with captured ships and cargoes, unpaid debts, confiscated property, or other individual grievances.[114]

The peace settlement between the European powers involved a comprehensive legal process but followed a fairly well-established form. On 3 September 1783, Vergennes, Manchester, and Aranda signed definitive treaties of peace between Britain and Spain and Britain and France at Versailles.[115] Both texts were composed of fairly standard clauses, such as affirmation of perpetual peace and general legal oblivion and amnesty in respect of all war-related claims and violations that were unaccounted for; the release of prisoners, hostages, and vessels captured after the end of hostilities; various colonial cessions and territorial settlements between the powers in the Americas as well as in Africa and India, with a blanket restoration of everything else to status quo ante; adjustments to fishing and logging rights between the parties; time limits for evacuations and the protection of private persons and their property in ceded or returned territories; and assurances of good faith and assumption of state responsibility by each party for enforcing the treaty upon their own nationals. The Anglo-Dutch treaty of 1784 took a similar form, though with additional clauses addressing Britain's insistence on the old flag salute near its coasts, relations between the colonial companies, and freedom of navigation in the Far East.[116]

112 Arnold McNair, 'Introductory' in II McNair, *Opinions* 197–198.

113 Ulpian in *Dig* 43.16.31.

114 Randall Lesaffer, 'Peace Treaties and the Formation of International Law' in Bardo Fassbender and Anne Peters (eds) *The Oxford Handbook of the History of International Law* (Oxford University Press 2012) 76–80.

115 48 CTS 437; 48 CTS 481.

116 49 CTS 65.

The peace treaties also addressed methods for settling private claims. The Franco-British treaty explicitly reconfirmed the jurisdiction of prize courts on both sides over their remaining cases and the finality of their judgments.[117] Special commissions of jurists were to be tasked with drafting further trade agreements and addressing colonial boundary questions between the parties and their colonial companies on the African coast.[118] Together, the peace settlements in Paris and Versailles also rendered the League of Armed Neutrality redundant, as they put an end to the state of war between Britain and the Continental states.

The peace of Paris between Britain and the United States, on the other hand, was designed to settle a revolutionary civil war. This turned out to be a different matter. The primary objective of the American negotiators was to secure international recognition of the United States as a sovereign state, marking the most historic example of state creation since perhaps the Dutch revolt. But even if the peace treaty formally established US sovereignty and peaceful international relations with Britain for the future, the substance of the legal settlement itself could be given meaning only by interpreting the circumstances of the civil war that had preceded it. Had the revolution been an unconstitutional rebellion in Britain or a justified prosecution of self-evident rights under *ius gentium*? Had rebel actions taken place by right and with the sanction of the law of nations, or had they been state crimes for which liability could still lie with the individuals and organs concerned? Should there be state responsibility for private damages caused by the rebellion? In this manner, the core problem of civil war persisted also in its aftermath. Even if a state of peace had now been attained, what exactly had been fought to reach it?

The peace negotiations lasted some two years and involved several rounds of international mediation. The points of contention included the boundaries of the new states, fishing rights on the Atlantic coast, and various property claims by loyalist refugees, bombarded civilians, and British creditors to whom debts were owed by persons in America.[119] Provisional articles of peace were signed in November 1782 and the final Treaty of Paris in September 1783.[120] Its first three articles covered

117 Franco-British treaty, arts XXI–XXII.

118 Franco-British treaty, arts XI, XVIII; Spanish-British treaty, art 9; Dutch-British treaty, art VII.

119 Bemis, *Diplomacy*, chs XIV–XVIII.

120 48 CTS 223; 48 CTS 487.

recognition of the United States by Great Britain, the delineation of US borders, and American fishing rights at the Newfoundland fisheries, while Britain was granted freedom of navigation on the Mississippi. Other articles concerned a general amnesty for acts during the war, the release of all prisoners of war, and an agreement on withdrawal of the remaining British troops and fleets.

The question of private claims turned out to be the most testing. It had been clear during the negotiations that there could be no recognition of the United States without an agreement on the fate of the debts allegedly owed to British creditors and loyalists. The legal bases for such claims were numerous, and conceivably related to the actions of colonial public authorities. During the war, the individual colonies had enacted laws that had led to broad confiscations of loyalist properties and lands that had then been sold or leased onwards in order to fund the war effort. Elsewhere, the insurgents had confiscated estates and inheritances under their power that were due to persons in British-occupied territories. Other measures had 'confiscated' debts owed to British subjects by authorising payments into the insurgent state treasuries instead.[121] The American negotiators also had a constitutional hurdle to overcome. As the Congress of the Confederation at the time could not overrule state legislative Acts dating from the revolution, it had difficulty agreeing on the settlement of private claims. In the end, the peace treaty proposed general wording that postponed immediate resolution of the foreign private claims: it recognised and protected them and provided for eventual recovery of all bona fide debts. The treaty allowed British subjects to visit the United States to recover their assets and the congress agreed to urge individual states to provide for the restitution of confiscated properties.[122]

These foreign property claims, together with questions about the boundaries of the United States, lingered on for a decade. In the end, the two parties returned to them in their treaty of friendship, commerce, and navigation of 1794 (commonly known as the Jay Treaty).[123] Outstanding issues at the time included defining the 'river St. Croix' boundary between the United States and Canada mentioned in the peace treaty, the withdrawal of Britain's troops from its former colonies, and trade and navigation rights on rivers and in the West Indies. There also

121 An exposition of the claims and a list of such Acts is found in Hammond to Jefferson, 5 March 1792, 1 Am Stat Pap For Rel 193–200.

122 Arts IV, V.

123 Treaty of Amity, Commerce and Navigation between Great Britain and the United States, signed in London, 19 November 1794, 52 CTS 243 ('Jay Treaty').

remained numerous British private claims over debts owed by Americans before and during the revolution and, to a lesser extent, Americans' counter-claims concerning property expropriated from them by the withdrawing British during the revolution and further depredations caused by Britain seizing ships during the French revolutionary wars. To settle these issues once and for all, John Jay and Lord Granville agreed to constitute three mixed claims commissions to resolve the issues of the boundary river, the unpaid debts, and contemporary matters of neutral rights and duties at sea.[124]

The St Croix river commission is remembered as a success story, rendering its unanimous award in October 1798.[125] The third commission was able to address a number of questions regarding neutral shipping, although Britain withheld its prize judgments from review by the commission and instead allowed claimants to go before the commission only for pecuniary compensation on account of decisions of the British admiralty courts.[126] By contrast, the second commission, which dealt with private debts, broke down without reaching conclusive results. The composition of the commission – its president drawn by lot[127] – favoured the British by a 3–2 majority. Its work was consequently dominated by the solid front of the three British members, who tended to favour rigid international standards of responsibility for revolutionaries. Early on, they proposed a series of general overarching principles that the commission could then apply across the claims. These propositions – such as 'that the *law*, or the defect of law, should not, *on either side*, stand between the fair creditor, and his unwilling debtor: that all laws which had been passed against such recovery, should be *repealed*' – were not accepted by the Americans. As time went by, disagreements accumulated over seemingly technical issues: whether the definition of 'debt' should include interest; whether the claimants should be required to exhaust local remedies; and who would actually count as a 'British national' eligible to lodge a claim. But beneath the surface, the disagreements ran deep into the essence of the revolution, in particular when the British commissioners suggested that during the war all Americans had nonetheless been

124 Jay Treaty, arts V, VI, VII.

125 Moore's *Adjudications*, vols I–II.

126 Moore's *Adjudications*, vol IV. For summaries, see Neff, *Rights and Duties of Neutrals*, 74–75; Samuel Flagg Bemis, *Jay's Treaty: A Study in Commerce and Diplomacy* (Macmillan 1923) 319–320.

127 Richard B. Lillich, 'The Jay Treaty Commissions' 37 *St. John's Law Review* (1963) 272; III Moore's *Adjudications* 18.

natural-born British subjects – that is, *rebels* – whereas the Americans felt that in 1776 they had become independent Americans, and only the loyalists had then deliberately chosen to side with the British adversaries. This discord proved insurmountable, and in 1799 the two American commissioners exploited the one last weapon they had: they left.[128] The commission disbanded and never met again; instead, the matter returned to the foreign offices of the two governments. Ultimately, a compromise was reached in a separate claims convention in 1802, in which the United States agreed to pay a lump sum of 600,000 pounds to satisfy an estimate of what they might have had to pay had the commission been able to conclude its work. For any remaining disputes, British citizens would have to seek redress from American courts.[129]

The aftermath of the American Revolution illustrates how the legal problem of civil war persisted far beyond the signing of peace treaties. It did so, in particular, through the recurrent question of the responsibility of states for damages caused to foreign private nationals by the civil war and its outcomes. After the peace settlement, both sides let justice run its course domestically, which accommodated their respective interpretations of the nature of the conflict. The British courts could deal with the consequences of a rebellion, and the Americans those of a war of independence. But when a selection of international private claims were to be resolved through an international settlement, the legal status of the conflict returned to haunt the jurists involved. Although the commissions were able to settle territorial questions and questions of prize or no prize on the high seas, they were unable to characterise the conflict even in retrospect. The only way out was through a bilateral lump-sum arrangement between the sovereign states.

Ultimately, the Anglo-British claims settlement provided an international precedent: a newly independent state in the wake of revolution paid a legal ransom for its freedom, addressing the private claims of individuals who were now foreign nationals. In the coming decades, the next transatlantic revolutions that reshaped the New World would see the emergence of new states through a similar process, their recognition being confirmed through the conclusion of treaties of friendship, commerce, and navigation with foreign powers. In these treaties the new republics would negotiate the terms of their international existence, deal

[128] *Allen's Case* in III Moore's *Adjudications* 238, esp 251–252, 279. See also Lillich, 'Jay Treaty Commissions', 272–275.

[129] US–Britain Claims Convention, 8 January 1802, 56 CTS 267. Background in III Moore's *Adjudications* 349–356.

with outstanding claims and disputes over public and private debts and prize cases, and draw up the terms of future commercial interaction between public and private actors. One persistent element in these settlements made revolutionary peacemaking different from inter-state wars: it was virtually indispensable for the new revolutionary republics to gain recognition from their former masters and the international community. Consequently, governments were in a position to wring significant concessions, compensations, and future guarantees in return. Such concessions might be demanded not only in connection with particular disputes, such as outstanding private debts or calculated pecuniary losses for loyalists who had vacated their estates in the former colonies, but also for future relations: continued access to resources, relief from customs duties, guarantees for the protection of foreign private property and investments. Consequently, new republics in the early decolonised world would go through a rite of passage that involved determining the price of their freedom under the law of nations settling it through claims conventions, mixed commissions, arbitrations, and occasional acts of punitive gunboat diplomacy. The result was a century of state practice that prepared the way for the emergence of a general law of state responsibility towards the end of the nineteenth century.[130]

[130] See Kathryn Greenman, *State Responsibility and Rebels: The History and Legacy of Protecting Investment against Revolution* (Cambridge University Press 2021); Alan Tzvika Nissel, *Merchants of Legalism: A History of State Responsibility* (1870–1960) (Cambridge University Press 2024).

3

The Age of Revolutions

3.1 The Politics of Neutrality, Legitimacy, and Revolution

The classical doctrine of civil war came of age in the 'age of revolutions'.[1] The main corpus of state practice for the classical doctrine emerged from the transatlantic theatre during the Spanish American revolutions, where the conditions were suitable for a law of war and neutrality to be applied to internal conflicts. The New World was customarily an area where facts of possession and control had been invoked to challenge claims of lawful title over territory, whether in terms of European conquistadors and settlers against the Native Americans, or Protestant interlopers against the Spanish Empire, or the colonial revolutionaries against the crown of England. As the wave of civil wars progressed, the Western Hemisphere was characterised by various types of republics born out of popular revolutionary movements (with the notable exception of Brazil and its migrant monarchy). This chapter explores the events in these transatlantic revolutions which gave rise to the abundant (often anglophone) state practice later on examined by continental civil war scholars.

State practice in the period was far from consistent. Before discussing the Spanish American revolutions, it will be useful to point out the important limitations on universality in this practice and, arguably, in the subsequent legal doctrine. The first of these was the geographic distinction just mentioned. In contrast to the New World and its traditional character as a land of conquest and colonisation, in the old continent of Europe the popular upheavals and internal conflicts were more commonly characterised as internal political events and debated on philosophical grounds rather than in courts of prize and booty. During the first half of the nineteenth century, these two hemispheres would give rise to two alternative forms of legitimist ideologies; in Europe the liberal revolutions would cause the establishments to rally behind monarchical legitimism, while in the New World the exceptionalist legitimism of the

[1] Eric Hobsbawm, *The Age of Revolution: Europe 1789–1848* (Weidenfeld & Nicolson 1962).

Monroe Doctrine would gradually grow out of the humble beginnings of the United States' neutrality policies. Apart from Europe, the nineteenth-century experience in Asia and Africa tended to follow altogether different priorities as well; in these parts of the world the dominant mode of the law of nations followed the practices of European empires and company colonialism.

A second limitation which may be made here concerns the uniformity of practice within Europe and America. The hemispheric divide was by no means absolute, especially where revolutions were underpinned by ethnic and religious hierarchies that always had their own weight in international law. To take two famous examples, we will first look at the Haitian revolution, which spearheaded the nineteenth-century civil wars in the Americas and which went unrecognised for decades largely due to racial reasons and the insistence of jurists on protecting the rights of the French proprietors against any Haitian right to human liberty. A contrasting example is the Greek War of Independence, a disordered insurgency in the Ottoman Empire between 1821 and 1832, which culminated in a multilateral European intervention, ostensibly for the protection of international trade, and the decimation of the Ottoman fleet in the Battle of Navarino during what was formally still called peacetime. The extent and circumstances of that reaction were clearly an exception to the otherwise solid anti-revolutionary position of the Concert of Europe.

3.1.1 Revolution and Legitimism in Europe

The French Revolution of 1789 had a fundamental indirect influence on the theories of possibility underlying the law of civil war. The 'revolution' as such was more a political period than a particular intra-state conflict, and its international significance is still primarily viewed through the international war it caused. For the world beyond France, the true impact of the French Revolution was its popular challenge to the monarchical state system, which led to a general counter-revolutionary reaction among the foreign powers. The French revolutionaries perhaps did not set out to change the world much beyond their borders, but the actual course of their movement ignited a profound transformation in international political and legal thought in Europe.[2] As the revolutionary

[2] Edward J. Kolla, *Sovereignty, International Law, and the French Revolution* (Cambridge University Press 2017) 33–34. Over the next few pages, I owe much to this brilliant and useful work, and I express my warm thanks for it.

government began to consolidate its new republic across its territories, it ended up annexing as full departments a number of regions in its periphery where old international treaty relations had limited the sovereignty of the French crown. In particular, the French Revolution abolished all noble titles in Alsace in an apparent violation of the 1648 Treaty of Münster (i.e. the Peace of Westphalia) and several other arrangements that were still guaranteeing titles to German *princes possessionnés* in the Holy Roman Empire.[3] They soon also annexed the ancient papal enclaves of Avignon and Comtat Venaissin, which, de jure, had been distinct from the French territory surrounding them since the Middle Ages.[4] Across these annexations, the French revolutionary logic arrived at the argument of popular sovereignty; in Alsace the revolutionary will of the people was mostly assumed by the National Assembly and unilaterally imposed on the abolished nobles, but in the case of Avignon the annexation was confirmed by a plebiscite that demonstrated the desire of the local population to declare their independence from Pope Pius VI and to join France.[5]

In the autumn of 1791, as France was annexing Avignon and the National Assembly finally turned against Louis XVI, foreign courts turned to ostracise French republican ambassadors and lent their ears to royalists and émigrés instead.[6] Leopold II of Austria and Frederick Wilhelm II of Prussia openly called for the restoration of the French monarchy as 'a matter of common interest to all the sovereigns of Europe',[7] and half a year later, in 1792, the French National Assembly declared war on Austria.[8] After initial incursions by the allied troops, the French armies managed to turn the tide of war and take the offensive through mass mobilisation and domestic terror. Around the same time, occupied towns within the Rhineland pleaded for France to offer them protection and union.[9] The National Convention replied at first with a declaration of 'fraternity and assistance to all peoples who shall wish to

[3] Ibid 50–55, 61–79.

[4] Ibid 88–94.

[5] On the significance of the plebiscite, see ibid 95–116.

[6] Harry Ammon, *The Genet Mission* (Norton 1973) 6–9.

[7] The Declaration of Pilnitz, 27 August 1791, in Frank Maloy Anderson, *The Constitutions and Other Select Documents Illustrative of the History of France 1789–1907* (2nd edn, Wilson 1908) 57–58.

[8] Declaration of War against Austria, 20 April 1792, ibid 103–104. Britain became involved through the French Declaration of War against Great Britain, 1 February 1793, ibid 148–151.

[9] Kolla *Sovereignty*, 166–170.

recover their liberty', and then with a comprehensive proclamation on the liberty and sovereignty of all peoples.[10] The proclamation stated that France would suppress all of the established authorities in occupied territories and only lay down its arms after the conquered peoples had established popular sovereignty and free and popular government. It was accompanied by a standardised declaration – a sort of liberal *requerimiento* – to be distributed in all conquered territories. In the eyes of the European monarchists, this total war threatened all conceptions about the lawful scope and purpose of warfare.[11]

Through this struggle for popular sovereignty, 'revolution' and the will of the people became the grand narrative for the mass movements opposing the traditional monarchies, and 'legitimism' the credo of those determined to defend the *ancien régime*. According to the ideology of the third estate, a popular revolution bore its own legitimacy, from the standpoint of which it was the king who was in rebellion against the people, and not vice versa.[12] In the face of this challenge, conservatives across Europe found themselves explicitly spelling out the immutable political principles which they had until then taken for granted. As Stephen Holmes explains, 'There were no Legitimists before the Revolution. Under the old regime, hereditary succession had been a custom; by the time of the Restoration, it had become an ideology.'[13] At the Congress of Vienna in 1814, Talleyrand advocated that the first need for Europe was to revive 'that sacred principle of legitimacy from which all order and stability spring'.[14] When Napoleon broke his exile, the allies declared their collective support to the 'legitimate sovereign' Louis XVIII and asserted their ability and willingness to execute an intervention by invitation anywhere in Europe.[15]

Legitimism and the confinement of liberalism became the particular lodestar of the Holy Alliance of Russia, Prussia, and Austria, which

[10] Declaration for Assistance and Fraternity to Foreign Peoples, 19 November 1792, and Decree for Proclaiming the Liberty and Sovereignty of all Peoples, 15 December 1792, both in Maloy Anderson, *Constitutions*, 130–133.

[11] Compare James Q. Whitman, *The Verdict of Battle: The Law of Victory and the Making of Modern War* (Harvard University Press 2012) 226–229.

[12] Victor Hugo, *Les Misérables* ([1862] Bibliothèque de la Pléiade, Gallimard 2018) IV.4.1.

[13] Stephen Holmes, 'Two Concepts of Legitimacy: France after the Revolution' 10 *Political Theory* (1982) 166.

[14] Charles Maurice de Talleyrand, *Memoirs of the Prince de Talleyrand*, vol II (G. P. Putnam's Sons 1891) 203. On Talleyrand's motives, see Holmes, 'Two Concepts', 176–178.

[15] Treaty of Alliance against Bonaparte, 20 November 1815, 2 BFSP 443.

pledged 'in front of the Universe' to defend what they called the Christian religion and values.[16] According to Prince Metternich, the 'moral essence' of the alliance rested on the 'principle of preserving everything that has a legal existence, and of a happy union between the great Powers'.[17] The concrete manifestation of the confrontation was the struggle over written constitutions in the mainland. The legitimist ideology found its clearest expression in the winter of 1820–1821, when the Concert of Europe met to discuss the security implications of the liberal Neapolitan revolt in the Kingdom of the Two Sicilies. The three Holy Allies attending did not hesitate to assimilate all revolutionary activities to the spectre of Bonapartism.[18] Exercising their 'indisputable right', they called for 'common measures of safety' against states in which the government had been overthrown by rebellion (and which must be made an example of). All revolutionaries were to be treated as 'hostile to all lawful constitutions and Governments' and prevented from 'scattering rebellion and confusion around' in the neighbouring countries.[19] The intervention in Naples was soon followed by a French intervention in Spain, again agreed among the foreign powers, which enabled the king of Spain to revoke the Cadiz constitution for a second time. This ideological confrontation over constitutionalism and absolute monarchy persisted in Europe until (and beyond) the continent-wide eruption of popular movements in 1848 and the eventual transition towards more constitutional and limited forms of monarchy.

Against this broad ideological background, it may be somewhat surprising that among the later generations of scholars who worked to define the rules and the jurisprudence of the classical doctrine of civil war, the French Revolution remained a relatively marginal precedent. This fact tells us perhaps more about the doctrine of civil war than about the significance of the revolution. The French Revolution took place at the heart of Europe, and thus for many authors evidently in the realm of politics and political philosophy rather than in the more peripheral sphere of rebellions and insurgencies. It also differed from the transatlantic revolutions in its practical circumstances, as it did not primarily manifest itself in terms of a well-defined naval or even territorial armed

16 Sainte Alliance, 26 September 1815, 3 BFSP 211–212.

17 Metternich to Esterhazy, 7 August 1825, in Prince Klemens Lothar Wenzel von Metternich, *Memoirs of Prince Metternich* (Mrs Alexander Napier tr, Richard Bentley & Son 1881) vol IV, 225. See also vol III, 453–476.

18 The Troppau Circular, 8 December 1820, ibid, vol III, 444–447.

19 Ibid.

struggle. It rather followed a cascading pattern of fast-paced *coups d'état* and constitutional reforms at the highest level of state institutions – six constitutions in a dozen years – which was amplified by incessant local uprisings, riots, tumults, and political murders in Paris and other major cities. Thus, scholars mostly by-passed the French Revolution and moved on from the American Revolution to the Spanish American revolutions. Even Antoine Rougier, who did explore the French Revolution in his book on the law of civil war, did not concern himself much with the question of when and how the revolutionary movement itself managed to become an international actor against the king's government. He rather considered the revolutionary government after the abolition of the monarchy simply as the lawful government of France and examined the internal dimension of the revolution through the smaller individual riots that took place within revolutionary France.[20] Among those internal upheavals, Rougier identified the war in the Vendée as a 'civil war' mainly on account of its scope, organisation, and goals.[21] For the most part, that finding did little more than confirm a mainstream historiographical assumption; it remained less clear what, if any, international legal effects Rougier saw emerging from this interpretation.

3.1.2 *The United States and the Law of Neutrality*

The revolution looked somewhat different from across the Atlantic. Much of the Americas remained both peripheral in international relations and firmly under the influence of European empires; for these empires, overseas colonies were viewed mostly as objects of history rather than their subjects. After the outbreak of the French Revolution, the recently founded United States began to gradually develop a new role in global politics from its remote geographical location. This role stemmed from policies of neutrality and free trade that were influenced by the continuing imbalance of power between the Atlantic coasts, and it increasingly took a legalistic form and relied on the language and argumentation of the law of nations. As the United States worked to fulfil its sovereignty through the Jay Treaty arbitrations and navigate its way through the fragile diplomacy of the revolutionary wars, it gradually introduced a new kind of legalistic neutrality that became characteristic of the nineteenth-century international law.

[20] Antoine Rougier, *Les guerres civiles et le droit des gens* (Larose 1903) 34–35.
[21] Ibid 41–42.

In 1793, Citizen Edmond Genet arrived in the United States to rally American privateers and volunteers to the cause of the French Revolution. He travelled up from Richmond by land, handing out privateer commissions and attending popular rallies celebrating the ties between the allied sister republics. But upon arriving in Philadelphia, he quickly encountered formal protests against French privateering and refusals of privateers' prizes in American ports.[22] President Washington's cabinet, torn internally between a desire to turn against British commercial dominance on the one hand and fears of British counter-reaction to any sign of American support for France on the other, had proclaimed neutrality with respect to the European war upon Genet's arrival in the United States.[23]

But what exactly did it mean for the United States to be neutral in the European conflict? Should Genet's privateers be refused access to US ports? Could individual citizens answer Genet's call and volunteer for the revolutionary cause? Cases soon began to arrive in courts concerning US citizens apprehended for their intentions to enlist with the French.[24] One Gideon Henfield, a volunteer on the French privateer *Citizen Genet*, was arrested after he brought a captured British vessel to the port of Philadelphia. As he stood accused of violating US neutrality, the circuit court had to begin by asking under which jurisdiction and under what law the defendant might be tried in the first place. It found that although no municipal law prescribed a punishment for the violation of neutrality, the defendant could be tried under the law of nations, as this was the binding and supreme law of the land according to both the new constitution and the old common law.[25] In the end, the local jury acquitted Henfield, stating that it was not convinced that, at the time of the capture, the declaration had become public enough to hold the defendant liable for breaching it. But on the point of law, the verdict recognised the possibility of universal standards of neutrality in international law and opened up the path for new, characteristically American interpretations about its substance.

22 Ammon, *Genet Mission*, 66–70.

23 Proclamations of neutrality (1793, 1794) in *A Compilation of the Messages and Papers of the Presidents* (J. D. Richardson ed, Bureau of National Literature 1897) vol I, 148–150; Neutrality Proclamation, 22 April 1793, I Am Stat Pap For Rel 140.

24 For a digest, see Dana's *Wheaton* 455–466.

25 *Henfield's Case*, 11 Fed Cas 1099, 1120. See Matthew P. Harrington, *Jay and Ellsworth, The First Courts: Justices, Rulings, and Legacy* (ABC-CLIO 2008) 157–158.

The product of these questions was the US Neutrality Act of 1794,[26] an early prototype for the municipally enacted neutrality laws of the nineteenth century.[27] The Act prohibited by statute citizens from accepting foreign commissions, enlisting in foreign forces, fitting out or augmenting warships or other armed vessels, and preparing military expeditions destined overseas. It was enacted for two years at a time in 1794 and 1797, and 'without limitation of time' in 1800. In its later variants it transformed from an ad hoc arrangement into a standing statutory instrument that spelled out what a presidential declaration of neutrality would mean for individual US citizens and how the obligations it placed on them would be enforced by federal officials in given instances of neutrality. More indirectly, the Act implicitly sketched out the particular duties and responsibilities that a neutral state might be obligated to bear under the law of nations. The Neutrality Act would later play a central role in defining official US positions on the law of civil wars: in 1818 the Act would be clarified so that it could also apply to foreign insurrections, and in 1823 the US neutrality policies would be consolidated in the Monroe Doctrine and its hemispherical assertion of popular self-determination. This development did not follow a smooth path, as the United States found itself in maritime quasi-war with France in 1798 and in an open war with Great Britain in 1812. But in the decades after the Vienna Congress neutrality became an ever more integral part of international politics in the context of the Concert of Europe and its monarchical balance of power.[28]

Beginning with the French *Code civil* in 1804 and the British Foreign Enlistment Act of 1819,[29] the European powers gradually adopted the American practice of declaring neutrality and contributed to the articulation of the international obligations of neutrals through their own statutory law. These statutes would offer a template for the practice of the law of civil war, as states would declare neutrality with respect to foreign insurrections and warn their citizens that anyone attempting contraband trade or running a blockade would not receive diplomatic protection in the event of capture. The practical implications flowing

[26] Neutrality Act, 5 June 1794, in *A Collection of Neutrality Laws, Regulations and Treaties of Various Countries* (Philip C. Jessup and Francis Deák eds, Carnegie Endowment for International Peace 1939) vol 2, 1079–1083.

[27] *Neutrality Laws*, vol I, xi. The United States was not entirely alone with neutrality laws; the Prussian *Allgemeines Landrecht* of 1794 included neutrality provisions regarding shipping (prohibiting contraband). See *Neutrality Laws*, vol I, 630–631.

[28] Maartje Abbenhuis, *An Age of Neutrals: Great Power Politics, 1815–1914* (Cambridge University Press 2014) 38–39.

[29] *Neutrality Laws*, vol I, 125, 582–583; vol II, 1085.

from these declarations would later culminate in the legal opinion that by proclaiming their neutrality third states actually recognised the belligerent status of both sides in these conflicts – including the insurgents.

3.1.3 *Limits of Universality: Civil War and the Peripheries of Empire*

The age of revolutions therefore produced two variants of legitimism. In Europe the establishments typically rallied behind monarchical legitimism, while in the New World the US neutrality policies and later the Monroe Doctrine gave rise to a distinct sense of American international law that rejected colonial empire and favoured ideals of popular self-determination. At their intersection were the Spanish American revolutions which, together with the revolution of the thirteen colonies, constituted the first wave of decolonisation. It was during the Spanish American revolutions that statesmen and jurists in Europe and the Americas became accustomed to debating and applying the formal principles of neutrality in foreign civil wars, and consequently produced a trail of opinions, decisions, and declarations that would eventually constitute the basic texts and principles for the doctrines of belligerent recognition and the rest of the law of civil war. But in the colonial peripheries of the world, state practice on neutrality and civil war was always subject to the dynamics of difference that continued to separate them from the sovereign core in Europe.[30] Especially when dealing with oriental kingdoms or indigenous populations, interpretations of general legal principles on both sides of the Atlantic often gave way to pragmatic considerations, prejudice, and casuistic pursuits of metropolitan interests. In these contexts, the open-ended nature of the legal principles concerning recognition and jurisdiction provided ample room for contradistinct legal arguments between lawyers, courts, and governments in different countries and situations whenever they did not share the same political priorities or perceptions of justice.

Although the law of war and neutrality in the context of civil wars had its origins in the Americas, it was not applied consistently in that hemisphere either. The most obvious example of a contrary treatment was the Haitian revolution, in which the slaves in the French sugar colony of Saint-Domingue revolted against their masters, established a new revolutionary government, and eventually seized their own sovereign liberty. The Haitian revolt was the first colonial revolution in the New World after

[30] See Antony Anghie, *Imperialism, Sovereignty and the Making of International Law* (Cambridge University Press 2005) 3–4 *et passim*.

that of the United States and a direct offshoot of the French enlightenment. Following the universal declaration of the rights of man and the citizen by the French National Assembly in 1789, restlessness spread into France's colonies. In Saint-Domingue, this restlessness first appeared among the colony's *petits blancs*, who radicalised to promote themselves against the propertied planters, the crown, and the people of colour, but it then spread among the black majority after the National Assembly in Paris refused to abolish slavery.[31] New constitutions in 1790 and 1791 claimed legislative authority in the colony,[32] while the French National Assembly momentarily recognised the full rights of the free blacks in its colonies.[33] A widespread insurrection erupted in Saint-Domingue in 1791, and by 1793 a British counter-revolutionary expedition began to seize the colony for Britain. To regain control, the French commissioners on the island declared the abolition of slavery in 1793,[34] which was affirmed by the National Convention,[35] and by 1798 the islanders, led by Toussaint Louverture, had repelled the British invasion. Napoleon Bonaparte, who became consul in 1799, soon began to lean towards the reinstitution of plantation slavery in the French Caribbean colonies. The Haitians hastened to attain complete abolition of slavery with a constitution of their own in 1801,[36] but their hopes were ultimately dashed when Bonaparte sent in Leclerc's expedition to reinstate imperial control.[37] After a bitter total war on their island, the Haitians declared independence in 1804 and promulgated a sovereign constitution in 1805.[38] But the factions and regions of the new republic continued to clash for many years, with periods

[31] Laurent Dubois and John D. Garrigus, *Slave Revolution in the Caribbean, 1789-1804: A Brief History with Documents* (2nd edn, Bedford 2017) 14–17, 55–65.

[32] Constitutional decree, 28 May 1790, in Laurent Dubois, Julia Gaffield, and Michel Acacia, *Documents constitutionnels d'Haïti 1790–1860* (De Gruyter 2013) 23–25; Draft constitution, 1791, ibid 27–51.

[33] Law on the Colonies, 15 May 1791, in Dubois and Garrigus, *Slave Revolution*, 70–71.

[34] Decree of General Liberty, 29 August 1793, ibid 110.

[35] Extract from the minutes of the National Convention, 4 February 1794, ibid 122.

[36] 16 BFSP 716.

[37] Carl Ludwig Lokke, 'The Leclerc Instructions' 10 *Journal of Negro History* (1925) 80–89; Proclamation, 8 November 1801, in *Correspondance de Napoléon Ier* (Imprimerie impériale 1861) vol 7, 401, doc 5859; Napoleon to Louverture, 18 November 1801, *Correspondance de Napoléon Ier*, vol 7, 410, doc 5867; Laurent Dubois, *Avengers of the New World: The Story of the Haitian Revolution* (Laurent Dubois 2004) 236–279.

[38] Haitian declaration of independence, 1 January 1804, in Dubois and Garrigus, *Slave Revolution*, 178–181; Constitution of the Empire of Hayti, 20 May 1805, 16 BFSP 728. On the war, see Philippe Girard, 'The Leclerc Expedition to Saint-Domingue and the Independence of Haiti, 1802–1804' (*Oxford Research Encyclopedia of Latin American History*, 23 May 2019) https://oxfordre.com/latinamericanhistory.

of internal strife punctuated by republican and imperial constitutions succeeding one another.[39] On the high seas, French privateers and capers from Cuba and Santo Domingo continued to harass international shipping around Haiti, benefiting from the unsettled legal status of its flag and coasts.[40]

The Haitians continued to receive very little international recognition in support of their statehood for another two decades,[41] it being assumed at the time that their independence would either be altogether impossible due to the slave revolt with which it originated, or at least conditional upon due compensation being paid to the former French slaveowners. At the Congress of Vienna in 1814, France was still asserting its right to reconquer Saint-Domingue, and it was only after the recognition of Spanish American republics that it began to lean towards the recognition of Haiti – for a price. In 1825, a French naval squadron delivered an ultimatum from Paris: France would recognise the Haitians in exchange for special trading privileges and the payment of 150 million francs to indemnify the French citizens for their losses in Haiti.[42] It was only after France recognised Haiti that other foreign powers did so, including the British Empire, which was never inclined to accept Haitian independence during its revolutionary wars against France and Spain.[43] A notable exception was the United States; not until 1862 and the civil war did the US government dare to recognise a black republic, even though in other circumstances it was prepared to recognise anti-colonial revolutions in the vicinity of the United States.[44]

The indemnity was impossibly high, and the Haitians defaulted immediately on the loan they had assumed. The debt was ultimately restructured in 1838 in the Franco-Haitian treaty of peace and friendship, in

[39] Constitutions of 1805, 1806, 1807, 1811, 1816, 1843, 1846, and 1849, in Dubois, Gaffield, and Acacia, *Documents constitutionnels*.

[40] Girard, 'Leclerc Expedition'. See also *Rose* v. *Himely* (1808) 8 US 241.

[41] The US prohibited trade to the rebel-controlled parts of Haiti in 1806, while Britain declared free trade during the war with France in 1808. See Acts of Congress (1806, 1807) 4 BFSP 328, 329; British Order in Council for a Free Trade with Hayti, 14 December 1808, in Baron de Vastey, *An Essay on the Causes of the Revolution and Civil Wars of Hayti* (Western Luminary Office 1823) app l, no 3, cxviii; General View of the Commerce of Cape Henry, Hayti, in Vastey, *Essay*, app l, no 2, cxvii.

[42] Royal ordinance of 17 April 1825 and the convention between France and Haiti, signed at Paris, 31 October 1825, 75 CTS 417.

[43] Benoît Joachim, 'La reconnaissance d'Haïti par la France (1825): Naissance d'un nouveau type de rapports internationaux' 22 *Revue d'histoire moderne et contemporaine* (1975) 381–384.

[44] 1 Moore's *Digest* 107.

which France also renounced the threat of military intervention.[45] Such renunciations notwithstanding, when earthquakes, fires, and insurrections prompted the Haitians to oust their president and call a halt to the payments in 1843, France quickly secured the continuation of the payment programme from 1849 onwards.[46] The Haitian payments to France continued until 1883, and it was only in 1893 that the French government finally certified that Haiti had paid off the indemnity.[47]

The Haitian independence debt has gone down in history as a notorious case of inequitable post-colonial domination. In the present context, it may be worth observing how significantly the origin of the Haitian debt differed from an analogous experience in the original French Revolution. After taking possession of the territories of Alsace and Avignon, the French revolutionaries for a while debated the question of proper indemnities for the *princes possessionnés* and the papacy, and initially they reserved the sum of forty million livres for potential relief. They ultimately rejected any obligation to indemnify, considering it an obsolete remnant of *ancien régime* international law. At one point, Prime Minister Montmorin instructed, first, that there could be no property rights over human beings (and therefore nothing to compensate), and second, that proprietors could not indefinitely have a right to refuse to consent to the general will of the people.[48] Thus, while in 1790s the French republic had argued that freedom from slavery and the will of the people were absolutes for which no compensation was due, the restored monarchy in 1815 had no desire to recognise such principles in favour of Haiti.[49]

***

If the story of the Haitian revolution highlighted the racial boundaries of the liberal revolutions in the Americas, then likewise the Greek Revolution of 1821 demonstrates the limits of legitimism on the fringes of Europe. This revolution, also known as the Greek War of Independence, emerged from a combination of popular enlightenment,

[45] Treaty of Friendship and Treaty Relative to an Indemnity between France and Haiti, signed at Port-au-Prince, 12 February 1838, 87 CTS 357.

[46] Convention between France and Haiti, 15 May 1847, 101 CTS 17; same, 1 October 1854, 112 CTS 211, François Blancpain, *Un siècle de relations financières entre Haïti et la France, 1825–1922* (L'Harmattan 2001) 75.

[47] Jeremy D. Popkin, *A Concise History of the Haitian Revolution* (Wiley-Blackwell, 2012) 153.

[48] Kolla, *Sovereignty*, 62–63, also 67 fn 97 for a brief summary of the debate.

[49] France was allowed to keep Alsace and Avignon under the 1814 peace of Paris (63 CTS 171) and the final act of the Vienna Congress (64 CTS 453); therefore, its title there was arguably no longer based on the revolutionary actions.

Greek nationalism, Russian power politics, and widespread support from Panhellenic enthusiasts and classical literati in European capitals. In this landscape, Greece's secession from the Ottoman Empire inspired many Europeans to exempt it from the general counter-revolutionary politics that the Holy Allies, and the Concert of Europe more broadly, were willing to enforce elsewhere on the continent.[50]

In many ways, the legal structure of the Greek revolt resembled that of the transatlantic revolutions. The insurgents asserted their existence under the law of nations by immediately constituting their prize jurisdiction,[51] while in return the imperial Ottoman fleet ordered a blockade of the Peloponnese.[52] Greece's makeshift navy attracted adventurers and filibusters of various nationalities, and its initial campaign at sea had some success, with the insurgents even declaring they would blockade several ports in the empire itself.[53] Britain and France ordered their subjects to respect the insurgent blockades in early 1823, while Metternich maintained a harder line and refused to instruct Austrian vessels to avoid the blockaded ports.[54] But in the long run, the Greek prize courts had difficulty managing the depredations by their privateers, and their war effort was generally viewed by foreign governments as rife with piracy. The insurgent leaders even contributed to this infamy by briefly adopting an overtly aggressive stance towards neutral flags that engaged in dealings with the Ottomans.[55] In 1824, the Royal Navy made preparations to seize insurgent vessels suspected of piracy.[56]

The Greeks tried to completely cancel their policies against neutrals, but did so too late to avoid the consequences.[57] By the end of the year, Western European powers were corresponding with Russia on the

[50] On the Greek war, see generally Viktorija Jakjimovska, 'Uneasy Neutrality: Britain and the Greek War of Independence (1821–1832)' in Inge Van Hulle and Randall Lesaffer (eds), *International Law in the Long Nineteenth Century (1776–1914): From the Public Law of Europe to Global International Law?* (Brill Nijhoff 2019) 45–71; W. Crawley, *The Question of Greek Independence: A Study of British Policy in the Near East 1821–1833* (Cambridge University Press 1930).

[51] Philip James Green, *Sketches of the War in Greece* (London 1827) 143; Samuel Howe, *An Historical Sketch of the Greek Revolution* (White, Gallaher & White 1828) 325.

[52] Proclamations of 7 May 1821, 8 BFSP 1282.

[53] Declaration of 25 March 1822, 9 BFSP 798.

[54] C. W. Crawley, *The Question of Greek Independence*, 27–28; 1 Smith 282.

[55] Proclamation of 27 May 1824, 11 BFSP 827. Reversed in Proclamation of 15 August 1824, 11 BFSP 828. See also proclamation of 16 August 1824, 11 BFSP 828–829, acknowledging the piracy problem.

[56] Ionian proclamation, 6 September 1824, 11 BFSP 829–830.

[57] Greek proclamation, 3 September 1824, 11 BFSP 830.

question of a joint international intervention, which the tsar's cabinet embraced wholeheartedly in the name of humanity and world peace.[58] Meanwhile, the Greek insurgents began to run out of luck by 1825 and 1826, when the sultan instructed the armies of his Egyptian vassal Muhammad Ali to subdue the rebellion. The Greek pleas for aid were rejected by Metternich,[59] though they still drew a formal proclamation of neutrality from Britain.[60] Upon Metternich's urging, Austria and Prussia refused to acknowledge the Greeks as viable interlocutors, while Britain, Russia, and France devised a plan for mediation backed up by an intervention, if needed. To justify their plan, they invoked humanitarian interests, arguing that pushing the insurgents below the reach of the law of nations might lead to 'indiscriminate rapine and massacre'.[61]

The 1827 Treaty of London avoided any suggestion of universal justice for the Greek cause, but instead it emphasised a seemingly apolitical need to protect neutral commerce.[62] The treaty contained a plan of cooperation between the three powers and a peace plan for implementation in the conflict. The plan demanded an armistice, offered good offices and mediation to the conflicting parties, and proposed an arrangement whereby the Porte would retain suzerainty over the Greeks and enjoy an annual tribute. In return, the sultan was asked to agree to 'a complete separation between the individuals of the two nations' and the transfer of all private property in Greece and its islands to Greek ownership against full indemnities to be paid by the Greeks. For their part, the three powers agreed not to seek new territory or other concessions that could not be granted to all.[63] The Greek insurgents eagerly accepted the armistice.[64] The Porte, not unexpectedly, rejected it outright as infringing its sovereignty and its exclusive right to deal with the rebels in accordance with its laws and without foreign interference.[65] This had been well anticipated by France, Britain, and Russia, which had included in the Treaty of London an additional and secret article for this eventuality. In the event of rejection, they would first establish formal diplomatic relations with the Greeks – thus recognising the Greek government – and then

[58] Mémoire, 31 May 1824, 11 BFSP 819 at 826.
[59] See Prince Metternich, *Memoirs of Prince Metternich*, vol III, 234–240.
[60] Proclamation of 30 September 1825, 12 BFSP 525–529.
[61] Canning to Wellesley, 31 December 1824, 1 Smith 294–297 at 296. Also cited in Lauterpacht, *Recognition*, 227.
[62] Treaty of London, 6 July 1827, 77 CTS 307, preamble.
[63] Ibid, arts 1, 2, 5.
[64] Proclamation of the provisional government, 21 August 1827, 14 BFSP 1048.
[65] Manifesto of the Sublime Porte, 9 June 1827, 14 BFSP 1042.

commit themselves to pacification through 'ulterior measures'. Their naval commanders would be instructed to 'exert all measures that circumstances may suggest to their prudence, for the purpose of obtaining the immediate effects of the Armistice'.[66]

In October 1827, the three powers copenhagened the Ottoman fleet at Navarino without ever declaring war. The following year, Tsar Nikolai I formally declared war on the Porte and brought the conflict overtly into the international realm, while France's Morea expedition pushed back the Egyptian troops from the Peloponnese. In the peace treaty between Russia and Turkey in 1829, the Sublime Porte finally submitted to the armistice and the principles of the Treaty of London as further developed by the allies in a separate protocol.[67] After three more years of conflicts in the Levant (including between Egypt and the Porte), the Kingdom of Greece was formally recognised in 1832 in the Treaty of Constantinople and was placed under the protection of the three allied powers.[68] But whatever the scale and human cost of the conflict, the allied powers never conceded that it was a situation of civil war or belligerency.[69]

***

The examples from Haiti, Greece, and the Two Sicilies illustrate how the age of revolutions occurred in a political landscape of commerce and empires. They also demonstrate the limited applicability of any European and US legal forms when dealing with colonial peripheries and the Oriental empires. The Haitian revolution, despite its liberal foundations and de facto successes, attracted little recognition and no allies from abroad; in particular, it was marginalised by the United States within US hemispheric policy for decades thereafter. The Greek revolution, on the other hand, culminated in a multilateral intervention by Europe to protect maritime trade at a moment when the Porte was gaining the upper hand against its Hellenic rebels. While neither case would be forgotten or excluded from the memory of the law of nations, they would in retrospect not constitute primary cases in scholarship on the law of civil war. Instead, the centre stage in this period belonged to the Spanish American revolutions. The convulsive implosion of the Spanish American empire led to an accumulation of various streams of diplomatic correspondence and legal

66 Treaty of London (1827), Secret and Additional Article.

67 Treaty of Adrianople, 14 September 1829, 80 CTS 83, art X; Protocol of conference, 22 March 1829, 79 CTS 361.

68 Arrangement for the settlement of the boundaries of Greece, 21 July 1832, 82 CTS 477.

69 Lassa Oppenheim, *International Law*, vol II (2nd edn, Longmans Green 1912) 48, § 44.

court practice on the questions of formal neutrality in civil wars, its legal effects, and its consequences. This implosion and the rise of the new republics constituted a legal encounter that would give rise to a major corpus of legal material for the classical doctrine of civil war.

3.2 The Spanish American Revolutions

After Nelson's victory at Trafalgar in 1805, France and Spain could exert little genuine blue-water control across the Atlantic, which left the Western hemisphere vulnerable in the face of a wave of enlightened revolution.[70] When in 1807 Napoleon ordered his armies into the Iberian Peninsula and put Joseph Bonaparte on Ferdinand VII's throne in 1808, he triggered a chain of events that culminated in the decolonisation of Spanish America. Soon, the French armies were fighting against the forces of Portugal, Spain, and Britain, as well as dealing with widespread popular resistance from irregular fighters who deployed techniques that came to be known as guerrilla warfare. While Spain and Portugal were occupied by the Peninsular War, the *americanos* established a chain of juntas and republics across the colonial territories and eventually declared their independence from the European motherland. At first, they did not aim for full independence: most of the new statesmen emerged as pro-monarchical loyalists, repudiating French rule and seeking autonomy or equal status with the regions of metropolitan Spain.[71] In the Spanish constitutional tradition, the juntas were intended to act merely as interim governments during the king's absence.[72] But within a few years, increasingly revolutionary sentiments spread throughout the viceroyalties of New Spain, New Granada, and Río de la Plata, and the first declarations of independence were delivered in 1811.[73]

70 Arthur Preston Whitaker, *The United States and the Independence of Latin America, 1800–1830* (Johns Hopkins Press 1941) 1, 19, 31. John Chasteen, *Americanos: Latin America's Struggle for Independence* (Oxford University Press 2008) 35–42.

71 Jaime E. Rodríguez, *The Independence of Spanish America* (Cambridge University Press 1998) 2–3; David Head, *Privateers of the Americas: Spanish American Privateering from the United States in the Early Republic* (University of Georgia Press 2015) 14–16.

72 Rodríguez, *Independence*, 75–106. See also Grotius after Covarruvias, *De jure praedae*, ch XIII (f 129).

73 Act of the Supreme Junta of New Granada, 26 July 1810, 1 BFSP 1237 and 1242; Declaration of independence of Carthagena (1811) 1 BFSP 1136; Federative Act of New Granada (1811) 1 BFSP 1069; Venezuelan Declaration of Rights (1811) 1 BFSP 1104; Venezuelan Declaration of Independence (1811) 1 BFSP 1108. See also I Moore's *Digest*, 74–80; Head, *Privateers*, 14–20. For subsequent declarations and constitutions, see 5 BFSP 804, 958; 6 BFSP 820, 1028; 9 BFSP 393, 407, 696, 698, 800, 854; 10 BFSP 945, 1023; 11 BFSP 874.

The revolutionary momentum was briefly reversed in 1812 when the Cádiz Cortes proclaimed in its new constitution 'a Spanish nation of all the Spanish of the two hemispheres' and promised the colonies in the new world (as well as the Philippines) equal status with the territories in Europe.[74] But soon after being reinstated on the throne in 1813, Ferdinand revoked the constitution and declared a reconquest of 'his' New World possessions.[75] This reconquest was not to last. In the face of the prospect of a return to colonial status, the previously disparate social and cultural factions in the New World rallied around charismatic rebel leaders such as Simón Bolívar and José de San Martín.[76] By 1820, despite swings of fortune, the revolutionaries managed to bring Spain's local representatives to agree to formal armistices, although Madrid itself refuted any state of belligerency and continued internationally to claim its dominion and sovereignty over its old empire.[77] Apart from in their engagements against Spain, the revolutionaries did not form a unified front; some of their rivalries were rooted far back in the past.[78] Factionalism and competition for power seemed inevitable; the problem was that as the republics' borders along the colonial administrative boundaries had been claimed mainly on an *uti possidetis juris* basis, the boundaries between the Spanish viceroyalties had never been settled very clearly. At the same time as the Spanish reconquest, the republics continued to confront each other under increasingly uncertain conditions.[79]

The Spanish American revolutions unleashed a period of uncertainty in the transatlantic world of commerce and shipping, which lasted well beyond the end of the war in Europe in 1815. The new republics and insurgent factions asserted themselves as legitimate governments against the remaining Spanish colonial officials, and soon buccaneering,

74 Constitution of 19 March 1812, 7 BFSP 237–279.

75 Manifesto of the king of Spain, 4 May 1814, 1 BFSP 1093; Royal proclamation to the transatlantic colonies, 24 May 1814, 1 BFSP 1310.

76 See Bolívar's manifesto of 30 July 1811, 1 BFSP 1113; Bolívar's Jamaica letter, 6 September 1815, in David Bushnell (ed), *El Libertador: Writings of Simón Bolivar* (Oxford University Press 2003) 12–30; Venezuelan declaration of independence, 20 November 1818, 5 BFSP 958.

77 For example, armistice agreements at 71 CTS 281 and 447; Stephen C. Neff, *War and the Law of Nations: A General History* (Cambridge University Press 2005) 256. See also 71 CTS 291.

78 Chasteen, *Americanos*, 66–94.

79 For example, Colombia and Peru, 11 BFSP 866; 15 BFSP 1190–1202; 15 BFSP 1202; 16 BFSP 1199. The Plata region, I Manning's *Dipl Corr* 590–591; 16 BFSP 1198.

filibustering, and piracy thrived one last time across the Spanish Main.[80] This prompted all the commercial states and empires to seek ways to adapt to the circumstances while still exercising their functions as responsible flag states and protecting the interests of their shipowners and merchants. The result was a period of diplomacy around various declarations of blockade, neutrality, reprisals, and diplomatic protest by maritime powers – an environment that subsequently led to a gradual understanding among jurists that an intermediate status for qualified insurgents seemed like a logical solution to the belligerent powers/neutral rights equation. During this crucial period of state practice, the maritime powers of the Atlantic began to consider themselves implicitly or explicitly as 'neutrals' vis-à-vis each other's colonial troubles. Out of this practice of neutrality a doctrine was eventually born for recognising belligerency.

3.2.1 *Recourse to Belligerent Rights*

3.2.1.1 Rebel Privateers and Blockades

The Spanish American insurgents fought for their independence with the most convenient maritime force available to them: commissioned privateers. These quickly became quite a cosmopolitan gathering of adventurers, rogues, slavers, and smugglers, especially as numerous veterans and decommissioned privateers from the Napoleonic Wars were looking for work.[81] When foreign powers began to declare neutrality or to conform to blockades by the Spanish government, the rebel governments began to offer citizenship, domicile, and commissions to foreign privateers and filibusters. Over time, these privateers and their financiers developed

[80] According to Matthew McCarthy, revolutionary privateers initiated as many as 1,688 encounters in the Americas, of which 1,074 involved insurgent privateers. Out of those 1,074 visited vessels, the insurgent privateers seized and brought ashore 527, while the rest were either let go of or 'plundered'. At least 266 of the vessels engaged by the privateers were neutrals. From 1816 to 1821, the Buenos Aires government deployed between 36 and 45 privateers, the Venezuelan fleet was 35 ships strong in 1817, and the Mexican squadron under Louis Aury in 1816–1818 numbered between 14 and 18 hulls and 1,000 men. See Matthew McCarthy, *Privateering, Piracy and British Policy in Spanish America 1810–1830* (Boydell Press 2013) 24–28. This remarkable work has been of great benefit for this chapter, and I owe a debt of gratitude to the author.

[81] Rafe Blaufarb, 'Arms for Revolutions: Military Demobilization after the Napoleonic Wars and Latin American Independence' in Alan Forrest, Karen Hagemann, and Michael Rowe (eds), *War, Demobilization and Memory: The Legacy of War in the Era of Atlantic Revolutions* (Palgrave Macmillan 2016) 100–116.

creative (and often cruel) strategies for managing the lawfulness and profitability of their operations.[82]

The insurgent governments also blockaded Spanish ports – an act the law of nations reserved strictly to lawful belligerents. Once they had gained a degree of tacit recognition in the region, or had themselves been torn asunder by rival factions that created civil wars within civil wars, the Spanish American republics issued declarations of blockades as though they were sovereign states with full belligerent powers.[83] The globally determined dates of entry into force of the blockages specified in the notifications of these declarations suggest that the blockades were meant to be enforced against neutral, as well as against Spanish, vessels. The blockades led to heated exchanges of legal opinions that exposed the opposing views of insurgents and neutrals. Foreign powers were often inclined to regard the rebel blockades as invalid paper blockades that could not be effectively enforced, even if in their actions they often avoided confrontations with the rebels and focused on the protection of their international commerce.[84] In 1817, the two American vessels *Tiger* and *Liberty* were taken as prize by Venezuelan insurgents on the Orinoco River and condemned for trading arms with the Spanish forces. The American 'special agent' Baptis Irvine sought their restitution.[85] In his exchanges with Bolívar, Irvine argued that neutral merchantmen enjoyed a customary right to engage in trade with all belligerents, as long as this could happen impartially with all of them. He also argued that free ships should make free goods. In contrast, Bolivar, whose privateers followed the customary *Consolato* rule in the absence of treaties, argued that trade in munitions and armaments constituted an unneutral act and contraband trade, and that in any event blockades applied under the law of nations to everyone, neutrals included.[86] That was the very

82 Head, *Privateers*, 42–50, 76–83, 92–99, 102–108, with commissions from Aury at 96 and 113; Brian Vale, *Cochrane in the Pacific: Future and Freedom in Spanish America* (I. B. Tauris 2008) 31–38.

83 For example, Capitulation at Amelia Island and declaration of blockade of the Floridas (1817), 4 BFSP 814–817 (for the form of the letters of marque, see 5 BFSP 768–769). Notifications of Chile's blockade of Peru, 1819, 6 BFSP 1109; Decree and declaration of Chile, 1820 and 1821, 8 BFSP 1218–1220; Peruvian declaration of blockade, 15 October 1821, 9 BFSP 804; Colombian decree of blockade, 6 July 1820, 7 BFSP 979; Mexican declarations of war and blockade, 8 October 1823, 10 BFSP 1026–1028.

84 Preston Whitaker, *United States*, 196.

85 Lewis Hanke, 'Baptis Irvine's Reports on Simón Bolívar' 16 *Hispanic American Historical Review* (1936) 360–373; Lewis Hanke, 'Simón Bolívar and Neutral Rights' 21 *Hispanic American Historical Review* (1941) 258–291.

86 Bolívar to Irvine, 6 and 20 August 1818, in Hanke, 'Bolívar and Neutral Rights', 260–268; Bushnell, *El Libertador*, 156–158; James F. Vivian, 'The *Paloma* Claim in the United States

point of blockades. Ultimately, the blockade was not accepted as valid by the United States – after all, it did not even acknowledge some of the insurgent flags.[87] Throughout the revolutions there continued to be considerable uncertainty over the question of whether insurgents could establish valid, binding blockades at all, and views in favour and against would perdure for the next fifty years.

Behind the insurgent privateer fleets the insurgents established prize courts in an attempt to control those fleets' activities under the law of nations. Foreign agents near the insurgent governments did not hide their interest in the establishment of rebel admiralty courts and reported back home on notable prize cases.[88] Accordingly, the republics issued detailed prize ordinances accompanied by instructions for privateers. An early example was the Venezuelan prize ordinance by Simón Bólivar in 1817, which (1) allowed privateer commissions to be granted to Venezuelan citizens in exchange for a bond of 6,000 pesos and an oath of fidelity; (2) subjected privateers to overall admiralty supervision and command; (3) laid out detailed rules for the proper handling and conservation of prizes until adjudication; and (4) prohibited plundering and piracy.[89] The Colombian ordinance of 1822 was along similar lines. It provided that every Colombian had 'the right' to fit out privateers, and that the same right could also be granted to foreigners provided they posted a privateer bond of sufficient value in exchange. It contained provisions on gun money, visit and search procedure, and the circumstances in which capture was permitted. It also prohibited the breaking of bulk, ordered that all prize must be taken to the nearest convenient port for adjudication, and laid out the prize procedure to be followed in court.[90] In terms of substance, the insurgents generally observed the *Consolato* rule in the absence of treaties to the contrary, making neutral

and Venezuelan-Colombian Relations, 1818–1826' 14(4) *Caribbean Studies* (1975) 60; Charles Carroll Griffin, *The United States and the Disruption of the Spanish Empire 1810–1822* (Octagon Books 1968) 150–151. On the question of free ships and free goods, Irvine and Bolívar repeated the same pattern of arguments as Edmond Genet and Thomas Jefferson during the French revolutionary war, concluding that in the absence of treaties the *Consolato* rule was customary.

87 *United States* v. *Klintock* (1820) 18 US 144.

88 II Manning's *Dipl Corr* 800–801, 950–951, 1193–1194.

89 'Documento 1850: Reglamento sobre el corso expedido por El Libertador en Barcelona el 4 de marzo de 1817', https://archivodellibertador.gob.ve/archlib/web/index.php/site/documento?id=2431.

90 Provisional Ordinance of the Republic of Colombia, Relative to the Equipment and Service of Vessels Bearing Letters of Marque, 30 March 1822, 12 BFSP 647–661.

vessels liable to seizure for carrying Spanish cargo. Once the Spanish property had been unloaded and condemned, the insurgent prize courts seem to have appropriately released these neutral ships.[91] The period also saw plenty of irregular captures and sheer piracy; the creative exploits of the Baltimore privateers and the Barataria and Amelia Island filibusters were often shady and in many ways reprehensible, while in the early 1820s the island of Cuba was favoured by Hispanic pirates, who liquidated their loot well beyond the reach of any admiralty judges.[92]

Foreign governments generally acquiesced to the rebel privateer activities, although the closer they came to neutrality, the greater their insistence on due process in prize procedure. Since the early years of the revolutions, Great Britain steered a mostly neutral course. But as its government became more and more aware of piratical depredations along the Main, it began to exert cautious measures of diplomatic protection against the insurgent governments, while its law officers were clear to caution against any formal recognition.[93] Throughout the period, the British government refrained from issuing definitive statements on the legitimacy of insurgent privateering and instead instructed the Royal Navy to protect British trade. As for the United States, its neutrality policy in the early years was constantly complicated by insurgent depredations that led to a number of private claims. As will be seen, the US would go to considerable lengths to recover compensation from the new republics through diplomatic and legal means. In the short term, insurgent privateering led to the passing of the 1819 Piracy Act, which at a stride asserted jurisdiction over foreign nationals too. Armed with this new assertive legal framework, the United States began sending agents to seek redress from the insurgents and to dispatch naval squadrons for anti-piracy patrols throughout the Caribbean.[94]

Despite the resistance and foreign opposition, the rebel privateering efforts helped to position the insurgent cause as a lawful candidate for a place among the nations of the world. By now it was settled that establishing prize jurisdiction was both the first step and the primary prerequisite for an insurgent government hoping to attain foreign recognition. It entailed both possession of belligerent rights among nations

[91] McCarthy, *Privateering*, 52–53.

[92] Ibid 39–45; Head, *Privateers*.

[93] For Christopher Robinson's legal opinions from 1817 and 1823, see McCarthy, *Privateering*, 68–69; I McNair, *Opinions* 133.

[94] Vivian, '*Paloma* Claim', 61–65; Mark C. Hunter, *Policing the Seas: Anglo-American Relations and the Equatorial Atlantic* (Liverpool University Press 2008) 74–80.

and a corresponding responsibility for wrongful acts. As in the thirteen colonies a generation earlier, the Spanish American prize jurisdictions emerged as the first sign of Latin American sovereignty, marking a transition from colonial rebellion to the status of an internationally recognized civil war, where the laws of belligerency and neutrality would apply. Yet such a status was not easily accorded to the insurgents, not even tacitly, and to many factions never at all. The Cuban pirates are a case in point. In 1822, a British naval squadron was deployed to the Greater Antilles to protect international trade, where they were joined by a task force of the US navy sent out on the same business. With Spain's reluctant consent, the piracy was suppressed within but a few years.[95]

3.2.1.2 The Spanish Colonial Blockade and Foreign Protests

In 1814, Ferdinand VII sent an expeditionary force to reconquer the Spanish Main. In 1815, Commander Morillo of the Cartagena expedition declared 'the most rigorous blockade of the ports of the viceroyalty of Santa Fé, including Carthagena', and warned that every neutral vessel found on those coasts would 'be made prize of, in order to prevent those who have revolted from His Majesty's authority receiving succors of any kind'.[96] The colonial blockades grew even stricter towards foreigners until, in 1816, a notification from Caracas decreed that foreigners dealing with the insurgents would be hanged at the yardarm. The notification rejected any suggestion of the rebels being lawful enemies or the blockade a state of war: 'as the Spanish Nation is at full Peace with all other Nations, it is not to be expected that they can be permitted to afford assistance to its Traitors.'[97]

By this time, Europe had been pacified and Napoleon exiled to Saint Helena. To Ferdinand, this may have seemed like a return to his traditional colonial monopoly in the New World, but for the other powers the invocation of the belligerent power of blockade raised questions about its legal basis – especially as the blockade was basically extended across the Spanish Main while excepting certain ports that were still 'left open to the commerce of neutrals'.[98] This begged the question of what sort of 'neutrality' this referred to. The foreign powers reacted to the matter in differing degrees. The European monarchies, led by the Holy Alliance, were reluctant to engage in diplomatic protests for fear that they might

[95] McCarthy, *Privateering*, 39–45, 144–148; Hunter, *Policing the Seas*, 84–89.
[96] Onís to Monroe, 5 September 1815, IV Am Stat Pap For Rel 156.
[97] Decree of the captain-general of Caracas, 29 January 1816, 3 BFSP 1112–1113.
[98] Onís to Monroe, 2 March 1816, IV Am Stat Pap For Rel 156.

implicitly legitimise the insurgents. In the wake of the alliances formed during the Napoleonic Wars, Britain was inclined to toe the same line, provided this did not prevent it from pursuing its free trade policies in Latin America. But the United States, which had considerable trade interests and opportunities in the area, and no monarchy, protested strongly against the blockade as 'evidently repugnant to the law of nations'.[99] The Spanish ambassador replied that the blockade was perfectly lawful, because it was 'not being directed against an enemy's country' but was rather a law enforcement measure meant to 'maintain the laws for the regulation of the Indies in their full force'.[100] Instead of protesting against the Spanish Empire, the ambassador recommended that the United States take a different approach – 'namely, that the President would be pleased to issue orders that no vessel should be cleared at the custom-houses save for a specified port, according to the general practice of nations'.[101]

The Spanish demands led eventually to the enactment of domestic neutrality laws and declarations by foreign states, but Spain kept on imposing strict penalties on foreigners. In 1818, a royal order from Madrid directed the colonies to treat all foreigners taken at arms or under insurgent banners in the revolted provinces equally severely as the insurgents themselves.[102] In 1822, the colonial blockade was again reinforced with a decree specifically banishing and punishing foreigners.[103] Foreign governors and admirals protested fiercely against such 'a manifesto so extraordinary, so hostile to the Rights of Nations'. They alleged Spanish state responsibility, holding Spain 'answerable to the world' for its 'acts of rapacity, cruelty, and oppression', and reserved for themselves the possibility of retaliation.[104] The blockading policy brought to a head the fragile balance between the anachronistic Spanish claim to Latin America, based on the ancient papal grants, and its tacit acquiescence to international trade with its colonies. In the early 1820s both the United States and Great Britain assumed de facto stances of neutrality with respect to the Spanish American rebels, and after the wars the impact of the Spanish blockades and Spanish privateering operations would be the subject of claims proceedings in which the alleged

99 Monroe to Onís, 20 March 1816, IV Am Stat Pap For Rel 156–157.
100 Onís to Monroe, 25 March 1816, IV Am Stat Pap For Rel 157.
101 Ibid.
102 Declaration of the king, 14 January 1819, 6 BFSP 1134.
103 Decree relative to the blockade of the Spanish Main, 15 September 1822, 10 BFSP 938.
104 See Dutch, American, and British protests, September to December 1822, 10 BFSP 939–945, citations at 941.

absence of a valid state of war that could have justified the use of blockades in the first place was examined.

3.2.2 *The Reactions of Foreign Powers*

3.2.2.1 Great Britain: Coping While Not Recognising

Although managing a colonial empire itself, the government in Great Britain never had any fundamental objection to revolution in the Spanish Main. By the beginning of the nineteenth century, the industrialised British economy was already pushing against the limits of demand for its products, and Latin America appeared as a promising overseas market for the emerging workshop of the world.[105] But the Napoleonic Wars in Europe remained the primary concern for British foreign policy, and the politics of legitimism among its continental allies deterred the island kingdom from taking aggressive action beyond the Line.[106] Two new opportunities emerged in 1810. First, the eruption of revolutions in Spanish America created favourable conditions for Britain to pursue its practical objectives of permissive trade relations in the Spanish Main while maintaining formal loyalty to the common cause in Europe. The government laid out this policy just as its foreign minister was meeting with Bolívar and Méndez in 1810 – an encounter that sparked strong Spanish protests even though at the meeting the minister explicitly refused to recognise the insurgents. Secondly, when the Royal Navy evacuated the Portuguese Braganzas from the mainland and helped them establish themselves in Brazil, the British gained what was essentially a vast client regime in South America, through which they could – and would – conduct their commerce also with the revolutionary republics perfectly lawfully.[107] The outcome was a British policy of intense commercial expansion in Brazil, unstable commercial relations with unrecognised Spanish American rebels, and a search for opportunities (in vain) to secure formal trade concessions from the Cortes in Spain.

When Napoleon abdicated in 1814, the widespread international war came to a close and, in a special treaty clause, Britain agreed to support Ferdinand's policies in Spanish America.[108] The relationship between

[105] William W. Kaufmann, *British Policy and the Independence of Latin America 1804–1828* (Yale University Press) 7–8.

[106] Ibid 13, 53, 103–105.

[107] Kaufmann, *British Policy*, 50–56, 63; Treaties of Rio de Janeiro, 19 February 1810, 61 CTS 41.

[108] Additional articles to Treaty of Madrid, 28 August 1814, 63 CTS 264, art III.

Spanish America and Madrid once again became a matter of domestic law in the eyes of the British. In practice, the counter-revolutionary crackdown in the Spanish Main had a significant impact on the continuation of commerce and the functioning of the British free port system in the West Indies, which led to protests in Parliament in defence of commercial and shipping interests.[109] At the same time, the lawyers of the Doctors' Commons were careful to maintain the ambiguous line of non-recognition and reminded the government about Britain's own past positions during the American Revolution.[110] As a result, Britain veered towards a domestically enacted neutrality, a policy of 'non-interference'.[111] In 1817, the crown acknowledged the 'state of Warfare between His Catholic Majesty and divers Provinces or Parts of Provinces in Spanish America' and prohibited all British subjects from serving or enlisting on either side of the war without a royal permission.[112] Spain reacted initially with satisfaction, welcoming the measure as a pledge of non-intervention in its internal affairs,[113] but in 1819 the British Parliament enacted the Foreign Enlistment Act,[114] which arguably put 'Spain and her colonies . . . on an equal footing'.[115] This opened a widening rift between London and Madrid, which in the 1820s escalated further when the revolutionaries finally gained the upper hand and any return to past colonial status was irreversibly out of the question.

The British also had to decide how to react to the insurgent privateers who visited and searched merchantmen at sea and pretended to exercise a valid prize jurisdiction over them. Throughout the conflict, the law officers of the crown refused to deliver definitive conclusions about the legal consequences of the government's neutrality policies, and they fully accepted the status of the insurgents only after British recognition of the

[109] McCarthy, *Privateering*, 12–16; Dorothy Burne Goebel, 'British Trade to the Spanish Colonies, 1796–1823' 43 *American Historical Review* (1938) 288–320. For Free Ports Act of 1766, see 6 Geo III c 49.

[110] For example, Report of Robinson, 1 July 1816, II McNair, *Opinions* 329.

[111] I Smith 266; Dana's *Wheaton*, 104.

[112] Proclamation, 27 November 1817, 4 BFSP 488.

[113] D. A. G. Waddell, 'British Neutrality and Spanish-American Independence: The Problem of Foreign Enlistment' 19 *Journal of Latin American Studies* (1987) 8–9.

[114] Foreign Enlistment Act, 3 July 1819, 59 Geo III c 69, also 6 BFSP 130. See also Instructions, 8 June 1818, 5 BFSP 963; Instructions, 9 July 1818, 5 BFSP 1224; Order in council, 12 July 1819, 6 BFSP 519; Orders in council, 18 May 1822 and 15 November 1822, 9 BFSP 363 and 364; Proclamation, 6 June 1823, 10 BFSP 648.

[115] Lauterpacht, *Recognition*, 179. Also Dana's *Wheaton* 448–449; Jean Siotis, *Le droit de la guerre et les conflits armés d'un caractère non-international* (LGDJ 1958) 69–70; I Smith 275–279.

first Spanish American republics resolved the matter through political fiat.[116] As a matter of policy, the British government on the whole considered it best not to accept the validity of the insurgent proceedings. While private individuals could in practice lodge their claims in prize proceedings in the insurgents' courts if any were available, there could be little guarantees of due process, and participating in the prize proceedings might be taken as an acknowledgement of their authority. The Foreign Office therefore prohibited its representatives from intervening in insurgent prize adjudications. In 1817, Robinson recommended that Britain should deploy a naval force of its own to protect its shipping from insurgents 'sailing under what is called the Independent Flag', noting that:

> Countries which have not acknowledged the Independence of the Insurgent Provinces cannot be supposed to recognize the establishment of their Tribunals so as to rely on their Power to administer justice according to the established rules of the Law of Nations. Without that security, no Country can be required to abstain from the right of protecting its own Trade by actual Force.[117]

He nonetheless made a distinction between cruisers 'actually fitted out by the insurgents' and privateers acting under foreign commissions, which for him were simply pirates. Another opinion advised that properly commissioned revolutionary privateers could not be tried as pirates; the matter would depend upon the character of the government that had granted their commission, and 'considering the situation of the Spanish American Provinces, as far as they are the subject of general observation, this would not be deemed a case of Piracy'.[118]

Overall, Great Britain would maintain its patient reserve towards the insurgent prize jurisdictions until the recognition of the Spanish American republics in 1825. After recognition, this position began to change. Although the British representatives in the new republics continued to issue protests and defend the rights of their merchants as far as their means allowed, the British government did not seek to enforce these protests on the new states through forceful diplomatic protection. Instead, the Foreign Office informed its consuls of its legal view that that free ships made free

[116] See reports of law officers in I Smith 265–281 and II McNair, *Opinions* 327–337; Roscoe R. Oglesby, *Internal War and the Search for Normative Order* (Martinus Nijhoff 1971) 13–16.

[117] Report of Robinson, 6 February 1817, II McNair, *Opinions* 329–331.

[118] Opinion of Robinson, Shepherd, and Gifford, 7 October 1817, III McNair, *Opinions* 333–334.

goods only where a treaty provided a derogation from the *Consolato* rule, and focused their attention on ensuring that British prizes received fair proceedings and that the substantive prize law applied in such proceedings was not repugnant to British interpretations. As the British government was now dealing with states whose sovereignty was recognised, it took to protecting its interpretation of neutral and belligerent maritime rights by allowing for their exercise by the new states.[119]

Another problem rose from Spain's use of belligerent rights even though it claimed no war was present. Unlike the revolutionaries, Spain was an established maritime power with valid admiralty courts. Here, the British acquiesced to Spanish prize jurisdiction, but reserved the right to issue diplomatic protests for any injustices and denials of justice suffered by their citizens. In practice, this meant that whenever British ships were taken by the Spanish, the Foreign Office requested opinions from the Doctors' Commons on a case-by-case basis. Occasional complaints were then made to Spain from 1813 onwards, and these would later form the basis of post-war claims.[120] The blockade was generally tolerated until the early 1820s, at least wherever it was being effectively enforced. A notable turning point in Anglo-Spanish relations was the affair of the merchantman *Lord Collingwood* in the summer of 1822, taken by a Spanish privateer and declared good prize not for a breach of blockade but rather because it had violated the old Spanish Laws of the Indies.[121] As the desperation of the Spanish captors increased and Bolívar and his peers won decisive victories, the path to British recognition of the Spanish American republics was open. The admiralty sent its reinforced squadron to 'protect trade' in the West Indies and issued general reprisals against Spain.[122] The measure was intended to intimidate Spain and reinstate the naval might of the British Empire as much as to result in compensatory prizes. At the very last minute, Spain flinched, and the Cortes gave in to a series of British demands, informing its colonies that British trade should be resumed and pledging a sum of 40,000,000 reals (half a million pounds sterling), to be put aside for compensating British merchants for spoliations.[123] This

119 McCarthy, *Privateering*, 82–90.

120 Ibid 92–97.

121 Ibid 101–113. There are brief citations from the judgment in *The Times* (3 July 1822) 4. See also Hansard, HC Deb 3 July 1822 and HC Deb 5 July 1822.

122 Notification of the sailing of a British squadron to take reprisals, 20 December 1822, 9 BFSP 897–898.

123 Decree of the Cortes of Spain on foreign trade with Cuba and the liquidation of claims of British subjects, 9 January 1823, 10 BFSP 867; Royal decree relative to foreign trade with Cuba, 27 January 1822, 10 BFSP 865.

rapprochement led eventually to the establishment of the Anglo-Spanish Claims Commission of 1823 tasked with determining these spoliations cases and appropriate compensation.[124]

3.2.2.2 The Concert of Europe and the French Intervention in Spain

Continental powers in Europe engaged with Spanish affairs primarily as a result their struggle against Napoleon's France. After the peace treaties of Paris in 1814 and the Congress of Vienna in 1815, their legitimist views and the balance of power placed Spanish America clearly within Spanish sovereignty and under Ferdinand's dominion. Well into the 1820s, Spanish American representatives toured Europe in the illusory hope of establishing diplomatic relations with foreign powers. When Spain appealed to Metternich to ensure the rebels were refused audience with the Concert of Europe, Metternich was confident that all powers would dismiss the Spanish American visitors.[125] Recognising the continuing threat of popular sovereignty, the Holy Allies laid out the principle of non-recognition of illegitimate governments – 'That the Powers would never recognise anything which is the work of the rebellion'.[126] However, European private parties were in fact faced with similar difficulties and prospects in the New World as the British due to the revolutions, and although the Latin Americans did not gain much political support in Europe, they did find supplies available and volunteers forthcoming in various quarters.[127]

European politics concerning the Spanish American revolutions took a momentous turn during the Spanish turmoil of 1820–1823, when the military's *coup d'état* reinstated a liberal government in Madrid and compelled Ferdinand to restore the constitution of 1812.[128] Fearing the revolution would spread, the Holy Alliance began to plan a collective intervention, notwithstanding Britain's concern that the Concert of Europe was 'never intended as a union for the government of the world

[124] Convention between Great Britain and Spain for the settlement of British claims, signed at Madrid, 12 March 1823, 73 CTS 131.

[125] William S. Robertson, 'Metternich's Attitude toward Revolutions in Latin America' 21 *Hispanic American Historical Review* (1941) 539.

[126] Metternich to Rechberg, 31 December 1820, in *Memoirs of Prince Metternich*, vol III, 447–450 at 449; see also 658–660.

[127] On the Swedish 'West India Relief' and trade of warships, see V Martens, *Causes célèbres* 229–254; Ordinance of the king of Sweden, 15 June 1822, 9 BFSP 819. On the trade in general, see Blaufarb, 'Arms for Revolutions', 100–116.

[128] Decree of the king, 9 March 1820, 7 BFSP 237.

or for the superintendence of the internal affairs of other States'.[129] After the Congress of Verona in 1822, the Holy Alliance gave quiet backing to an intervention by France in Spain. The intervention proved successful and permitted a return to absolutism in Spain. But following the restoration of the monarchy in mainland Spain France was unable to pursue the reconquest into the Spanish American colonies, where the British West India squadron was now protecting its free trade by force and the threat of reprisals.

Besides restoring Ferdinand to his former position, the continental intervention contributed to the British and Americans becoming alienated from the legitimist front, which opened the way to their recognition of the new republics soon thereafter.[130] In 1823, France and Britain came to a mutual understanding over the Spanish Americas. Both confided that they would not try to intervene in the insurrections or obtain new colonies from Spain; instead, they would seek free trade rights there on a most-favoured-nation basis.[131] When President James Monroe of the United States heard of the agreement, the news precipitated his drafting of the famous passage in his 1823 presidential address that became the Monroe Doctrine.[132] The Polignac understanding and the Monroe Doctrine marked the end of international acquiescence to a Spanish reconquest. Ferdinand nonetheless invited all the members of the Concert to a multilateral conference in Paris, where he offered trade concessions in exchange for an assurance of continued Spanish dominion in the colonies from the Europeans.[133] But it was too late. By 1827, Britain had already signed treaties of commerce and navigation with Buenos Aires, Colombia, and Mexico, and others were to follow.[134] An instantaneous 'mania of speculation' swept across Europe: vast mining companies and public loans were immediately set up to finance this conquest of the resources of the New World, and the first speculative bubble burst as early as 1826.[135]

[129] Castlereagh to Austria, France, Prussia, and Russia, May 1820, 10 BFSP 71.
[130] C. W. Crawley (ed), *The New Cambridge Modern History*, vol IX (Cambridge University Press 1965) 674–681.
[131] Extract from Memorandum of a conference between the Prince de Polignac and Mr Canning, 9 October 1823, 11 BFSP 49.
[132] McCarthy, *Privateering*, 20.
[133] Count Ofalia to ambassadors in Paris, Saint Petersburg, and Vienna, 11 BFSP 55.
[134] Britain and Rio de la Plata, 2 February 1825, 75 CTS 75; Colombia and Britain, 18 April 1825, 75 CTS 195; Britain and Mexico, 26 December 1826, 77 CTS 39; Brazil and Britain, 17 August 1827, 77 CTS 375.
[135] Kaufmann, *British Policy*, 179–180.

3.2.2.3 The Neutrality Policy of the United States

In 1807, the United States was still a relative newcomer among the family of nations. Many of its statesmen had long had an interest in Latin American independence, although the most they could offer initially was support in principle but not in action.[136] Whatever their own desires, the United States could not afford to turn a blind eye given the proximity of the Spanish American revolutions, especially as the rebels sailed straight into US ports as soon as insurrections broke out, bringing with them calls for volunteers, privateer commissions, captured prizes, blockade runners, and plenty of diplomatic trouble. Since the early years of their revolutions, the Spanish American republics attracted filibusters, adventurers, mercenaries, and privateers from the United Sates, many of whom could often contribute to the revolutionary cause by operating from their own ports and nearby territories. Sailing under various insurgent flags, US citizens operated from domestic ports such as Baltimore, island outposts such as Amelia Island, and later, as naturalised Latin Americans, from the capitals and ports of the revolutionaries themselves.[137]

Between 1815 and 1818, the United States refashioned its policy of neutrality towards the French revolutionary war to suit the circumstances of civil war and revolution. The Spanish American privateering campaigns began to thrive during this period, and new and passionate voices encouraged the United States to pursue a sort of manifest destiny of world leadership that could rival the European powers.[138] At the same time, the Spanish counter-revolutionary campaign threatened foreigners with interceptions at seas and demanded acquiescence to increasingly strict interpretations of Spain's old monopoly. What followed was a succession of proclamations, presidential and otherwise, that established the standing of the United States as formally neutral under the law of nations with respect to both Spain and the insurgents. A basic question for the US administration was, once again, whether the insurgents were lawful belligerents or *piratae et latrones.* There were already legal precedents at hand from the Haitian revolt and the recent war between Great Britain and France, but the accumulation of cases from the Spanish

[136] Henry Adams, *The History of the United States of America*, vol IV (Scribner's Sons 1889) 340–342; Whitaker, *United States*, 42–43.

[137] Head, *Privateers*, 122–148.

[138] Griffin, *United States*, 121–132.

American revolutions would gradually turn the principles of neutrality into a somewhat consistent practice.

Two weeks after the Battle of Waterloo had taken place in Europe, the United States instructed its customs authorities to grant the Spanish American insurgents access to its ports, because there was 'no principle of the law of nations' and no treaty provision requiring them to exclude from their ports 'the subjects of a foreign power, in a state of insurrection against their own government'.[139] But when volunteers began to organise expeditions from Louisiana to the Spanish Main, Madison and Monroe prohibited them from intervening and brought the old Neutrality Act of 1794 back into force for the insurgence.[140] As the Spanish government continued to pressure the United States over the question of foreign privateers sailing under insurgent flags, an expanded Neutrality Act was passed by Congress in 1817.[141]

In retrospect, it has been argued that the proclamation of 1815 amounted to US admission of belligerent rights accruing to the South American insurgents, or a proclamation of strict neutrality.[142] But the official position of the US at the time was to portray its neutrality as an impartial measure of non-intervention: it was not favouring the insurgents, as all vessels were welcome to their ports regardless of their flag, 'pirates excepted'.[143] This was an assertive invocation of the status of neutrality, one that sought to shield independent operators with a presumption of neutral rights. The United States would reassess and abandon this assertive interpretation in the latter half of the century, when the idea of declaring neutrality often became synonymous with intervention in US parlance.

The task of interpreting US neutrality laws fell time and again on the shoulders of the Supreme Court, which at the time was dominated by John Marshall. In the cases the footprints of the privateers are apparent everywhere alongside questions of American neutrality and recognition. The terrain in which Marshall's court now manoeuvred was formed by

139 Instructions, 3 July 1815, I Moore's *Digest* 170–171.

140 Presidential proclamation, 1 September 1815, IV Am Stat Pap For Rel 1.

141 An Act More Effectually to Preserve the Neutral Relations of the United States, 3 March 1817, in *Neutrality Laws*, vol II, 1084. For the *travaux préparatoires*, see Message of the President and Correspondence Relative to the Neutral Obligations of the United States towards Belligerent Powers, 1816–1817, 4 BFSP 833– 841; IV Am Stat Pap For Rel 103–105; extracts of the same in 1 Moore's *Digest* 172–173.

142 Erik Castrén, *Civil War* (Suomalainen Tiedeakatemia 1966) 41; Oglesby, *Internal War*, 9; I Moore's *Digest* 172.

143 Correspondence between Monroe and Onís, 1816, I Moore's *Digest* 172, IV Am Stat Pap For Rel 424–426, 3 BFSP 119–120.

precedents dealing not with Spanish America but with the Haitian revolution, the question of the status of Saint-Domingue having ended up in admiralty courts in several countries.

When dealing with Haiti, admiralty courts tended to uphold the principle that questions of recognition were to be left to the executive and not the judiciary; accordingly, the application of the law of nations could become indistinguishable from state policy. This was the essence of *The Immanuel*, a British case from 1799 involving a Hamburg ship that sailed to Saint-Domingue stopping en route in Bordeaux to take aboard French wares to be shipped to the Indies. The vessel was captured at sea under the rule of the war of 1756, according to which, although neutrals were allowed to continue their ordinary trade with the enemy, they were not allowed to assume internal colonial trade on behalf of the enemy itself. Before the admiralty court the claimants 'denied that St. Domingo was to be considered in its present state as a French colony'.[144] But when they attempted to produce evidence in the form of general newspaper articles, Judge William Scott would not permit them to be read, noting that 'the *Gazette* is the only authority of this species admitted and respected by the Court'. Based on other, 'more legitimate' evidence, Scott held that, despite the disturbances, Saint-Domingue continued to be a French colony.[145] With this referral to executive authority – we might call it the *Gazette* principle – the court signalled its refusal to determine the legal status of the insurgents, leaving that question for the crown to define.

The same principle emerged in the US case *Rose* v. *Himely* from 1808, which saw non-recognition of the Haitian insurgents as going hand in hand with non-recognition of French belligerent rights against the insurgents. The matter concerned the cargo captured in early 1804 by a French Caribbean privateer from the American schooner *Sarah*, which was trading with 'the brigands, or rebels of St. Domingo'.[146] The cargo was sold onwards by a French prize commissioner stationed in Cuba and then appeared in an American port, where it was put up for sale as French property. There, it was libelled by its original owners for restoration. The claimant argued that France could not condemn the *Sarah* and its cargo as prize because 'there was no feature of public war' but 'merely an insurrection'. Consequently, unless France had recognised the rebels as

[144] *The Immanuel* (1799) 165 Eng Rep 284.
[145] Ibid 286–287.
[146] *Rose* v. *Himely* (1808) 8 US 241.

enemies under the law of nations, the blockade of Haiti was merely a municipal measure, which France could not enforce on the high seas.[147] The respondent took the opposite view: the Haitian revolution was 'a *civil*, or rather a *servile* war, but not to be distinguished from other wars as to belligerent rights', and France was 'to be considered as a belligerent with respect to *Hayti*'.[148] Like Scott in *The Immanuel*, Chief Justice Marshall held that 'it is for governments to decide whether they will consider St. Domingo as an independent nation, and until such decision . . . courts of justice must consider the ancient state of things as remaining unaltered'.[149] He thus held that Saint Domingue remained a French colony despite the insurrection, and consequently the French seizure could only be a municipal measure and not a capture *de jure belli*. The key issue in *Rose* v. *Himely* was whether or not the US Supreme Court could examine the matter despite the French decision having made it res judicata under the law of nations.[150] Here, Marshall replied by drawing a distinction between a foreign court's jurisdiction to decide the substance of a matter and its right to determine its jurisdiction. In a controversial judgment, the Supreme Court found that as the *Sarah* had been captured on the high seas, it followed that the French prize court had wrongly retained jurisdiction, making the condemnation not just mistaken but null and void.[151]

In 1818, the case of *United States* v. *Palmer*[152] gave the Supreme Court an opportunity to re-examine its findings in *Rose* v. *Himely* in the context of the Spanish American revolutions. *Palmer* was a piracy trial, in which the defendants were American-born mariners who had adopted the nationality of one of the Spanish American insurgent republics and captured a Spanish ship and its cargo. In their defence, the sailors referred to their status as foreign privateers. Questions now before the Supreme

147 Ibid 244, 248.

148 Ibid 255.

149 Ibid 272.

150 Ibid 268.

151 Ibid 279–281. Justice Johnson dissented, observing the contrived distinction between substance and jurisdiction and pointing out that any compensation for a French miscarriage of justice in prize matters should be a matter brought up between the two governments, not in the claimant's courts (282–289). Marshall's decision to review a foreign prize court's jurisdiction was glaringly at odds with 'the unquestionable principle of public law, that the judicial cognizance of prizes belongs exclusively to the tribunals of the captor's country' (*The Divina Pastora* (1819) 17 US 52; Dana's *Wheaton* 66 fn.).

152 *United States* v. *Palmer et al.* (1818) 16 US 610.

Court included, first, whether a revolted colony might have authority at all to issue commissions for effecting captures on the high seas; second, whether a state's courts could treat a revolted colony as an independent or sovereign nation before it had been acknowledged as such by the government of the state (i.e. the *Gazette* principle); and third, whether, in the event of civil war, the subjects of the different parties could claim the rights of war.[153] In its decision, the Supreme Court acknowledged that the Piracy Act provided no basis on which the US could assert jurisdiction over foreign warships as such. To be able to draw a distinction between pirates and privateers, the court restated the *Gazette* principle: since questions concerning the recognition of rebels were 'generally rather political than legal in their character', the authority to decide upon them belonged to Congress rather than the courts.[154] When dealing with foreign insurgencies, 'a nation may engage itself with one party or the other – may observe absolute neutrality – may recognize the new state absolutely – or may make a limited recognition of it'. If a government declared neutrality, then courts could not rule against belligerent acts. Persons employed in the service of an insurgent government 'maintaining its separate existence by war' could be protected if their commission was found convincing.[155] A distinct international legal personality could emerge for the insurgents through sustained armed resistance; they could have belligerent powers over the subjects of the recognising neutral; and duly recognised insurgent privateers would have standing equal to those of the mother country.[156] In conclusion, the Supreme Court found in favour of the defendants, identifying them as privateers rather than pirates.

Over time, the rationale of *Rose* v. *Himely* and *United States* v. *Palmer* gained acceptance as the authoritative position. In the similar case of *The Divina Pastora,*[157] a capture had been made 'under a regular commission from the government established at Buenos Ayres', by a vessel that had not violated US neutral rights. The Supreme Court referred directly to *United States* v. *Palmer*, which it said

> establishes the principle that the government of the United States, having recognized the existence of a civil war between Spain and her colonies, but remaining neutral, the Courts of the Union are bound to consider as

153 Ibid 614–617.
154 Ibid 634.
155 Ibid 634–635.
156 Ibid 635, 643–644.
157 *The Divina Pastora* (1819) 17 US 52.

> lawful, those acts which war authorizes, and which the new governments in South America may direct against their enemy.[158]

Not all scraps of paper with a seal on them were accepted as valid privateer commissions. The case of *United States* v. *Klintock*[159] was another piracy indictment where the defendant claimed to be a lawful privateer. His commission, however, was from the French renegade Louis-Michel Aury, who at the time professed himself to be 'Brigadier of the Mexican Republic and Generalissimo of the Floridas'.[160] The state attorney demanded that the facts of the case be deemed incompatible with any blanket recognition of revolutionary commissions; Mexico had not been included among the republics at the time they were recognised by the US.[161] Marshall agreed. The Supreme Court ruled that Aury had no power to commission privateers and that 'the whole transaction taken together' was not a belligerent capture but a robbery on the high seas.[162] *Klintock* stands as a reminder that no court could be totally relieved of the need to assess whether or not the facts on the ground matched what was purported in the documents provided by the belligerents.[163] No matter how intent the courts were on adopting a purely constitutive stance on recognition, there were always situations in which the facts were so glaring that they could not be overlooked. What *exactly* had the government declared and whom had it recognized? And who was to review this question, if not the courts? Cases like *Klintock* and *Palmer* underline the inherent indeterminacy of all legal reasoning regarding the identification and recognition of non-state belligerents. Matters involving recognition under the law of nations always tended to fall between pure fact and pure form.

Although US neutrality policy was officially presented as minimising American involvement in foreign wars under the law of nations, in reality

158 Ibid 63–64. See also *The Estrella* (1819) 17 US 298; *The Nuestra Señora de la Caridad* (1819) 17 US 497.

159 *United States* v. *Klintock* (1820) 18 US 144.

160 See Head, *Privateers*, 106–114.

161 *United States* v. *Klintock* 146–147.

162 Ibid 149–150. See also *The Nueva Anna and the Liebre*, (1821) 19 US193.

163 In the matter of *The Fourth-of-July Privateer*, the attorney general, making reference to *Palmer*, advised indicting a group of Baltimore privateers commissioned by Artigas at La Plata for piracy. See attorney general's opinion in *Fourth-of-July Privateer* (6 November 1818) 1 Op Atty Gen 249. In *Consul of Spain* v. *The Conception* (C Ct D South Carolina 1819) F Cas 3, 137, a circuit court asserted its competence to recognize the belligerency of the insurgents *proprio motu*, but its decision was overturned by the Supreme Court in *La Conception* (1821) 19 US 235.

it provided a legal framework that permitted American filibustering in the service of Spanish American rebels. This is epitomised in the case of the *Santissima Trinidad* and the Baltimore adventurer James Chaytor, who sailed under commission from Buenos Aires but continued to frequent Baltimore, where his family continued to live. After examining his numerous captures in 1822, the Supreme Court found Chaytor at fault only for having augmented his fleet at Baltimore by acquiring a consort ship, but not for having taken up the commission. In the eyes of the court, he was a naturalised person in the service of the Buenos Aires navy and commanding a public man-of-war, which was not to be confused with foreign enlistment or privateering prohibited by the United States.[164] A key passage from Justice Story deserves to be quoted in full:

> The government of the United States has recognized the existence of a civil war between Spain and her colonies, and has avowed a determination to remain neutral between the parties, and to allow to each the same rights of asylum and hospitality and intercourse. Each party is therefore deemed by us a belligerent nation, having, so far as concerns us, the sovereign rights of war, and entitled to be respected in the exercise of those rights. We cannot interfere to the prejudice of either belligerent without making ourselves a party to the contest, and departing from the posture of neutrality. All captures made by each must be considered as having the same validity, and all the immunities which may be claimed by public ships in our ports under the law of nations must be considered as equally the right of each, and as such must be recognized by our courts of justice, until Congress shall prescribe a different rule. This is the doctrine heretofore asserted by this Court, and we see no reason to depart from it.[165]

3.2.3 The Recognition of Spanish American Independence and the Monroe Doctrine

International recognition of the Spanish American republics was a remarkably slow process, which arguably continued right up to the Spanish-American War of 1898. At first, recognition did not seem inevitable, but by the early 1820s the insurgents appeared to have established permanent control over their territories and managed to force

[164] *The Santissima Trinidad and the St Ander* (1822) 20 US 283. See also *The Bello Corrunes* (1821) 19 US 152.

[165] *The Santissima Trindad*, 337–338. The passage is also cited in Oglesby, *Internal War*, 11, with further analysis of the aforementioned cases.

Spain to sign armistices that could be seen as de facto recognition of their territorial possessions.[166] In 1820, Bolívar's insurgents in Colombia even managed to negotiate a treaty with Spain in which they agreed to apply the laws and customs 'followed by civilised nations' in the 'war' existing 'between the two governments' and guaranteed that captives would be treated as prisoners of war.[167] Such implicit recognition *de jure belli* was a notable achievement for the insurgents. But when, in 1824, Ferdinand VII again abolished the constitutional order with the backing of other European monarchs, he reinstated absolutism and halted any progress towards recognition. Only after Ferdinand's death did Spain formally acknowledge the sovereignty of its former American colonies when the Cortes instructed the government to negotiate permanent peace treaties in 1836.[168] A few weeks later, Mexico and Spain signed a treaty in which Spain recognised the Mexican Republic 'as a free Nation, sovereign and independent'.[169] In further provisions of the treaty, the parties consigned their disagreements to oblivion, laid down principles that allowed private citizens to seek satisfaction of debts and claims, and agreed on basic trade arrangements, which included a most-favoured-nation clause.[170] They furthermore confirmed Mexico's responsibility for its debts and released each other from further state responsibility.[171] Similar treaties of friendship and recognition followed between Spain and the other revolutionary republics.[172]

From the perspective of the classical doctrine of civil war, the Spanish American revolutions were noteworthy for bringing about formal recognition of the new foreign republics first by a number of influential foreign powers, long before they were recognised by the Spanish crown. Of particular significance was recognition by the United States and Great Britain, which occurred simultaneously with, and in reaction to, policy

[166] For example, 61 CTS 343; 71 CTS 557; 73 CTS 261; 75 CTS 67, 75.

[167] Armistice and treaty between Colombia and Spain, 25 and 26 November 1820, 71 CTS 281, 291.

[168] William S. Robertson, 'The Recognition of the Spanish Colonies by the Motherland' 1 *Hispanic American Historical Review* (1918) 72–80.

[169] Treaty of peace and friendship between Mexico and Spain, 28 December 1836, 86 CTS 361, art I.

[170] Ibid, arts II–VI.

[171] Ibid, art VII. Mexico seems to have quickly defaulted on these debts. See Mexico–Spain debt convention, 17 July 1847, 101 CTS 193.

[172] For example, Spain–Ecuador, 1840, 89 CTS 389; Spain–Urugay, 1841, 89 CTS 389; Spain–Chile, 1844, 97 CTS 1; Spain–Venezuela, 1845, 98 CTS 109. See also Robertson, 'Recognition by the Motherland', 83–91, counting a total of fifteen treaties.

reversals by Madrid and led to significant transformations in the international legal standing of the new Latin American states.

The United States' sympathy with the Latin American insurrections was perhaps always to some extent connected to visions of hemispheric emancipation and the downfall of the Spanish trade monopoly.[173] In 1818 and 1819, the US had made indirect overtures about recognising the Spanish American republics together with the Europeans, but the idea had been rejected, especially by the legitimist Holy Allies, which at the time had been busy intervening in the constitutionalist Neapolitan revolt in the Mediterranean.[174] Recognition was postponed also because the priority of the US government was to first secure Spanish ratification of the Adams-Onís treaty and the transfer of Florida.[175] But in the spring of 1822 despite European objections, the US recognised the republics and established formal diplomatic relations with them. The decision was thoroughly debated in Congress, which then granted public funds for legations to the Spanish American republics;[176] this seemingly innocuous act was patently based on a pro-revolutionary interpretation of the law of recognition, as it extended the right of legation to the rebels.

The significance of the moment was evident in President Monroe's message to Congress. With concision and perspicuity born of hindsight, he reframed the US neutrality policy on insurrectionaries: 'As soon as the movement assumed such a steady and consistent form as to make the success of the provinces probable, the rights to which they were entitled by the law of nations, as equal parties to a civil war, were extended to them.'[177] He then explained the view of his administration with words that were declarative of recognition: 'When the result of such a contest is manifestly settled, the new Governments have a claim to recognition by other Powers, which ought not to be resisted.'[178] Recognition was soon translated into concrete action through the establishment of embassies

[173] For example, Report of a committee concerning the expediency of recognising the independence of the Spanish American provinces, 10 December 1811, III Am Stat Pap For Rel 538.

[174] Whitaker, *United States*, 259–264, 338–343.

[175] Griffin, *United States*, 209–220; Kaufmann, *British Policy*, 122–123. See also Message of the President, 17 November 1818, 6 BFSP 92 and documents at 557–959

[176] Act for the Financing of Diplomatic Missions, 4 May 1822, *Annals of Congress*, 17th Congress, 1st session II, 2603–2604; I Moore's *Digest* 82-86; William Spence Robertson, 'The United States and Spain in 1822' 20 *American Historical Review* (1915) 781–783.

[177] Monroe to Congress, 8 March 1822, IV Am Stat Pap For Rel 818–819.

[178] Ibid; I Moore's *Digest* 85.

and the conclusion of treaties of friendship, commerce, and navigation with several Spanish American republics.[179]

Predictably, the Spanish ambassador protested vociferously against Monroe's message. The exchange of views between the governments became something of a textbook example of international argument on recognition. The Spanish protest was grounded in two contentions: first, that the colonies had no right to secede, and second, that there was no stability in the facts upon which the Americans were about to base their decision. On the rights question, the ambassador referred to the recent reinstatement of the constitution of 1812 and argued that, having now been protected by law and granted all the rights and prerogatives of Spanish citizens and the 'rank of freemen', the Spanish colonists had no lawful grounds for seceding, as the United States had in 1776. On the facts question, the protest cited anarchy, oppression, and infighting across the insurgent colonies and put it to Monroe that if the facts nonetheless justified recognition, then surely the European powers would have taken that step already.[180] In a prompt reply, John Quincy Adams argued the opposite. He noted that: 'In every question relating to the independence of a nation, two principles are involved: one of *right*, and the other of *fact*; the former exclusively depending upon the determination of the nation itself, and the latter resulting from the successful execution of that determination.' In the matter at hand, facts would triumph over formal rights: the United States had maintained 'most impartial neutrality' until finally 'the civil war . . . ha[d], in substance, ceased to exist'. Facing the facts, the US had 'yielded to an obligation of duty of the highest order' and granted its recognition as a 'mere acknowledgment of existing facts' and in the hope of establishing 'those relations, political and commercial, which it is the moral obligation of civilized and Christian nations to

179 For example, 74 CTS 455; 75 CTS 433; 79 CTS 249; 82 CTS 413; 86 CTS 1; 86 CTS 257. These treaties already bore the hallmarks of nineteenth-century American trade treaties. The Colombian treaty, for example, provided for most-favoured-nation treatment (art 2); access to ports and interior markets (art 3); expropriation clause (art 5); safe harbour in distress (art 6); *postliminium* of goods taken from pirates (art 7); assistance to the shipwrecked (art 8); national treatment and repatriation (art 9); access to courts and due process (art 10); freedom of religion (art 11); free ships and free goods (arts 12–13); narrow contraband lists and the effective blockade rule (arts 14–15); procedure for visit and search, documents etc., and the immunity of convoys (art 20); prize courts and *toute prise doit être jugée* (art 21); non-confiscability of private debts in wartime (art 24); rules on diplomatic relations and an obligation to exhaust local remedies before issuing reprisals or declaring war (art 31). Article 22 obliged both parties to prevent their citizens from taking up commissions as privateers in the service of each other's enemies.

180 Anduaga to Adams, 9 March 1822, IV Am Stat Pap For Rel 845.

entertain reciprocally with one another'.[181] By this time, Spanish protestations met opposition elsewhere as well; upon receiving news of the US recognition and Spanish complaints, the British prime minister responded rather coldly that 'His Catholic Majesty must be aware that so large a portion of the world cannot, without fundamentally disturbing the intercourse of civilised society, long continue without some recognised and established relations' in the absence of effective control by Spain.[182] British recognition of the republics followed in 1825 through the establishment of commercial treaties.[183]

The US neutrality policy culminated in the Monroe Doctrine of 1823, 'asserting, as a principle in which the rights and interests of the United States are involved, that the American continents, by the free and independent condition which they have assumed and maintain, are henceforth not to be considered as subjects for future colonization by any European power'.[184] The doctrine originally emerged as a retrenchment of US neutrality against European colonial and commercial interests, including such possibilities as British and Russian expansion in unsettled territories in the West.[185] Here, the old idea of a hemispheric difference was turned to the advantage of the Americans: the formal and legalist tone of the principle could be deployed to justify declarations of neutrality in colonial civil war situations even when this would seem like an unfriendly act towards Europe. But by further declaring European expansion 'as dangerous to our peace and safety',[186] Monroe also presented a challenge to the monarchical legitimism of the European empires. Over time, the Monroe Doctrine laid the basis for US aspirations to act as 'Supreme Judge of the world'[187] in its hemisphere, and thus to determine the legitimacy of insurgent intentions on the basis of universal principles that it alone had the right to interpret.[188]

The opposite concern, of course, was the potential arbitrariness of any such 'external' judgment, and the fear among European reactionaries of

181 Adams to Anduaga, 6 April 1822, IV Am Stat Pap For Rel 846.
182 Kaufmann, *British Policy*, 131.
183 See treaties listed in n 134.
184 James Monroe to Congress, 2 December 1823, in *Journal of the Senate*, 18th Congress, 1st session, 1823, 9–24 at 11.
185 Dana's *Wheaton*, 82 fn 36.
186 Monroe to Congress, 2 December 1823, at 22.
187 See US Declaration of Independence, 4 July 1776, last paragraph.
188 For example, Alejandro Alvarez, 'The Monroe Doctrine from the Latin-American Point of View' 3 *St Louis Law Review* (1917) 135–146; Jay Sexton, *The Monroe Doctrine: Empire and Nation in Nineteenth-Century America* (Hill and Wang 2011) 5–8.

the day that the new stance could spread back across the Atlantic to the old continent. If any state might declare a rebel faction in another country as equal to its government, then what was left of the principle of sovereignty? After American recognition of the Spanish American republics, Metternich wrote with concern:

> If the political systems upon which these declarations are founded should be generally approved in Europe, it is evident that henceforth the most illegal and the most audacious enterprises will be judged only by their material success, that any revolt would be sanctioned by the mere fact that the results existed *de facto*, and finally that there would no longer prevail among men any other right than that of force or any other bonds than those imposed by the victorious usurpation of a particular moment – bonds which might be dissolved the following moment.[189]

As predicted, the wave of revolutionary momentum finally overtook European monarchies in 1848, the year Metternich himself resigned from office and took flight.

3.2.3.1 Foreign Claims and the Aftermath

The revolutionaries soon learned that the first mark of sovereignty in the New World was a state's capacity to bear its international responsibility for foreign property claims. The various mixed claims commissions established after the Spanish American revolutions continued the developments that had begun with the Jay Treaty commissions, binding together the recognition of new states and their responsibility into a common rite of passage for statehood in international law. As one arbitrator summarised fifty years later:

> Holding a State responsible reflects no disgrace to the nation; on the contrary [it] is calculated to advance her reputation in the eyes of the world, as it shows her willingness to adopt, for the solution of difficulties, the enlightened course which has found favor, especially of late years, with powerful countries which could have trusted with confidence to the arbitrament of the sword.[190]

189 Cited in Robertson, 'Metternich's Attitude', 540.

190 *The Montijo (United States v. Colombia)*, 2 Moore's *Arbitrations* 1421, at 1442–1443. The expression 'rite of passage' comes from Tzvika Nissel, *A History of State Responsibility: The Struggle for International Standards (1870–1960)* (University of Helsinki 2016) 192. See also Tzvika Nissel, *Merchants of Legalism: A History of State Responsibility (1870–1960)* (Cambridge University Press 2024) 60–64. The link between revolution and state responsibility is examined in detail in Kathryn Greenman, *State Responsibility and Rebels* (Cambridge University Press 2021) 5–18 *et passim*.

Besides the new republics, the Spanish crown, too, found itself responding to foreign legal claims over the inconveniences caused to international commerce by its counter-insurgency campaigns. Together, the legal disputes and consequences arising from the revolutions reverberated for decades, some of them going through several rounds of arbitrations and settlements and paved the way for the rise of the international arbitration movement later in the nineteenth century.

During the war, Spain had assured itself of Britain's ambiguous neutrality policy by tacitly permitting British free trade into South America. When the Spanish colonial fleet began to seize foreign merchant vessels in the final years of the conflict, British sentiment turned decidedly against it. The West India squadron of 1822 was instructed not only to combat the Cuban pirates but also to re-establish free trade in the West Indies, and by force if need be. The assault was called off only at the eleventh hour, when the Spanish government agreed to compensate the British merchants for any unlawful depredations. A mixed claims commission was to be established to examine these private claims, and 40 million reals (approximately 500,000 pounds) was to be deposited in the Bank of England for that purpose.[191] In March 1823, Britain and Spain signed a treaty constituting the commission, which would sit in London 'for the purpose of taking into consideration and deciding in a summary manner, according to equity, upon all cases that shall be brought before it, properly authenticated, of the capture or seizure of British Vessels, or detention of Property belonging to the Subjects of his Britannick Majesty' between 1808 and 1823.[192] In return, the commission was also to receive Spanish claims for seizures by the British. The commission was to consist of two British and two Spanish members; any split cases would be referred to two umpires and, in the very last resort, determined by lot.[193] In preparation for the proceedings, the British commissioners published a call for claims and arranged the claims they received in seven categories: captures for alleged infractions of the Spanish Laws of the Indies; condemnation of vessels on the grounds of

[191] McCarthy, *Privateering*, 112–114.

[192] Anglo-Spanish claims convention, 12 March 1823, 73 CTS 131, art 1. Also in *London Gazette*, 11 October 1823, at 1665–1667. The records of the Anglo-Spanish claims commissions of 1823 and 1828 have not received sufficient attention from legal scholars. Matthew McCarthy's groundbreaking study has recently brought the subject out of obscurity, and I would like to recommend the records for further research. They can be found at TNA FO 316.

[193] Ibid, art. 2.

having connections with Spanish American insurgents; captures made by pirates in Spanish colonial waters; British ships captured prior to 1815 by Britain's enemies and detained by Spanish authorities; property originally captured prior to 1808 but continuing to be detained beyond that date; forced loans and seizures for public service or alleged irregularities in trading; certain claims acknowledged by the Spanish government but not yet paid; and private contractual arrangements with the Spanish government or commanders.[194] Neither party therefore seems to have held Spain responsible for captures by the insurgents; instead, potential insurgent liability was to be examined as a separate matter.

Throughout its existence, the Anglo-Spanish mixed claims commission kept stumbling on difficulties and disagreements. After the French intervention in Spain, the Spanish commissioners asked Madrid to confirm their legal status and the reserved funds, but the Spanish government was in no hurry to answer. When the commission finally got to work, its members split over a range of issues varying from the payment of interest to the admissibility of the Spanish counter-claims from the Peninsular War. Following a mixture of private and public negotiation, the stalled work of the commission was ultimately settled in 1828 through a lump-sum payment under a separate treaty.[195] Spain would pay 900,000 pounds to Britain and Britain 200,000 pounds to Spain. The two governments would then use those funds to satisfy the claims of their respective citizens through domestic claims commissions, which would determine the validity and merits of the individual claims under the law of nations.[196] Working within national jurisdiction, each side was able to maintain its own precedents and interpretations concerning the events. Though perhaps not a procedural success, one key outcome of the Anglo-Spanish claims was Spain's recognition of its responsibility for harm to foreigners caused by its counter-revolutionary actions on the high seas.

The United States also pursued a number of private claims against Spain. Several vessels had been seized by Governor Morrillo when the Spanish expeditionary force had captured the port of Cartagena in 1816.[197] The seizures led to several spoliations claims, which the US government quickly took advantage of when negotiating the borders

[194] McCarthy, *Privateering*, 120.

[195] Anglo-Spanish claims convention, 28 October 1828, 79 CTS 181; McCarthy, *Privateering*, 126–131.

[196] Ibid 132–135.

[197] Message of the president, 3 December 1816, 4 BFSP 10; Lowry to Monroe, 22 January 1816, in II Manning's *Dipl Corr* 1169; Griffin, *United States*, 98–99.

between Louisiana and Spanish possessions in Florida, Texas, and Mexico. In his negotiations with Ambassador Luís Onís, Secretary of State Adams weighed the private claims against the Spanish counter-complaints, which included territorial claims, protests against Andrew Jackson's Florida expedition, and the consequences of Spanish-American privateers operating in, near, and out of the United States.[198] Adams proposed that instead of Spain compensating *in specie*, the territory of Florida might be ceded to the United States so that its land could be sold and the proceeds used to compensate the claimants.[199] In 1819, Adams and Onís eventually settled on the transfer of Florida in exchange for making Sabine the western border of Louisiana (with Spanish Texas) and settling all private claims on both sides.[200]

Florida was thus traded in part to compensate for ships captured in Spain's colonial civil war. Both parties to the treaty agreed to reciprocally renounce all further claims for damages or injuries, including 'all claims of Citizens of the United-States upon the Government of Spain, arising from the unlawful seizures at Sea, and in the ports and territories of Spain or the Spanish Colonies'. The Spanish renunciation, in return, covered the Miranda expedition and all claims 'arizing from unlawful seizures at Sea or within the ports and territorial Jurisdiction of the United-States'.[201] As the United States exonerated Spain from all of its private claims, it also undertook to satisfy those claims from its own pocket up to an amount of five million dollars through a domestic US claims commission.[202] The US commission handed in its final report in 1824, having satisfied over 90 per cent of the claims using the funds assigned to it. Although its proceedings were domestic, the commission professed to having examined the private claims in the light of what it understood as the applicable law of nations and the lawful rights and duties of Spain.[203] In this sense, the Florida settlement provided a platform for the emergence of procedural and substantive precedents, which the United States could try to redeploy in its future arbitrations on the international arena.

198 Adams to Onís, 12 March 1818, IV Am Stat Pap For Rel 463–474. The letter states that '[t]here is no principle of the law of nations more firmly established than that which entitles the property of strangers within the jurisdiction of a country in friendship with their own to the protection of its sovereign by all the efforts in his power' (ibid 476).

199 V Moore's *Arbitrations* 4495–4496.

200 Florida Treaty, 22 February 1819, 70 CTS 1.

201 Article 9.

202 Article 11.

203 The final report of the commission is in V Moore's *International Arbitrations* 4500–4518.

3.2.3.2 Latin America and the Law of Diplomatic Protection

During the war, the United States exerted relatively little pressure on the revolutionaries, as President Monroe calculated that the benefits gained from open insurgent ports outweighed the necessity to call for compensation over individual depredations.[204] But after recognising the Spanish American republics, the United States turned to concluding comprehensive treaties of friendship, commerce and navigation with them. In this process of forging friendly relations and rules of equitable investment protection and commercial intercourse, it also raised some of the old wartime claims. One known example was the US–Colombia claims convention of 1825, in which it was simply agreed that 'there shall be paid to the owners' of various vessels and cargo certain sums as compensation.[205] The convention required no ratification on either side and it was definitive upon signature. The amounts of the claims were not disputed but rather agreed directly on the basis of the claimants' figures, and payment with interest was made to the United States government for onward payment to its citizens.[206] The settlement never referred to Colombia as a faulty party, but rather reaffirmed its 'rights and actions against any person or persons, whose irregular conduct may have been the cause of the claims'.[207] The payment was thus framed as a discretionary one-off settlement based on goodwill and not liability per se. Despite this contrivance (or precisely because of it), the affair shows an early example of the principle according to which a successful insurgent rebel government might be found responsible for claims arising from civil war irrespective of whether the damage was caused by the insurgents themselves or actors beyond their immediate control. For the remaining claims, the US signed an additional claims convention in 1829 with Bolívar,[208] and when Venezuela and Ecuador separated from Colombia in 1830, the three republics divided the remainder of the debt between themselves through a treaty provision.[209] Some of the revolutionary era claims kept returning to arbitration at least until

[204] Vivian, '*Paloma* claim', 57–72.

[205] United States–Colombia claims convention, 16 March 1825, 75 CTS 161.

[206] David Hunter Miller (ed) *Treaties and Other International Acts of the United States of America*, vol III (US Government Printing Office 1933) 196–198.

[207] United States–Colombia claims convention, art 6.

[208] Claims Convention between Colombia and the United States, signed at Bogotá, 25 November 1829, 80 CTS 225.

[209] Miller, *Treaties*, vol III, 527–528.

the 1850s.[210] At least thirteen claims were settled between the United States and Brazil in a similar manner through a separate convention in 1829.[211]

Protection of foreign private claims against revolution became an integral part of the international law of the Americas.[212] After the recognition of the Spanish American republics, Bolívar's Panama Congress in 1826[213] provided the next opportunity for the foreign powers to establish treaty relations that promoted the peaceful settlement of disputes through arbitration and compensation.[214] To some extent, the US vision of free trade and abolition of European colonialism in the Western hemisphere found a fertile terrain in Latin America; as internal and external pressures led many of the republics into continuous cycles of regime changes and intestine discord, legalist safeguards and property protection through settlements seemed to promise at least an alternative to forceful reprisals and what they saw as the threat of colonial intervention. Such concerns were still very valid at the time. To take the example of France, let us recall that the Haitian 'independence debt' was restructured and reconfirmed by treaty in 1838, with another five decades of payments and special trade concessions to follow.[215] That same year, France raised a diplomatic complaint against Mexico, alleging that Mexico had failed to protect the rights of French citizens during its internal conflicts.[216] France demanded 600,000 pesos in compensation and, when Mexico refused, declared a blockade,[217] claiming that as a sovereign state Mexico was responsible for guaranteeing a minimum standard of fair treatment to foreigners. When Mexico still refused, a French armada shelled San Juan de Ulloa

210 For example, the claims of Clark and Daniels in *La Constanca*, the *Medea*, and the *Good Return*, which went back to 1817 but were arbitrated in 1865 and reviewed in 1885, in III Moore's *Arbitrations* 2729–2751, 29 RIAA 99.

211 United States–Brazil clams convention, 15 June 1829, 79 CTS 453.

212 Generally on this, see the excellent Greenman, *State Responsibility and Rebels*, esp. Chapter 2.

213 Treaty of Perpetual Union, League, and Confederation between the Republics of Colombia, Central America, Peru, and the United Mexican States, 15 July 1826, in James Brown Scott (ed), *The International Conferences of American States 1889–1928* (Oxford University Press 1931) xxiv.

214 For example, British instructions for the Panama Congress, in C. K. Webster, *Britain and the Independence of Latin America* (Oxford University Press 1938) vol I, 403–409; Arnulf Becker Lorca, *Mestizo International Law: A Global Intellectual History 1842–1933* (Cambridge University Press 2014) 89–93.

215 Treaty of Port-au-Prince, 12 February 1838, 87 CTS 357.

216 Treaty of commerce between France and Mexico, 8–9 May 1827, 77 CTS 181.

217 'Notification du blocus', 15 Avril 1838, 26 BFSP 1099. 'Extrait de la notification', 31 Mai 1838, in *Nouveau recueil de traités* (G. F. Martens ed) vol VI (XV) 1830–1838 (Dieterich 1840), 830, doc 113.

for five hours until Veracruz capitulated.[218] 'When a nation knows not how to maintain order within its bosom, it must learn how to punish itself', pontificated the French rear admiral Charles Baudin from aboard his flagship.[219] In the end, France returned San Juan de Ulloa to Mexico in exchange for submitting to arbitration the fate of the Mexican ships taken by France and the private claims arising from the confrontation.[220] Mexico finally agreed to pay France the original claim sum of 600,000 piasters.[221] Concerning the vessels, the 1844 arbitral award of Queen Victoria of England found that at the time there had been 'a state of war between the two countries' and that the French acquisitions had therefore been valid *de jure belli*.[222] Meanwhile in 1838, after having failed to secure free trade and most-favoured-nation treatment from Buenos Aires, France declared a blockade ostensibly to protect French citizens there.[223] This blockade went on for nearly two years until the government of Buenos Aires finally signed a capitulation in which it recognised the French right to indemnities, agreed to a mixed commission of six arbitrators, and accorded France most-favoured-nation rights.[224] The commission processed the claims without delay and in 1841 Buenos Aires settled them for the sum of 173,725 piasters.[225] Altogether, these French ventures in America were local instances of a broader wave of imperial use of force at the turn of the 1840s, where European armed forces extracted compensations and trade privileges in many parts of the world, including China and North Africa.

In contrast to the spectre of European gunboat diplomacy, the United States' apparent decision not to resort to arms in its indemnification efforts might look like a civilised method of dispute resolution. In 1839, Mexico signed a convention to deal amicably with US private claims.[226] However, a real threat of intervention hung over the negotiation of the convention. Back in 1837, the United States had already recognised the independence of the Mexican breakaway republic of Texas, which it

[218] Capitulation between France and Mexico, 28 November 1838, 88 CTS 179.
[219] Baudin to Cuevas, 27 October 1838, 27 BFSP 1176, 1178.
[220] Peace of Vera Cruz, 9 March 1839, 88 CTS 345.
[221] 'Convention relativement aux indemnités', 9 March 1839, 88 CTS 348.
[222] Victoria's arbitral award between France and Mexico, 1 August 1844, 97 CTS 153.
[223] Correspondence in 26 BFSP 920–1083; Notification of blockade, 26 BFSP 727.
[224] Convention between Buenos Aires and France, 29 October 1840, 91 CTS 111.
[225] Accord between Argentina and France, 26 April 1841, 91 CTS 349.
[226] United States–Mexico claims convention. 11 April 1839, 88 CTS 397. The 1838 treaty is in Miller, *Treaties*, vol IV, 198–204.

would later annex.[227] In the establishment of the US–Mexico mixed claims commission, the interest in protecting foreign property was expressed in the shape of general principles derived from the law of nations. Unlike the discriminatory manner in which the so-called Turkish capitulations and the Chinese treaty port system were imposed in other parts of the world, the treaties of friendship, commerce, and navigation signed with the Latin American states were established on the basis of formal equality.[228] A state's capacity to bear its international responsibility was an essential part of its sovereignty among equals. When negotiating the legal principles to be applied in the arbitration, Mexico proposed that 'a government is not responsible for losses incurred in political convulsions unless it has failed to take all the precautions necessary for preserving order [and] that there should be no responsibility unless the judicial decision was either notoriously unjust or notoriously contrary to the principles of international law'. The United States disagreed, explaining that 'it would not be proper for the commissioners to receive instructions from the executive of either country',[229] which meant that the commission should interpret and apply common standards of international law. By the end of its mandate, in 1842, the US–Mexican mixed claims commission had resolved some fifty claims out of the eighty-four submitted to it.[230] When Mexico began to fall behind in its payments in 1843, it pledged to pay the remaining sum directly from the proceeds of the taxes of the republic.[231] War broke out when the United States annexed Texas in 1845.[232] It led to the Treaty of

[227] Greenman, *State Responsibility*, 41–44. On Texas, see I Moore's *Digest* 96–103, 176–178; Declaration of independence, 2 March 1836, 24 BFSP 1269; Constitution of Texas, 24 BFSP 935; Texas' proclamation of blockade, 21 July 1836, 24 BFSP 1288; United States–Texas claims and boundary treaties in Charles I. Bevans (ed), *Treaties and Other International Agreements of the United States of America 1776–1949*, vol 11 (US Department of State 1974) 974–977; Texas' proclamation of blockade, 26 March 1842, 34 BFSP 1261.

[228] Becker Lorca, *Mestizo International Law*, 88.

[229] II Moore's *Arbitrations* 1216–1217.

[230] Reported in II Moore's *Arbitrations*, 1209–1286. Cases from 1839 include at least *The Ann* and *Augusta* (unlawful detention), vol IV, 4346; G. G. & S. Howland (seizure of goods), vol III, 3227; *The Galaxy* (detention), vol IV, 3265; Harmony (seizure of money), vol III, 3044; *The Jane* (detention), vol III, 3119; Mercy Mitchell (seizure of money), vol IV, 4227; Santangelo (illegal expulsion), vol III, 3333; Baldwin's case (deprivation of liberty, responsibility of de facto authorities), vol III, 2859; *The William* (detention, damages), vol IV, 4226.

[231] Convention for the payment of awards between Mexico and the United States, 30 January 1843, 94 CTS 139, arts 4, 5.

[232] Correspondence relating to the annexation in 33 BFSP 232–300, II Moore's *Arbitrations* 1246–1249.

Guadalupe Hidalgo, which settled the remaining grievances at great cost: in exchange for peace and a payment of fifteen million dollars, the United States not only kept Texas but also annexed California and other territories in the west.[233]

Not long after, the United States took the definitive step of empire building by putting boots on the ground in Latin America during peacetime to secure its 'first American protectorate'.[234] In 1846, New Granada agreed to guarantee uninterrupted access to and across the Panamanian Isthmus for the US, which in return pledged to 'guarantee positively and efficaciously ... the perfect neutrality of the before mentioned Isthmus'.[235] When a domestic riot broke out in a railway company boomtown in 1856, the United States fulfilled its responsibility to protect the isthmus by having its forces make landfall to occupy the railway properties.[236] In 1857, New Granada acknowledged its liability 'arising out of its privilege and obligation to preserve peace and good order along the transit route', and submitted to arbitration 'in conformity with general principles of the law of nations'.[237] In the ensuing arbitration more than 100 US claims were settled for a total of 496,235.47 dollars.[238]

By the middle of the eighteenth century, international lawyers regularly considered private pecuniary claims as a matter of the law of nations and were accustomed to debating their applicability to states that had suffered from internal hostilities. As Rear Admiral Baudin noted after bombarding Veracruz:

> France is now acting towards Mexico, as she did to Portugal in 1831, to Carthagena of Colombia in 1834, and as at present she is acting towards Buenos Ayres. In all these States, Frenchmen have been the victims of oppression more or less violent, and France would have been wanting in

233 Treaty of Guadalupe Hidalgo, 2 February 1848, 102 CTS 29, arts III–V, XII–XV.

234 Brian Loveman, *No Higher Law: American Foreign Policy and the Western Hemisphere since 1776* (University of North Carolina Press 2010) 52–56 and 104–108.

235 United States–New Granada treaty of peace, amity, navigation and commerce, 12 December 1846, 100 CTS 363, art 35.

236 See II Moore's *Arbitrations* 1362–1366; Loveman, *No Higher Law*, 108–110; Mercedes Chen Daley, 'The Watermelon Riot: Cultural Encounters in Panama City, April 15, 1856' 70 *Hispanic American Historical Review* (1990) 85–108.

237 United States–New Granada claims convention, 10 September 1857, 117 CTS 245, also 47 BFSP 353.

238 See II Moore's *Arbitrations* 1361–1396. A second tribunal awarded a further 88,000 dollars in 1865; see ibid 1396–1420.

> the most imperative duties towards her citizens, had she not exacted fit redress for these injuries.[239]

France's actions in Latin America were part of the broader trend of gunboat diplomacy conducted by the Europeans in the wider world in the mid nineteenth century. Under Palmerston (harking back to 'civis romanus sum'), the British Empire became fully aware of its seapower through the Opium Wars and the *Don Pacifico* affair, while the black ships of the US commodore Perry pried open the markets of Edo.[240] The legal provisions that were increasingly included in claims conventions and the international work of mixed commissions provided standard solutions transplantable to these situations, which promised to at least minimise violence on the way to a settlement. In this manner, the first decades of Latin American independence served as an incubator for the system of international state responsibility that was to have growing influence in the years to come. Although the mixed claims commissions often failed to conclude their mandates and gave way to directly negotiated settlements, they nevertheless contributed to the process of 'legalising' these questions for the future: the commissioners framed private claims as apolitical issues of legal responsibility rather than as matters of inter-sovereign discretion, extortion, or goodwill.[241]

3.3 Conclusion

By the year 1848, the world had witnessed the first wave of decolonisation, and this wave had revolutionised the legal vocabularies of neutrality, recognition, and responsibility that were essential to the classical doctrine of civil war. Well into the eighteenth century, the law of neutrality had existed mainly as a doctrine of conduct for a sovereign who sought to maintain peaceful relations with two or more friendly sovereigns who happened to be at war with one another. In the mid nineteenth century it came to be seen as a body of rules in international law from which scholars and jurists might derive concrete rights and obligations for states and for private actors depending on the formal positions assumed by their governments with respect to international conflicts. When more and more states enacted domestic neutrality laws, and when they then

[239] Rear Admiral Baudin to Cuevas, 27 October 1838, 27 BFSP 1176, 1180.

[240] Martti Koskenniemi, *To the Uttermost Parts of the Earth* (Cambridge University Press 2021) 777–794.

[241] See Tzvika Nissel, *Merchants of Legalism* (Cambridge University Press 2024) 44–45, 86–89, 108–112.

began to adopt formal or tacit positions of neutrality with respect to foreign civil wars, they found their citizens and courts debating the limits and consequences of neutrality in the language of international law, which had previously dealt only with international conflicts.

The decades of revolution also broke the immemorial order of the *ancien régime*, which, despite being defended by legitimists and conservatives, no longer remained uncontested. The spectre of popular sovereignty had come to haunt Europe. Locke's old prediction that 'where there is no judge on earth, the appeal lies to God in heaven' had been proven right by the independence of the United States, the French and Spanish American revolutions, and even Bonaparte's legalised conquests and orchestrated plebiscites – all of which drew connections between governmental legitimacy and the popular will and testified to the capacity of revolutionary movements to turn into sovereign entities. The consequence had been a return to the ancient problem of how to distinguish between lawful authority and *piratae et latrones*, and attempts to address the problem led jurists to grapple with the interminable question of recognition in international law. A generation of philosophers who had witnessed Napoleon's victories reimagined international law as a community of sovereign states that existed not by divine fiat but rather because they validated each other through mutual recognition, which was also their primary absolute right.[242] As this view foregrounded the act of recognition, the principles of revolutionary legitimacy took the shape of a declaratory view of recognition (states were recognised because they first existed in fact), while the old legitimist principles assumed that of a more constitutive view (the act of recognition was what validated statehood). In the context of civil wars, the legal profession found refuge in delegating the question to the executive branch. As far as legal practice in prize cases or arbitration was concerned, the status and legal subjecthood of revolutionaries and insurgents could be determined by exploring the relevant governmental declarations and diplomatic enactments.

Finally, questions of diplomatic protection and the problem of responsibility sprouted from the indeterminate intersection between war, peace, and neutrality on the one hand and the law of recognition in civil wars on the other. Whether governments opted for tacit or overt responses to the legal status of foreign insurgencies, the losses and damages caused by those conflicts were real and inescapable for their victims. As private

[242] G. W. F. Hegel, *Philosophy of Right* ([1820] Batoche 2001) §§ 330–331; Martti Koskenniemi, *Uttermost Parts*, 873–878, 947–948.

claims for diplomatic protection mounted, they transformed the problem of revolution into a problem of responsibility, which governments could seek to allocate legally to one another through combinations of legal argumentation and diplomatic leverage. In these encounters, the age of revolutions provided many useful vocabularies for allocating liability between the metropolitan empires engaging in counter-revolutionary actions, the neutral states obliged to maintain their impartiality, and the insurgent factions seeking to assume sovereignty over their territories through force and ideology.

***

When, in the late nineteenth century professional international lawyers in America and Europe fashioned the classical doctrine of civil war, they were greatly influenced by precedents from the Spanish American revolutions. But by then, their sources had been further enriched by a multitude of disputes arising from the *cause célèbre* of the American Civil War in 1861–1865, which not only surpassed prior civil wars through the scale of the hostilities but, most importantly, led lawyers to coin the concept of recognition of belligerency. This concept referred to the crucial moment when an insurgency transcended its domestic limits and became a civil war and when the insurgent parties acquired status as belligerents under international law. It is to this conflict that we turn next.

4

The American Civil War and Recognition of Belligerency

In November 1860, Abraham Lincoln, a vocal opponent of slavery, was elected president of the United States, despite resistance from what were soon to become the Confederate states. The way was now paved to imminent rebellion. Within six months, seven Southern states had announced their secession, constituted their own Confederate States of America under the presidency of Jefferson Davis, and begun to disarm federal troops in their territories. On 12 April 1861, the new Confederate army opened fire on Fort Sumter in Charleston, which had refused to surrender and join the secession. So began the American Civil War.

The war would in many ways be remembered as a milestone in the field of the international law of war and neutrality more generally. It was to have lasting legal effects as Great Britain and the United States suddenly found their customary roles reversed, with the US acting as the belligerent, and Britain taking on the role of a neutral. The war both consolidated and signified a high-water mark in the recognition of belligerency, while also cementing the law of civil war in the consciousness of international jurists. The American Civil War saw the establishment of Confederate prize jurisdiction and privateer fleets, the declaration of a massive Union blockade, and the expedient declarations of neutrality that followed. Of course, the war's significance went far beyond that of a case study in international law. It was a climactic moment in American history, marking a crucial triumph for the abolition of slavery and heralding the impending conquest of the remaining western frontier territories and the suppression of the Native American ways of life there. Less famously perhaps, it was also the last war in which privateers were commissioned on the high seas. The war's many legal aspects were extensively argued in courts and diplomatic fora the world over, and many of its consequences, such as the *Alabama* arbitration and the Lieber Code, soon became enshrined in the foundations of the emerging discipline of liberal international law.

The legal history of the American Civil War blends dimensions of international law and the United States constitutional law in ways that are often not separable. This intermingling was often a deliberate part of Union government strategy. Throughout the war the Union maintained that the Confederate States of America were not international belligerents but rather domestic rebels, and therefore their fate was ultimately to be decided in accordance with the Constitution, sheltered by state sovereignty from excessive international pressures. Yet in the conflict the Union repeatedly followed or applied the laws of war, even if the Lincoln administration claimed to be doing so of its own will in its sovereign capacity, rather than by obligation, and specifically denied any implication of recognition under international law.[1] An illustrative example is the issuing of the Lieber Code in 1863: although the substance of the code was a synthesis of the civilised international laws of war at the time, the Union framed it as conceding to such rules of engagement only on a municipal legal basis; the interpretation of those rules in the domestic sphere was clearly in the hands of the Union.

Thus, the American Civil War stands also as a definitive reference on the *limitations* of neutrality and belligerent recognition in civil wars. The Union claimed a right to wage war concurrently as both sovereign and belligerent. It insisted that it could treat the insurgents as traitors or rebels, if need be, and at the same time blockade their ports. As it turned out, the Union gradually conceded to the application of the laws of war in its conflict, codified them for its use and, whenever necessary, cited the authority of international law in defence of the Union cause.[2] In the aftermath of the civil war, Union officials even invoked the international legal rule of non-responsibility for rebel actions when arguing in the Senate against a set of claims emerging from Southern citizens.[3] But that was only after an outcome had been reached in the conflict; during the hostilities, the Union position remained strictly opposed to any belligerent status for the

[1] On the dual nature of the conflict, see generally Stephen C. Neff, *Justice in Blue and Gray: A Legal History of the Civil War* (Harvard University Press 2010); John Fabian Witt, *Lincoln's Code: The Laws of War in American History* (Free Press 2013). This chapter has benefited greatly from the thorough and outstanding research on which those works are based and for which I am deeply grateful.

[2] James G. Randall, *Constitutional Problems under Lincoln* (2nd edn, University of Illinois Press 1951) 65–73.

[3] Charles Sumner, 'Claims of citizens in the rebel states: Speeches in the Senate, January 12 and 15, 1869' in Charles Sumner, *Complete Works* (1872) vol XVII, 10 at 10–16.

Confederacy, even in the face of a finding by the Supreme Court that war under the law of nations existed between the two sides.[4]

4.1 War, Prize Jurisdiction, and Blockade

In the beginning there was prize jurisdiction. On the same day the Confederate States of America promulgated its permanent constitution, its congress passed an act establishing a court of admiralty and maritime jurisdiction at Key West, Florida.[5] Less than a week later, it assigned to all the district courts 'original cognizance of all civil causes of admiralty and maritime jurisdiction', with a right of appeal to the Supreme Court in matters of prize or no prize.[6] By the time the war began, preparations for a Confederate privateer fleet were well under way.

Within a week of the attack on Fort Sumter, both sides issued proclamations that framed their legal positions in the coming civil war. Abraham Lincoln called up 75,000 militiamen 'to repossess' the forts, places, and property seized from the Union.[7] For the Confederates, who were by now claiming sovereignty of their own, the Union mobilisation provided a pretext for invoking self-defence under the law of nations. According to them, their takeover of Union facilities had been a lawful sovereign action by the seceded states. Two days after Lincoln's proclamation, Jefferson Davis offered Confederate commissions to privateers willing to capture merchant vessels flying the Union flag, in order 'to repel the threatened invasion, and defend the rights and liberties of the people by all the means which the laws of nations and usages of civilized warfare place at its disposal'.[8] The preparation of letters of marque began on the following day.[9] The practical aim of the Confederacy was to play

[4] *Prize Cases* (1863) 67 US 635.

[5] Act to Establish a Court of Admiralty and Maritime Jurisdiction, 11 March 1861, in *Acts and Resolutions of the First Session of the Provisional Congress of the Confederate States, Held at Montgomery, Ala.* (Enquirer Book and Job Press 1861) 93–95; Constitution of the Confederate States of America, 11 March 1861, 51 BFSP 879.

[6] *Acts and Resolutions*, 115–132, ss 39 and 42. See also *Acts and Resolutions*, 110–111; J. Thomas Scharf, *History of the Confederate States Navy from Its Organization to the Surrender of Its Last Vessel* (Rogers & Sherwood 1887) 132.

[7] Lincoln's militia proclamation, 15 April 1861, 51 BFSP 268.

[8] Davis' proclamation, 17 April 1861, 51 BFSP 183–184; James McPherson, *War on the Waters: The Union and Confederate Navies, 1861–1865* (University of North Carolina Press 2012) 20.

[9] Correspondence on Confederate letters of marque and reprisal, 18 April 1861 onwards, in 2:1 OR Naval 329–335. See also correspondence in 51 BFSP 189–192. Privateer instructions and the form of privateer bonds are shown in 2:1 OR Naval 340–342. A Confederate

the role of underdog in a naval war, and to do so in the way that role always had been played: by issuing privateer commissions, they hoped to quickly enlist a fleet sufficient to cripple the Union's shipping and overburden its navy.

A day later, Lincoln declared the Confederate privateers as pirates who sailed under a 'pretended authority'.[10] His definition was carefully constructed: in compliance with the Union's insistence that the civil war was an internal insurrection, a gigantic police operation aimed at quelling the rioting populations in the South, the definition referred to Union law rather than piracy under the law of nations. This refusal to acknowledge a state of war was somewhat inconsistent with the second part of the proclamation – the declaration of 'a blockade of the ports within the States aforesaid, in pursuance of the laws of The United States, and of the law of nations in such case provided'.[11] What exactly the law of nations provided for was open to debate. But in due course this Union blockade would determine the nature of the conflict under international law and the attitude of the outside world towards the belligerents. Blockade, as we know, was an unmistakable exercise of belligerent powers under the law of nations. Resorting to it contradicted the assertion that the Confederation was an entirely illegal construction of municipal rebels and pirates. This blurred the character of the Confederacy: were the Southern ports occupied by a band of criminals or by a lawful enemy? If they were criminals, then how could the Union apply belligerent measures under the law of nations to subdue them? And if they were enemies, then by what logic could the Union declare them pirates and disregard the protection they were entitled to under the law of nations?

In response, the Confederate congress declared – or, to use its own words, recognised the existence of – war.[12] The declaration was essentially a prize act, accompanied by instructions for privateers and the blank form for privateer bonds. Noting the existence of war between the Confederacy and the Union, it authorised the president to deploy 'the

letter of marque is pictured in the frontispiece of William Morrison Robinson, Jr, *The Confederate Privateers* (Yale University Press 1928).

10 Proclamation of the Union blockade, 19 April 1861, 51 BFSP 185–186. The blockade was extended by a second proclamation on 27 April 1861, 51 BFSP 269. For its part, Congress approved all of Lincoln's proclamations and actions regarding the army and the navy on 6 August 1861. See 12 US Stat 326 (1861), 37th Congress, 6 August 1861, ch 63, s 3.

11 51 BFSP 185.

12 An Act Recognizing the Existence of War between the United States and the Confederate States, and Concerning Letters of Marque, Prizes, and Prize Goods, 6 May 1861, in 2:1 OR Naval 355–340 and 4:1 OR Armies 281–287.

whole land and naval force' against the Union and to issue privateer commissions against its vessels and citizens. A series of prize provisions followed, the first of them being that free ships would make free goods.[13] This, then, provided the legal basis for Confederate privateering and the expansion of the American Civil War to the high seas.[14]

4.1.1 Insurrection at Sea: Pirates or Privateersmen?

It was not long before the war produced the first court cases to test Lincoln's hard line on rebel privateers. In June 1861, the Confederate privateer schooner *Savannah* took the Union brig *Joseph* and was then captured itself. The schooner was brought to Hampton Roads and her crew put on trial for piracy in the Circuit Court of New York, where the case aroused considerable public interest.[15] Producing a letter of marque from Jefferson Davis, the defendants claimed to be lawful privateers, not pirates. According to them, the seizure of the *Joseph* had been a maritime capture under the law of nations and not an act of armed robbery at sea. Their view received little sympathy from the Union court: Judge Nelson instructed the jury to decide the case on the grounds of the old US Piracy Acts of 1790 and 1819/20, according to which citizens engaging in robbing American property at sea could be tried as pirates even if they

[13] Act of 6 May 1861, s 1.

[14] There was one idiosyncratic exception to the Union and Confederate positions on the insurrection. The House of Representatives in Kentucky declared 'strict neutrality', resolving 'that this State and the citizens thereof should take no part in the civil war now being waged, except as mediators and friends to the belligerent parties; and that Kentucky should, during the contest, occupy the position of strict neutrality'. This exceptional position was not destined to last: the Confederate army wasted no time in seizing the state in September 1861. Upon being occupied, however, Kentucky declared its allegiance to the Union, while the Confederates, for their part, established an alternative government, which declared secession and won recognition from the South. The Union forced the Confederation to abandon the state, whereupon Kentucky sided with the Union for the rest of the war. See A. C. Quisenberry, 'Kentucky's "Neutrality" in 1861' 15 *Register of Kentucky State Historical Society* (1917) 9–21.

[15] *United States* v. Baker (30 October 1861) 24 Fed Cas 962. For court transcripts and documents, see A. F. Warburton, *Trial of the Officers and Crew of the Privateer Savannah on the Charge of Piracy in the United States Circuit Court for the Southern District of New York* (Baker & Goodwin 1862); 'THE PRIVATEER SAVANNAH; Copy of her Letter-of-Marque, and of the Vessel's Log' *New York Times* (17 June 1861); 'THE SAVANNAH PRIVATEER; Trial for Piracy Great Throng in Court UNITED STATES DISTRICT COURT. Before Judges Nelson, C. J. and Shipman' *New York Times* (24 October 1861).

were holding a 'foreign' commission.[16] Although Nelson acknowledged that the law of nations would protect privateers in the event of an international war, he specifically refused to recognise the Confederates as lawful belligerents. Relying on the familiar position that international recognition was up to governments and not the courts, he held that since the government of the United States had never recognised the Confederacy, the law of nations could not come to their aid: 'Until this recognition of the new government, the courts are obliged to regard the ancient state of things as remaining unchanged'.[17] Despite these directions, the jurors had some difficulty affirming the official line of reasoning. A few hours after retiring, the jury reappeared to seek further clarification on whether or not a civil war existed. They were once more instructed to limit their deliberation to domestic piracy legislation. This, however, they could not bring themselves to do: after twenty hours of inconclusive deliberation the jury was discharged without its having reached a verdict.[18]

A similar case arose in Pennsylvania.[19] This matter concerned privateersmen from the Confederate privateer *Jefferson Davis*, sailing as a prize crew aboard a captured Union schooner, which was then recaptured on its way to port. As in the case of *Savannah*, circuit judge Grier instructed the jury to consider a Confederate captor's fate only from the perspective of domestic piracy laws. He recalled the provisions of international law under which 'Turks and Algerines, though acting as free-booters on the ocean ... could not be treated as pirates, because they acted under a commission from states with whom the government had treaties, and had acknowledged to be states'. Reflecting the *Gazette* principle, he reminded the jury how 'the courts of the United States must view such contested government as it is viewed by the legislative and executive departments of the government of the United States'.[20] Grier's colleague, Judge Cadwalader, concurred: measures granting the protection of civilised laws of war to combatants were 'not, in a civil war, founded in any

16 Piracy Act (1790) 1 US Stat 112; Piracy Act (1819) 3 US Stat 510; Piracy Act (1820) 3 US Stat 600.

17 *United States* v. *Baker* (1861) 965–966.

18 Ibid 966–967; Warburton, *Trial of the Officers and Crew*, 373–376.

19 United States v. Smith (25 October 1861) 27 Fed Cas 1134; D. F. Murphy, The Jeff Davis Piracy Cases: Full Report of the Trial of William Smith for Piracy as One of the Crew of the Confederate Privateer the Jeff Davis (King & Baird 1861); 'THE SOUTHERN PRIVATEERS; Trial of the Pirates of the Jeff. Davis in Philadelphia' New York Times (27 October 1861).

20 *United States* v. *Smith* (1861) 1135; Murphy, *Jeff Davis Piracy Cases*, 96.

rules of absolute legal right, but are measures of governmental policy'. The question of their observance was a matter for the legislative or executive departments of government to decide, not for judges to opine on.[21] In the end, the crew of the *Jefferson Davis* were less fortunate than the men of the *Savannah*: after deliberating for three-quarters of an hour, the jury rendered a guilty verdict for the master and certain crew members.

The legal treatment of the Confederate privateers led to something of a land–sea anomaly between the treatment of soldiers and that of privateersmen. While the United States refused to acknowledge the existence of a war under the law of nations, it nonetheless treated the defeated Confederate soldiers on land as prisoners of war.[22] There were practical reasons for this: to treat every Confederate soldier as a criminal would have meant they were entitled to a full and impartial trial under the federal constitution, with full procedural rights that might prove not only burdensome but also counter-productive for the war effort. Granting protection under the laws of war meant that foot soldiers could be interned without individual prosecution. Despite the fact that these practices reflected the treatment of prisoners of war under the law of nations, the Union would throughout the war maintain that in granting these rights to persons who after all were fellow citizens it did so at its discretion in the expectation that those persons would respect them in return. Even the Lieber Code of 1863, which provided a baseline for the humane treatment of captives, subjected its provisions to military necessity and strictly maintained that the humane treatment of insurgents would 'in no way whatever imply a partial or complete acknowledgement of their government'.[23] If such was the case with men captured in the field, then why should the Union not offer similar treatment to captured mariners?

The contrast between the treatment of captured soldiers (as enemies) and privateersmen (as pirates) did not escape the attention of all lawyers concerned. Among the first of those it frustrated were the judges Grier and Cadwallader back in Philadelphia, as one Confederate crew after another was brought before them. 'Why not try all those taken on land

[21] Murphy, *Jeff Davis Piracy Cases*, 98.

[22] Neff, *Justice in Blue and Gray*, 20–21; *Revised United States Army Regulations of 1861* (Government Printing Office 1862) paras 745–747; General Orders No. 32 and No. 67 in *General Orders of the War Department, Embracing the Years 1861, 1862 & 1863* (Derby & Miller 1864) vol I, 247 and 29.

[23] Lieber Code, arts 152–154; Witt, *Lincoln's Code*, 142–151.

and hang them?' burst out Justice Grier, and declared he would thenceforth refuse to hear another prize case in his court.[24] The sentiment that the Confederate privateers should be treated as combatants just as soldiers were soon spread wide and afar in the North, becoming intertwined with public debates on the civilised laws of warfare in general. In late 1861, Charles Daly, a New York judge, raised the question in an eloquent open letter entitled 'Are the Southern Privateersmen Pirates?'.[25] In it he argued that the Confederate privateersman was not a freebooter, as he was acting under the authority, and was subject to the control of, what he himself at least regarded as a government. He recalled how Edmund Burke had defended the colonial insurgent privateers during the American Revolution and argued that the Union had no reason to complain about European recognition of Southern belligerency as it had conducted itself in precisely the same way towards the Spanish American republics in the previous decades. Consequently, the Union could not ignore 'the fact, that war, and war upon a more extensive scale than usually takes place between contending nations, actually exists'.[26]

Together, these cases illustrate the difficulties the Union courts faced in applying their government's ambivalent legal position, which was to support non-recognition of the Confederates while at the same time treating them in fact as lawful enemies in the manner required under the law of nations. While the debate never caused the government to back down from its stance, the realities of war saved the accused individuals from being hanged. Following newspaper reports of the New York trials of the *Savannah* privateers, Jefferson Davis threatened retaliation in kind against Union captives if any of the privateers were hanged.[27] This pressure, together with public opinion in the North, eventually bore fruit: the Union refrained from executing the privateersmen as traitors and instead spared them for the emerging prisoner exchanges.[28] Though perhaps pirates in the eyes of the (reluctant) courts, these prisoners in the end received treatment that resembled that of privateersmen.

As regards the Confederate privateering campaign itself, the adventurous mariners soon found out that the world had moved beyond their classical method of warfare. Most of the world's seafaring nations – the US being an

24 See the dialogue reproduced verbatim in Randall, *Constitutional Problems*, 93.

25 Charles P. Daly, *Are the Southern Privateersmen Pirates? Letter to the Hon. Ira Harris, United States Senator* (James B. Kirker 1862).

26 Daly, *Are the Southern Privateersmen Pirates?*, 5–9.

27 Davis to Lincoln, 6 July 1861, in 2:3 OR Armies 5–6.

28 Neff, *Justice in Blue and Gray*, 23–24, 64.

exception – had signed or acceded to the Declaration of Paris, which in its first article imposed a total ban on privateering. As a consequence, notwithstanding the foreign states' various positions of neutrality, Confederate privateers were either unwelcome in foreign ports or faced considerable constraints there. After initial enthusiasm, the privateering effort quickly withered as the private adventurers transitioned towards the more lucrative business of running the Union blockade.[29] To make up for the restrictions encountered in the privateering campaign, the Confederacy succeeded in purchasing or building several commerce raiders for its navy; as public ships of war, these were not prohibited by the Declaration of Paris. The great success of some of these individual raiders ignited a bitter dispute between the Union and the United Kingdom, leading to the famous Geneva arbitration of the 1870s. The commerce raiders aside, the Confederate navy's ability to suppress trade in the North remained limited. When the Confederacy accepted the 'free ships free goods' principle to win the favour of foreign powers, it allowed regular Union merchants a workaround through the shipment of their goods in neutral bottoms.[30]

4.1.2 Insurrection on Land: From Formality to Necessity

Out of the large-scale land operations of the American Civil War was born the initiative to comprehensively codify the laws of war. It culminated in General Orders No. 100: Instructions for the Government of Armies of the United States in the Field, which, commonly known as the Lieber Code, was a restatement of the laws of war that would serve international lawyers for several generations to come. Its author, Professor Francis Lieber, was a renowned international lawyer, himself a veteran of the Napoleonic wars, and father of two sons who fought for the Union and a third who fought for the Confederacy. Lieber took a serious, matter-of-fact attitude towards warfare, rejecting idealistic pacifism. When, in 1861, he began to outline the modern laws of war, he was inspired not so much by sentiment as by practicalities: 'There is no sickly philanthropy in this; you know that I have no morbid feeling about war; what I wish, I wish as an earnest publicist, and in the name of international statesmanship.'[31]

29 Jan Martin Lemnitzer, *Power, Law and the End of Privateering* (Palgrave MacMillan 2014) 132–134.

30 Confederate resolution on maritime law, 13 August 1861, 55 BFSP 584; Lemnitzer, *End of Privateering*, 129–134; Neff, *Justice in Blue and Gray*, 177–178.

31 Lieber to Sumner, 27 December 1861, in Thomas Perry (ed), *The Life and Letters of Francis Lieber* (Osgood 1882) 323–325 at 325. On Lieber's later views, see Ville Kari, 'A

During the *Savannah* and *Jefferson Davis* trials, Lieber was lecturing at Columbia University, exploring the martial ideas that would later inform his code.[32] In his lectures, he maintained that the world had just entered a new period in the history of ideas on warfare: 'We had better call the period which preceded it the anti-war period, which began at the battle of Waterloo and ended with the Crimean war.' The anti-war period had been 'distinguished by the almost universal opinion that war was inadmissible under any circumstances, that it brought nothing but misery to man'. Yet, Lieber concluded, as people in America were now involved in an arduous war and preparing for conflicts in Europe, the time had come to once again recommence the study and development of the laws of war: 'The history of this law is really one of the histories of human progress, and it is a blessed thing that even in a time when men are arrayed against one another to kill and destroy, that humanity cannot be perfectly rejected.'[33] These views reflected Lieber's fatalistic view of warfare, which he had derived in part from Carl von Clausewitz – namely, that the path towards humane and moral warfare lay in keeping wars fierce and short.[34] The general overarching principle in the Lieber Code was, and would always be, the principle of military necessity: 'Military necessity, as understood by modern civilized nations, consists in the necessity of those measures which are indispensable for securing the ends of the war, and which are lawful according to the modern law and usages of war.'[35] Although Lieber acknowledged limits to necessity – cruelty, especially torture, was never justified by necessity[36] – the main guideline in his teachings would be that war was a grim, destructive business where the permissibility of actions depended on their purposes, causes, and circumstances.[37]

Military necessity was a principle that served not only to legitimise the destructive methods of war but also to restrict them. This suited the Union government's needs well. Facing widespread public pressure from

Less Elevated Cosmopolitanism: Victor Hugo, Francis Lieber, and the Franco-Prussian War of 1870' in Jan Klabbers, Maria Varaki, and Guilherme Vasconcelos Vilaça (eds), *Towards Responsible Global Governance* (University of Helsinki 2018) 31–52.

32 *New York Times* (27 October 1861, 1 November 1861, 16 November 1861, 13 January 1862, 10 February 1862, 16 February 1862, 3 April 1862, 17 March 1862).

33 'Lecture by Dr. Francis Lieber on the Laws and Usages of War' *New York Times* (27 October 1861).

34 Witt, *Lincoln's Code*, 184–186.

35 Lieber Code, art 14.

36 Ibid, art 16.

37 Famously, ibid, art 15. See also Witt, *Lincoln's Code*, 191–196.

the outside world, whose neutral stance threw the international status of the Union into question, the Lincoln administration found itself obliged to explain its actions and defend the United States' status and reputation as a civilised state. One way to achieve this was to boldly restate the laws of war, with the necessities of the Union war effort as their core. Besides, military necessity was not always invoked to destructive ends: Abraham Lincoln famously relied on military necessity to justify his emancipation proclamation, arguing that the liberation of all slaves was not only the right thing to do but also necessary to the Union war effort.[38] The principle's ambivalence allowed the Union to continue pursuing its goals with little external restraint and in the hope of winning over the spirits and imaginations of domestic and foreign lawyers.

Although Lieber's work was primarily a story of the laws of war in general rather than the doctrine of civil war per se, it certainly had an impact on the question of internal conflicts. Its final section set forth the legal basis of the Union's opposition to the Confederacy, as well as the elementary principles of occupation in the war. For the Union, the Lieber Code established that the application of the laws of war or the granting of prisoner-of-war status could in no way be taken to imply partial or full recognition of the insurgent government, and that the lawful government could still try the rebel commanders for treason.[39] Its articles reflect a legal position increasingly present in the practice of the courts where the Union argued that since the Confederates were both traitors and enemies, it could engage with them by both sovereign and belligerent means. On the question of occupation, the Lieber Code permitted discrimination between loyal and disloyal civilians, and accorded the lawful government's military commanders the discretion to distinguish between the two.[40] The final article characterised as treason any resistance or obstruction against the occupying troops.[41] Altogether, the Lieber Code asserted a strong 'legitimist' preference, rejecting any equality of rights before the law and instead firmly insisting on the sovereign authority of the central government.

Lieber's treatment of irregular fighters was also of particular relevance for civil wars. Previously, the old laws of war had distinguished between brigands or *banditti* and lawful combatants, primarily on the basis of

[38] Neff, *Justice in Blue and Gray* 135–142, Witt, *Lincoln's Code*, 203–213, 237–239; Proclamation of 22 September 1862, 12 US Stat 1267.

[39] Lieber Code, arts 152–154.

[40] Ibid, arts 155–156.

[41] Ibid, art 157.

whether or not they held proper commissions from a sovereign authority. Rejecting the old approach, Lieber considered properly authorised partisans as being generally entitled to belligerent status, but independent guerrilla fighters as being liable to any punishment meted out by the government suppressing them.[42] In the background were the Union's experiences with Mexican guerrillas and the Confederate bushwhackers earlier in the war, which had led Union commanders to treat guerrillas as 'highway robbers under another name' – that is, *piratae et latrones* – and to deal with them through summary trials and executions.[43] Although Lieber recommended that these individuals be treated with a minimum of humanity as well, he decoupled such treatment from the rights and obligations flowing directly from international law.[44] In the Union laws of war, irregular troops' acceptability as belligerents became increasingly dependent on factual elements, such as their organisation, uniforms and insignia, and their adherence to the laws of war.[45] However, all such considerations remained secondary to military necessity.

4.2 Foreign Reactions and the Recognition of Belligerency

4.2.1 Declarations of Neutrality by European Powers

When Abraham Lincoln declared the Union blockade in April 1861, his invocation of the law of nations caused a great deal of concern among his own advisors and constituents. Prior to the declaration, his administration had instructed its representatives abroad to warn against recognition of the Confederates and had sought a preliminary understanding with foreign diplomats in Washington that a formal blockade under the law of nations would be the clearest and most transparent way to pursue the Union's operations against Confederate commerce if a war began.[46] This was particularly to please the British, who had uncontested sea power in the world and would likely welcome another international precedent

[42] Ibid, arts 81–85; Francis Lieber, *Guerrilla Parties Considered with Reference to the Laws and Usages of War* (D. Van Nostrand 1862) 18–21.

[43] On the Mexican war, see Witt, *Lincoln's Code*, 122–129.

[44] Lieber Code, arts 152–154.

[45] Witt, *Lincoln's Code*, 193–194, 234–237. Tracey Dowdeswell, 'The Brussels Peace Conference of 1874 and the Modern Laws of Belligerent Qualification' 54 *Osgoode Hall Law Journal* (2017) 805–850, at 821.

[46] Lynn M. Case and Warren F. Spencer, *The United States and France: Civil War Diplomacy* (University of Pennsylvania Press 1970) 46; Witt, *Lincoln's Code*, 143–145; Neff, *Justice in Blue and Gray*, 21.

confirming the blockading rights of belligerents. Yet when European powers began to respond to belligerent actions on the part of the Union by adopting a public stance of neutrality – thus implicitly recognising a civil war and a state of belligerent equality between the Union and the Confederacy – this caused great alarm and consternation among US officials and publicists, who, as the war progressed, would come to see the Europeans' neutrality as a potentially unfriendly act. From the European perspective, as the Union blockade had been enacted at least in part to attract foreign acceptance, there seemed to be solid grounds for declaring neutrality. On the other hand, the signatories of the Declaration of Paris of 1856 had an alternative avenue through which to position themselves – namely, the prohibition of privateering. The result was a range of stances among European powers, from neutrality to non-intervention to recognition.[47]

The events developed very quickly in Great Britain. Within weeks of the outbreak of the war, the first Confederate merchant ships reached European ports, where both Union and Confederate diplomats were already busy pushing their causes. The government referred the question of neutrality to the law officers of the crown on the very day news of the Union blockade reached London. While the officers were deliberating, the British prime minister Lord Russell met unofficially with a small Confederate delegation that was requesting recognition of Confederate independence.[48] When the Union representatives enquired whether European governments would assist them in detaining insurgents, they received the answer that no action would be taken against the Confederates for the time being.[49] On 6 May, the law officers delivered their opinion that the government should consider the Civil War in America as regular war and that all the rules concerning blockade and letters of marque that were applicable to neutrality during a war should be applied.[50] Accordingly, the crown issued a proclamation of neutrality on 13 May – that is, less than two weeks after receiving news of the Union blockade.[51] In her proclamation, the queen expressed determination to

[47] Mountague Bernard, *A Historical Account of the Neutrality of Great Britain during the American Civil War* (Longmans, Green, Reader, and Dyer 1870) 135–136, 144–150.

[48] Rob Merkin, *Marine Insurance: A Legal History* (Edward Elgar 2014) vol II, 284–285.

[49] Bernard, *Historical Account*, 247ff.

[50] I McNair, *Opinions*, 138–139.

[51] 51 BFSP 165; *London Gazette* (14 May 1861); Bernard, *Historical Account*, 135–143; Francis Deák & Philip C. Jessup, *Collection of Neutrality Laws* (Carnegie Endowment 1939) vol I, 161–162.

maintain 'a strict and impartial neutrality' in the 'contest' between the Union and 'certain States styling themselves the Confederate States of America'. To ensure all British subjects observed strict neutrality in and during the hostilities, the Foreign Enlistment Act of 1819 was brought into force.[52] Six months later, the policy was extended to a total prohibition on the export of arms and other military stores from the United Kingdom.[53] To the disappointment of the Confederates, however, British neutrality was not accompanied by the creation of diplomatic relations with them, and the insurgents would be received by the Foreign Office only on an informal basis.[54]

The Union government was not at all pleased with British neutrality. Extensive correspondence on the law of neutrality and the question of belligerent recognition followed between the British foreign minister Lord Russell, the British ambassador to Washington Lord Lyons, the US minster in London Charles Francis Adams, and the secretaries of state William Seward and Hamilton Fish, as well as between the governments and legislative bodies on both sides of the Atlantic. After the war, these exchanges received a long afterlife in the Geneva arbitration and eventually formed a basis for subsequent academic explorations into the origins of the recognition of belligerency doctrine.[55] The Union representatives expressed concern that the queen's proclamation of neutrality had been 'hasty and premature'[56] and disappointment that although Britain had not recognised the Confederates, it had not denounced the insurgents either.[57] Britain, of course, took the opposite line, arguing that the civil war was a well-known fact and recognition had been necessary for clarity and precisely to avoid making final determinations about Confederate statehood; in declaring its neutrality, Britain had simply conceded that the Confederacy had 'a belligerent character', which it understood as 'an

52 51 BFSP 165.

53 British proclamation of 29 November 1861, order in council of 30 November 1861, Proclamation of 4 December 1861, and order in council of 4 December 1861, 51 BFSP 170–173. By January 1862, ships of either belligerent were prohibited from using British ports as their bases; arrivals and departures of such ships were separated by intervals of twenty-four hours, to avoid the risk of encounters; and all ships were prohibited from stocking any arms or war-related supplies, other than just enough coal to reach the next friendly port. See Russell to commissioners of the Admiralty, 31 January 1862, 51 BFSP 265–268.

54 Russell to Lyons, 11 May 1861, 51 BFSP 186–187.

55 For example, Dana's *Wheaton* (1866) § 23 fn 15; Bemis, *Hasty Recognition*; Bernard, *Historical Account*, 152–170; I Smith 302–312; I McNair, *Opinions* 138ff.

56 Noted in Russell to Lyons, 21 June 1861, 51 BFSP 198.

57 Russell to Lyons, 21 May 1861, 51 BSFP 192.

intermediate position' that could be revised if the circumstances required.[58] As the war went on, the British view was increasingly reinforced as a result of the prize adjudications in United States, where the Union courts derived the factual existence of war from the Union blockade and justified their observations by referring to past court practice in the Spanish American revolutions. The US government would nevertheless continue to challenge the propriety of the British declaration until the end of the war.

The French approach to neutrality was influenced by Napoleon III's aspiration to regain a French colonial presence on the American mainland and to challenge the Monroe Doctrine. While the United States was pre-occupied with its civil war, he decided to go ahead with his machinations for invading Mexico. In respect of the American Civil War, the French seemed willing to acknowledge a state of international belligerency, and even went so far as to propose its mediation between the Union and the Confederacy.[59] Once war broke out, the French foreign ministry sought to form a unified neutral front with Britain and to insist on the importance of implementing the principles set forth in the Declaration of Paris; as in London, the ministers in Paris received a stern diplomatic protest from the Union.[60] France declared its neutrality vis-à-vis the American Civil War in early June 1861 and, like Britain, adopted a position of formal impartiality with respect to both sides in the conflict.[61] The French declaration was similar to that of Britain, with France avowing 'to maintain strict neutrality in the ongoing struggle between the Union Government and the States that pretend to form a particular Confederation'. It was made chiefly on the basis of relevant neutrality provisions in the navigation law of 10 April 1825, the *Ordonnance de la marine* of 1681, and the *Code pénal*. Except in situations of distress, belligerent vessels were permitted to use French ports for no longer than twenty-four hours, and the sale of prizes was prohibited in French ports. Enlisting men to fight in the war, equipping warships and accepting commissions from either belligerent party were all prohibited, too.

The Confederate privateers favoured the Caribbean colonies of Spain and the Netherlands for supply ports; the Union therefore had a particular interest in securing their cooperation. Spain proclaimed neutrality by royal

[58] Ibid 192–193. See also Hersch Lauterpacht, *Recognition in International Law* (Cambridge University Press 1947) 177.

[59] Stève Sainlaude, *France and the American Civil War: A Diplomatic History* (University of North Carolina Press 2019) 1–27.

[60] Case and Spencer, *Civil War Diplomacy*, 52–58.

[61] French declaration of neutrality, 10 June 1861, 51 BFSP 1137.

decree in June 1861; following the French model, it avowed 'to maintain the most strict neutrality on the contest begun between the Federal States of the Union and the states confederated at the South'.[62] Citing the 1856 Declaration of Paris, it made equipping privateers and accepting letters of marque from either belligerent illegal. Spanish subjects were warned not to enlist with the belligerent forces on pain of losing any protection from the Spanish government.

Trade needs in Cuba prompted the secretary of state Seward to request that Spain grant the Union consular jurisdiction over all Confederate vessels in Spanish ports until the end of the war.[63] Spain refused, referring to its duties as a neutral. Their dissension intensified when the infamous Confederate commerce raider *Sumter* stopped in Cuba with six prizes in tow. After unloading the prizes with their crews, the raider replenished its supplies and headed out to resume its hunt. The Union protested that allowing the *Sumter* to stock up and set sail again was 'in violation of the Treaties existing between this Government and Spain, as well as of the law of nations'. It further demanded the release of the prizes and 'reserv[ed] the subject of indemnity for the injury inflicted upon the United States by the transaction'.[64] This time Spain complied, reporting that the prizes were freed as they had ostensibly been 'captured in waters within the jurisdiction of the island, and under unlawful circumstances'. The excuse seems artificial; the move is better understood as a concession made by Spain.[65] In contrast to the forthright pressure exerted by the Union, the Spanish neutrality decree remained deliberately ambiguous on the question of Confederate belligerent rights, which shows that the Confederates were still clearly cast in the role of contender. Most importantly, Spain's commitment to the Declaration of Paris led to a de facto repudiation of the services of Confederate privateer vessels.

Other states displayed varying degrees of de facto neutrality. While not openly declaring strict neutrality, the Netherlands acknowledged the 'doubtful complications in the United States of North America' and ordered that no privateers or their prizes would be admitted to their ports, except in distress.[66] Dutch subjects engaging in privateering would

[62] Ministry of State – Royal Decree, Madrid, 17 June 1861, in Mr Perry to Seward, 19 June 1861, 51 BFSP 97–98.

[63] Bernard, *Historical Account*, 248–249.

[64] Seward to Tassara, 15 July 1861, in Bernard, *Historical Account*, 250.

[65] Tassara to Seward, 9 August 1861, in Bernard, *Historical Account*, 250–251 and fns.

[66] Pike to Seward, 16 June 1861, 51 BFSP 117.

be tried as pirates.[67] Since the Netherlands still possessed valuable colonies in the West Indies, the king ordered a new squadron to stand ready in case the colonies needed protection. Dutch shipmasters, consignees, and freighters were warned of the risk that they would forfeit their insurance as well as government protection if they engaged in blockade violations or contraband trade.[68] This therefore amounted to a position of neutrality in all but name. The Netherlands stressed that it had not recognised the Confederates as belligerents, but this did not prevent it from expressing concern over the Union's inconsistent treatment of insurgent privateers.[69] Like the Dutch, the Kingdom of Denmark dispatched a man-of-war to the Danish West Indies 'for the purpose of preventing privateering and preserving the neutrality of Denmark'.[70] Russia, on the other hand, continued to regard Confederate merchantmen as simply 'American vessels' no different from any others and to apply to them the treaties in force with the United States.[71]

States could also skirt around the question of neutrality by focusing on the prohibition of privateering under the 1856 Declaration of Paris. The Senate of Bremen reacted to the civil war primarily by passing an ordinance prohibiting its subjects from 'meddling in any way with privateering',[72] while the Senate of Hamburg tersely reminded the public that privateers were abolished.[73] The king of Portugal prohibited his subjects from engaging or assisting in privateering and refused privateers, prizes, or other armed vessels entry to Portuguese ports, other than in situations of distress.[74] Another maritime state that, unlike the aforementioned, made a formal declaration of neutrality was the Kingdom of Hawaii.[75]

4.2.2 Questions between the Belligerents and Neutrals

US courts soon found themselves seised of cases concerning neutral shipping. They had already been treading a thin line between Union policy

67 Ibid 117–118.
68 Ibid 118.
69 Pike to Seward, 11 September 1861, 51 BFSP 118–121.
70 Wood to Seward, 19 July 1861, 51 BFSP 102.
71 Correspondence between Appleton, Clay, and Seward, April–August 1861, 51 BFSP 98–102.
72 Ordinance of Senate of Bremen against privateering, 2 July 1861, 51 BFSP 1138.
73 Ordinance of Senate of Hamburg against privateering, 19 July 1861, 51 BFSP 1139.
74 Portuguese decree of neutrality, 29 July 1861, enclosed with Harvey to Seward, 25 August 1861, 51 BFSP 130–131.
75 Proclamation of 26 August 1861, 51 BFSP 136–137.

and the facts of civil war in the Confederate privateer cases they had dealt with. Now they had to address the rights and views of foreign merchants and states as well. The Union never recognised the Confederacy in any capacity other than that of domestic rebel, and it ruled out the possibility of rights and duties arising from international relations between the Confederacy and foreign powers. Most foreign powers aligned themselves to some extent with this view and consequently never established formal diplomatic relations with the Confederates. But in their practice most states cultivated a de facto relationship of belligerency and neutrality with the Confederates and, from time to time, sought to have this acknowledged by the Union. As might be expected, disagreements between the Union and the neutrals persisted throughout the civil war.

One such disagreement was the diplomatic row that erupted in November 1861 when the Royal Mail steam packet *Trent* was boarded by a Federal frigate while en route from Havana to Southampton.[76] The commanding officer, Captain Wilkes, had forcibly removed from the ship a group of Confederate diplomatic representatives who were on their way to Britain and France.[77] This raised problems in respect of the law of nations: Wilkes had boarded a neutral ship travelling between neutral ports while it was in neutral waters and had removed its passengers by force. The *Trent* itself had not been captured, nor even properly investigated, so what had happened could be qualified as an intrusion into the jurisdiction of a foreign sovereign, besides being an affront to the sacrosanct immunity of postal ships.[78] The British law officers put it baldly: the boarding of the *Trent* had been illegal and unjustifiable under international law.[79] Britain formally demanded the release of the captured men and a public apology,[80] while other neutrals in Paris, Berlin, and Vienna issued diplomatic notes expressing their 'utmost astonishment and no little

[76] Generally on the *Trent* affair, see Neff, *Justice in Blue and Gray*, 171–172; McPherson, *War on the Waters*, 44–46; III McNair, *Opinions* 275–291; 'The Affair of the Trent' 12 *Law Magazine & Law Review* (1862) 324–255; Richard Henry Dana, 'The Trent Affair: An Aftermath' 45 *Proceedings of the Massachusetts Historical Society* (1911–1912) 508–530; Dana's *Wheaton*, 539–542.

[77] Cmdr Williams to Cpt Patey, 9 November 1861, in 1:1 OR Naval 158–159.

[78] The British found the whole affair profoundly insulting. See e.g. 'Seizure of the West India Mail by an American Frigate' *The Times* (28 November 1861); 'The American Outrage on Our Flag' *Manchester Guardian* (29 November 1861); 'Art. VII: The Affair of the Trent' 12 *Law Magazine and Law Review* (1862) 326: 'Within the memory of those now living no public event has aroused the anger of the nation to so high a pitch.'

[79] Reports of Harding, Atherton, and Palmer, 12 and 28 November 1861, in III McNair *Opinions* 276, 278.

[80] Russell to Lyons, 30 November 1861, in 1:1 OR Naval 159–160.

sensation' at the affair.[81] In response, the Union initially contended that the Confederate envoys were 'human contraband'[82] but then receded by admitting that while the capture itself had been lawful, Wilkes had not conducted the seizure at sea properly.[83] The Confederate representatives were therefore to be 'cheerfully liberated'.[84] What could not be conceded in substance was conceded by finding fault in the procedure. The resolution of the *Trent* affair was given a favourable reception in Europe, and, in light of the formal explanation, Britain did not press its original claim for a public apology. However, despite considering the US reaction sufficient reparation for the time being, the British government recorded its disagreement over the way in which the law of neutrality was applied in the case and intimated that it might well revisit the question after the war.[85]

4.2.3 The Union Blockade and the Legal Status of the War

The major bone of contention between the Union and the neutrals was the Union blockade. No sooner had it been put into effect than the first prize cases began appearing on court dockets in the summer of 1861. Because a blockade implied a distinctively belligerent power, courts could not avoid addressing the question of the legal nature of the conflict from this angle too. Unlike the question of the Confederate privateersmen, which concerned 'merely' the legal status of insurgent mariners at the hands of their compatriots, the enforcement of the Union blockade involved the forcible capture of foreign vessels and foreign property, which brought with it obvious diplomatic risks. As a matter clearly governed by the law of nations, the blockade prompted insistent calls from the neutrals for the Union to recognise the Confederates as belligerents. From classical textbooks it was clear that the exercise of belligerent powers indicated the existence of a state of war, and where there was war belligerent rights belonged to both sides in the conflict.[86] Great Britain, in particular, urged the United States to recognise Confederate prize jurisdiction. Its law officers rejected the US claim that rebels could not have a prize court and saw denying them this as 'destructive of the

[81] Correspondence reproduced in 10 *Supplement to the American Journal of International Law* (1916) 67–72.
[82] Seward to Lyons, 26 December 1861, in 1:1 OR Naval 177–187 at 180–181.
[83] Ibid 186.
[84] Ibid 187. See also III McNair *Opinions* 279–287.
[85] Russell to Napier and Lyons, 10 January 1862, in 1:1 OR Naval 188–190.
[86] For example, Vattel, *Droit des gens*, III.12.191.

Belligerent Rights and status' on the basis of which the United States itself operated.[87] The law officers put their case in no uncertain terms:

> Neutral States will not accord the Status of a Belligerent, and the right to visit on the high Seas, try, and condemn Neutral Vessels, to the United States Government, unless it recognizes the usual obligations which, according to International Law, accompany and balance those rights; unless they also concede to their enemy the *status* of a belligerent for all *international* purposes, and as to all matters that relate to the necessary intercourse of Neutral States with that enemy, preeminent among which is the recognition of a duly constituted Prize Court, the existence of which the Neutral has a right to demand at the hands of *every* belligerent.[88]

As the Union government continued to deny the Confederacy international status, this opened up the possibility for lawyers representing the claimants of neutral prizes taken by the Union to challenge the very legality of the Union blockade. In a decisive case before the Supreme Court in 1863, James Carlisle, on behalf of the appellants, invoked the *Gazette* principle with a view to deploying it against the Union. He argued that as the Lincoln administration, in its foreign policy, had consistently ruled out the notion of belligerency (and as the Congress had originally not declared war), its 'position was that it was purely a *municipal* question; and of course, there could be no blockade, in the international sense, and no capture *jure belli*'.[89] Therefore:

> To justify this condemnation, there must have been *war* at the time of this so-called capture; not war as the old essayists describe it . . . but war as known to international law – war carrying with it the mutual recognition of the opponents as *belligerents*; giving rise to the right of blockade of *the enemy's* ports, and affecting all other nations with the character of neutrals, until they shall have mixed themselves in the contest. War, in this, the only sense important to this question, is matter of law, and not merely matter of fact.[90]

To properly understand the response of the Union to this international challenge, it is worth briefly recalling the metaconstitutional conflict[91] at the root of the Southern states' secession, and, by way of consequence, the civil war. The secession crisis of 1860–1861 had brought to the surface the unsettled question of sovereignty in the United States – namely, that it

[87] Report by Atherton, Palmer, and Phillimore, 17 January 1863, in I McNair, *Opinions*, 139.
[88] Ibid 140.
[89] *Prize Cases* (1863) 67 US 635, 641–643.
[90] Ibid 648–649.
[91] On this term, see Christine Bell, *On the Law of Peace: Peace Agreements and the Lex Pacificatoria* (Oxford University Press 2008) 291–293.

had never been fully settled whether the federal Union had been constituted as a sovereign entity (by 'We the People'), in parallel to its individual constituent states, or whether sovereignty remained with the states alone. Whether or not the federal state bore marks of sovereignty mattered a great deal. During the secession crisis the two views collided; if only the states had sovereignty, secessions by individual states would be effective ipso facto, whereas if sovereignty belonged to the Union, then it would have a constitutional right to use force to protect the unity of the federation against secession.[92]

In November 1860, Attorney General Jeremiah Black submitted a legal opinion to the outgoing president Buchanan on the extent of presidential powers to enforce the laws within the Union, having in mind the question of what the president might be able to do if individual states began to secede.[93] In his opinion, Black affirmed that the president and federal authorities would have the power to use force to ensure the execution of the laws of the United States whenever opposed, including by sending the militia whenever the obstruction was caused by forces 'too powerful to be suppressed by the ordinary course of judicial proceedings'.[94] But things would be more difficult in a situation where the opposition in a state became 'so universal' that federal judges and legal officers refused to continue to dispense justice and instead resigned from their positions: 'Under such circumstances, to send a military force into any State, with orders to act against the people, would be simply making war upon them.'[95] Stressing that the president could not determine the rightfulness of secessions, Black observed that the Constitution's purpose was to protect the states and not to authorise attacks and conquests of some by others: 'If it be true that war cannot be declared, nor a system of general hostilities carried on by the Central Government against a State, then it seems to follow that an attempt to do so would be *ipso facto* an expulsion of such State from the Union.'[96] Black's opinion basically adopted the Southern constitutional compact theory and prohibited the Union from protecting the federation's integrity; in retrospect, it has been characterised as 'perverse' and 'defeatist'.[97]

92 Neff, *Justice in Blue and Gray*, 6–15.

93 Jeremiah S. Black, 'Power of the President in Executing the Laws', 9 Official Opinions of the Attorneys General (1860) 516.

94 Ibid 522.

95 Ibid 523.

96 Ibid 525.

97 Andrew Kent, 'The Constitution and the Laws of War during the Civil War' 85 *Notre Dame Law Review* (2010) 1839–1930 at 1862 and 1891.

What makes Black's constitutional analysis remarkable in the present context is that it reflected many of the principles of the classical doctrine of civil war in the law of nations. First, Black associated a state of civil war with the moment when civil courts could no longer dispense justice within the state. In so doing, he introduced into the American Civil War the old Roman law maxim of *silent enim leges inter arma*, which Coke had similarly introduced into the common law.[98] Second, in suggesting that the waging of war by some states against others would break the Union in two, his narrative resembled Vattel's description of a mature civil war under the law of nations.[99] At the same time, Black's conclusions highlighted the inescapable indeterminacy of the classical doctrine of civil war: in the event of secession, the Union would either let it go ahead without putting up any resistance or, if it chose to oppose it with force, then that very act would amount to treating the rebels as independent legal subjects.[100]

From as early as the onset of war, it seemed likely that the courts would consider declarations of a Union blockade as evidence of civil war and belligerency. The case of the *Tropic Wind* in June 1861 concerned a British vessel that its captors accused of violating the blockade. Predictably, the claimants challenged the lawfulness of the Union blockade as a whole on the grounds that since there had been no declaration of war the insurgency was a municipal affair, which in turn meant that the president had no power to order a blockade.[101] After examining Lincoln's blockade declaration, Judge Dunlop concluded that it amounted to a declaration of the existence of civil war: 'Blockade itself is a belligerent right, and can only legally have place in a state of war, and the notorious fact[s] . . . attest the executive declaration that civil war exists, a sad war which if it must go on, can only be governed by the laws of war.'[102] He pointed out that the United States' referral to domestic jurisdiction for the prosecution of Confederate privateers did not affect his overall conclusion 'averring the existence of civil war'.[103]

A month later, in Philadelphia, Judge Cadwalader reached a similar conclusion in the matter of the *Parkhill*, condemning a South Carolina

[98] Marcus Tullius Cicero, *Pro Milone*, IV.11; Coke, *Institutes*, I.412.
[99] Vattel, *Droit des gens*, III.18.292.
[100] Kent, 'Laws of War', 1891.
[101] *The Tropic Wind* (13 June 1861) 28 Fed Cas 218 at 218–219.
[102] *The Tropic Wind* (1861), 221.
[103] Ibid.

merchant ship as good prize.[104] Although the case involved a Confederate ship and not a neutral vessel, the court's reasoning is particularly telling. At first, Cadwalader tried to circumvent the question of the lawfulness of the Union blockade by examining instead whether or not confiscation of the prize on the high seas was possible simply on account of its being enemy property.[105] However, to answer this, he still had to determine whether or not an 'enemy' – and thus a civil war – existed in the first place. Cadwalader embarked on a long tour into past insurgencies and their treatment under the law of nations and the common law, revisiting precedents from, inter alia, the American Revolution, the Glorious Revolution of 1688, the Black Book of the Admiralty, and some of the disputes concerning the War of the Roses recorded in Thomas Rymer's *Fœdera*. Like Attorney General Black before him, Cadwalader turned towards Coke's rule on the recognition of civil war: when a state's courts were open and functioning, it was ordinarily a time of peace; but when the regular course of justice was interrupted by rebellion or insurrection 'so that the courts of justice cannot be kept open', a civil war existed.[106] The presence of war was thus a matter of fact, not of governmental fiat, and recognition thereof could be a declarative, as opposed to a constitutive, act. Relying on this rule, Cadwalader saw no problem in his determining the existence of a state of war in his judicial capacity, independently of the government. The Southern states having declared that their ties with the federal courts and federal court jurisdiction were severed, it could be said that war, and thus a state of belligerency, was at hand.

Union courts quickly also responded to the underlying metaconstitutional question of the civil war by rejecting the compact theory, which posited that individual states were sovereign with respect to the Union and free to secede at will. In the case of the British bark *Hiawatha*,[107] the New York judge Betts took a stance strongly in favour of the full sovereignty of the federal state represented by the central government. 'The Union is not composed of subtleties and abstractions', he determined, 'It was formed with the purpose to render it practical and efficacious.' When adopting the Constitution, it had been the 'manifest purpose of the people . . . to constitute and perpetuate a government of national powers' and precisely to overturn the previously ineffective

[104] *The Parkhill* (23 July 1861) 18 Fed Cas 1187.
[105] Ibid 1188.
[106] Ibid 1191.
[107] *The Hiawatha* and *The Crenshaw* (29 August 1861) 12 Fed Cas 95 at 99.

construction of separate sovereignties. 'The whole extent of the country is one nation and one government. In respect to the United States and its constitutional laws, there are no state lines, and state sovereignty is a nonentity.'[108] Consequently, the insurrectionists had become enemies of the United States by openly committing hostilities against it while legally still subjects of the central government. The government was repressing the 'rebellion and treason' legitimately through war, 'because the magnitude and force of the revolt [was] beyond the control of the law and the civil magistracy'.[109] In the matter of the *Amy Warwick*,[110] Judge Sprague in Boston went further and affirmed the Union's 'double character' theory, according to which the Union was waging war against the Confederacy both as a sovereign and as a belligerent, and could thus exercise its powers and jurisdiction in either capacity. Sprague observed how the classical doctrine of civil war as explained in Wheaton's *Elements* 'so strongly maintains belligerent rights in civil war, that some of his language would imply that there are no other rights'. But this could not have been the intention, because civil war as such 'imports that sovereign rights are not relinquished, but insisted on. The war is waged to maintain them.' He found:

> In this war, the rebels are, at the same time, belligerents and traitors, and subject to the liabilities of both. The United States sustains the double character of a belligerent and sovereign, and has the rights of both. The temporary non-user of any such rights is not a renunciation of them, but they may be called into practical exercise at pleasure. The United States has full belligerent rights, which are in no degree impaired by the fact that their enemies owe allegiance, and have added the guilt of treason to that of unjust war.[111]

It was clear that a precedent from the Supreme Court would be needed to resolve the legal nature of both the Union blockade and the entire civil war in a satisfactory way. This came about in the winter of 1862–1863 in the joined cases of the *Amy Warwick*, the *Crenshaw*, the *Hiawatha*, and the *Brilliante*, collectively known as *The Prize Cases*.[112] Of these ships two were Confederate vessels, one was British, and one Mexican; the case thus combined belligerent captures of both enemy and neutral ships. Overall,

[108] Ibid.
[109] Ibid 100.
[110] *The Amy Warwick* (April 1862) 1 Fed Cas 799.
[111] Ibid, syllabus and 803.
[112] *The Brig Amy Warwick; The Schooner Crenshaw; The Barque Hiawatha; The Schooner Brilliante* (1863) 67 US 635 (*Prize Cases*).

the case hinged on the validity of the blockade, which in turn depended on whether or not the Union government could exercise belligerent rights against the insurgents. Much in the substance of the *Prize Cases* concerned constitutional questions of whether and when, as president, Lincoln had held the constitutional right to engage in a civil war. For present purposes, however, the significance of the *Prize Cases* was that it examined the very central question of belligerency status and the existence of war in relation to the neutral powers.

The case represented a final challenge against the view that belligerent rights could ever have been lawfully available to the Union. The appellant shipowners argued – to use the words of Carlisle quoted earlier – that the government's consistent refusal to recognise the Confederacy meant that the war was 'purely a *municipal* question', so there could be no lawful blockade.[113] Referring to the wording of the Constitution on war powers, they also argued that the lawfulness of the capture was ruled out by the fact that Congress had not declared or confirmed war at the time of the captures.[114] For the Union, Richard Henry Dana, Jr, who had already acted successfully in earlier phases of *Amy Warwick*, responded with the 'double character' argument.[115] On the question of the president's authority, Dana asserted that war was '*a state of things*, and not an act of legislative will', and that the factual state of war had been brought into existence by the Confederacy itself.[116] This, then, was the crux of the *Prize Cases*: whether the legal existence of civil war was a matter of form alone or could be a question of fact. At issue, therefore, was the *Gazette* principle.

By a 5–4 majority – including Justice Grier, allegedly persuaded by Dana's eloquence[117] – the Supreme Court affirmed the lawfulness of the Union blockade and adopted the Vattelian view that, by virtue of its factual circumstances, an insurgency could acquire the status of a civil war under the law of nations. The court emphatically rejected the appellants' view that in a civil war a sovereign could not, 'for some unknown reason, exercise the rights of belligerents'.[118] For the Union to exercise lawful prize jurisdiction against neutral vessels on the high seas, the court

113 Ibid 641–643.
114 Ibid 649.
115 Ibid 654–657.
116 Ibid 659–660.
117 Stuart Benrath, *Squall across the Atlantic: American Civil War Prize Cases and Diplomacy* (University of California Press 1970) 27.
118 *Prize Cases*, 673–674.

held that 'a war must exist *de facto*.'[119] Formal recognition or declaration was not necessary, especially in an internal war:

> A civil war is never solemnly declared; it becomes such by its accidents – the number, power, and organization of the persons who originate and carry it on. When the party in rebellion occupy and hold in a hostile manner a certain portion of territory; have declared their independence; have cast off their allegiance; have organized armies; have commenced hostilities against their former sovereign, the world acknowledges them as belligerents, and the contest a *war*.[120]

As legal sources, the Court cited Vattel's threshold for civil war,[121] as well as Coke's old common law definition, according to which civil war existed '[w]hen the regular course of justice is interrupted by revolt, rebellion, or insurrection, so that the Courts of Justice cannot be kept open'.[122] In these sources the court found language allowing it to confirm the validity of the Union's belligerent war. By not contradicting the government's non-recognition of the Confederacy, the court nominally conformed to the customary practice of deferring to governments the question of war or no war, thereby upholding the *Gazette* principle. But in practice its conclusion – that the conflict was indeed a civil war as such under the law of nations – went beyond the government's official policy by giving judicial backing to the Union's use of belligerent rights on the high seas. However, throughout the war the government, for its part, would continue to reject any legal recognition of belligerency, insisting that it alone could exercise rights of war but that not they could not be exercised against it.[123]

For the Lincoln administration, the Supreme Court's findings in the *Prize Cases* turned out to be quite opportune. They confirmed the legality of the Union blockade and the applicability of the 'double character' doctrine permitting the Union's use of sovereign and belligerent powers at its pleasure.[124] Concerning relations with neutrals, the

119 Ibid 666.
120 Ibid 666–667.
121 Vattel, *Droit des gens*, III.18.292.
122 *Prize Cases*, 667–668. Compare Coke's *Institutes*, I.412.
123 Compare Neff, *Blue and Gray*, 26–27. Four judges dissented, as they were not so eager to let the essence of the *Gazette* principle yield to autonomous judicial review of the question of war or no war; in their view, it was the formal endorsement of Congress on 13 July 1861 that marked the start of war. Although this may seem a minor adjustment, it could have led to the Union bearing considerable liability for early captures in the war. See *Prize Cases*, 688–695, 698–699.
124 Compare Witt, *Lincoln's Code*, 155–156.

Supreme Court noted the formal declarations of neutrality that had been made abroad and considered neutrals to be bound by such declarations regardless of the Union's views. Neutral claimants were thus estopped from questioning the existence of their duties as neutrals and from 'ask[ing] a Court to affect a technical ignorance of the existence of a war, which all the world acknowledges to be the greatest civil war known in the history of the human race'.[125] Thus, the Supreme Court's ruling provided legal arguments for the Union government to assert its territorial sovereignty internally and internationally, defend its use of sovereign and belligerent rights against the Confederates, and hold neutrals responsible for the conduct of their nationals – all without lending any legal character to the Confederates. The findings were creatively indeterminate and open to debate, which left room for interpretation and manoeuvre on the Union's part, including the possibility of treating individual insurrectionists humanely without according them any status under international law.[126]

From the perspective of the classical doctrine of civil war, the *Prize Cases* represents a remarkable precedent, vindicating the doctrine's very existence. The decision showed how the act of blockading a port was to become a keystone in the recognition of belligerency and, thus, in the classical doctrine as a whole. When dealing with captured privateersmen, the courts could determine their status and fate by either the sovereign or belligerent route; as either rebels or insurgents, the men were at their mercy. Yet a blockade was an international, public act of commercial warfare having physical existence on seas that were common to all mankind. Even if scholars might debate whether the Union should have formally accepted the Confederacy as belligerents, the Supreme Court's findings were a clear acknowledgement that the war itself fell within the domain of Vattel's *Droit des gens* and the chapter on the classical law of civil war. And from the correspondence between the belligerents and neutrals it is clear that jurists and statesmen did in fact believe that a common doctrine of civil war existed in the law of nations, even if they might disagree on its details.

***

After the *Prize Cases*, the civil war continued on the high seas and on land for another two years, but from 1863 onwards the war took place mostly in the manner of an international war rather than a civil war. The Lieber

[125] *Prize Cases*, 669.

[126] Compare Randall, *Constitutional Problems*, 515–517.

Code is telling in this respect. Aside from the passages guaranteeing the Union's right to wage war on rebels and rely on military necessity against insurgents, the Lieber Code was essentially a synthesis of the general laws of war and, although born of the American Civil War, was arguably most famous for its legacy to international law. In the law of neutrality, most new legal developments likewise had more to do with general questions of neutrality than the problem of civil war.[127] The American Civil War saw the United States adopt the continuous voyage doctrine with respect to contraband cargo, to prevent neutrals from shipping goods via blockade runners through the West Indies, or landing their goods in the Mexican port of Matamoros and then transhipping them by land to Texas.[128] In the case of the *Circassian* (1865), the Supreme Court found that a vessel sailing from a neutral port 'with intent to violate a blockade' was liable to capture 'from the time of sailing'.[129] And in its *Springbok* decision, perhaps the most contentious expansion of US prize rules, it applied the continuous voyage and intended destination doctrines not to the ship but to its cargo irrespective of the ship.[130] This decision drew fierce criticism across all parts of Europe, both Britain and the continent.[131] Fifteen years after the decision, the Institut de droit international published a retrospective dissent rejecting the decision as 'subversive of an established rule of the law of maritime warfare' and, to use the words of Bluntschli, threatening to 'annihilate' neutral trade.[132] Even American textbooks thereafter began to admit that the decision had been extreme.

At a broader level, the driving legal principle in the expansive enforcement of the Union blockade and other belligerent measures was clear: these were matters of military necessity. From this perspective, the formal rules in the books had to be leveraged in pursuit of whatever ends the war effort required. At the time, this was far from scandalous; jurists (including Bluntschli) admitted, in principle, the imperatives of warfare,

127 For general treatises, see Stephen C. Neff, *The Rights and Duties of Neutrals* (Manchester University Press 2000) 115–123; Benrath, *Squall across the Atlantic*, esp 47–98.

128 *The Bermuda* (1865) 70 US 514; *The Peterhoff* (1867) 72 US 28, 59; Benrath, *Squall*, 47–62, 65; Neff, *Rights and Duties*, 116–117.

129 *The Circassian* (1865) 69 US 135.

130 Benrath, *Squall*, 85–98; *The Springbok* (1867) 72 US 1, 27–28, I Moore's *Arbitrations* 694–695.

131 See 7 Moore's *Digest* 726–739.

132 'Principes appliqués par la Cour suprême des États-Unis dans l'affaire du Springbok: Consultation' 14 *Revue de droit international et de législation comparée* (1882) 328–331. Translated in 7 Moore's *Digest* 731–732.

whether at sea or on land,[133] and although continuous voyage was always a disputed doctrine – based as it was on presumptions about hidden intentions – it continued to be invoked in the context of maritime warfare. Similar difficulties of enforcement had emerged at the time of the Napoleonic wars, with the British naval blockade and the Continental System, and would arise again in the future, such as in the Boer War of 1899 and between 1914 and 1945 in the world war era.[134] In 1865, when close blockade was still the ultimate weapon of war from a legal perspective, the doctrine of continuous voyage remained highly contentious to the core, rejected by most jurists, and if accepted, then only as a rare exception to the customary rules.

4.3 Aftermath: Belligerency and Responsibility

The American Civil War ended in April 1865 with the surrender of the forces under Robert E. Lee at Appomattox Court House, Virginia. Once again, the end of hostilities in a civil war was only the beginning of a long trail of post-conflict litigation. The majority of this legal aftermath took place within the constitutional domain of the newly reunited federation. As Union victory was total, there was no negotiated peace treaty or final settlement. Instead, the Confederate government was declared 'null and void' in its entirety by a presidential executive order.[135] Slavery was abolished once and for all through the Thirteenth Amendment to the Constitution, and various legal mechanisms emerged to address the lingering property issues caused by the civil war.[136] Among these was the Southern Claims Commission, which considered claims from former Union loyalists in Southern states, who requested compensation for losses caused by the Union forces.[137] Other key post-war projects included criminal prosecution of top Confederate leaders; here, a key question would again be whether a trial for treason was possible after

[133] Bluntschli, *Das moderne Völkerrecht der civilisirten Staaten als Rechtsbuch dargestellt* (Beckschen 1868) art 549.

[134] John W. Coogan, *The End of Neutrality: The United States, Britain, and Maritime Rights 1899–1915* (Cornell University Press 1981) 30–42, 53, 155–168, 213 *et passim*.

[135] Executive order of 9 May 1865, 13 US Stat 777.

[136] For an overview, see Neff, *Justice in Blue and Gray*, 238–245.

[137] Act of 3 March 1871, 16 US Stat 521; Randall, *Constitutional Problems*, 323–341; Frank W. Klingberg, 'The Southern Claims Commission: A Postwar Agency in Operations' 32 *Mississippi Valley Historical Review* (1945) 195–214. For the Supreme Court, loyalists included those who had originally been hostile to the Union but who had later become loyal. See *United States* v. *Klein* (1871) 80 US 128.

a formally recognised civil war, and once more the Union's case would be based on the 'double character' argument.[138] Trials for treason became less frequent as the restoration process advanced and Southern states were quietly rehabilitated. In the case of Jefferson Davis, as the federal laws would have led to the trial taking place in Virginia, the Union attorneys, including Richard Dana, gradually abandoned criminal proceedings in light of the risk of an obstinate Richmond jury mi finding Davis innocent of having taken part in the war.[139]

Throughout the post-war legal proceedings, the Union government benefited from a broad array of legal bases for asserting its policies as the victorious lawful government. The *Prize Cases* had affirmed the dual characterisation of the conflict as both rebellion and war, and thus helped legitimise the Union's exercise of both sovereign and belligerent rights against the Confederacy. At the same time, having consistently not recognised the Confederacy during the war, the Union could repudiate any attempts to invoke the laws of war and belligerent recognition against it. In 1867, a federal circuit court found that any payments to the Confederate government in accordance with insurgent debt sequestration laws had not discharged the debtor from their original lawful obligation towards the creditor, and thus the debt was still valid.[140] Chief Justice Chase, presiding, concluded on the validity of insurgent legal acts by distinguishing between successful revolution and suppressed insurgencies: 'If they succeed, rebellion becomes revolution, and the new government will justify its founders. If they fail, all their acts hostile to the rightful government are violations of law, and originate no rights which can be recognized by the courts of the nation whose authority and existence have been alike assailed.'[141] Notwithstanding this principle, the Supreme Court predictably held that ordinary administrative actions by the Confederacy and 'transactions in the ordinary course of civil society . . . are without blame, except when proved to have been entered into with actual intent to further invasion or insurrection'.[142] A similar proviso was included in the famous case of *Texas* v. *White*, in which the

[138] On these generally, see Nicoletti, *Secession on Trial*; Randall, *Constitutional Problems*, 96–117.

[139] Randall, *Constitutional Problems*, 113–116.

[140] *Shortridge* v. *Macon* (1867) 22 Fed Cas 20. For analysis, see Cynthia Nicoletti, *Secession on Trial: The Treason Prosecution of Jefferson Davis* (Cambridge University Press 2017) 217–219.

[141] *Shortridge* v. *Macon*, 23.

[142] *Thorington* v. *Smith* (1869) 75 US 1, 12.

Supreme Court found the Texas ordinance of secession to be 'absolutely null' but nevertheless recognised, *obiter*, that ordinary civil actions ought to be regarded as valid.[143]

No matter how null and void Confederate legal enactments were deemed, the Union courts still recognised Confederate belligerent actions at sea as having binding legal effects in terms of maritime and insurance law. When the merchantman *Golden Rocket* was captured and burned by the Confederate raider *Sumter*, a dispute arose over whether the owners could recover the loss under a policy that did not insure against belligerent capture but did insure against 'pirates and assailing thieves'.[144] Before a district court in 1864, Dana argued on behalf of the shipowners that the Confederates had not been recognised as belligerents and were thus pirates under the law of nations. The insurance company in turn contended that the insurance policies used 'the word "pirates" in that simple and ordinary sense in which it now is and immemorably has been known to the general commercial law of the civilized world; and not to describe offenders against some municipal criminal law, of some particular country'. The Supreme Court agreed with the respondents; citing US jurisprudence from the Spanish American revolutions that had recognised belligerent rights on both sides, it found that the capture and destruction of the *Golden Rocket* were not acts of piracy within the meaning of the policy.[145] In 1867, similar reasoning was applied by the Supreme Court in the case of *Mauran* v. *Insurance Company*. The arguments put forward were similar to those in the *Golden Rocket* and occasionally even used the same wording. Referring to past US practices in the Spanish American conflicts, the Supreme Court found that 'the so-called Confederate States' were 'as a matter of fact … in the possession of many of the highest attributes of government, sufficiently so to be regarded as the ruling or supreme power of the country, and hence captures under its commission were among those excepted out of the policy by the warranty of the insured.'[146]

The United States also found itself before international tribunals, responding to foreign claims arising from the American Civil War. In 1868, the United States and Mexico signed a claims convention and agreed to establish an arbitral tribunal to settle various private claims between the

143 *Texas* v. *White* (1869) 74 US 700, syllabus, 726, 733; Neff, *Justice in Blue and Gray*, 213.
144 *Dole* v. *New England Mutual Marine Ins Co* (1864) 7 Fed Cas 837; Dana's *Wheaton* 167.
145 *Dole* v. *New England Mutual Marine Ins Co* (1864) 842 and 850–851.
146 *Mauran* v. *Insurance Company* (1867) 73 US 1, 14.

nations.[147] Among the matters that came before the tribunal was the case of Prats, Pujol & Co., owners of the brig *M.A. Stevens*, which, together with its cargo of cotton, had been destroyed in Barataria by Confederate naval forces after the Union had taken possession of nearby New Orleans.[148] Prats based his claim specifically on the absence of formal recognition of belligerency by the United States and Mexico; according to him, this meant that the United States remained responsible for the damages.[149] The US commissioner Wadsworth recognised that the conflict had de facto been a civil war and that the relevant question was 'that of the responsibility of a government for injuries committed by its rebel enemies against aliens in time of civil war'.[150] But '[n]onresponsibility on the part of the United States . . . resulted from the *fact* of belligerency itself, and whether recognized or not by other governments'.[151] Citing Thomas Rutherford's lectures on Grotius, Wadsworth held as follows:

> The principle of non-responsibility for acts of rebel enemies in time of civil war rests upon the ground that the latter have withdrawn themselves by force of arms from the control and jurisdiction of the sovereign, putting it out of his power, so long as they make their resistance effectual, to extend his protection within the hostile territory to either strangers or his own subjects, between whom, in this respect, no inequality of rights can justly be asserted.[152]

The Mexican commissioner Palacios concurred, finding it 'self-evident' that there was no violation on the part of the United States, 'because the authors of the fact [were] neither *de facto* nor *de jure* authorities of the United States, nor of any of the States of the Union'.[153]

147 US–Mexico Claims Convention, 4 July 1868, 137 CTS 331. The majority of the claims before the tribunal were directed against Mexico, where internal disturbances continued long after the Treaty of Guadalupe Hidalgo and which only recently had seen the overthrow of the French puppet empire under Maximilian.

148 *Salvador Prats* v. *United States* (1868) III Moore's *Arbitrations* 2886.

149 Ibid 2888.

150 Ibid 2887.

151 Ibid 2888–2889.

152 Ibid 2890, citing Thomas Rutherford, *Institutes of Natural Law; Being the Substance of a Course of Lectures on Grotius de Jure Belli et Pacis* ([J. Bentham 1756] 2nd American edn, Baltimore 1832) 509: 'But such neglect does not make a nation accessory to the acts of subjects, that are in a state of rebellion, and have renounced their allegiance; or that are not within its territories: for, in these circumstances, the subjects, whatever they may be of right, are not under its jurisdiction in fact.'

153 *Prats* v. *United States*, 2893. Palacios' version of the rule was: 'It is the duty of the governments to protect in an efficient manner, against all kinds of unjust aggression, all persons residing within their jurisdiction and under the shelter of their laws. To this protection the alien

The question also came before a separate Anglo-American mixed claims commission on civil war claims, which sat in Washington during and after the Geneva arbitration of 1872.[154] When a joint commission convened in 1871 to draft the Treaty of Washington, the United States laid down its general proposition 'that no government is responsible for injuries done to the inhabitants of the country whether citizens or foreigners, by rebels or by alien enemies exercising in the particular locality or for the time being superior force against such government'.[155] When the mixed claims commission got to work in Washington in 1872, a total of 478 British and 19 American claims (amounting to approximately sixty million and one million dollars respectively) had already been filed by the claimants or would be filed shortly thereafter; of these, only seven claims were for property alleged to have been destroyed by the Confederate forces.[156]

Early on in its proceedings, in December 1871, the Commission made two decisions that had a particular bearing on the question of state responsibility over rebels. The case of Edward Barritt concerned a small claim of 200 pounds for unpaid 'cotton bonds' issued by the Confederates. Though insignificant in amount, the matter involved a principle of the highest importance. After deliberating, the commission unanimously dismissed the claim and affirmed that the United States was not liable for the payment of debts contracted by the Confederate authorities.[157] Its reasoning was straightforward: 'Persons contracting with the so-called Confederate States voluntarily assumed the risk of

residents are no less entitled than the citizens, but it would be wrong, however, to pretend a better right to it in the former case than in the latter.' There are interesting parallels between Palacios' opinion and the case made in Carlos Calvo, 'De la non-responsabilité des États à raison des pertes et dommages éprouvés par Étrangers en temps de troubles intérieurs ou de guerres civiles' 1 *Revue de droit international et de législation comparée* (1st ser 1869) 417. See also Greenman's reading of Prats at Greenman, *State Responsibility and Rebels*, 89–107.

154 Like the Geneva arbitration, the Washington claims commission was also constituted under the Treaty of Washington (arts 12–17). Its purpose was to investigate the remaining claims unrelated to the Confederate cruisers.

155 I Moore's *Arbitrations* 684. Moore notes: 'On this proposition the following citations were made: Lord Stanley, June 17, 1870, Hansard, 3d series, III. 1306; Rutherford's Institutes, 509; Vattel, Book 2, ch. 6, sec. 73; Phillimore Int. Law, I. sec. 218; Calvo, Derecho Internacional, I.387, Torres Caicedo, Union Latino-Americano, 343, 348 (dispatches of Prince Schwartzenberg to Baron Hotter, April 14, 1850, and Count Nesselrode to Baron Brunnow, May [?], 1850), Mauran *v.* Insurance Co., 6 Wallace, 14, Opinions of At. Gen. XII. 21, Mr. Marcy to the Count de Sartiges, Sen. Ex. Doc. 9, 35 Cong. 1 sess.'

156 I Moore's *Arbitrations* 692. Some 167 claims had already been adjudicated during the war in US prize courts, and Britain mostly accepted the prize decisions, with the exception of the *Springbok* affair. See I Moore's *Arbitrations* 685–686, 694–695.

157 I Moore's *Arbitrations* 695.

such failure and accepted its obligations, subject to the paramount rights of the parent state by force to crush the rebel organization and seize all its assets and property, whether hypothecated by it or not to its creditors.'[158] In the case of John Hanna, the commission ruled more broadly that the United States could not be held liable for injuries caused by the acts of rebels over whom they could exercise no control, and which acts they had no power to prevent.[159] As a consequence, a large number of claims concerning the responsibility of the United States over damages caused by the Confederacy were never presented to the commission. The US commissioner Frazer opined that because Britain had recognised the Confederates as belligerents, its subjects were bound by that act of recognition. He added that the outcome might been the same even if there had been no recognition, as it was 'public history' that the Confederacy had engaged in a 'formidable rebellion' at the time.[160] In a hark back to *Shortridge* v. *Macon*, Frazer also noted the distinction between ultimately successful insurgents, who might bear the responsibility of civil war as the new lawful government, and the Confederates, who had ultimately been defeated and whose rebellion had merely 'interrupted the course of lawful government without the fault of the latter'.[161] The work of the tribunal therefore focused primarily on damages caused by the US armed forces and its authorities to British nationals and their vessels and property interests. In its final award, the mixed claims commission recorded that it had disallowed all US claims on various grounds and awarded a sum of 1,929,819 dollars, to be paid in gold by the United States to the government of Great Britain.[162]

As a whole, the post-war claims commissions concluded that the United States could not be held liable for injuries caused by the acts of rebels over whom they could exercise no control and whose actions they had no power to prevent. One can easily understand why the United States would categorically refuse to be held responsible for a civil war that had been waged on the broadest scale imaginable. At the same time, the

[158] *Barrett's Case*, award of 14 December 1871, in *Papers Relating to the Treaty of Washington* (US Government Printing Office 1874) vol 6, 154–159 at 157.

[159] *Hanna's Case*, award of 13 December 1871, in *Papers Relating to the Treaty of Washington*, vol 6, 56 at 58; III Moore's *Arbitrations* 2982; 29 RIAA 143.

[160] Frazer's opinion in *Papers Relating to the Treaty of Washington*, vol 6, 239–240; 29 RIAA 144–145.

[161] Ibid.

[162] Final award, 25 September 1873, I Moore's *Arbitrations* 698; *Papers Relating to the Treaty of Washington*, vol 6, 229–230. We should also note that the Geneva tribunal, working in parallel, awarded 15,500,000 dollars to the United States. See Chapter 5.

precedent of the civil war consolidated its own legal position for the future. In the coming decades, US lawyers would argue that non-responsibility for rebels was the main rule in international law, but state responsibility could arise through a government's proven lack of due diligence in suppressing an insurrection. Carlos Calvo also included the case of the United States in his famous 1869 article, in which he argued for giving precedence to state sovereignty, as the customary rule, over investment protection in civil wars.[163] But as Kathryn Greenman has shown, during the following decades the exception became the dominant rule in much of US foreign policy and, by extension, in the international law of state responsibility more generally.[164]

***

The Geneva arbitration was instructed to examine whether or not Great Britain had breached its neutral duties during the war. At the outset of the conflict, the Confederacy had constructed a small fleet of agile vessels in British shipyards. They sailed them out to the high seas, where they had them refitted as armed commerce raiders. These ships had proven to be the insurgents' most effective naval arm, with the *CSS Alabama* tallying more than eighty victories. The Geneva arbitration enquired into the duty of care that required Britain, as a neutral, to prevent the fitting of such vessels and the liability commensurate with any breach of that duty. Ultimately, the *Alabama* arbitrations led to a restatement of the international law of neutrality and constituted another *cause célèbre* for the international arbitration movement, enthralling the new Institut de droit international and the international legal community around it as a welcome relief from the grim tragedies of the contemporaneous Franco-Prussian War.

The Geneva arbitration will be discussed in Chapter 5. But it is useful to mention here another important by-product of the war: the first common synthesis of the classical doctrine of civil war since Vattel. During the war, American jurists involved in the various litigations generally reaffirmed the validity of Vattel's familiar principles on civil war, after which European scholars then re-imported them into Europe alongside Francis Lieber's code on the laws of war. To use the words of Arnold McNair, international legal doctrine concerning the recognition of belligerency and its consequences 'can be said to "crystallize out"' with

[163] Calvo, 'De la non-responsabilité des États', 422, 427.

[164] Kathryn Greenman, *State Responsibility and Rebels: The History and Legacy of Protecting Investment against Revolution* (Cambridge University Press 2021) 10–18, 120–136.

the American Civil War.[165] The irony was that its crystallization in the broader field of international legal scholarship came just as it was falling out of use in state practice.

4.4 The Men of 1866 and the Doctrine of Belligerent Recognition

4.4.1 *An American Synthesis: From Wheaton to Dana*

At the start of the American Civil War, the law of civil war was still a subject of debate, but its fundamental components were already available in legal scholarship. In their attempts to ally state practice to a presumed international body of norms, jurists adopted various approaches, which often depended on how closely affiliated they were with the Union war effort. One example was Henry Halleck's *International Law*[166] and its abridged version *Elements of International Law* (1866). In his original *International Law*, Halleck produced his own broad taxonomy of the different kinds of wars from a military scholar's perspective, according to their scale, aims, and other features.[167] His approach followed Vattel on the distinction between insurrections – which were internal affairs – and civil wars, where the laws of war might apply; any recognition of the independence or sovereignty of a revolted province was 'a question of policy and prudence only' to be made by the sovereign legislative or executive power of the state and not by any subordinate authority.[168] By 1866, Halleck had incorporated the Union position into his *Elements*. While, as a general rule, the laws of war might apply to belligerent intercourse in a civil war, the use of belligerent rights would as such imply no recognition of the insurgent government, 'nor does it afford any ground whatever to neutrals for acknowledging or treating such rebels or their government as constituting an independent or belligerent power'.[169] This was both a reflection of the Union's 'double character' doctrine and a rejection of the view that the use of belligerent powers by the lawful government would in itself imply tacit recognition of the rebels. Halleck also reflected the Union's views by considering guerrilla and irregular troops as prohibited by the modern laws of war and by defining their military actions as unlawful robbery and

165 I McNair, *Opinions* 138.

166 H. W. Halleck, *International Law; Or, Rules Regulating the Intercourse of States in Peace and War* (D. Van Nostrand 1861).

167 Ibid 330.

168 Ibid 73–76; see also 184 on legation.

169 H. W. Halleck, *Elements of International Law and Laws of War* (Lippincott 1866) ch XIV, esp 153.

murder – which did not include 'levies en masse' and properly commissioned privateers.[170]

Like Halleck's *Elements*, the Lieber Code was closely aligned with the Union's positions on questions relating to the legal status of insurgents. It explicitly rejected the use of belligerent powers as constituting tacit recognition of belligerency. Although the code briefly distinguished between civil wars, insurrections, and rebellions in a Vattelian manner, it contained no clear affirmation that the international laws of war and neutrality could apply to both belligerents on an equal footing by virtue of the factual scale and circumstances of the conflict. Lieber mostly avoided the basic issue of belligerent recognition, and instead explored the laws of war irrespective of the characterisation of individual conflicts. Apart from the protection of military necessity, which pervaded its provisions, the Code's legacy on the law of civil war lay essentially in protecting the position of a lawful and organised government against irregular insurgents. Its focus was less on ensuring non-discriminatory humanitarian protection for all combatants in armed conflicts. In the end, the Lieber Code was not a study of the law of civil war but rather a treatise on the public laws of war, and this is how it was received among European jurists, who were soon reading it as a representation of the customary laws of land warfare in international wars.[171]

In posthumous editions of Henry Wheaton's *Elements of International Law* the doctrine of the recognition of belligerency was separated from Union policies and defined as a concept of international law.[172] The original *Elements* studied the law of civil war mainly on the basis of Vattel and Martens, which Wheaton accepted for the most part, with some additions of his own related to the time of the Spanish American revolutions. A state might acquire sovereignty by separating from another state, and for the duration of a civil war foreign states would be free to remain neutral under the law of nations, provided they maintained their neutrality impartially.[173] Foreign powers also had a right of intervention, based on the general sovereign right of states to make war upon one another, 'as the positive law of nations makes no distinction, in this respect, between a just and an unjust war'.[174] This of course

[170] Ibid 174–175.
[171] Witt, *Lincoln's Code*, 342–345; James Crossland, *War, Law and Humanity: The Campaign to Control Warfare, 1853–1914* (Bloomsbury 2018) 121–122.
[172] Henry Wheaton, *Elements of International Law* (2 vols, B. Fellowes 1836).
[173] Ibid, vol I, 91–99. Compare Halleck, *International Law*, 74.
[174] Wheaton, *Elements of International Law*, 93.

conformed with experiences from the American Revolution, and the generally favourable position Wheaton took on revolutions fought by 'a province or colony shaking off its sovereignty' also reflected his experience as reporter to the Supreme Court during the Spanish American revolutions.[175] But any choice between recognition and non-recognition of insurgents remained, in accordance with the *Gazette* principle, the preserve of governments, 'a question of policy and prudence only'.[176]

Wheaton's *Elements* was revised by William Beach Lawrence in 1855 and 1863 and by Richard Henry Dana in 1866. Each of these two glossators added hundreds of pages of footnotes and commentary to the text, and in their 1863 and 1866 editions they understandably covered several matters touching on the contemporaneous civil war.[177] They also elaborated recognition of belligerency into a concept of international law, probably for the first time in textbook form.[178] This took the form of lengthy footnotes below the passage where Wheaton originally discussed the legal options open to foreign states during a revolution. In 1863, Lawrence inserted there his own analysis, which ran to some four pages and in which he stated that 'the *recognition of belligerent rights* in a colony or portion of a State, in revolt from, or in opposition to the metropolis, is not to be confounded with the acknowledgement of the absolute independence of such province or colony'.[179] He then listed a number of precedents and sources for legal arguments on this distinction, beginning with John Paul Jones' prizes taken to Texel during the American Revolution, and concluded with his own tentative remarks about the status of recognition 'in the pending hostilities between the United States and the so-called Confederate States of America'.[180] The sixth edition, by Dana, with its famous footnote 15 in the same place, was published shortly after the conclusion of the war and therefore benefited from the

175 Ibid 96.

176 Ibid 98.

177 There is significant overlap between the work of the two authors. Dana's edition ultimately became the definitive one and is reproduced in the Classics series in 1936. On the bitter copyright disputes between the two editors, see *Lawrence* v. *Dana* (1869) 15 Fed Cas 26; G. G. Wilson's preface to Dana's *Wheaton*, 22a–23a.

178 The expression 'recognition of belligerency' was probably coined earlier. It is example prominent, for example, in George Bemis' pamphlet *Hasty Recognition of Rebel Belligerency and Our Right to Complain of It* (A. Williams 1865), but this was a broadside focussed on the *Alabama* dispute rather than a general exposition of the doctrine in international law.

179 Henry Wheaton, *Elements of International Law* (William Beach Lawrence ed., Little, Brown 1863) I.2.7, 40 fn 16. Emphasis added.

180 Ibid.

author's intimate knowledge of the case law and state practice.[181] Dana chose 'recognition of belligerency' as the explicit heading of his gloss, presenting the concept as a principle of law, and argued that recognition was ultimately a question of fact rather than discretion (as the *Prize Cases* had done). He paid particular attention to the maritime nature of the doctrine and briefly recounted the ways in which the legal status of belligerents and neutrals differed from that of friendly powers in peace, distinguishing between rules that applied in situations of war and those that applied where there was no war:

> If the contest is a war, all foreign citizens and officers, whether executive or judicial are to follow one line of conduct. If it is not a war, they are to follow a totally different line. If it is a war, the commissioned cruisers of both sides may stop, search, and capture the foreign merchant-vessel; and that vessel must make no resistance, and must submit to adjudication by a prize court. If it is not a war, the cruisers of neither party can stop or search the foreign merchant-vessel; and that vessel may resist all attempts in that direction, and the ships of war of the foreign State may attack and capture any cruiser persisting in the attempt. If it is war, foreign nations must await the adjudication of prize tribunals. If it is not war, no such tribunal can be opened. If it is a war, the parent State may institute a blockade *jure gentium* of the insurgent ports, which foreigners must respect; but, if it is not a war, foreign nations, having large commercial intercourse with the country, will not respect a closing of insurgent ports by paper decrees only. If it is a war, the insurgent cruisers are to be treated by foreign citizens and officials, at sea and in port, as lawful belligerents. If it is not a war, those cruisers are pirates, and may be treated as such. If it is a war, the rules and risks respecting carrying contraband, or despatches, or military persons come into play. If it is not a war, they do not. Within foreign jurisdiction, if it is a war, acts of the insurgents, in the way of preparation and equipments for hostility, may be breaches of neutrality laws; while, if it is not a war, they do not come into that category, but into the category of piracy, or of crimes by municipal law.[182]

Dana portrayed belligerent recognition as both a right and a responsibility for foreign states and noted the potential unfriendly nature of premature recognition. While endorsing the *Gazette* principle, he also stressed that merchants and citizens looked to their governments for clarity and guidance in respect of foreign civil wars. Foreign governments were under pressure or possibly even duty-bound to either recognise or deny belligerency:

> It is not fit that cases should be left to be decided as they may arise, by private citizens, or naval or judicial officers, at home or abroad, by sea or

[181] Dana's *Wheaton*, pt I § 23 fn 15, pp 29–32 in 1936 Classics edn.

[182] Ibid 30–31 fn 15.

> land. It is, therefore, the custom of nations for the political department of a foreign State to make the decision. It owes it to its own citizens, to the contending parties, and to the peace of the world, to make that decision seasonably.

The effects of belligerent recognition followed the logic that international laws of war could, and should, apply to a civil war. Dana argued that insurgents were not the only ones to benefit from these effects: while insurgents would acquire '*quasi* political recognition', the lawful government would in return be relieved of any future international responsibility for acts of the insurgent government – a principle that was to be reaffirmed by the post-war mixed claims commissions.[183]

Dana's summary was based on a review of correspondence between the British and American governments during the American Civil War He now had the benefit of hindsight when addressing questions remaining open from the time of his involvement in the *Prize Cases*. He was also free to record his position on those questions for the post-war world as a jurist and scholar less directly dependent on his government's view. Although what he wrote did not directly contradict the US position, his summary is a masterly synthesis of the basic principles underlying the belligerent and neutral views. It also included key references to several first-hand sources, which would be taken up in later treatises on civil war. Dana's edition marked a high point in the classical doctrine of civil war and continued to reverberate in monographs on the law of civil war well into the twentieth century.[184]

4.4.2 From America to Europe

Lieber's teachings from the American Civil War were transplanted to Europe by his loyal correspondent Johann Caspar Bluntschli, who held the chair of international law in Heidelberg.[185] Prior to the American

[183] In addition to the summary on the recognition of belligerency, Dana also produced a thirty-five-page general summary on neutrality and non-intervention. Ibid 450–484 fn 215.

[184] For example, Carlos Wiesse, *Reglas de derecho internactional aplicable a las guerras civiles* (Viuda Galland 1893) 15–16, 142–143; Marquis Ramón de Dalmau y de Olivart, *Del reconocimiento de beligerancia y sus efectos inmediatos* (Tipolitografía de L. Péant é Hijos 1895) 61–64, 97–99; Antoine Rougier, *Les guerres civiles et le droit des gens* (Larose 1903) 374 fn 1; Hans Wehberg, 'La guerre civile et le droit international' 63 *Collected Courses of Hague Academy of International Law* (1938) 24, 89, 107.

[185] On Bluntschli's influence, see Dietrich Schindler, 'J. C. Bluntschli's Contribution to the Law of War' in Marcelo G. Kohen (ed), *Promoting Justice, Human Rights and Conflict*

Civil War, textbooks in Europe continued to explain that a state of war could lawfully exist only between sovereigns, who had exclusive access to public war, the highest degree of self-help under the law of nations.[186] After the war, Bluntschli's major textbook on international law – initially published in part as *Das moderne Kriegsrecht* (1866) and then in full as *Das moderne Völkerrecht* (1868) – revised such thinking with a summary of the new doctrine of belligerent recognition. Although Bluntschli defined war as primarily a legal dispute between belligerent states over public law,[187] he now added that in an insurrection an armed party not authorised by any established state power to exercise violence is nevertheless to be considered a belligerent, insofar as it has been organised as an independent military force, and is fighting in a state's stead and in good faith towards public law.[188] In his 1868 version, *Das moderne Völkerrecht*, he likewise justified belligerent recognition on the grounds of the general interests of humanity.[189] Bluntschli refined his thinking on the preconditions for recognising belligerency in his famous opinion on the *Alabama* affair, where he suggested that recognition of belligerency could be given when the insurgent faction 'a) is organised as a military force; b) observes the laws of war in their conduct of hostilities, and c) believes to be fighting in good faith in place of a State ["an States statt"] in defence of its public law'.[190] This was an early prototype in developing formal criteria for the recognition of insurgents who might deserve the protection of the laws of war. *Das moderne Völkerrecht*, especially in its French translation, helped disseminate the principles of the law of civil war across sovereign European states just as international law was emerging as a profession to give voice to the legal conscience of the civilised world.

Resolution through International Law: Liber Amicorum Lucius Caflisch (Martinus Nijhoff 2007) 437–454; James Crossland, *War, Law and Humanity: The Campaign to Control Warfare, 1853–1914* (Bloomsbury 2018) 121–122. On the transplantation and adoption of the Lieber Code in Europe, see Eyal Benvenisti and Doreen Lustig, 'Monopolizing War: Codifying the Laws of War to Reassert Governmental Authority, 1856–1874' 31 *European Journal of International Law* (2020) 165 fn 261.

186 See August Wilhelm Heffter, *Das europäische Völkerrecht der Gegenwart* (G. H. Schroeder 1867) § 114, making an exception for the Hanseatic League.

187 Johann Caspar Bluntschli, *Das moderne Kriegsrecht der civilisirten Staaten als Rechtsbuch dargestellt* (Beckschen, 1866), § 2.1.

188 Ibid § 3.

189 Ibid § 512.1.

190 Johann Caspar Bluntschli, 'Opinion impartiale sur la question de l'Alabama et sur la manière de la résoudre' 2 *Revue de droit international et de législation comparée* (1870) 452.

Thanks to British recognition of the Confederacy during the war, the *Trent* affair, and the *Alabama* affair, Britain was the United States' principal European interlocutor on questions of belligerency and neutrality. The American Civil War reversed the roles in which British and American lawyers were customarily cast, for during those years the vocabulary of neutrality informed the work of the British civilians rather than their usual imperial interests of prize law. During the war, public commentators like Vernon Harcourt ('Historicus') and John Stuart Mill commented on the war from several angles, defending the British position in the matter of the *Trent* while asserting the justice of the Union anti-slavery cause and seeking justifications for British neutrality in past US case law.[191] Their ranks were not united, with some defending the Confederacy in the interests of the British textile and cotton trade and others calling for diplomatic intervention in the conflict. Pressure mounted when critics from the United States, who were following these discussions, published scathing indictments of British neutrality policies.[192] In return, the Oxford professor Mountague Bernard released in 1870 a comprehensive treatise on British neutrality policy during the American Civil War,[193] which earned him a place on the joint commission that negotiated the Treaty of Washington in 1871. In his treatise Bernard goes into the beginnings of Confederate privateering and the declaration of the Union blockade. Among the many US documents included in the annexes are the *Prize Cases* judgment finding that the specific nature of the blockade made it justified as the exercise of a belligerent right.[194] The war, he argued, 'came as a fact, which [Britain] could not help recognizing'.[195] Against accusations of premature recognition, Bernard stressed the unitary character of belligerent rights and the tacit recognition that their exercise would imply.[196] He portrayed the recognition of belligerency as an essentially American doctrine and suggested that '[w]e have now seen how painful and difficult it may be for a nation to submit its own feelings and interests to a rule which seems just and expedient when applied to others'.[197]

[191] Vernon Harcourt, *Letters by Historicus on Some Questions of International Law* (Macmillan 1863); John Stuart Mill, *The Contest in America* (Little, Brown 1862).

[192] George Bemis, *Precedents of American Neutrality in Reply to the Speech of Sir Roundell Palmer* (Little, Brown 1864); George Bemis, *Hasty Recognition of Rebel Belligerency and Our Right to Complain of It* (A. Williams 1865).

[193] Bernard, *Historical Account* .

[194] Ibid 78–105.

[195] Ibid 41.

[196] Ibid 113; the following pages cover the theory of belligerent recognition.

[197] Ibid 500.

Mountague Bernard's advocacy of the British position continued in Geneva, where he was counsel to the British delegation. During the work of the Geneva tribunal, the doctrine of the recognition of belligerency was confirmed as a settled principle of international law. As Bluntschli had already suggested in his famous legal opinion in 1870, after the conclusion of the American Civil War there remained no credible grounds to deny that the conflict satisfied the factual requirements of civil war under international law, whether measured according to the criteria of Vattel, Bluntschli, or any other author. The fact that Britain's recognition of Confederate belligerency was ultimately accepted as lawful made it possible for international lawyers to consider their doctrine of civil war as valid law in a manner that transcended political expediency. In 1873, Mountague Bernard and Johann Caspar Bluntschli were both among original founders of the Institut de droit international, and both were involved when that body adopted the 'Three Rules of Washington' as international law and resolved to promote their acceptance among all civilised nations.[198] Yet, as the states appearing before the Geneva tribunal had agreed on future principles of neutrality, to which they pledged to adhere, the process of eradicating irregular warfare from the high seas begun a decade and a half earlier with the Declaration of Paris had reached its conclusion. This transformation of the laws of maritime war and neutrality set in motion the rapid decline of the classical doctrine of civil war in state practice.

198 Resolution of 30 August 1875, in 1 *Annuaire de l'Institut de droit international* (1877) 33; James Brown Scott, *Resolutions of the Institute of International Law* (Oxford University Press 1916) 12–14.

5

The Decline of the Classical Doctrine in State Practice

The classical doctrine of civil war began to decline immediately after the American Civil War. Recognition of belligerency – its new central tenet – failed to become a regular practice among states even though scholars embraced it and stressed its validity and importance.[1] The more formal and explicit became the law of civil war, the more state practice gravitated into an indeterminate grey zone of non-recognised insurgencies, with governments reluctant to take a formal stance or accept binding obligations in respect of foreign civil wars. The reasons for this were manifold, ranging from changes in attitudes towards the laws of war and neutrality to new developments in technology, communications, and the industrialisation of warfare.

The latter half of the nineteenth century was altogether transformative for the international system and the law governing it. It was an 'age of capital' heralding new ideals about free trade and the international protection of private property, but also an era of empire and of public nation-states.[2] After 1848, continental Europe shifted gradually from reactionary legitimism towards enlightened monarchies, constitutionalism, and even popular sovereignty, and, increasingly, the fault-lines dividing legitimate governments and revolutionary malcontents ran not only between crowned elites and the people but also between factions within the popular masses themselves.[3] Recourse to popular will, measured through plebiscites in individual territorial disputes and in the Italian and German unifications, saw calls for revolution and self-determination challenge the sanctity of formal treaty arrangements that had defined the boundaries and territories of the continent since the

[1] See Roscoe Oglesby, *Internal War and the Search for Normative Order* (Martinus Nijhoff 1971) 102, 108–110.

[2] See Eric Hobsbawm, *The Age of Capital 1848–1875* ([1975] Vintage 1996) and *The Age of Empire 1875–1914* (Vintage 1989).

[3] Bo Stråth, *Europe's Utopias of Peace* (Bloomsbury 2016) 132–139; Karl Marx and Friedrich Engels, *The Manifesto of the Communist Party* ([1848] Progress (Moscow) 1977).

Middle Ages.[4] Amidst all this, the monarchs and emperors of Europe found mutual support through international law, codifying modern laws of war and modelling them in such a way as to give preference to formal, organised, and public warfare conducted by regular armed forces over irregular popular resistance. The result was an internationalised state monopoly on violence that resembled a new form of legitimism, a cosmopolitan vision to defend the sovereign authorities of the 'civilised world' against radical challenges from below, within, and outside their familiar establishments.[5]

We can identify at least four key elements in this period that led to the decline and desuetude of the classical law of civil war in state practice. The first of these was the gradual monopolisation of war, beginning with the abolition of privateers in the 1856 Declaration of Paris. Since privateers were usually the only marine arm available to insurgents, their abolition – and consequently their non-recognition and rejection in foreign ports – meant that insurgents' access to the concrete means of bringing about a condition of belligerency and neutrality in a conflict was restricted. The model was replicated on land during the negotiation of the modern laws of war, where states defined lawful war primarily as one taking place among their regular troops, and relegated irregular citizen fighters to the periphery of humanitarian law.

Secondly, the widespread approbation the Treaty of Washington and the Geneva arbitration received from international lawyers helped propagate the conviction that there were common international standards for neutral duties and that disregard of the obligations they entailed might constitute unlawful acts and lead to state responsibility. As the standards and stakes of neutrality rose higher, states lost their appetite for it. During international wars neutrals often had no choice about their role, but when foreign insurrections were at issue they could choose simply to reject the duties neutrality imposed. This is indeed what they did.

Consequently, instead of declaring neutrality, states increasingly chose to treat all foreign civil wars as de facto disturbances and internal matters of states. This was the third element. The United States, in particular, developed its own doctrine – 'recognition of insurgency' – which

[4] Edward J. Kolla, *Sovereignty, International Law, and the French Revolution* (Cambridge University Press 2017) 285–289.

[5] Eyal Benvenisti and Doreen Lustig, 'Monopolizing War: Codifying the Laws of War to Reassert Governmental Authority, 1856–1874' 31 *European Journal of International Law* (2020) 127–169. My thanks are due to Benvenisti and Lustig for their thorough research and excellent findings, from which I have drawn great benefit in this chapter.

essentially meant that it enacted its neutrality laws without conceding any belligerent rights to the insurgents or acknowledging any other binding effects under international law. This served their regional interests well and gave legal scholars much to debate about, but it meant that US foreign policy towards rebels was consigned to the indeterminate realm of state discretion and legal pragmatism.

Fourthly, the consequence was that most civil wars were from then on fought under formal peacetime conditions. In an era of free trade and increasing protection of private property on the high seas, this 'normalisation' of colonial and counter-revolutionary violence was paralleled by a corresponding rise and proliferation of general principles of state responsibility. In addition to neutral governments incurring responsibility for private actions of their nationals, governments of states fighting rebels could be held liable for damages caused to foreign nationals resulting from the state's failure to maintain order in its territory.

5.1 The Monopolisation of War and the Internationalisation of Neutrality

5.1.1 *The Abolition of Privateers and the Question of Guerrilla Warfare*

The Declaration of Paris had its roots in the Crimean War, during which long-time maritime rivals France and Britain found themselves temporarily united in an alliance against Russia. To enable them to reach a mutual understanding on neutral rights in the conflict, Britain agreed to momentarily waive part of the belligerent rights it customarily exercised under the *Consolato* rule, accepting instead that free ships made free goods, whereas the French, for their part, conceded that enemy colours would not taint neutral cargoes.[6] At the 1856 peace conference this merchant-friendly consensus was then perpetuated in the open multilateral treaty known as the Declaration of Paris, in which there were also provisions on the effectiveness of blockades and the prohibition of privateers.[7] The declaration created considerable dissension domestically, especially in Britain. Scholars have indeed occasionally asked why the maritime hegemon chose to submit to the treaty's limitations on belligerent powers. This could be explained, for example, by the obvious

[6] British declaration, 28 March 1854, 46 BFSP 36; Stephen C. Neff, *Rights and Duties of Neutrals* (Manchester University Press 2000) 97–99.

[7] Declaration of Paris, 16 April 1856, 115 CTS 1.

benefit to free trade for the world's largest merchant fleet, or by Britain's calculation that by the mid nineteenth century the Royal Navy would have the capacity to establish effective blockades in any part of the world and thus less need for the general law of visit and search in its operations.[8] Lemnitzer's research points to a particular privateering scare in Britain during the early Crimean War, as it was thought that Russia might try to commission US privateers against Britain and that the US had an interest in maintaining the legality of privateering in case of any future conflicts with Britain or other Europeans.[9] The Crimean War apart, Britain and the other European powers stood to benefit greatly from the permanent abolition of privateers, as this would offer them legal guarantees against colonial insurgents and neutral interventionism in the remote parts of their empires. As it happened, the impact of the Declaration of Paris was soon demonstrated by the difficulties the American Confederacy encountered. Lacking access to foreign ports, it was forced to abandon its privateering war and to replace it with commerce raiders and private blockade runners.[10] After the war, the United States, too, integrated the principles of the declaration in its policies for good, even if it never actually signed the document.

This privateers' sunset was further precipitated by technological revolutions that caused privateering to become largely obsolete, besides being prohibited. The superiority of new ironclad steamships was evident after the Battle of Hampton Roads, and during the second half of the nineteenth century the construction of warships and merchantmen diverged significantly. Warships and their armaments had to be designed and constructed exclusively as such, and the conversion of civilian vessels for armed cruising became less practicable. At the same time, the proliferation of railroads challenged the usefulness of sporadic maritime depredations and even blockades. It was no longer necessary for very heavy cargoes, including arms and other contraband, to be shipped directly to the recipient; they could instead be offloaded at some convenient port and transported overland to the regions where the armies or insurgents needed them. This meant that contraband could be shipped under

8 Neff, *Rights and Duties of Neutrals*, 98; Maartje Abbenhuis, *An Age of Neutrals: Great Power Politics, 1815–1914* (Cambridge University Press 2014) 88–93.

9 Jan Martin Lemnitzer, *Power, Law and the End of Privateering* (Palgrave MacMillan 2014) 36–43.

10 Lemnitzer, *End of Privateering*, esp 179, 129–134. See also Mountague Bernard, *A Historical Account of the Neutrality of Great Britain during the American Civil War* (Longmans, Green, Reader, and Dyer 1870) 247–282.

neutral flags to neutral ports, which complicated their capture at sea and circumvented traditional 'close' maritime blockades. Further inventions after the turn of the century rendered private maritime depredations not only ineffective but essentially impossible; the wireless telegraph, the torpedo submarine, the aeroplane, and the practice of aerial bombing took economic and infrastructural warfare to entirely unprecedented levels. From its inception in 1911, aerial bombardment was found to be a particularly cost-effective weapon for suppressing colonial resistance and insurgencies, with the 'pilot as policeman, bomb as baton'.[11] The air soon superseded the sea as the decisive arena for civil wars, and aviation became a favourite method of asymmetric warfare favoured by governments and used against rebels and civilians.

The abolition of privateering formed the backdrop to a global transition from civil wars fought at sea to land-based guerrilla insurrections. Deprived of the opportunity to fly their flags on the high seas, insurgents lacked a practical means to impose a condition of belligerency and neutrality in the international domain. In land war, the legality of irregular and non-state troops was similarly under pressure from states that sought to impose their ancient monopoly of violence on the battlefields as well as in peacetime. The term 'guerrilla warfare' had been coined during the Peninsular War, and irregular methods had constituted a significant challenge for the United States army in both the Mexican War and the American Civil War. According to Witt, uncertainty over the legal treatment of partisans, bushwhackers, and other irregular fighters was a major reason for the commissioning of Francis Lieber's research, out of which his famous code was born.[12] The dilemma facing Union forces was not just whether or not the laws of war should protect commissioned irregular combatants, but rather how to legally challenge the manner in which the Confederates had embraced irregular partisan rangers and handed out such commissions to self-organised guerrilla bands. The response of the Union forces was to reserve the possibility of determining the legal status of combatants and captives on the basis of their factual circumstances and behaviour rather than whether they held a formal

[11] Thomas Hippler, *Governing from the Skies: A Global History of Aerial Bombing* (Verso 2017) xix, citing Sven Lindqvist, *A History of Bombing* (New Press 2003) 74 and R. P. Hearne, *Airships in Peace and War* (John Lane 1910).

[12] John Fabian Witt, *Lincoln's Code: The Laws of War in American History* (Free Press 2013) 187–196.

commission or not.[13] In this regard, the monopolisation of war went further on land than at sea. Although admiralty courts had in the past occasionally rejected the legality of individual privateer commissions,[14] they usually followed the *Gazette* principle and applied the government's recognition policy when considering the ship's papers in each case. By contrast, field officers on land were now at liberty to invoke a wider margin of discretion.

***

Debates over the distinction between lawful combatants and unlawful criminals continued throughout the major peace conferences of the late nineteenth century. Typically, civil society actors, pacifists, humanitarians, and representatives from smaller states would propose broad protection of all human life in conflict, while the delegates of the major powers and army experts would defend the principle of military necessity and advocate the minimum requirements of civilised warfare. Such debates transplanted the problem of recognition from the abstract international plane to the scale of the battlefield. Governments trying to determine the limits of the legitimacy of popular movements often looked to theories of sovereign statehood for answers. These theories were notable for the legal distinction they drew between the authoritative public realm, on the one hand, and the private sphere and civil society, on the other. Having lost ground in the domestic sphere, the monarchs and emperors of Europe believed that by relying on international law in the conferences on the modern laws of war they would be able to restate their monopoly of violence in new universal terms that would be acceptable to the legal conscience of the entire civilised world.[15]

The Geneva Conference of 1864 elaborated the basic principles of humanitarian aid for the wounded in the field and led to the founding of the International Committee of the Red Cross, but it did little to establish protections for civilians and non-combatants in armed conflict, let alone in civil war. By contrast, the question of the protection of civilians – and consequently the distinction between civilians and combatants – was very much at the core of the Brussels Conference of 1874. The conference's catalyst was the Franco-Prussian War of 1870–1871 and in its aftermath the Paris Commune. During that conflict, the bloody fate

13 Francis Lieber, *Guerrilla Parties Considered with Reference to the Laws and Usages of War* (D. Van Nostrand 1862); Witt, *Lincoln's Code*, 192–195.
14 For example, *United States* v. *Klintock* (1820) 18 US 144.
15 Benvenisti and Lustig, 'Monopolizing War', 138–139.

suffered by loosely organised groups of French *francs-tireurs* and communards had highlighted a fundamental distinction between the French defenders (who saw such armed citizens as entitled to the protections of the laws of war) and the victorious Prussian army (which had them shot on sight as rebels and outlaws).[16] The plenipotentiary delegations convened in Brussels to give shape to new laws of war in such circumstances, but their perspectives continued to diverge on the question of irregular fighters. The 'stronger' military powers advocated military necessity and broad discretion for occupying forces, while voices from the 'weaker' states sought to promote broad protection for participants in any forms of resistance. In the absence of a clear consensus, the exchange drifted to the indeterminate middle ground and converged around broad principles that promoted war as the privilege of organised, regular armies, but left open the exact limits of and exceptions to this principle, as well as the question of whether irregular fighters might still be protected by customary international law.[17]

In the end, all the Brussels conference could come up with was a draft, which its participants offered as a basis for future codification efforts. The draft included a set of principles for distinguishing lawful combatants, which may sound familiar to modern readers. According to its Article IX, the laws, rights, and duties of war were applicable 'not only to the army, but likewise to militia and corps of volunteers' if they were responsibly organised, wore distinctive and recognisable badges, carried their arms openly, and conformed to the laws and customs of war in their operations. Under Article X, also the population of a non-occupied territory taking up arms to resist an approaching enemy would be 'considered as belligerents, if they respect the laws and customs of war'.[18] Albeit a draft, the outcome of the conference has been applauded as a significant milestone in international humanitarian law because it provided the wording of criteria for identifying belligerents and distinguishing between civilian and military targets as later adopted with minimal change by the Hague Conference of 1899.[19] The fact remains, however, that the Brussels

[16] Ibid 145–148; Tracey Leigh Dowdeswell, 'The Brussels Peace Conference of 1874 and the Modern Laws of Belligerent Qualification' 54 *Osgoode Hall Law Journal* (2017) 808–810, 824–825.

[17] *Actes de la conférence de Bruxelles de 1874 sur le projet d'une convention internationale concernant la guerre* (A. Wittersheim 1874), Protocole 18 (22 August) at 45, Protocole 4 (26 August) at 50–51.

[18] Draft of an international declaration, Brussels, 27 August 1874, in 1(S2) *American Journal of International Law* (1907) 96.

[19] Dowdeswell, 'Brussels Peace Conference', 841–843.

Conference failed to conclude the binding treaty that was its original objective. It may have provided a promising first draft for future negotiations, but its legacy to future generations was also a pregnant silence on the limits of, and exceptions to, the laws of war in internal conflicts. Even Articles IX and X remained vague on the status of irregular insurgents and guerrilla fighters in occupied areas – a reticence designed to permit powerful armies to treat such fighters as *piratae et latrones* and at the same time allow smaller states and other potential targets of occupation to continue arguing for protection of their resistance movements under customary law. This indeed appears to have been the original intention of the convenors.[20]

The tension between the interests of humanity and the acknowledgement of a public monopoly on violence also preoccupied successive generations of international lawyers in their efforts to develop the laws of war. We have seen how limiting war to nations and states was an imperative whenever they worked closely with governments to develop civilised laws of war for the modern age, as did Lieber in the United States or Martens and Bluntschli at the Brussels Conference. Yet these international lawyers (and civil society more broadly) also wanted to see international law applied to all warfare, including civil wars, and they often invoked humanitarian principles in doing so. In 1870, Bluntschli reflected this sentiment when noting how 'the great march of the history of the world' had shown 'how impracticable and foolish' it was to view great revolutions 'with penal code in hand'. He advised that the 'only thing to be done, then, is to place one's self in the point of view, not of criminal procedure, but of public law and the law of nations'.[21] The Institut de droit international adopted and embraced the Brussels declaration as a basis for its work, which eventually led to the Oxford Manual in 1880 and the Hague Conferences of 1899 and 1907.[22] Yet, notwithstanding this new language of humanitarian law, pacifists and liberal internationalists still found it difficult to persuade governments to compromise on their immediate policy interests. When unrest and riots broke out in

[20] Benvenisti and Lustig, 'Monopolizing War', 157–160.

[21] Johann Caspar Bluntschli, 'Opinion impartiale sur la question de l'Alabama et sur la manière de la résoudre', 2 *Revue de droit international et de législation comparée* (1870) 455. Translated as J. C. Bluntschli, *An Impartial Opinion on the Alabama Question and the Manner of Settling It* (US Government Printing Office 1871) 5.

[22] 1 *Annuaire de l'Institut de droit international* (Annuaire IDI) (1877) 133–138; James Brown Scott, *Resolutions of the Institute of International Law* (Oxford University Press 1916) 7–12.

the Balkans in 1876, Gustave Moynier published a circular on behalf of the International Committee of the Red Cross, in which he called out the Ottomans on their alleged violations of the Geneva Convention of 1864 and demanded that the Porte respect the treaty to which it had acceded in 1865.[23] Rejecting the Turkish claim that this was a civil war and therefore an matter internal to the Ottoman Empire, Moynier pleaded that the convention should nonetheless be applied in the very name of humanity. 'Can we truly say that a State party to the Geneva Convention is free to not grant its subjects or rebelling vassals the benefit of this Convention?' he asked. The Geneva Convention was 'more than' a technical arrangement or a postal treaty; it represented 'a sort of profession of humanitarian faith, a moral code, which could not be obligatory in some cases and optional in others'.[24]

The Porte eventually resolved the matter by equipping its own humanitarian volunteers with the symbol of the red crescent instead of the red cross. But no matter how insistent nineteenth-century pacifists and humanitarians were on making the application of the laws of war binding in internal conflicts, governments continued to treat the distinction between public international wars and domestic rebellions as sacrosanct. The classical concepts of civil war continued implicitly to have importance in state practice even if they were rarely applied affirmatively; for example, they served in justifying empire or the protection of vital national interests against rebels and insurgents. The ambiguity cast into the modern laws of war in Brussels became the decisive factor contributing to the continued denial of standing before the law of nations for insurgents. As, internationally, there was no longer any widespread recognition of internal conflicts as satisfying the prerequisites of belligerency, any plea by land-based insurgents for the protection of the laws of war was ultimately at the mercy of the government trying to subdue them. As succinctly stated by Benvenisti and Lustig, '[w]hile the 1856 Paris Declaration abolished privateers at sea, the Brussels Declaration abolished, in so many words, privateers on land and, by implication, all other individuals who took up arms'.[25] In the end, it would take until the middle of the twentieth century for the classical concepts of insurgency,

[23] Gustave Ador and Gustave Moynier, 'Les destinées de la Convention de Genève pendant la guerre de Serbie' 7 *Bulletin International des Sociétés de la Croix-Rouge* (1876) 164. List of accessions to the convention in 70 BFSP 1156–1175 at 1160.

[24] Ador and Moynier, 'Les destinées', 168.

[25] Benvenisti and Lustig, 'Monopolizing War', 153–154.

belligerency, and civil war to be finally abandoned and superseded by the principles of international humanitarian law.

The Brussels draft had a second coming at the Hague Conference of 1899. Friedrich Martens famously manoeuvred the question of the protection of irregular fighters into the margins by introducing in the second Hague Convention the 'Martens clause'.[26] The clause was a non-binding, preambular call for cases not mentioned explicitly in the regulations to be treated with humanity; in such cases, populations and belligerents would 'remain under the protection and empire of the principles of international law', whatever that might mean.[27] As in Brussels, the smaller countries could draw little comfort in The Hague from measures prohibiting desperate actions such as sabotage and irregular warfare, which might be their only means of defence. Reassuring them of the sanctity of treaties, Martens appealed to the conference 'not to try to formulate a code for cases which cannot be foreseen and codified'. The purpose of the Martens Clause was to guard against including in the conventions any provisions containing explicit recognition of the right to resist, and thus to insist on the incompleteness of the law.[28] Although ostensibly designed to expand the scope of the laws of war beyond public international war, the actual outcome could hardly be hidden, which was rather to further reinforce the status quo that the laws of war really applied to international wars only.

5.1.2 The Rules of Washington and the Transformation of Neutrality

Another factor accelerating the decline of the classical law of civil war was the general transformation of the law of neutrality that took place in the second half of the nineteenth century. In the early nineteenth century neutrality had been a discretionary tool allowing states to wash their hands of troubles arising from the transatlantic colonial conflicts. By asserting neutral rights, states could expect belligerents to respect them, which would simplify dealings with insurgent merchantmen and privateers whenever they appeared in foreign ports or with various de facto officials in territories controlled by insurgents. Governments might

[26] See Rotem Giladi, 'The Enactment of Irony: Reflections on the Origins of the Martens Clause' 25 *European Journal of International Law* (EJIL) (2014) 847–869; Antonio Cassese, 'The Martens Clause: Half a Loaf or Simply Pie in the Sky?' 11 EJIL (2000) 187–216.

[27] Hague Convention (II) on the Laws and Customs of War on Land (1899) 187 CTS 429, preamble.

[28] Giladi, 'Enactment of Irony', 853–859, citing Martens at 856.

disagree over details, such as which rules or treaty provisions should apply to contraband between the two states concerned, or how they should be interpreted and by whom, but these were matters that jurists at the time were accustomed handling bilaterally. After the Crimean War and American Civil War years, however, international lawyers and governments began to conceptualise neutrality as a formal status governed by universal standards of care that were part of international law, as reflected in the increasingly verbose neutrality statutes adopted by the major maritime powers. In particular, the Geneva arbitration of 1872 initiated a move away from neutrality as a means of avoiding responsibility and recast it as a potential source of international state responsibility in itself, exposing future neutrals to unprecedented complaints and claims from belligerents. This greatly diminished its appeal, and insofar as states were free to declare or not declare their neutrality with respect to foreign civil wars, the Geneva arbitration had a chilling effect on the practice of neutrality in civil wars.

The Geneva arbitration concerned alleged violations of neutral duties on the part of Great Britain, not just through formal recognition of Confederate belligerency but particularly through practical aid given to the Confederacy, some of whose warships, including the notorious CSS *Alabama* and the CSS *Florida*, had been constructed in Liverpool.[29] The Confederate middlemen in Britain had interpreted the British Foreign Enlistment Act of 1819 as prohibiting the fitting of warships in British ports but not the acquisition of British vessels, which would then be taken out to the high seas and there armed for cruising.[30] The Foreign Office and the courts were uncertain as to how to deal with the situation; the *Alabama* apparently still docked in Jamaica without disturbance, while the *Florida* was even released by the vice-admiralty court at Nassau after being seized for violating the Act.[31] Some of these Confederate raiders became very successful, and the *Alabama* took or sank as many as sixty-four Union prizes before being sunk in a duel with the *USS Kearsage* off Cherbourg.[32] Throughout the war, US agents in London appealed to the

[29] The Geneva arbitration documents are in *Papers Relating to the Treaty of Washington* (6 vols, US Government Printing Office 1872); I Moore's *Arbitrations* ch XIV.

[30] 59 Geo III 69, s 7.

[31] It was still called the *Oreto*. The decision is held in The National Archives; see Foreign Office: Confidential Print collection 881/2017 at 38–52.

[32] For an overview of the construction and fitting of the Confederate cruisers, see Tom Bingham, 'The *Alabama* Claims Arbitration' 54 *International & Comparative Law Quarterly* (2005) 4–11. See also Raphael Semmes, *The Cruise of the Alabama and the Sumter* (Saunders, Otley 1864) app I.

British government to seize these Confederate builds, but the ships tended to slip away before the officials were instructed to take action, or were released on the grounds of a narrow interpretation of the Neutrality Act by the courts.[33] Internally, a royal commission in 1867 reviewed the Act of 1819, and a new Foreign Enlistment Act of 1870 extended the prohibition on fitting warships to anyone 'having reasonable cause to believe' that the vessel might end up being used in war against a friendly government.[34] In retrospect, this amendment was understood as a tacit admission of the inadequacy of the Neutrality Act during the war.

Union claims concerning the depredations and captures made by the Confederate raiders accumulated in the course of the war, and diplomatic tensions mounted even further thereafter. Negotiations took a particularly ill turn in 1869, when US politicians led by Henry Sumner rejected the initial Clarendon–Johnson draft settlement and began to attribute to the cruisers indirect damages in amounts that were astronomically high due to the inclusion of excessive insurance expenses and even the assumed cost of an alleged prolongation of the war.[35] In 1870, the Oxford professor Mountague Bernard published his comprehensive study on British neutrality during the war; politely, he did not agree.[36] Also in 1870, Bluntschli's influential legal opinion on the *Alabama* claims appeared in the *Revue de droit international et de legislation comparée.*[37] Reciting the doctrine of civil war, Bluntschli maintained that since the condition of civil war was a matter of fact (as had been held in the *Prize Cases*), its recognition by Britain was not a constitutive or partisan act but simply the consequence of a civil war that existed irrespective of the actions of the neutrals.[38] The declaration of neutrality therefore did not constitute a violation of international law. On the question of Britain's responsibility for its negligence in respect of

[33] *The Alexandra* (1863) 176 Eng Rep 295; *Oreto* trial (n 31).

[34] 33 & 34 Vict 90, s 8.

[35] Gustave Rolin-Jaequemyns, 'Moyens pacifiques de régler les difficultés pendantes', 1 *Revue de droit international et de législation comparée* (1869) 153–154; Rolin-Jaequemyns, 'Rejet par le sénat américain du traité Clarendon–Johnson pour le règlement des réclamations anglo-américaines' 1 *Revue de droit international et de législation comparée* (1869) 449–456; Charles Sumner, 'Claims on England: Individual and National' [1869] in *Works of Charles Sumner* (Lee and Shepard, 1880) 53–93. See also Bingham, '*Alabama* Claims Arbitration', 12–13; I Moore's *Arbitrations* 509–512.

[36] Bernard, *Historical Account*, 492–496, also citing Esperson.

[37] Bluntschli, 'Opinion impartiale', 452–485.

[38] Ibid 13.

the Confederate cruisers, Bluntschli found Britain possibly liable and thus recommended a solution through arbitration. However, since a formal admission of guilt would hardly be a realistic option, 'however laudable it may be in the eyes of morality and justice', Bluntschli suggested an arrangement whereby Britain and the United States would jointly and expressly recognise neutral duties and Britain would then declare itself ready to pay a just indemnity to the Union and the damaged proprietors.[39] This is what the two states eventually set out to do.

As Bluntschli had predicted, the British government continued to refuse any formal admission of fault. But as a result of negotiations it began to favour an amicable settlement of the dispute in which it would offer no-fault compensation for the damage caused by the cruisers.[40] In 1871, a joint commission drafted the Treaty of Washington, which provided for the settlement of the remaining claims by a panel of five arbitrators in Geneva.[41] Its most enduring legacy was its Article VI, which contained the tribunal's working rules for the laws of war and neutrality. Governments were required 'to use due diligence' to prevent the arming and fitting of vessels that they had 'reasonable ground to believe' were intended to cruise against friendly powers (first rule). They were also instructed not to permit use of their ports as bases for operations (second rule) and to exercise due diligence by policing their waters for violations of the rules (third rule). Britain's negotiators took care to ensure that the three rules were not to be understood as customary international law at the time of the American Civil War, but rather as forward-looking principles 'in order to evince [Britain's] desire of strengthening the friendly relations between the two countries and of making satisfactory provision for the future', to be used by the arbitrators as a mutually accepted framework within which to decide the matters at issue.[42] The parties pledged to uphold the three rules in the future as the new restatement of neutral duties under international law and to encourage all other nations to adhere to them.[43]

In the end, the Geneva tribunal awarded the United States a sum of 15,500,000 dollars – an estimated 5 per cent of Britain's annual budget,[44] equivalent to around 50 billion pounds sterling today. The award

39 Ibid 20–21.
40 Bingham, '*Alabama* Claims Arbitration', 13; I Moore's *Arbitrations* 519–532.
41 Treaty of Washington, 8 May 1871, 143 CTS 145.
42 Ibid, art VI (fourth para of the rules).
43 Ibid, art VI (fifth para of rules).
44 See Bingham, '*Alabama* Claims Arbitration', 1.

grounded Britain's obligation in an 'omission, to fulfill the duties prescribed in ... the rules established by the VIth article of the treaty of Washington'.[45] Although the final figure was in itself remarkable, the Geneva arbitration was noteworthy above all as a breakthrough for international law and the principle of the pacific settlement of disputes. It represented a major turning point in transatlantic relations, because it brought an end to almost 100 years of potentially adversarial relations between the United States and Great Britain and opened the way to a new Anglo-American partnership in the Atlantic and beyond. Taking its cue from the Treaty of Washington's emphasis on advancing the three rules in international relations, the Institut de droit international embraced the rules in 1875. It recommended that future infringements of neutral duties be referred to arbitration, where 'the arbitral tribunal decides *ex aequo et bono* on the questions of damages which the neutral State should, by reason of its responsibility, pay to the injured State, either for the State itself, or for its nationals'.[46] In the eyes of international lawyers styling themselves as the legal conscience of the civilised world,[47] the law of neutrality became internationalised, understood as a set of universal standards that were independent of the subjective sovereign discretion of individual states. International arbitration was held up as a beacon of hope and civilisation against war and barbarism, in stark contrast to the siege of Paris and the bloody Commune in 1871.

But as the full ramifications of the *Alabama* precedent began to reveal themselves, international lawyers gradually understood how very demanding and potentially risky it was to adopt a position of neutrality, for considerable state responsibility might follow from the slightest negligence. The day after the completion of the Geneva arbitration the world returned to the familiar configuration of British domination as chief belligerent on the high seas. If anyone benefited from the notion of a truly universal standard of neutrality, it was the British Empire, for in the *Alabama* arbitrations, as Travers Twiss is said to have observed, Britain had purchased an invaluable precedent for the future.[48] It is no

[45] Decision and award, *Papers Relating to the Treaty of Washington*, vol IV, 49–53. Several of the original claims were dismissed in the award.

[46] Resolution on the International Duties of Neutral States – Rules of Washington (Hague 1975) arts 6 and 7. Reproduced in 1 Annuaire IDI (1877) 139; Scott, *Resolutions*, 12.

[47] Martti Koskenniemi, *The Gentle Civilizer of Nations* (Cambridge University Press 2001) 11.

[48] Cited in Stephen Neff, *Justice in Blue and Gray: A Legal History of the Civil War* (Harvard University Press 2010) 184.

coincidence, then, that as the price tag on neutrality rose, the state practice of belligerent recognition fell into disuse.

5.2 Abandonment of Belligerent Recognition

Looking back a century after the Geneva arbitration, Roscoe Oglesby reached a blunt conclusion on its consequences: 'Immediately following the American Civil War recognition of belligerency went into desuetude.'[49] His assessment seems largely correct, at least in practical terms. Although governments in Latin America continued to issue occasional recognitions of belligerency in their region until the end of the century, the United States and the European empires no longer resorted to them after 1865. As a consequence, civil wars in the late nineteenth century were conducted increasingly on the basis of what was considered formally as peacetime international law, and were thus dealt with through diplomatic exchanges that fell short of conditions of belligerency. As insurrections and civil wars continued to lead to practical problems and legal encounters between states, new practices and concepts of law emerged to facilitate the management of rebellions under international law. The preferred approaches varied depending on the actors and geographical regions. While the Europeans for the most part continued to treat insurgencies in the Orient as their internal colonial affairs or otherwise distinct from the customary law of nations, new techniques of international law began to develop in the Western Hemisphere, where the management of conflicts and property interests took place among nominally sovereign equals.

5.2.1 *The Doctrine of Recognition of Insurgency*

The doctrine of recognition of insurgency emerged in US state practice as a substitute for recognition of belligerency. At the core of this doctrine was the idea that foreign insurrectionaries could be recognised de facto entities without being accorded any belligerent rights. A foreign state might bring its domestic neutrality laws to bear on a foreign insurrection, but would not consider itself bound by the international duties of neutrals nor accept the use of belligerent rights by the warring parties against its vessels. The doctrine's principal function 'was to entitle nationals of

[49] Roscoe R. Oglesby, *Internal War and the Search for Normative Order* (Martinus Nijhoff 1971) viii.

foreign states to accept the validity of any government-like measures promulgated by insurgents in areas which they actually controlled'.[50] The foreign state would assume that any customs duties that foreign private actors paid to the insurgents and any decisions, licences, and receipts issued by the insurgents were valid and binding on the lawful government. But because there was no recognition of belligerency, any further costs or losses caused by government action (such as collecting payments twice) could potentially give grounds for pecuniary claims. Thus, during the first and second Peruvian wars in the 1850s,[51] US vessels importing nitrites from rebel-held areas dealt with the local insurgent officials in a regular manner, paying their fees and obtaining licences as usual. When these vessels were then captured by the Peruvian government and sanctioned for trading without a 'valid' licence, the US government strongly protested that foreigners had 'a right to claim protection, and also to be exempted from all vexatious interruption when the ascendancy of the parties is temporarily changed by the events of the [armed] contest'.[52]

In relation to the law of neutrality, recognition of insurgency was an attempt to have the best of both worlds: the adoption of a de facto 'neutral' stance towards a foreign insurgency but no de jure recognition of the consequences of war and neutrality. Its profound indeterminacy was its greatest strength. Scholars in later years were never able to agree on how precisely to define recognition of insurgency, though they did perhaps agree that recognised insurgents need not be considered pirates or bandits.[53] Domestic neutrality laws enabled a foreign power to still have its own officials sanction private parties in the event they interfered in the foreign insurrection.[54] Their motivation might be to preserve good relations with the government of the country in which the civil war was taking place, but any enforcement of neutrality laws would be carried out by the state itself independently of the government fighting the civil war.

50 Stephen C. Neff, *War and the Law of Nations: A General History* (Cambridge University Press 2005) 269.

51 Meredith Reid Sarkees and Frank Whelon Wayman, *Resort to War* (CQ Press 2010) 363–364 (cases 557 and 560).

52 Cass to the Peruvian minister (1858), cited in Neff, *War and the Law of Nations*, 270. See also II McNair, *Opinions*, 395–396. The British courts followed a similar logic elsewhere; e.g. *Republic of Peru* v. *Peruvian Guano Co* (1887) 35 Ch D 489.

53 Carlos Wiesse, *Le droit international appliqué aux guerres civiles* (B. Benda 1898) 114–115; Erik Castrén, *Civil War* (Suomalainen Tiedeakatemia 1966) 208, 216; Hersch Lauterpacht *Recognition in International Law* (Cambridge University Press 1947) 270; Hans Kelsen, *Principles of International Law* (Rinehart 1952) 292.

54 Francis Wharton, 'Insurgents as Belligerents' 33 *Albany Law Journal* (1886) 125–131.

The doctrine had its origin in the Cuban insurrections in and after 1868.[55] On the whole, there was broad support for the Cuban revolt in the region. By 1870, at least five Latin American republics had formally recognised the Cuban insurgents as belligerents or as forming an independent nation.[56] The revolt was also supported by sympathisers in the United States. The public mood in postbellum US was in favour of the emancipation of Cuban slaves, and the Cuban revolutionary junta operated out from New York. (This was the time when also Haiti received its recognition.) The federal government, however, decided to stand back and avoid intervening in the conflict. It gradually developed a policy line according to which it would domestically activate its own neutrality laws with respect to the Cuban insurgency but internationally would not recognise any neutral duties nor tolerate belligerent interference with its shipping.[57] At the time, the United States was involved in two simultaneous international disputes relating to civil wars, and the protection of its interests called for careful deliberation. Its own *Alabama* claims were founded on the rights governments involved in civil war could exercise against neutrals, and its complaints in Geneva relied on the position that premature recognition of belligerency could give rise to state responsibility. At the same time, it was relying precisely on state responsibility for rebels in its pursuit of foreign private claims before the US–Mexico mixed claims commission. Meanwhile, Spain made persistent protests over the shipment of arms and foreign fighters from the United States to Cuba. Any formal actions by the US in respect of the Cuban conflict (but also the Franco-Prussian War two years later) might have a bearing on its existing and future cases against Britain, Mexico, and Spain. Out of these contradictory positions emerged a policy line that sought to demonstrate

[55] On the origins of the Cuban insurrection, see Marquis de Olivart, 'Le différend entre l'Espagne et les États-Unis au sujet de la question cubaine' 4 *Revue générale de droit international public* (1897) 577–620; Ada Ferrer, *Insurgent Cuba: Race, Nation, and Revolution, 1868–1898* (University of North Carolina Press 1999) 17–22.

[56] In April 1869, both Mexico and Chile recognised Cuba as an independent republic; Venezuela recognised both Cuban independence and belligerency; Peru declared its recognition of belligerency in April 1869, Bolivia in June 1869, and Colombia on 14 March 1870. See Olivart, 'Le différend', 617–618; Gustave Rolin-Jaequemyns, 'Chronique du droit international' 2 *Revue de droit international et de législation comparée* (1870) 299 at 302–303; Olivart, *Del Reconocimiento del Beligerancia* (L. Péant é Hijos 1895) 33; cf Hans Wehberg, 'La guerre civile et le droit international' 63 *Collected Courses of Hague Academy of International Law* (1938) 33.

[57] On efforts to prevent filibustering, see Cuban correspondence, 1866–1871 in FRUS (1872) 759–856.

a credible domestic policy of non-interference while at the same time escaping the obligations of neutrals internationally.

That policy line took shape at the intersection between the Monroe Doctrine and the abolition of privateers. Early in 1869, a proclamation is said to have been signed by President Grant recognising the Cubans as belligerents, but the proclamation was never finally promulgated owing to opposition from the secretary of state.[58] In the Senate, the influential Charles Sumner rejected the call for recognition of belligerency, arguing that belligerency was a question of 'fact' and was not at hand, 'no matter what our sympathy'. The decisive criterion for Sumner was none other than the lack of a rebel prize jurisdiction: 'whatever the strength of the Rebellion on land, it remained . . . without those Prize Courts which are absolutely essential to recognition by foreign powers'.[59] Accordingly, Grant ultimately rejected the option of recognising the Cuban civil war, stressing that the United States was 'its own judge when to accord the rights of belligerency, either to a people struggling to free themselves from a government they believe to be oppressive or to independent nations at war with each other'.[60] The US calculated that declaring formal neutrality would imply acceptance of Spain's prize jurisdiction over American vessels.[61] In March 1869, the Spanish colonial commanders issued a decree to the effect that any vessels captured near Cuba bearing men, arms, and ammunition without a licence would be treated as 'pirates' and their crews would be immediately executed. This exceeded what the United States could expect on the basis of the 1795 treaty, and the ensuing maritime incidents added to the long list of US private and public claims against Spain.[62] Hamilton Fish informed the Spanish, in no uncertain terms, that 'while Spain disclaims a state of belligerency, or until the United States may find it necessary to recognize her as a belligerent', interference with US ships on the high seas 'cannot but be regarded as a violation of their rights that may lead to serious complications'.[63]

[58] J. T. Morgan, *Belligerent Rights for Cuba* (Washington 1897) 5.

[59] Charles Sumner, 'National Affairs at Home and Abroad' in *Complete Works* (1872) vol XVII, 122.

[60] Message of the president, 6 December 1869, 59 BFSP 186 at 190.

[61] Stephen McCullough, *The Caribbean Policy of the Ulysses S. Grant Administration: Foreshadowing an Informal Empire* (Lexington Books 2017) 99–103.

[62] On the notorious *Virginius* affair, see 2 Moore 967–968; correspondence in 65 BFSP 98–229 and FRUS (1875) 922–1117; McCullough, *The Caribbean Policy*, 145–168. The indemnities to Britain are in 65 BFSP 225–229.

[63] Fish to Lopez Roberts, 16 July 1869, in *Correspondence of the Department of State in Relation to the Seizure of American Vessels and Injuries to American Citizens during the Hostilities in Cuba* (US Government Printing Office 1870) 234.

Under these circumstances, the principle of non-intervention, once a cornerstone of the Monroe Doctrine, appeared in a new light. Whereas in 1823 the United States had formally declared neutrality as a demonstration of non-intervention, the situation had by 1870, changed such that it was now expedient for the US to assert a position of non-intervention by precisely not giving a formal declaration of neutrality. To this end, Grant restated in June 1870 that there was 'not a de facto government in the island of Cuba sufficient to execute law and maintain just relations with other nations'. Yet, protests were being made about the 'serious complications growing out of the seizure of American vessels upon the high seas'. The United States reserved its right to seek compensation, as the issue of belligerent recognition was 'entirely different from and unconnected with' questions of state responsibility.[64] By refusing to declare its neutrality, the United States could claim it was entitled to grant diplomatic protection to its nationals against captures and seizures by Spain. And by enforcing its neutrality laws at home, it might prevent uncomfortable references in the Geneva arbitration and elsewhere to its own shortcomings with Cuba. This policy was soon tested in the famous case of the rebel ship *Hornet*,[65] which had been acquired by men linked to the rebel junta in New York and, according to Spanish intelligence, was destined for the high seas, where it would be armed for privateering under a letter of marque. This was to the horror of the United States, which, in Geneva, was accusing Britain of precisely having enabled such actions. The *Hornet* was therefore seized, detained, and libelled for violating the Neutrality Act of 1818. The district court upheld the seizure by faithfully reciting the *Gazette* principle: as the United States had not recognised the republic of Cuba, the court would not take into account the claim of the Cuban commander. After the dust had settled around the matter, the *Hornet* was released in exchange for a marine bond and assurances of good behaviour. Its owners immediately broke those assurances: the *Hornet* undertook a filibustering expedition to Cuba in 1870 before being chased and blockaded in Port-au-Prince by the Spanish and from there brought home for condemnation by an embarrassed United States.[66]

64 Message of Ulysses S. Grant regarding insurrection in Cuba, 13 June 1870, in James Richardson, *A Compilation of the Messages and Papers of the Presidents*, vol VIII, 4018, at 4022–4023.

65 *The Hornet* (1870) 12 Fed Cas 529.

66 Correspondence relating to the *Hornet* in FRUS (1872) 827–856; see also 'The Seizure of the Cargo of the Hornet', *New York Times* (26 January 1871).

This US policy was maintained virtually unchanged throughout the ten years of war in Cuba. As time passed, the language of neutrality became equated with that of non-recognition. In his 1875 speech to Congress, Grant again recited the classical doctrine of civil war to explain what the options on recognition were, but maintained that he was still 'unable to see that any notable success, or any marked or real advance on the part of the insurgents, has essentially changed the character of the contest'. In particular, '[t]he contest, moreover, is solely on land; the insurrection has not possessed itself of a single sea-port whence it may send forth its flag'. This being the case, he believed a declaration of neutrality 'still to be as unwise and premature [and] indefensible as a measure of right'.[67]

***

During the first Cuban insurrection, the emerging US policy was referred to as neutrality or non-intervention. The expression 'recognition of insurgency' was coined only retrospectively, following a dispute over the case of the *Ambrose Light* in 1885.[68] The *Ambrose Light* was captured by the US gunboat *Alliance* on the high seas near Cartagena. It had been flying 'a strange flag' belonging to Colombian insurgents and was carrying a letter of marque from one of their leaders. The captors, represented by Elihu Root, claimed 'the forfeiture of the ship as piratical, under the law of nations, because she was not sailing under the authority of any acknowledged power', whereas the claimants argued that it was belligerent and had been subsequently recognised as such by the United States.[69] Once again, a court was asked to rule on whether or not a foreign insurgency constituted a civil war. And once again, the response was recourse to the *Gazette* principle. In his judgment, Justice Brown stressed that it was not for the court but rather the government to decide whether foreign insurgents ought to be considered lawful belligerents, and that in the absence of such recognition they were pirates, against whom the ships and tribunals of every nation had a right to act.[70] This *had* to be so, for otherwise:

> The whole significance and importance of the doctrine of recognition of belligerency would be gone, since the absence of recognition could be safely disregarded; the distinction between lawful and unlawful war would

[67] Message of the president, 7 December 1875, 66 BFSP 243 at 248–250.

[68] *The Ambrose Light* (30 September 1885), 25 Fed Cas 408.

[69] Ibid 410–411.

[70] Ibid 412–413.

> be practically abolished; and the most unworthy revolt would have the same immunities for acts of violence on the high seas, without any recognition of belligerent rights, as the most justifiable revolt would have with it. The right to treat unlawful and unauthorized warfare as piratical, seems to me, therefore, clearly imbedded in the very roots of international law.[71]

On this basis, the seizure of the *Ambrose Light* would have been lawful. However, the outcome took a different turn when Brown addressed the doctrine of implied recognition. In the correspondence between the United States and Colombia he identified a tacit recognition of belligerency by Colombia. Observing that the United States had refused to acknowledge any closures of port *save and except* 'only through the exercise of the belligerent right of blockade, i.e., by war,' and since Colombia had in his understanding tacitly recognised belligerency, Brown now concluded that the US, too, had 'recognized, by necessary implication, the existing insurrection as a state of war, and the insurgent forces as a *de facto* power, having the counter-rights of a belligerent'.[72] He therefore released the *Ambrose Light* as a belligerent vessel that had done no piratical harm. The judgment rejected as unfeasible the notion of legally meaningful neutrality without belligerency; on the contrary, it held that a court might find a tacit recognition of belligerency whenever government policies seemed indeterminate. Such an outcome may well have reflected the way in which legal professionals wished the doctrine of civil war and belligerency to operate when brought before a court, but it was starkly at odds with actual US foreign policy.

The fallout was quick to follow in the form of an article by the senior state department jurist Francis Wharton on the law of insurgent recognition.[73] Wharton argued that the correspondence that Justice Brown had taken as evidence of a tacit recognition had precisely meant that the United States *refused* any belligerent recognition, just as it had rejected the Colombian paper blockade and refused to comply with Colombia's wishes to engage with the insurgents as pirates.[74] Wharton admitted that the Colombian insurgents were not entirely unrecognised, as that would mean, for example, that they could not be hosted in US ports. But mere 'non-intervention' did not indicate an intent to grant belligerent rights: 'the government of the United States unquestionably

71 Ibid 413.
72 Ibid 446–447.
73 Wharton, 'Insurgents as Belligerents', 125.
74 Ibid 126.

recognized the *insurgency* of the forces arrayed in April last against the Colombian titular government. But it expressly declares that it did not recognize their *belligerency*.'[75] Wharton offered his own suggestions on how to use this new policy doctrine in the future. First, he recommended that the United States should never grant belligerent recognition until an insurgency had established itself on 'an apparent parity' with the government. Second, the United States should never 'cast aside that policy of non-interference in foreign systems which we have heretofore followed with scrupulous conscientiousness' – except in two cases: to prevent new European conquests in America and, 'when necessary', on the Panamanian isthmus.[76] Here lay the politics of the new American policy of insurgent recognition. It was a policy ostensibly based on thorough and cautious legal impartiality and the calm assessment of facts alone. At the same time, the Monroe Doctrine rose from the depths as an ultimate measure of legitimacy and necessity.

The doctrine of recognition of insurgency was restated in 1895 after guerrilla columns led by José Marti and others set steam from Florida to start a new rebellion in Cuba.[77] Spain blamed foreign interference and irresponsible international public opinion, while the US House and Senate debated the question of Cuban belligerency extensively and with explicit reference to the law of civil war. In early 1896, they passed concurrent resolutions affirming that a condition of public war existed between Spain and Cuba, that the United States should maintain strict neutrality and respect the belligerents' rights on both sides, and that the president should offer his good offices to achieve recognition of the belligerency or independence of Cuba.[78] There was at the time no doubt about the legal effects of belligerent recognition, including the creation of neutral duties under international law as well as domestic

[75] Ibid.

[76] Ibid 131.

[77] Arthur Desjardins, 'L'insurrection cubaine et le droit des gens' 3 *Revue de Paris* (1896) 354–366; John L. Offner, An *Unwanted War: The Diplomacy of the United States and Spain over Cuba, 1895–1898* (University of North Carolina Press 1992) 2–4; George W. Auxier, 'The Propaganda Activities of the Cuban Junta in Precipitating the Spanish-American War, 1895–1898' 19 *Hispanic American Historical Review* (1939) 286–305; Olivart, 'Le différend' (pt IV) 7 *Revue générale de droit international public* (1902) 541–629, esp 580.

[78] Congressional Record, vol 28, pt 3, Senate, 28 February 1896, at 2256, House, 2 March 1896, at 2359; J. T. Morgan, *Belligerent Rights for Cuba* (Washington 1897); Amos Hershey, 'The Recognition of Cuban Belligerency' 7 *Annals of the American Academy of Political and Social Sciences* (1896) 74–85.

neutrality laws. However, the resolutions were not binding on the administration. Instead of complying by declaring formal neutrality, President Cleveland followed the ambiguous doctrine of recognition of insurgency: he proclaimed that domestic neutrality laws were to be enforced against potential volunteers and shipments, but conceded no belligerent rights.[79] In 1897, the Supreme Court affirmed the legality of the policy of insurgent recognition in the matter of the steamer *Three Friends*.[80] It maintained that unlike traditional declarations of neutrality, recognition of insurgency did not affect the right of the United States to protect its nationals and their property in the event of Spanish seizures or other belligerent measures or of losses due to administrative acts by Spain. Accordingly, private parties began to press for claims on the grounds that as peace and not war existed in Cuba, any damages caused by the insurgency and not paid for by Cuba or Spain should fall within state responsibility under international law.[81]

By the early twentieth century, legal scholars had mostly accepted insurgent recognition as a valid concept in the law of civil war.[82] They did so as it might have been counter-productive to ignore the state practice that was actually taking place, especially in the Americas. This development opened the way for them to dissociate neutrality from recognition of belligerent rights. Now, something resembling neutrality could be declared during what was formally still considered a time of peace. This new conception allowed the United States to openly exercise discretion over whether or not to respect the rights of the belligerents *jure gentium* and whether in fact a war existed or not.

Successive US administrations would in the future build on this diplomatic leeway in the inter-American conferences as they began to develop an ‘American international law’. In its regional initiatives related to the principles and doctrines of recognition, the US could play the role of objective arbiter or except itself, depending on whichever was necessary. Thus, it responded to Luis Drago’s appeal for a principle of non-use of force for the collection of debts by agreeing

[79] Proclamation by the president, 12 June 1895, 87 BFSP 733; 1 Moore’s *Digest* 242.

[80] *The Three Friends* (1897) 166 US 1, esp 63–66. See also *Underhill* v. *Hernandez* (1897) 168 US 250, 253.

[81] Desjardins, ‘L’insurrection cubaine’, 379–381.

[82] For example, George Grafton Wilson, ‘Insurgency and International Maritime Law’ 1 *American Journal of International Law* (1907) 46–60 at 51; Wehberg, ‘Guerre civile’, 60–61; Lauterpacht, *Recognition*, 270–278; Jean Siotis, *Le droit de la guerre et les conflits armés d’un caractère non-international* (LGDJ 1958) 117–128, Castrén, *Civil War*, 207–223.

with the principle in diplomatic terms but in fact continuing to reserve its right of intervention in Latin America.[83] In 1907, in Washington, it hosted the drafting of a general treaty of peace between several Latin American states, which provided for mutual counter-revolutionary cooperation and established the Tobar Doctrine on non-recognition of revolutionary regime changes. The US was not itself a party to the treaty, however.[84] At the Havana conference of 1928, the US participants ensured that an unconditional prohibition of intervention would not be adopted.[85] When, in 1933, the United States did sign and ratify the Montevideo Convention (famously stating the criteria for statehood, the declarative theory of recognition, non-intervention, and mutual non-recognition of territorial acquisitions by force),[86] it still ensured that the outcome necessarily prioritised recognition over factual criteria, and thus facilitated a system where US recognition would remain pivotal in determining the legitimacy of states in the Americas.[87] The inter-American conventions were, of course, not imposed unilaterally; through their active participation, the Latin American countries were participants in the creation of their hemispheric legal arrangements on a basis of pragmatic legalism, which sought to release the New World from European predominance and to channel regional disputes away from potential use of force towards arbitration and state responsibility. Yet the conference outcomes verged on trade-offs to meet the special interests of the northern side of the continental equation.[88]

The academic world was not blind to the potential for empire that the United States projected upon the Latin American countries.[89] As

[83] H. Edward Nettles, 'The Drago Doctrine in International Law and Politics' 2 *Hispanic American Historical Review* (1928) 218-219.

[84] General treaty of peace and amity, 2 December 1907, and additional convention, 20 December 1907, in 206 CTS 63.

[85] James Brown Scott, 'The Sixth Pan-American Conference' 22 *American Journal of International Law* (1928) 356. See also Juan Pablo Scarfi, *The Hidden History of International Law in the Americas: Empire and Legal Networks* (Oxford University Press 2017) 121–131.

[86] Montevideo Convention on the Rights and Duties of States, 26 December 1933, 165 LNTS (1936) 19.

[87] Scarfi *Hidden History*, 158–168.

[88] Arnulf Becker Lorca, *Mestizo International Law: A Global Intellectual History 1842–1933* (Cambridge University Press 2014) 327–352; Alan Tzvika Nissel, *Merchants of Legalism: A History of State Responsibility (1870–1960)* (Cambridge University Press 2024) 108–118.

[89] See Desjardins, 'L'insurrection cubaine'; Olivart, 'Le différend'; Alejandro Alvarez, 'The Monroe Doctrine from the Latin-American Point of View' 2 *St Louis Law Review* (1917)

Alejandro Alvarez observed in 1917, the United States had built up, alongside the Monroe Doctrine, 'a policy of hegemony' that '[did] not represent the interests of the continent, but quite the reverse'.[90] Although the concepts of the classical doctrine of civil war were largely brushed aside into the background, they nonetheless remained relevant – not because governments would have made use of belligerent recognition or neutrality in civil wars, but because of the benefits governments might receive by *not* applying them. Thus the *fin-de-siècle* scholarly doctrine of civil war would continue to insist on the continuing centrality of the recognition of belligerency, while the doctrine of recognition of insurgency and the fragmentation of the law of recognition would provide governments with practical excuses and escape routes from any consequences of such insistence. Given these circumstances, it is not difficult to criticise the doctrine of insurgent recognition as excessively ambiguous and apologetic: it was a sublimation of indeterminate international legal argument, a recognition of non-recognition, the granting of a status of no status. In the end, the law of recognition in situations of foreign civil war could now be used either way, in any argument, and at any point in time.

5.2.2 *Empire and Colonial Insurrections*

The United States was not the only one to separate neutrality from its binding legal consequences. European empires, in particular Britain, improvised similar approaches, sending gunboats to oversee the commercial interests of their nationals in unstable areas of the world and resorting to provisional de facto (as opposed to de jure) recognition of internal political changes in peripheral nations.[91] Such imperial approaches towards insurrection were rooted in the fundamental dynamic of difference between encounters in the Orient and the 'civilised' world, as part of which the European scholars counted the Latin American states, with some qualification on questions of state responsibility.[92] In the Western Hemisphere, the practice of European powers gradually adapted to the principles and examples laid out by the

135–146. For a critique in retrospect, see Carl Schmitt, *The Nomos of the Earth* ([1950] G. K. Ulmen tr, Telos Press 2006) 304–308.

90 Alvarez, 'Monroe Doctrine', 139.

91 Lauterpacht, *Recognition*, 274–276.

92 Famously, James Lorimer, *The Institutes of the Law of Nations* (Blackwood and Sons 1883) vol I, 101–103. See also Antony Anghie, *Imperialism, Sovereignty and the Making of International Law* (Cambridge University Press 2004) 4–6.

United States; they mostly reined in their ambitions for new colonial appropriation in the Americas and opted for the new methods of free trade and diplomatic protection. Thus, the French interventions in Mexico in 1838 and the 1850s as well as the Franco-British rivalry over the Río de la Plata ended by reparations, trade concessions, and local regime changes instead of direct imperial appropriation. During the disturbances and civil war in Venezuela in the 1860s and 1870s, the British law officers delivered an opinion suggesting that the insurgents were belligerents, but still reserved the British government's right to exact compensation from Venezuela for unjust captures.[93] They also advised the crown to respect Venezuelan blockades against insurgents.[94] What exactly that respect entailed is unclear, since a recognition of belligerency seems never to have been issued, and in 1868 Britain and Venezuela constituted a mixed claims commission to examine British private pecuniary claims, leading to awards totalling more than 300,000 dollars.[95] During the Brazilian naval revolt of 1893, Europeans and Americans alike seem to have rejected the validity of the government's blockades, denied the insurgents any right against foreign shipping, and left the question of formal recognition unanswered.[96]

Whenever civil wars took place within indigenous kingdoms or empires in Africa or Asia, the classical doctrine of civil war received only superficial application at best. In the so-called Orient, straightforward protection of interests remained a valid and accepted approach for the Europeans when dealing with the local peoples and indigenous kingdoms, and in these parts of the world the United States, too, accommodated its approach to the prevailing circumstances. Imperial governments and their jurists avoided the international law of civil war in colonial revolts and insurgencies and relied instead on a firmly Eurocentric understanding of hierarchical relationships between the metropolitan thrones and their dominions. This was in line with events such as the Berlin Africa conference of 1884 and the failure of the Institut de droit international to decide whether or not 'the Orient' was ready to

93 Opinion of Twiss, 28 June 1871, in Lauterpacht, *Recognition*, 202–203.

94 Opinion of Phillimore, 21 October 1864, in Lauterpacht, *Recognition*, 207; Opinion of Twiss, 13 November 1871, in Lauterpacht, *Recognition*, 208. Compare Opinion of Twiss, 1 July 1870, in Lauterpacht, *Recognition*, 216–217. Notifications of Venezuelan blockades in 66 BFSP 939, 67 BFSP 520–521, 67 BFSP 601.

95 UK–Venezuela claims convention, 21 September 1868, with final report, 15 November 1869, in 138 CTS 75.

96 1 Moore's *Digest* 203. See also opinions from 20 July 1893 and 4 August 1894, in II McNair, *Opinions*, 393.

participate in the customary law of nations.[97] Instead of debating the legal standing of various insurgents, Europeans mainly focused on the protection of their commercial and private interests through a mixture of treaty concessions, extraterritoriality, capitulations, and the occasional use of force. It would generally have been out of character for the Western powers to recognise belligerent rights or prize jurisdiction of Oriental peoples over European flags: indeed, up until the Japanese prize cases from the Sino-Japanese War of 1894–1895 the very idea of belligerent rights exercised by Orientals seems to have been out of question.[98] (Nor were Asians themselves much protected by the customary limits of European belligerent rights; when, in 1885, France blockaded China in the Tonkin area, it resorted to declaring food as contraband cargo – unthinkable in wars between 'civilised' peoples – and did so without even declaring an official state of war.[99])

In China, Europeans mostly considered the massive Taiping rebellion as an internal matter of the Celestial Empire, and prioritised their own trade interests in the Second Opium War. In 1858, they accommodated the situation of Nanking in the Treaties of Tianjing by agreeing to impose their privileges of free passage only after it had been recaptured by the Qing government and then assisted in the suppression of the rebellion.[100] When the anti-foreigner Boxer rebellion escalated in 1900 to threaten foreign embassies in Beijing, an international coalition (including Japan) intervened by force. On 7 September 1901, China agreed to pay an enormous indemnity of 450,000,000 taels, which the foreign powers divided among themselves.[101] Similarly, internal disturbances in the

97 1 Annuaire IDI (1877) 141–142; report of 1879 in 3–4 Annuaire IDI (1879–1880) 298–311. After sending this manuscript to print, I have came across Lauren Benton's remarkable *They Called it Peace: Worlds of Imperial Violence* (Princeton University Press, 2024). I warmly recommend it as a further reference on the following pages.

98 Sakuyé Takahashi, *Cases on International Law during the Chino-Japanese War* (Cambridge University Press 1899). Prize law was introduced into Japan through correspondence with Western scholars, including John Westlake and Thomas Erskine Holland. The legal statute constituting the Japanese prize court was issued in 1894, marking the birth of that jurisdiction. In the Republic of China, the first prize courts appeared in 1917 in the context of the First World War. See F. T. Cheng (tr) *Judgments of the High Prize Court of the Republic of China* (High Prize Court 1919).

99 Nicholas Mulder and Boyd van Dijk, 'Why Did Starvation Not Become the Paradigmatic War Crime in International Law?' in Ingo Venzke and Kevin Jon Heller (eds) *Contingency in International Law* (Oxford University Press 2021) 373.

100 Sino-British treaty of Tientsin, 26 June 1858, 119 CTS 163, art IX; Sino-French treaty of Tientsin, 27 June 1858, 119 CTS 189, art 6; Andrew Wilson, *The 'Ever-Victorious Army': A History of the Chinese Campaign under Lt.-Col. C. G. Gordon and of the Suppression of the Tai-ping Rebellion* (Blackwood and Sons 1868) 49–67.

101 Peking final protocol, 7 September 1901, 190 CTS 61, art VI. See also 191 CTS 296, 198 CTS 406. One Haikwan tael was the equivalent of about 33 grams of silver.

Ottoman Empire raised issues of a more pragmatic nature for the Europeans rather than doctrinal questions of belligerency and neutrality. When insurrections erupted in the Balkans in the 1870s, Russia took the opportunity to intervene on the side of the insurgents; the situation led to the Russo-Turkish War and the Berlin Congress of 1878, and the diplomacy of the war had more to do with the inter-imperial balance of power and humanitarian assistance than with the formal legal standing of the insurgents.[102] A few decades later, the policy of the British Empire towards the Young Turks at the turn of the century remained pragmatic, cautious, and supportive of the sultanate as long as its own imperial interests, such as naval bases and trade concessions, were secured.[103]

The European jurists and statesmen probably came the closest to applying the law of civil war to an Oriental insurrection in the Japanese civil war that followed the 1868 Meiji Restoration.[104] When the emperor declared war on the shogunate, foreign representatives stationed on the islands complied by giving preliminary notifications of strict neutrality to their nationals. These were in fact quite remarkable in their language, warning, among other things, that subjects violating neutral obligations might forfeit all claims to the protection of their governments and the rights and privileges of their respective treaties with Japan, expose their ships and transports to capture and confiscation, and find themselves judged by the rules of war for violations of the principles of international law.[105] The European governments eventually scaled down their neutrality when expressing their official positions, such as when Queen Victoria declared 'a strict neutrality' during the hostilities but avoided any mention of submission to Japanese jurisdictions, prize or otherwise, and also did not invoke the Foreign Enlistment Act.[106] When the dismissed

[102] Treaty of Berlin, 13 July 1878, 153 CTS 171; documents in 68 BFSP (1876–1877); Bela L. Kiraly and Gale Stokes (eds), *Insurrections, Wars, and the Eastern Crisis in the 1870s* (Columbia University Press 1985); Murat Birdal, *The Political Economy of Ottoman Public Debt: Insolvency and European Financial Control in the Late Nineteenth Century* (I. B. Tauris 2010) 25–62.

[103] John Burman, *Britain's Relations with the Ottoman Empire during the Embassy of Sir Nicholas O'Conor to the Porte, 1898–1908* (Isis Press 2010) 191–218.

[104] On the Meiji restoration, see Mark Ravina, *To Stand with the Nations of the World: Japan's Meiji Restoration in World History* (Oxford University Press 2017); Oona Hathaway and Scott J. Shapiro, *The Internationalists: How a Radical Plan to Outlaw War Remade the World* (Simon & Schuster 2017) 134–148.

[105] US, British, Italian, Prussian, and French notifications of neutrality in FRUS (1868–1869) vol I, 672–677, see also 661.

[106] British order in council, 14 May 1868, in 58 BFSP 33. Also in *Collection of Neutrality Laws*, vol. I, 174; Foreign Office Confidential Print collection881/1588. See also order in

shogun retreated with his supporters to the short-lived Republic of Ezo, the imperial government declared this as 'an act of rebellion' and any further rebel activities as 'piracy'.[107] A brief civil war took place at sea and ended after the Meiji government managed to purchase a new fleet, including a flagship originally ordered from the United States by the shogunate but which the US now delivered to the imperial navy.[108] From this point onwards, sources tend to fall silent on neutrality. British law officers now advised denying both the lawful government and the insurgents any belligerent rights, the reason being that although the existence of civil war was 'a question of pure fact', the definition of civil war 'is essentially European, and can not be strictly applied with exactness or rigour to communities where the action of the central Government is different'.[109] In the end, a dynamic of difference prevailed, with Western powers refusing to see the Japanese as possessing belligerent rights against foreign flags until the Russo-Japanese War and Japan's elevation into the family of 'civilised' nations.

In Africa, the concept of civil war seems to have carried little weight with European empires on the rare occasions when it might have benefited insurgents or indigenous peoples. In 1870, when local tribes in Benin engaged in sustained warfare, Travers Twiss delivered an opinion suggesting that the situation might warrant a British declaration of neutrality.[110] But when he discovered that a British ship had already intervened in the conflict, he reviewed the evidence and characterised the intervention as having been 'rather an act of armed mediation, the propriety of which can hardly be measured by the ordinary European standards'.[111] Here again, the distinction between Europe and the rest of the world proved more decisive to the legal mind than the facts on the ground.

By contrast, the law of civil war proved quite useful to European lawyers for justifying and defending their own overseas imperial interests. This was particularly so in Africa after the British concept of colonial protectorates became equated with sovereignty in the Berlin Final Act of 1885 and then

council correcting an error, 13 May 1869, in 59 BFSP 1259 and Foreign Office Confidential Print collection881/5265.

107 FRUS (1868–1869) vol I, 831–832.

108 G. A. Ballard, *The Influence of the Sea on the Political History of Japan* (John Murray 1921) 119–124; Ravina, *To Stand with the Nations*, 122–128.

109 Opinion of 19 April 1869, Lauterpacht, *Recognition*, 214.

110 Opinion of 29 September 1870, Lauterpacht, *Recognition*, 205.

111 Opinion of 7 October 1870, Lauterpacht, *Recognition*, 206.

gradually developed into a shield used to protect empires against indigenous resistance and international competition.[112] The notion of a colonial protectorate, which formally suggested a voluntary agreement of protection and allegiance between natives and foreign crowns, developed into a deliberately ambiguous species of legal relations, the practical effect of which was to enable imperial governments to claim sovereignty over their colonies internationally and at the same time, within their domestic legal systems, treat the colonies as foreign countries that could be made to bear legal responsibility and excepted from constitutional rights and guarantees.[113] The classical law of civil war fitted this equation well: by arguing that a colonial insurrection was an internal matter that had nothing to do with the law of nations, European capitals could use the doctrine of civil war to insulate their monopolies on colonial violence from international scrutiny and foreign interference. Furthermore, at a time when territorial titles and claims were often in a state of flux, and where the distinction between peaceful trade relations and protectorates over indigenous peoples could be blurred, Europeans were sometimes happy to invoke the doctrine of civil war to keep their rivals away from territories where they were in fact waging an aggressive war of conquest. Britain and France used the concept of civil war in this manner to shield new colonial conquests from international interference when establishing protectorates respectively in Transvaal and Madagascar.[114]

The independence of the kingdom of Madagascar had not been in serious doubt before 1883. France itself had maintained a treaty of peace and commerce with the kingdom since 1868.[115] An initial French conquest led to the cession of a piece of Hova territory to France and, in 1885, to the signing of a treaty providing for France to represent Madagascar in foreign relations and placing the Malagasy people under France's protection.[116] (France was also to be paid 10 million francs as indemnities, and French troops were to remain posted on the kingdom's soil until payment.) When the Second Franco-Hova War began, French jurists and statesmen argued

[112] General Act of the Berlin Conference, 26 February 1885, 165 CTS 485; Martti Koskenniemi, 'International Law and Imperialism' in David Freestone (ed), *Contemporary Issues in International Law: A Collection of the Josephine Onoh Memorial Lectures* (Brill 2002) 202–209; Koskenniemi, *Gentle Civilizer*, 124–125.

[113] See James Crawford, *The Creation of States in International Law* (2nd edn, Oxford University Press 2006) 299–303.

[114] Siotis, *Le droit de la guerre*, 94–96; Antoine Rougier, *La théorie de la guerre civile dans le droit international* (Recueil Sirey 1903) 103–104.

[115] Treaty of peace and commerce, 8 August 1868, 137 CTS 489.

[116] Treaty between France and Madagascar, 17 December 1885, 167 CTS 133.

that it was now a civil war and therefore a matter internal to the French empire.[117] Indeed, under the General Act of the Berlin Conference of same year Europeans committed themselves to establishing authority in the regions they occupied on the coasts and to protecting the freedom of trade and of transit there.[118] In this scramble for Africa, rival powers recognised the French claim in exchange for recognition of their own similar claims in other parts of Africa.[119] No foreign government seems to have recognised any form of belligerency for the Africans, although the British law officers may perhaps have advised their government to insist on the applicability of the laws of war to the insurgents and any foreign subjects assisting them.[120] The principal concern for the European empires was the protection of the rights of their subjects and securing them access to justice in the colonies.[121] The formal French protectorate was finally established in all of Madagascar by treaty in 1895,[122] concluding a fait accompli, even if the views expressed publicly by lawyers at the time tended to suggest that the so-called colonial rebellion had already been an international aggression from the outset.[123]

Something similar happened with the South African Republic. After the First Boer War in 1881, the British crown accorded the Transvaal burghers 'complete self-government, subject to the suzerainty of Her Majesty'.[124] After 1884, Britain expanded this autonomy to a prima facie independence in foreign policy, subject only to a veto by the queen.[125] The South African Republic consequently had its own diplomatic representatives abroad and signed treaties with foreign sovereign powers.[126] Then, in 1886, gold was struck in the Transvaal. The influx of uitlanders that followed gave rise to

[117] See citations in Siotis, *Le droit de la guerre*, 94.

[118] General Act of the Berlin Africa Conference, 26 February 1885, 165 CTS 485, arts 34, 35.

[119] Joseph Dubois, 'La France à Madagascar' 28 *Revue de droit international et de législation comparée* (1895) 477–501; Fauchille's 'Chronique' in 2 *Revue générale de droit international public* (1895) 140–158 On foreign interests, see, for example, the declaration and lifting of the British blockade at Zanzibar, 81 BFSP 97 and 1291.

[120] Opinion of 16 April 1895, II McNair, *Opinions*, 370–371.

[121] British and French correspondence in 89 BFSP 1036–1094 and 90 BFSP 457–514.

[122] Treaty of protectorate between France and Madagascar, 1 October 1895, 182 CTS 74.

[123] Report of the law officers to the crown, 16 April 1895, in II McNair, *Opinions*, 370–371; Siotis, *Le droit de la guerre*, 95; Rougier, *La théorie de la guerre civile*, 104.

[124] Convention between Great Britain and the Transvaal Burghers, 3 August 1881, 159 CTS 57; cf British proclamation annexing the Transvaal Republic, 12 April 1877, 68 BFSP 140.

[125] Convention between Great Britain and the South African Republic, 27 February 1884, 163 CTS 345.

[126] For example, treaty with Germany (1885) 76 BFSP 512; treaty with France (1885) 76 BFSP 188; accession to the Universal Postal Union (1893) 84 BFSP 69.

internal tensions and grievances. Britain eventually intervened to protect the interests of its colonists against the Boer authorities. When the Second Boer War began in 1899, the question arose as to whether it was an international war, a civil war, or both.[127] International lawyers – many of whom were at the time debating the law of civil war under the auspices of the Institut de droit international – ruled out any idea of the war being an internal conflict. John Westlake, for one, maintained that it was an international war and dismissed the notion of a colonial insurgency as 'perfectly absurd'.[128] Frantz Despagnet agreed.[129] Even though the Boers were landlocked and had no navy, Britain invoked the doctrine of continuous voyage and began to enforce belligerent rights against neutral ships heading to nearby ports. The conflict was thus fought as a protracted guerrilla war on land with naval blockades and the search of ships at sea, which reignited a number of familiar legal controversies concerning the rights of neutrals.[130] In the end, the defeated Boer republics reverted to colonial status under the British sovereign, with the acquiescence of foreign powers.[131]

The United States as well became a colonial empire in this period. Just as the Europeans complied with American principles of free trade in the Western Hemisphere, so conversely the Greater United States followed European examples in the subjugation and pacification of new colonial possessions. At the turn of the century the US expanded into the Caribbean and all across the Pacific as it annexed Spanish colonies in the wake of the Spanish-American War.[132] The colonies brought with

[127] For example, HC Deb 17 October 1899, *Hansard* vol 77 cols 60–160; 'The War', *The Times* (16 October 1899) 7; 'The Transvaal on the Eve of War', *The Times* (23 October 1899) 10.

[128] John Westlake, *The Transvaal War: A Lecture Delivered in the University of Cambridge on 9th November 1899* (C. J. Clay and Sons 1899) 33–34.

[129] Frantz Despagnet, *La guerre sud-africaine au point de vue du droit international* (A. Pedone 1902) 91–97.

[130] John W. Coogan, *The End of Neutrality: The United States, Britain, and Maritime Rights 1899–1915* (Cornell University Press 1981) 30–42; See also Robert Granville Campbell, *Neutral Rights and Obligations in the Anglo-Boer War* (Johns Hopkins Press 1908).

[131] Treaty of Vereeniging, 31 May 1902, 191 CTS 232, art 1. Claims commissions were to be set up to settle claims arising from the war, but 'no foreigner or rebel' was entitled to their benefits (art 10). Records of the peace negotiations in Rev. J. D. Kestell and D. E. van Velden, *The Peace Negotiations between the Governments of the South African Republic and the Orange Free State, and the Representatives of the British Government* (Clay & Sons 1912).

[132] See Daniel Immerwahr, *How to Hide an Empire: A History of the Greater United States* ([2019] Vintage 2020) 11; Treaty of peace between Spain and the United States, 10 December 1898, 187 CTS 100.

them their internal disturbances, and with the disturbances came an impulse to respond with repression. The island of Cuba gained formal independence in 1902, with the Guantánamo Bay area leased to the military presence of the United States, though in reality it remained greatly dependent on the United States until the revolution of 1959.[133] Matters were different in the Pacific colonies, and especially the Philippines, where local insurgents had been waging war against the Spanish for a long time and were expecting independence after playing a crucial role in the capture of Manila. When the US finally decided instead to purchase and annex their islands from Spain, the result was a new colonial insurgency.[134] Like the French in Madagascar and the British in South Africa, the US dismissed any idea of recognising the Filipino insurgents and considered them only as local guerrillas engaged in internal rebellion.[135] Any laws of war applied to them were granted at the government's discretion, and the Lieber Code was 'revised' to better enable brutal responses.[136] The insurgents looked abroad to plead for international support and 'formal recognition of the belligerency of the Revolution and the Independence of the Philippines',[137] but there seem to have been no positive replies. The war on the islands descended into a bitter guerrilla campaign, which was met with punitive and systematic mass atrocities inflicted by the colonising power.[138] Although the US navy blockaded Manila and other parts of the Philippines for the duration of the war, it seems there were no formal relations of neutrality in force.[139] The outside world appears to have accepted the war in the Philippines as an internal matter of colonial pacification similar to the conflicts in the Transvaal and Madagascar.

133 Commercial convention between Cuba and the United States, 11 December 1902, 95 BFSP 791, 192 CTS 255; supplementary convention, 26 January 1903, 192 CTS 342; land lease agreement, 16/23 February 1903, 192 CTS 429; treaty between Cuba and the United States, 22 May 1903, 193 CTS 198.

134 Treaty on the cession of the Philippines to the United States, 7 November 1900, 92 BFSP 814; protocol for retaining Spanish nationality, 29 March 1900, 92 BFSP 1128; declarations in Murat Halstead, *The Story of the Philippines and Our New Possessions, Including the Ladrones, Hawaii, Cuba and Porto Rico* (Our Possessions Publishing Co 1898) 69ff.

135 Annual message of the president in FRUS (1899) xliv–xlii; correspondence with Spain in FRUS (1899) 679–720.

136 Witt, *Lincoln's Code*, 358.

137 Halstead, *Story of the Philippines*, 80–81.

138 Immerwahr, *How to Hide an Empire*, 88–103.

139 Halstead, *Story of the Philippines*, 112, 120.

5.3 The Legal Conscience of the Civilised World

By the late nineteenth century, the classical doctrine of civil war constituted a formal legal language whose most practical function was that it helped governments avoid the application of the international laws of war in intra-state conflicts. After the abolition of privateers in 1856 and the successful conclusion of the Geneva arbitration in 1872, the major powers of Europe and America distanced themselves from their former neutrality policies, now opting instead for deliberately indeterminate, discretionary, and unilateral policies that they could define themselves and under which they could not easily be held liable. In this sense, the concept of belligerent recognition became another 'trap for the innocent and a signpost for the guilty'[140] – a passage of law whose validity was broadly accepted but whose utility was based precisely on the possibility of its inapplicability in any given circumstance. All lawyers agreed that there was a formal threshold to be met for civil war to exist under international law, but in practice states were able to interpret that threshold very much in whatever way they preferred. With few exceptions, late-nineteenth-century internal conflicts took place in the absence of a state of war and, therefore, within the sphere of peacetime international law.

***

The gradual decline in state practice does not represent the full picture, however. While the classical doctrine receded in practice, the law of civil war became an integral part of the broader humanitarian project embodied in the laws of war. New popular sensibilities were now at play in a world where wars had become national affairs involving countless citizens, auxiliaries, journalists, and unknown soldiers whose fates shook the consciences of learned men and women.[141] Matters of state responsibility were of increasing interest, too, and as early as 1869 the *Revue de droit international et de législation comparée* carried Carlos Calvo's famous opening article on the subject.[142] For the liberal internationalists gravitating around the Institut de droit international, who wrote and worked in an era marked by imperial rivalry and staunch

[140] The words of Austen Chamberlain, albeit in a different context; see Hansard HC Deb 24 November 1927, vol 210 col 2105. See also Martti Koskenniemi, 'A Trap for the Innocent . . .' in Claus Kreß and Stefan Barriga (eds), *The Crime of Aggression: A Commentary* (Cambridge University Press 2016) 1359–1385.

[141] Benvenisti and Lustig, 'Monopolizing War', 132–136.

[142] Carlos Calvo, 'De la non-responsabilité des États à raison des pertes et dommages éprouvés par des étrangers en temps de troubles intérieurs ou de guerres civiles' 1 *Revue de droit international et de législation comparée* (1st series 1869) 417.

protection of sovereign prerogative by States, civil war was still an urgent problem, but they sought to ameliorate the rigid status quo by becoming genuinely open to international cooperation and aspiring to higher ideals. Styling themselves as 'the legal conscience of the civilized world',[143] these individuals strove to temper nationalism with liberal internationalism by pushing back against states' self-serving policies and promoting longer-term, liberal ideals such as integration, free trade, and human rights.[144] Though they were often eager to work alongside their governments in justifying sovereign policies, they could equally often deliver critiques of sovereignty, with a view to taming and educating their societies, rulers, and political institutions.[145] To the modest extent that safeguarding their professional credibility would allow, these lawyers were committed to creating legal visions speaking truth to power, so as to steer international politics increasingly towards peaceful cooperation, the settlement of disputes, and economic integration.

The inversion in state practice would not become acknowledged in legal scholarship on civil war until the twentieth century. Even if states did not want to be legally bound by the laws of belligerency, jurists saw this as a problem for states, not the law. For them, the civilised rules and principles on the law of civil war existed beyond all doubt, as evidence from the first wave of decolonisation amply showed. If international lawyers aspired generally to promote a law-abiding attitude or *Gesetzestreue* among narrowly self-interested governments, then it would make sense for the legal profession not to abandon the legal principles it inherited from the past but rather to put their efforts into furthering them. And so it came about that the classical principles laid out by Gentili and Vattel enjoyed a new resurgence, even a second coming, in the scholarly teachings of international lawyers in later decades. It was in these later writings that the law of civil war was synthesised as what had the semblance of a complete legal doctrine with its own history and distinct principles. This second coming in the domain of scholarly writings forms the final act in the story of the classical doctrine of civil war in international law.

143 Koskenniemi, *Gentle Civilizer*, 41.
144 Ibid 4.
145 Ibid 4–5, 13–14.

6

The Second Coming: Academic Doctrine 1891–1939

While the governments of sovereign states lost their appetite for formal neutrality with respect to foreign civil wars, international lawyers, unperturbed, maintained the classical distinction between rebellions, insurgencies, and recognised belligerencies at the core of their doctrine. From the 1890s onwards, they constructed a dedicated corpus of academic literature on the law of civil war, which consolidated the doctrine as part of the broader system of international law as they understood it. Antoine Rougier relates the following:

> A Peruvian author, Mr Wiesse, compiled the first comprehensive volume on the subject, comprising a large number of facts and documents borrowed from Latin American history together with a legal commentary. The Institut de droit international debated and passed resolutions on two important topics on the subject of civil wars. In short, a new chapter in the law of nations was born.[1]

Despite mounting evidence of the classical doctrine's fall from favour in the external world – and to push back against the disinterest of states to make use of the legal concepts available to them – legal scholars continued to centre the doctrine of civil war around the concept of belligerent recognition, its effects, and the question of what rules should apply in its absence. As a whole, this scholarship constituted a second coming of the classical doctrine of civil war in international law.

This second coming peaked when the Spanish Civil War threw into stark relief the irreconcilable gap between state practice and scholarly doctrine, and international lawyers largely failed in their attempts to address the conflict in any non-partisan or meaningful way. The Spanish war tore Europe apart along political fault-lines and became a test laboratory for modern total warfare, intervention, and extreme ideologies. In this context, the old laws of neutrality and non-intervention lost their traditional meanings, and the classical doctrine

[1] Antoine Rougier, *Les guerres civiles et le droit des gens* (Larose 1903) 2.

of civil war never regained credibility after the disillusionment over Spain. Although it continued to influence legal writings well into the 1960s, it did so mostly through force of habit and the lack of any settled alternatives, until eventually the modern post-war regime of the law of non-international armed conflicts took its place.

The canonical textbooks on the law of civil war took on the appearance of systematic black-letter studies on the valid rules and principles of law, reflecting late nineteenth- and early twentieth-century positivism in continental legal literature. They were exercises in law-speaking rather than lawmaking; the scholar's purpose was the systematisation and interpretation of norms: to make manifest the meaning of the law as set down in valid sources but which was always in need of clarification by the legal profession. Accordingly, these writings remained largely silent or unclear on the broader ambitions or sensibilities of their authors or those of the intellectual movements that influenced them. Monotony and detachment were hallmarks of competent scholarship; the expression of a subjective or political opinion might be seen as detrimental to an author's professional credibility. Yet, although scholarly tradition was characterised by its purported value-neutrality, the codified doctrine of civil war in international law was the product of a particular movement of cosmopolitan, liberal international lawyers. The laws of war, the arbitration movement, and the pacific resolution of disputes were intrinsic to the project they pursued, and their call for a rule of enlightened law over the short-term impulses of governments was essential in giving momentum to their cause. If states were sometimes reluctant to follow the civilised principles of law, that did not make those principles void; on the contrary, enlightened individuals were expected to shepherd them back to the flock, or at least persevere in their knowledge of the law so as to keep open the possibility of future atonement and amends through adjustments in state behaviour.[2]

When explaining the importance and usefulness of their work, the scholars stressed the interests of humanity and the need to mitigate the cruelty of war. Writing in 1903, Antoine Rougier observed that although prior to then states and scholars had generally refused the application of the law of nations in unrecognised internal conflicts, this was no reason for concluding that such reticence confirmed the desuetude of the

[2] See Martti Koskenniemi and Ville Kari, 'A More Elevated Patriotism: The Emergence of International and Comparative Law (Nineteenth Century)' in Heikki Pihlajamäki, Markus D. Dubber, and Mark Godfrey (eds), *The Oxford Handbook of European Legal History* (Oxford University Press 2018) 974–999.

classical doctrine. Abandoning the laws of civil war might lead only to permitting cruelty and savagery in internal conflicts: 'The evolution of the law consists precisely in replacing imperfect and violent forms [*formes*] with more refined forms as humanity progresses.' In events of civil war, this human progress could be advanced through respect for the practice of belligerent recognition, which, Rougier argued, was theorised both in response to practical needs and to protect the rights and interests of humanity.[3] In any event, he concluded, 'the regulation of civil war is possible, useful, and let us add, desirable'.[4] This was a sentiment shared by his contemporary Paul Sadoul:

> The interest of both parties [in a civil war] is therefore in line with that of humanity. For the one and the other, it is advantageous to apply the rules of the law of nations and to banish from this fratricidal struggle all the useless cruelties ... This is why the recognition of belligerency got invented in doctrine and diplomacy.[5]

In 1932, Georges Scelle, one of the foremost utopians of his profession, was still referring to the classical principles of insurgent and belligerent recognition in his *Précis de droit des gens.*[6] Scelle pinpointed the same internationalist spirit of speaking truth to power across all domains of international law:

> Without question, the law is in a period of regression. Is this a reason to refrain from setting forth the rules? Quite the contrary, it is important not to weaken their expression. Nothing could be more pernicious than to imagine that the violation of positive law can be confused with its evolution. Already in the history of humanity there have been several periods of regression followed by enlightened stages of progress. It is while waiting for the return of these enlightened stages that we are continuing with the academic study of legal phenomena.[7]

Writing in 1938 on the Spanish Civil War, the Norwegian professor Frede Castberg asked whether 'what we call international law [was] nothing more than an ideal, a program of action for peace advocates,

3 Rougier, *Les guerres civiles*, 6, 165–166.
4 Ibid. 559.
5 Paul Sadoul, *De la guerre civile en droit des gens: Reconnaissance de belligérance* (Imprimerie Paul Scheffer 1905) 71.
6 Georges Scelle, *Précis de droit des gens*, vol I: *Principes et systématique* ([Sirey 1932] Dalloz 2008) 98–99.
7 Georges Scelle, *Précis de droit des gens*, vol II (Sirey 1934) 15. Translation: Hubert Thierry, 'The European Tradition in International Law: Georges Scelle' 1 *European Journal of International law* (1990) 196.

or a utopia'. His answer was a clear no: 'The vital needs of interaction between states demand the order and regulation that international law strives to achieve.'[8] After the world wars, Hersch Lauterpacht openly admitted that the recognition of belligerency was more an exception than the rule, for several reasons. He nonetheless diligently gave it much attention in his *Recognition in International Law*, even arguing in favour of an international duty incumbent on states to grant belligerent recognition in certain situations.[9] Published in 1947, *Recognition* still remains one of the most resourceful examinations of the core concepts of the classical doctrine. And Lauterpacht was by no means the last of the classical scholars; as late as 1966, Erik Castrén was still maintaining that although the traditional legal rules of civil war had been 'slow to develop', there still remained a way forward through sheer hard work by committed legal publicists.[10]

This chapter examines the second coming of the classical doctrine of civil war in four sections. First, it traces the appearance of the first dedicated academic textbooks on the subject in the 1890s. It then describes developments within the Institut de droit international, where some of the publicists came together to formulate resolutions and proposals that they hoped might guide and ameliorate state practice in the world. Thirdly, it discusses the comprehensive synthesis of the classical doctrine that emerged in the early twentieth century as a product of the earlier developments. And lastly, it observes how the classical law of civil war failed to remain relevant in the Spanish Civil War of 1936, which led to general disillusionment over the doctrine.

6.1 'A New Chapter in the Law of Nations'

In the early 1890s, a series of naval revolts broke out in Chile and Brazil, prompting a fresh debate about neutrality and belligerent rights during a maritime insurrection. The Chilean Civil War of 1890–1891 was no shady privateer campaign but a major insurrection by Admiral Montt's revolutionary junta against President Balmaceda's government. The insurgents promptly blockaded Valparaiso and several other ports and

[8] Frede Castberg, 'Folkrettslige spörsmål omkring den spanske borgerkrig' 8 *Nordisk Tidsskrift for International Ret* (1937) 160.

[9] Hersch Lauterpacht, *Recognition in International Law* (Cambridge University Press 1947) 182–184. See also 175–176, 228–230, 236–238, 240–246.

[10] Erik Castrén, *Civil War* (Suomalainen Tiedeakatemia 1966) 78–79.

proceeded to interfere with foreign shipping on the high seas.[11] The insurgent government established its seat in the nitrate-rich province of Iquique and appealed for international recognition, citing the criteria for recognition in Bluntschli's *Das moderne Völkerrecht* and in Lawrence's *Wheaton*.[12] While the Iquique government gained no support from European powers or the United States, it was eventually recognised as belligerent by Bolivia, in a move that became arguably the last formal recognition of belligerency in world history.[13] The United States and Great Britain mainly instructed their commanders to permit the insurgents to conduct their war without foreign interference, provided international commercial shipping was not interfered with and any damages caused to foreign nationals could be later reclaimed from Chile on grounds of state responsibility.[14] Considering the Iquique government as the de facto authority in the region, they dispatched their representatives to oversee the interests of their merchants and investors in the rebel-held areas and accepted the local authorities as representing the Chilean state on practical questions such as licensing, fees, and taxes. Later, after the war had ended in insurgent victory, Chile agreed to establish a series of mixed claims tribunals to adjudicate and oversee the compensation of outstanding foreign private claims arising from the war in Iquique and earlier. These followed a now familiar pattern, with awards of compensation to foreign nationals at the turn of the century.[15]

[11] Hugo Kunz, *Der Bürgerkrieg in Chile* (Brockhaus 1892) 28–38; Harold Blakemore, 'Chile from the War of the Pacific to the World Depression, 1880–1930' in Leslie Bethell (ed), *The Cambridge History of Latin America*, vol V (Cambridge University Press 1986) 508–521.

[12] Chiefs of the Revolutionary Party to Hotham, 26 March 1891, in *Correspondence Respecting the Revolution in Chile 1891* (British Foreign Office 1892), The National Archives, Foreign Office: Confidential Print collection 420/116, 198–200.

[13] Informes de la comisión mixta de relaciones exteriores sobre el reconocimiento de beligerancia de la junta gubernativa de Iquique hecho por el Gobierno de Bolivia (Tipografia de La Nueva Era 1891) 1–20. See also M. H. Geffcken, 'Incidents de droit international dans la guerre civile du Chili' 23 *Revue de droit international et de legislation comparée* (RDI) (1891) 577; Rougier, Les guerres civiles, 215; Hans Wehberg, 'La guerre civile et le droit international' 63 Collected Courses of Hague Academy of International Law (1938) 34. But see Alonso Gurmendi, 'The Last Recognition of Belligerency (and Some Thoughts on Why You May Not Have Heard of It)' Opinio Juris (10 December 2019) https://opiniojuris.org/.

[14] 2 Moore's *Digest* 1107–1112; Lauterpacht, *Recognition*, 218–219, 275; *Correspondence*, The National Archives, Foreign Office: Confidential Print collection 420/116, 99–102.

[15] Claims conventions at 177 CTS 281; 184 CTS 474; 179 CTS 135; 181 CTS 423; 182 CTS 280; 183 CTS 314; 183 CTS 336; 183 CTS 333; 182 CTS 363; 183 CTS 321; 184 CTS 256; 184 CTS 473; 196 CTS 334. Arbitrations at 2 Moore's *Arbitrations* 1470–1484; 3 Moore's

Two similar, if more localised, naval revolts took place in Brazil in 1891 and 1893–1894. Brazil had only just transformed from an empire into a republic when, in 1891, its navy forced President Manuel Deodoro da Fonseca to step down after he attempted to close the congress. Vice-president Floriano Vieira Peixoto took his place, but when Floriano tried to extend his term, refusing to organise new elections, the navy revolted again in 1893 and prepared to bombard the loyalist troops in Río de Janeiro. Given Río's central location along trans-oceanic shipping lanes, foreign imperial navies maintained a regular presence in the area, and the insurgents found themselves operating in the proximity of significant British, German, and US squadrons, which refused to accept an insurgent blockade. In exchange for their ad hoc neutrality, the foreign commanders jointly prohibited the rebels from bombarding commercial ports and directed that all foreign merchant shipping be permitted to continue. On at least one occasion, a US warship used force against the insurgents to ensure this protection.[16] Although the two sides in the conflict eventually engaged in full battle against each other, the foreign powers continued to prevent the formation of an effective blockade and never recognised the naval insurgents as belligerents.[17] The war ended in 1894 after the government managed to obtain new naval units and gradually brought the diplomatically isolated insurgents to surrender.

During these events, the Peruvian diplomat Carlos Wiesse published his monograph *Reglas de derecho internactional aplicable a las guerras civiles*, which his contemporaries credited for being the first dedicated treatise on the subject.[18] Aspiring to offer a systematic examination of the topic, Wiesse harvested applicable passages and principles from classical authors, such as Grotius, Pufendorff, and Vattel, as well as his contemporaries, including Lieber, Bluntschli, and Calvo, and combined these

Arbitrations 2318–2322, 2781–2799; 2938–2944; 2990–2992, 3001–3002, 3067–3071; 4 Moore's *Arbitrations* 3261–3265, 3569–3571, 3571–3590, 3711–3712, 3712–3714, 3744–3745, 4329–4332, 4930–4936; 29 RIAA 305–319, 322–326.

16 Joseph Smith, 'Brazilian Diplomacy and Foreign Intervention in the Brazilian Naval Revolt, 1893–94' 26 *Revista Complutense de Historia de América* (2000) 119–120, 124; 1 Moore's *Digest* 201–205. A joint communication is cited in 1 Moore's *Digest* 203.

17 Smith, 'Brazilian Diplomacy', 128–129, 133; 1 Moore's *Digest* 204–205; British law officers' opinions from 20 July 1893 and 4 August 1894 in II McNair, *Opinions* 393.

18 Carlos Wiesse, *Reglas de Derecho Internactional aplicable a las guerras civiles* (Viuda Galland 1893). Translated into French as *Le droit international appliqué aux guerres civiles* (B. Benda 1898). See also 'Bulletin bibliographique' 5 *Revue générale de droit international public* (RGDIP) (1898) 877–878; Ernest Lehr, 'Notices bibliographiques' 30 RDI (1898) 645–646; Rougier, *Les guerres civiles*, 1.

with fresh examples from diplomatic practice. After briefly exploring the way belligerent communities were formed and recognised, Wiesse presented the law of civil war as a system of legal rules that were applicable when there existed a state of belligerency, while a handful of principles applied to non-recognised insurgencies and situations where a government might be accepted de facto. The distinction between recognised belligerencies and unrecognised insurgencies became the structural spine of the book and an enduring trope in the subsequent literature on the classical doctrine of civil war.

Wiesse's theory of belligerent recognition was closely connected to questions of diplomatic protection and state responsibility in internal conflicts, because Wiesse insisted on the utility of belligerent recognition precisely as a formal means by which a government could exonerate itself from state responsibility. 'The primary and most immediate effect of the recognition of the belligerency of an insurgent party is to detach the Government from responsibility for acts carried out in the territory of the insurgents',[19] he wrote, and cited the US policy of non-responsibility for the Confederacy, which the Washington claims tribunal had adopted in *Hanna's Case*. Wiesse accepted that the duty to protect foreigners and their property was incumbent on the state as a consequence of its sovereign statehood, but this obligation could cease when the state itself (or foreign states for their own part) conceded belligerent recognition to an internal conflict. As long as there was no such recognition, the state and its government remained responsible for the damages suffered by foreigners, because the international personality of the state rested on the criterion that it possessed public organs capable of effectively fulfilling its international duties. Acts that were prejudicial to foreigners could be prima facie considered as taking place with the sanction – or, at least, through the negligence – of the public authorities. Should they wish to avoid that responsibility, there was a way of doing so: the price to be paid for non-liability would simply be the applicability of the laws of war and neutrality on both sides – hardly an undesirable outcome from a liberal cosmopolitan perspective.[20] Wiesse is sometimes remembered as a proponent of strict government responsibility for rebels (as opposed to the presumption of non-responsibility favoured by Calvo and other Latin American scholars),[21] but his approach gave international lawyers a means

[19] Wiesse, *Reglas*, 67.

[20] Ibid 61, 72–76, also citing Carlos Calvo, *Le droit international*, vol III, § 1262. See also Sadoul, *De la guerre civile*, 178–181.

[21] Alberto Ulloa, 'Wiesse, internacionalista' 1 *Nueva Revista Peruana* (1929) 322, 326–328; Carlos Calvo, 'De la non-responsabilité des États à raison des pertes et dommages

of circumventing difficult political tugs-of-war over questions of fact concerning the scale, duration, intensity, and legitimacy of the rebels' actions. In his view, a clean, formal procedure of recognition might appeal more to governments than tortuous scholarly debates – and, in addition, encourage them to adhere to the laws of war.[22]

Two years later, the Marquis of Olivart published his study of belligerent recognition, which had been commissioned by the Spanish foreign minister during the Cuban insurrection.[23] A renowned bibliophile and scholar, Olivart was able to put together an impressive synthesis of the relevant literature. The book's historical journey begins with Grotius and the English Civil War before moving on, via Vattel, to the American and Spanish American revolutions. Although focussing predominantly on state practice, case references, and diplomatic documents, Olivart highlights key authorities such as Henry Wheaton's *Elements*, which he describes as representing 'perfectly the final state of the science before the question of 1861'.[24] In the second part of the book, Olivart systematically surveys German, Italian, French, British, North American, and Spanish scholars, noting, however, the scarcity of scholarship and theory in their works. Olivart had praise mainly for the Anglo-American and German publicists; credit for 'the first scientific exposition' on the subject was given to Richard Henry Dana's footnote in Wheaton's *Elements*, which accordingly featured in several parts of the book.[25]

Written from the perspective of a waning Spanish empire, *Del reconocimiento de beligerancia* was motivated less by questions of state responsibility and more by the containment of neutral interference in civil wars: it revisited the doctrine of civil war to defend Spanish sovereignty in Cuba against encroachments by the United States and other foreign powers. When discussing the nature of belligerent recognition, in particular by neutrals, Olivart took a position that in many ways contrasted with that of Wiesse. Instead of advocating for belligerent recognition as a policy option that states

éprouvés par des étrangers en temps de troubles intérieurs ou de guerres civiles' 1 RDI (1st series 1869) 417.

22 One can also speculate on the relevance of Wiesse's contribution to the Tacna and Arica question and the prospect of Chile's incurring responsibility for the effects of its recent civil war. See Carlos Wiesse, *El asunto de Tacna y Arica; primera conferencia histórico-geográfica sobre las negociaciones diplomáticas entre el Perú y Chile de 1887 a 1894* (Imprenta Torres Aguirre 1905).

23 Marqués Ramón de Dalmau y de Olivart, *Del reconocimiento de beligerancia y sus efectos inmediatos* (Péant & Hijos 1895).

24 Olivart, *Del reconocimiento de beligerancia*, 18–20.

25 Ibid, esp 25, 61–64, 94, 97–99, 108.

could exercise at will, Olivart argued against arbitrary or premature recognition of belligerency by foreign powers, which he considered as intervening in the internal affairs of a state that was putting down a rebellion. Belligerent recognition by foreign powers without a clear and urgent motive of self-interest – which in practice would be the case where the incumbent government and the insurgents were exercising prize jurisdiction against neutrals – was 'a gratuitous and unnecessary offense' against the nation in which the insurgency was occurring.[26] That a legitimate state of belligerency could exist at all in connection with a revolution was a significant concession from an author writing under the auspices of the Duke of Tetuán. Above all, Olivart's conclusions were intended to discredit indeterminate, partway recognitions, such as the American position towards Cuba, and to restrict the possibility of formal recognition by foreign powers.

As the US intervention in Cuba became imminent and then reality, Olivart continued his work by publishing a series of articles on the Cuban question, in which he argued legal counter-positions against the United States.[27] Though the Spanish-American War of 1898 became a total defeat for mainland Spain, Olivart's scholarly efforts earned him a good amount of professional attention. *Del reconocimiento de beligerancia* was given a favourable reception in leading journals, which connected it to the urgency of the Cuban situation and recommended that Olivart's twelve conclusions be shared with a wider audience for broader discussion.[28] It was not long before Olivart brought these twelve points before the Institut de droit international, where they served as a basis for the work of a dedicated study commission on the law of civil war.

6.2 Hamburg to Neuchâtel: The Institut de Droit International and the Law of Civil War

Acting on a proposal by Olivart and his colleague Arthur Desjardins, the Institut de droit international established the 'commission on the rights

[26] Ibid 122–123.

[27] Marquis de Olivart, 'Le différend entre l'Espagne et les États-Unis au sujet de la question cubaine' (7 parts): 4 RGDIP (1897) 577; 5 RGDIP (1898) 358; 5 RGDIP (1898) 499; 7 RGDIP (1900) 541; 9 RGDIP (1902) 161; 10 RGDIP (1903) 577; 12 RGDIP (1905) 469.

[28] Ernest Lehr, 'Question de la reconnaissance des insurgés comme belligérants, suivant un mémoire récent de M. le Marquis d'Olivart' 28 RDI (1896) 100; 'Bulletin bibliographique' 3 RGDIP (1896) 503; Amos S. Hershey, 'The Recognition of Cuban Belligerency' 7 *Annals of the American Academy of Political and Social Science* (1896) 74–85; Arthur Desjardins, 'L'insurrection cubaine et le droit des gens' 3 *Revue de Paris* (1896) 347–383; Louis Le Fur, 'Chronique des faits internationaux: Espagne et États-Unis' 6 RGDIP (1899) 196–229.

and duties of foreign powers and their nationals with respect to established governments in the event of them experiencing insurrectionary movements' at its 1897 session in Copenhagen.[29] The commission was to work in parallel with a separate working group on state responsibility, which had already begun its work in 1891.[30]

The civil war commission presented its draft articles to the Institut in 1898.[31] The eight articles, covering barely two pages, represented a first joint attempt to codify the classical doctrine of civil war. The first three articles laid out general obligations of foreign states in their relations with states struggling with an insurgency, while the rest dealt with the question of belligerent recognition. The opening articles asserted that the law of nations applied in situations of civil war in sovereign states, confirmed the principle of non-intervention in the internal affairs of sovereign states, and prohibited any assistance to foreign insurgents.[32] The articles on belligerent recognition acknowledged the possibility of implicit and explicit recognition, stated the principal effects of such recognition according to whether it was granted by the incumbent government or by third states, and noted that recognition by one government did not oblige others to follow suit. A particular provision confirmed Lieber's old maxim that conceding to insurgents simple considerations of humanity or the basic laws of war would not in itself constitute a formal recognition of belligerency.[33] Recognition by a third power 'produced all the ordinary effects of neutrality', but this right of a foreign state to recognise belligerents was not unlimited: alongside the familiar prerequisites for belligerent recognition (territory, government, organisation of forces, a political goal, and adherence to the essential laws of war),[34] the articles also included Olivart's additional requirement of 'a just cause, that is to say, necessary for safeguarding a national interest'.[35] The commissioners reported that the work had been achieved consensually for the most part; there were just a handful of disagreements, which concerned indeterminacy in the language and the question of who should have the power to interpret the criteria laid down in the convention.

29 16 *Annuaire de l'Institut de droit international* (Annuaire IDI) (1897) 313.
30 11 Annuaire IDI (1889–1892) 15, 487–488.
31 *Projet* of the fourth commission, 17 Annuaire IDI (1898) 71–95.
32 Arts 1 and 2.
33 Art 4 § 2.
34 Art 8.
35 Art 9.

Consensuality was lacking two years later at Neuchâtel when the general meeting of the Institut debated the report for two days. The discussion had barely commenced when John Westlake took the floor and proposed limiting the applicability of the law of civil war to relations 'between States belonging to the European civilization', lest the Europeans be 'disarmed' against 'inferior' states.[36] Brusa and Kebedgy, in their turn, pressed for outright exclusion of non-Christians from the scope of the law.[37] Gustave Rolin-Jaequemyns, who at the time was in the service of the king of Siam, objected to both proposals and demanded the inclusion of all civilised nations without distinction.[38] The question of Japan's status was soon in people's minds, whereupon Westlake conceded that all rules came with exceptions.[39] More specific interests entered the debate, too: one member suggested special exceptions for wars of reunification, another a distinction between 'dynastic' and 'constitutional' insurrections, while certain members wanted to raise the possibility of humanitarian intervention against the Ottoman Empire. In the end, however, the abundance of options was to prove their undoing: when the numerous alternative amendments were put to a vote, they were rejected or withdrawn one by one until Desjardins' original formulation, which made no reference to civilisation, was left unchanged.[40]

Another debate erupted over, as might be expected, the preconditions for recognition of belligerency. The three principal requirements (territory, military organisation, and government) caused no particular dissension and were accepted as points of established law. But the two remaining criteria – that the insurgents fight for a political purpose and that they follow the Institut's 1880 Oxford rules for warfare – proved controversial. The problem with them was their inevitable over- and under-inclusiveness. Some felt that the reference to 'political goals' as a criterion for recognition was at odds with the very purpose of the report, which was to define impartial rules; after some debate, that reference was struck out.[41] By contrast, the reference to the Oxford rules was felt to be too specific. How absolute would adherence to those rules need to be? Could one ill-disciplined unit prevent an entire insurgency from being recognised? And should the rules not refer to the Geneva Convention instead of the Institut's

[36] 18 Annuaire IDI (1900) 182.
[37] Ibid 188–189.
[38] Ibid 183, 187, 189.
[39] Ibid 184.
[40] Ibid 189.
[41] Ibid 217–219.

own principles? After all, the Geneva Convention was legally binding and ensured the involvement of the Red Cross. Ultimately, the meeting settled for a general standard of 'military discipline and conforming to the laws and customs of war',[42] and Olivart's requirement of a just cause was rejected. Ludwig von Bar argued that such a requirement would be impossible to enforce among states that were in disagreement with each another and that the decision to grant recognition lay with the recognising state alone.[43] Olivart opposed this view. Referring directly to the war in Cuba, he urged the Institut to 'clearly establish the nature of the responsibility incumbent on friendly governments'.[44] By this, he meant that the Institut should extend the state responsibility of neutrals, which had been the subject of the Geneva arbitrations, beyond situations of recognised belligerency to cover unrecognised insurgencies. Instead of having only states suffering from civil war compensate foreign investors, Olivart wanted foreign states, too, to have to compensate a state or empire fighting internal insurgents for any interference in its sovereign efforts to protect its integrity. Once the Institut rejected Olivart's additional article, the threshold for foreign powers to incur responsibility in non-recognised insurrections was left without a written description. The Institut bit by bit cut away at the edges and corners of the report until it was finally able to approve the resolution.[45]

The Desjardins commission deferred the topic of state responsibility for insurgents to Emiliano Brusa's parallel commission, which had been working on the subject since 1891. The work of that group was part of a broader debate on state responsibility, which would continue for several years to come.[46] Ever since Calvo's famous 1869 article that opened the debate and the Washington arbitrations in the 1870s, international lawyers and mixed claims commissions had generally accepted that states were prima facie not responsible for damages caused by rebels and insurgents, provided the injury or non-suppression of the revolution could not be attributed to a proven fault or lack of due diligence on the part of their authorities.[47] (US lawyers were among those that took this

[42] Ibid 219–222.
[43] Ibid 222–223.
[44] Ibid 43–44 (Olivart's supplementary note).
[45] Resolution on the rights and duties of foreign powers in the event of insurrectionary movements, 8 September 1900, ibid 227–229.
[46] On that wider picture, see Alan Tzvika Nissel, *Merchants of Legalism: A History of State Responsibility (1870–1960)* (Cambridge University Press 2024) 185–247; Kathryn Greenman, *State Responsibility and Rebels: The History and Legacy of Protecting Investment against Revolution* (Cambridge University Press 2021), 144–148.
[47] For a summary, see Edwin Borchard, *The Diplomatic Protection of Citizens Abroad* (Banks Law Publishing 1919) 229–233.

view, mindful of the precedent of their own government regarding Confederate actions in the past.) The difficulty, however, lay in defining what was to be understood by due diligence. Here, the lawyers diverged: while some (in the manner of Calvo) held that minimum standards should be determined by a state's own domestic legislation and the principle of equal treatment with nationals, others maintained that international law itself provided universal minimum standards that were common to all civilised states. In actual fact, there was a great deal of overlap between the arguments on each side. The matter turned ultimately on who got to define the limits and exceptions, and thus determined the terms considered legitimate for holding states liable.[48] At its meetings in Hamburg and Neuchatel, the Institut examined the commission's work and debated the legal nature and underlying theory of state responsibility at some length. Its members eventually shaped the draft into a fairly moderate resolution aimed at setting down in words a limited set of conditions for state responsibility. These included situations where a state combating rebels had directed its harmful acts against foreign individuals as such, where damage to foreigners was caused by unlawful acts by public officials, where damage was caused through the closure of ports, or 'when the obligation to compensate is well founded on the general principles of the law of war'.[49] The Institut also expressed a wish (*voeu*) for states not to include in their treaties clauses providing for reciprocal exoneration from responsibility and for them to respect the duty of protection they owed to their citizens.[50]

It is difficult to say how much impact the resolution had beyond the Institut, as the question took on a new urgency in the following years. In 1902, several Latin American states signed a multilateral convention concerning the rights of aliens, in which they agreed that states bore no responsibility towards foreigners other than as established in their domestic laws, and that states were not liable for damages arising from acts of war, 'whether civil or national, unless the constituted authority has been negligent in fulfilling its duties'.[51] At the same time, however, the infamous Venezuelan blockade that year led to international arbitrations on a large scale and ushered in an era of strong diplomatic protection, which prompted Latin American lawyers to demand, but with little

48 Greenman, *State Responsibility and Rebels*, 18, 89–108.
49 18 Annuaire IDI (1900) 254–256.
50 17 Annuaire IDI (1898) 96, 134–137; 18 Annuaire IDI (1900) 253–254.
51 Convention concerning the Rights of Aliens, 29 January 1902, 190 CTS 445, art 2.

practical success, a prohibition on the use of force by Europeans for the collection of public debts.[52]

6.3 The French Synthesis of the Classical Doctrine of Civil War

Between 1903 and 1905, a new generation of French *doctorants* produced what can be considered a synthesis of the classical doctrine of civil war. The most prominent was Antoine Rougier, who set out to combine the theories of Wiesse and Olivart with the latest developments at the Institut de droit international and in state practice. Like his predecessors, Rougier considered legal relations between a lawful government and insurgents to be centred primarily on the question of belligerent recognition.[53] Rougier emphasised the overall interests of humanity as a compelling reason for granting belligerent recognition and opposed the idea that governments could repudiate neutral duties at will.[54] Focusing chiefly on empires, he studied cases in which wars involved protectorates, vassal states, and colonial insurrections. His perspective on colonial conflicts remained staunchly Eurocentric: while pointing out that theorising protectorates as 'semi-sovereign' was a contradiction in terms, he resolved this contradiction in favour of empire, readily observing that local colonial revolts had generally been equated with provincial rebellions – and thus illegitimate wars – whose instigators could be punished as rebels.[55]

As regards major colonial uprisings, Rougier took note of contemporary authors such as Despagnet and Dubois who, by analogy with private law, had proposed that since a protectorate was established by treaty between two states, it must follow that the protectorate was dissolvable by either party.[56] However, from the perspective of the law of civil war proper, Rougier found such a theory 'very juridical ... but too ideal, too theoretical, too detached from facts'; underlying any protectorate was a relationship of compulsion and force, and even if there was mutual

[52] Jackson H. Ralston and W. T. Sherman Doyle (eds), *Venezuelan Arbitrations of 1903* (US Government Printing Office 1904); *The Venezuelan Preferential Case*, 22 February 1904, 9 RIAA (1959) 99–110; Drago to García Merou, 29 December 1902, 1 *American Journal of International Law* (1907) 1; H. Edward Nettles, 'The Drago Doctrine in International Law and Politics' 8 *Hispanic American Historical Review* (1928) 217–223.

[53] Rougier, *Les guerres civiles*, 2. Paul Fauchille applauded Rougier for having 'treated his subject with great talent, so well that after his work there remain very few things to say'. 10 RGDIP (1903) 161.

[54] Rougier, *Les guerres civiles*, 165–166, 193–196.

[55] Ibid 85–91.

[56] Ibid 92–93.

agreement between the parties on protection and tutelage, the same could not be said of the subordination of the one to the other. Furthermore, he noted that the very idea of a protectorate was based on a responsibility to protect the indigenous population, not merely against foreign threats but also against the population's own internal failings. Therefore, as a matter of logic, just as tutors represented their wards in the international arena, so they also bore responsibility for them and were thus entitled to apply disciplinary force, when necessary, in carrying out their duties.[57] The pedigree of French punitive colonialism was clearly visible here, for the interventions France was conducting in Madagascar and continental Africa were framed precisely as police operations in defence of civilisation.[58] The idea of colonial intervention for a just cause and in the name of humanity had a particular appeal to Rougier. In his monograph he examined Calvo's and Pradier-Fodéré's ideas and taxonomies concerning interventions and, during the following years, continued to promote the civilising mission that inspired them and to further develop Pradier-Fodéré's theories of humanitarian intervention.[59] Rougier imagined that, with sufficient international support, it might be acceptable one day to protect human society as a whole from an individual state either by a collective intervention or by a single state acting with a mandate from the others.[60]

By the end of the first decade of the twentieth century the new scholarly synthesis of the classical doctrine of civil war was complete. Together with the French edition of Wiesse's book (1898) and the two Institut resolutions from 1900, the doctoral theses by Rougier and his contemporaries L. N. Stéfanesco and Paul Sadoul (both of whom followed a very similar approach)[61] compiled and systematised the law of civil war in a manner that would become something of an archetype for the law of civil war. They established a pattern that, for several decades, other authors would follow in their writings not only on internal wars but also on recognition more broadly,[62] and which was still framing legal

57 Ibid 101–103.

58 Ibid 98–99.

59 Ibid 320–349; Antoine Rougier, 'La théorie de l'intervention d'humanité' 17 RGDIP (1910) 468–526; Compare Paul Pradier-Fodéré, *Traité de droit international public européen et américain*, vol I (Durand et Pedone 1885) §§ 383–388.

60 Rougier, *Les guerres civiles*, 344–345.

61 L. N. Stéfanesco, *La guerre civile et les rapports des belligérants* (A. Rousseau 1903); Sadoul, *De la guerre civile*.

62 See James Lorimer, 'La doctrine de la reconnaissance, fondement du droit international' 16 RDI (1st series 1884) 333–359; Julius Goebel, *The Recognition Policy of the United*

debates at the time of the Spanish Civil War. The framework sought to combine recent developments in the laws of war and state responsibility with a push for a transparent, public, and formalistic diplomacy of recognition in situations of insurgency and belligerency. Although the French synthesis had little immediate impact on state practice, the legal precedents it brought together were firmly rooted in the age of sail, in many ways inseparable from the transatlantic revolutionary experiences of the early to mid nineteenth century. Further, scholars made regular references to contemporary cases and examples, such as the British and French expeditions in Transvaal and Madagascar. However, these experiences did not – and could not – have any direct bearing on principles that were based on a set of outdated policy options that governments now systematically refused to take. It was as if, by describing contemporaneous events in the language of the classical doctrine, scholars hoped to show that upon closer inspection there was less discrepancy between their doctrine and the contemporary world than one might otherwise assume.

The legal principles of civil war were embraced in prominent anglophone literature too. In 1905, the first edition of Lassa Oppenheim's *International Law* dealt with the question of neutrality in civil war by reference to Rougier.[63] John Bassett Moore's monumental *Digest of International Law* (1906) devoted lengthy sections to civil war and belligerent recognition from a US perspective. The question of civil war was also of particular interest to Herbert A. Smith, whose *Great Britain and the Law of Nations* mobilised archived opinions of British law officers for the use of international legal professionals. Smith presented his work as something of an experiment; when it came to the rich, but contradictory, materials on civil wars, he openly gave up any attempt to systematise them, opting instead for a chronological approach. His disciple Arnold McNair did likewise in his *International Law Opinions*, which presented questions of civil war and insurgency mostly in chronological order. In 1947, Hersch Lauterpacht revisited these materials in his more systematised treatise *Recognition in International Law.* On questions of state responsibility, American scholars like Edwin Borchard and

States (Columbia University 1915); René Le Normand, *La reconnaissance internationale et ses diverses applications* (Imprimerie Camis 1899); Rafael Erich, 'La naissance et la reconnaissance des États' 13 *Collected Courses of Hague Academy of International Law* (1926) 431–507; Ferdinand Schlüter, *De-facto Anerkennung im Völkerrecht* (Verlag Konrad Triltsch 1936); Lauterpacht, *Recognition*, 175–201.

[63] Oppenheim, *International Law* (1st edn, 1905) vol II, 86 and 321 (§§ 76 and 298).

Clyde Eagleton ultimately came to dominate the literature, debating whether the contours of state responsibility should be codified internationally or were best left for arbitrators and the most distinguished publicists to determine.[64]

The continental textbook model of the law of civil war remained remarkably unchanged beyond the First World War and the second wave of decolonisation which followed the peace of Paris. When Roberto Domenech's doctoral thesis on the law of civil war in the Americas was published in 1915, the presentation it chose was not fundamentally different, though the thesis covered only situations where belligerency had not been recognised.[65] Luis Podestá Costa, the renowned Argentinian scholar on civil wars, started with the question of state responsibility in his *El extranjero en la guerra civil*, published in 1913. The book became emblematic of the Latin American perspective, as he argued that civil wars were similar to situations of force majeure and made the case that state responsibility should be determined in accordance with domestic standards (as opposed to a hypothetical international measure).[66] But in 1926, in his general manual on the law applicable to civil strife, he adopted a very familiar structure: there, the systematic distinction between insurgency and civil war – and thus the applicable law – hinged on the 'voluntary but not arbitrary' condition of belligerent recognition, and the part devoted to state responsibility followed the reasoning from his previous publications.[67] These scholars writing on the law of civil war were motivated by various and often divergent projects – be it the question of state responsibility in relation to insurgencies, the expansion or containment of neutral rights, or articulation of the legal principles applied by governments in managing colonial insurgencies – yet, broadly speaking, they shared a common belief in a certain culture of formalism that could advance transparency and legal certainty in international relations. In particular, their reliance on the recognition of belligerency as an organising principle for legal relations between states in times of civil war would remain a central tenet of the teaching of the classical scholars until the doctrine's ultimate demise in the post-war years.

[64] Nissel, *Merchants of Legalism*, 238–241.

[65] Roberto Domenech, *Las guerras civiles americanas ante el derecho internacional* (thesis, University of Buenos Aires 1915).

[66] Luis A. Podestá Costa, *El extranjero en la guerra civil* (De Coni 1913). See also Greenman, *State Responsibility and Rebels*, 133–136.

[67] Luis A. Podesta Cosa, *Ensayo sobre las luchas civiles y el derecho internacional* (Rezzónico 1926).

But the very same formalism that gave their doctrine its structural clarity and principled appeal also produced its fundamental flaw. If belligerency was a convenient tool for states to use responsibly and respectfully when circumstances so required, then it followed that sovereign states could also decide not to use it and demand that the rest of the world respect their decision. According to Wiesse, governments of sovereign states remained 'sovereign judges' in their own affairs.[68] This contrasted with Olivart's view that, despite this freedom, even states that might want to recognise a foreign belligerency were forbidden to abuse such recognition for self-interested ends.[69] Between the two, who would decide when the use of state discretion was appropriate? No matter how hard the international lawyers may have hoped to become the chosen arbiters of international justice, none of them could force states to grant or refuse recognition against their will. This left the position of formalism with very little normative weight; on the contrary, it opened the door to ever more discrepant and self-interested state practices. In sum, the scholarship of the law of civil war provided a broad vocabulary of legal rules and principles through which states and scholars could engage in debates concerning ongoing internal conflicts in the world. Their teachings had more effect in describing and giving reasons for the actions and inaction of states and insurgent factions than in directly influencing their behaviour. They themselves were aware of this; positivist scholars at the time sought to provide authoritative and useful overviews of the law as it was, not to challenge or reject contemporary state practice. The fate reserved for their work, which laid such emphasis on the utility of recognising belligerency in civil wars yet provided ample scope for not doing so, was in their view due ultimately not to its own shortcomings but to the shortcomings of the world of sovereign states that they sought to both serve and guide. The contradictory nature of their legal materials was in other words due less to faults in their thinking and more to the fragmentary and opportunistic nature of state practice in their century.

6.4 An Age of Disillusionment

Depending on one's perspective, the Spanish Civil War of 1936–1939 was either the last of the classical civil wars or the first of the (post-)modern ones. In some ways, it was still very much a classical civil war as described

[68] Carlos Wiesse, *Le droit international appliqué aux guerres civiles* (1898) 18–22, 29.
[69] Olivart, *Del reconocimiento de beligerancia*, 89, 93–94.

by Vattel: a faction within the state ceased to obey the government and was strong enough to make a stand against it, whereby the republic was split in two, each side taking up arms against the other. Likewise, the world outside initially approached the conflict through the language of neutrality and belligerency, debating whether such recognition should be granted or neutrality declared. However, neither of these legal concepts seemed to make sense in the context of the Spanish Civil War. No declarations of neutrality were made, nor was there any recognition of belligerency. Instead, the entire conflict took place in what, legally speaking, was peacetime. The war divided the international community not into belligerents and neutrals, but rather into ideologically opposed sides, where the international response – to the extent there was any – centred around multilateral diplomacy and collective security. The Spanish war was thus also an 'international' civil war of a new kind.

The war forced international lawyers to finally face the bankruptcy of the classical doctrine of civil war. Even against the generally catastrophic backdrop of the interwar 1930s – the onset of the Cold War; the Japanese and Italian aggressions in Manchuria and Ethiopia; the imminent failure of the mandate system in Palestine, Syria, Southern Africa, and elsewhere; and, of course, the rise and expansion of the murderous Nazi regime – the Spanish war stood out as a particular failure of international law. By all appearances, this was a true civil war in a metropolitan European state, a case where both the laws of civil war and humanitarian law should have demonstrated the full legal and 'civilising' impact they potentially could have on real events. Yet amidst the ideological chaos created by fundamental political confrontations, arcane formalities like belligerent recognition or insurgent prize jurisdiction proved to be of little significance.

The war in Spain proved to be disastrously divisive for the interwar lawyers who continued to profess being voices of the cosmopolitan legal conscience of the civilised world. The war turned out to be violent and uncontrollable, and in state practice the international non-intervention efforts served as much as a smokescreen for intervention as they did as a mechanism for preventing it. The decisions taken by the foreign powers, such as their de facto recognition of the Nationalist regime, seemed to either disregard the old international laws of civil war or promote novel ideas that contradicted the views of legal publicists. Ultimately, all such bargains failed to secure international peace in Europe, and posteriority would remember the Spanish war as nothing but a fiasco, throwing doubt on the validity of the very concept of belligerent recognition, which seemed to have lost all practical significance in international law.[70]

The legal abolition of war between 1919 and 1928 completely uprooted the conceptual foundations of the classical doctrine of civil war, as it marked a fundamental transition in the structure of legal argument regarding war and peace under modern international law.[71] Before the interwar period, under what this book has called the 'classical' law of nations, public war remained a lawful (if regrettable) means of dispute resolution between states. If all other means of settlement failed, then lawful transfers of territory, rights, or title could still legitimately be enforced through aggressive acquisitions such as conquest, annexation, and capture or through coercion. However, with the founding of the League of Nations in 1920, the renunciation of war as a means of national policy in the Pact of Paris of 1928,[72] and the rise of collective international sanctions against aggressors in the 1930s, states gradually overturned the formal legal basis of war. After the end of the Second World War, the UN Charter sought expressly to constitute something resembling an international monopoly on violence through collective security, leaving individual states with mainly just the language of self-defence to justify their autonomous uses of force.

The prohibition of war reframed unilateral use of force as a legal problem: it meant that the credibility of international law required someone – be it a state, group of states, or other collective entity – to enforce the prohibition and to have the means of doing so.[73] This led to the adoption of international sanctions against those deemed to be aggressors and the formulation of the Stimson Doctrine, which called for states not to recognise any coercive acquisitions of territory, property, or treaty concessions.[74] If unjust aggression had become an act of armed

[70] Castrén, *Civil War*, 136, discussing Jean Siotis, *Le droit de la guerre et les conflits armés d'un caractère non-international* (LGDJ 1958) 222–223.

[71] Generally, see Stephen Neff, *War and the Law of Nations* (Cambridge University Press 2005) 286–313; Oona Hathaway and Scott Shapiro, *The Internationalists* (Simon & Schuster 2018) pt II.

[72] General Treaty for Renunciation of War as an Instrument of National Policy, signed at Paris, 27 August 1928, 94 LNTS 57.

[73] This resembles a new just-war tradition. See e.g. Neff, *War and the Law of Nations*, 279–281; Hans Kelsen, *Law and Peace in International Relations* (Harvard University Press 1942) 51–55.

[74] Henry L Stimson, 'The Pact of Paris: Three Years of Development' 11 *Foreign Affairs Special Supplement* (1932) vii. Stimson's cables are printed in FRUS (Japan 1931–1941) vol I, 76; Hathaway and Shapiro, *The Internationalists*, 165–168.

robbery among states, then no proceeds from such crime could be legitimate. The long journey to collective security had begun. Only once war was replaced with an organised system of collective enforcement involving the use of armed force could it be thought of as abolished as the ultimate sanction under general international law. The prohibition of war as an instrument of national policy gave way to the use of force as an instrument of international policy to be directed against violations of international law and in defence of an international rule of law.[75] This reversal led to a great deal of criticism and resistance among legal professionals. Some found such a 'discriminatory' concept of just war a scandalous abandonment of sovereign equality,[76] while others suggested a codification of international law was the only way forward or stressed the vital importance of reinforcing international judicial institutions.[77] A particularly bitter pill for many international lawyers was the gradual realisation that the abolition of war also meant an abolition of neutrality. Some senior scholars continued to defend and redefine the law of neutrality for many years after the Pact of Paris.[78] Yet, as attested by the words of Politis on the eve of the Spanish Civil War, the legal profession was well aware of the doctrinal about-turn that was taking place at the time.

> A new era began with the Pact of Paris of 1928. The war of aggression – that is to say, the unjust war – is henceforth proscribed. It has ceased to be a lawful act. War is no longer permitted except as a measure of legitimate defense or of sanction applied by the body collective, or in its name. Therefore, neutrality as it was previously understood has ceased, in principle, to exist.[79]

Although the renunciation of war primarily concerned relations between states, it inevitably raised questions about the legal status of civil war as well. When 'war' ceased to be a legal concept, it was not at all obvious what this would entail for the sub-concept of 'civil war'. During the Spanish Civil War scholars noted with exasperation that any proper functioning of the classical law of civil war needed war to be a lawful

75 Hans Kelsen, *Principles of International Law* (Rinehart 1952) 42–44.
76 Famously Carl Schmitt, 'The Turn to the Discriminating Concept of War (1937)' in Carl Schmitt, *Writings on War* (T. Nunan ed, Polity Press 2011) 30–74.
77 For example, Hans Wehberg, *The Outlawry of War* ([1928] Carnegie Endowment for International Peace 1931) 94–96; Hersch Lauterpacht, *The Function of Law in the International Community* ([1933] Oxford University Press 2011) 431–439.
78 Hathaway and Shapiro, *The Internationalists*, 168–171; Kelsen, *Principles*, 81–89.
79 Nicolas Politis, *Neutrality and Peace* (Carnegie Endowment for International Peace 1935), 8.

state of affairs, and since this seemed no longer to be the case, the outcome would almost certainly be some form of an indeterminate condition of insurgency for intra-state conflicts.[80] In this respect, the interwar transformation of the law of war also upended the law of recognition (insofar as it had ever been settled). It contributed to a dilution of the formalist and straightforwardly constitutive understanding of recognition in international law, which had been relatively clear about governments being responsible for their discretionary policies. As recognition became increasingly expressed as declarative – we recognise things because they exist[81] – their policies risked becoming even more vulnerable to criticisms of selectivity and hegemonism than before. Although states had always tended to justify their actual acts of recognition with arguments that cited tangible, objective facts ('under these circumstances we find ourselves *obliged* to recognise ... '), when there were disagreements their different interpretations had been easier to explain through the constitutive theories in the nineteenth century ('in the end each state makes its own sovereign decision'). Little surprise, then, that the new practices of collective recognition and non-recognition might cause resentment among jurists in those countries that became targets of collective liberal criticism and sanctions.

The turn to declarative theories of recognition was articulated particularly clearly at the inter-American conferences. In 1928, participants resolved to renounce the legality of war and established in the Habana Convention a new hemispheric, anti-revolutionary legitimism: the contracting states bound themselves to use all means at their disposal to prevent their nationals from supporting foreign insurgents and could take punitive action towards insurgent vessels at sea or disarm insurgents found in their territories.[82] In the 1933 Montevideo Convention, they expressly adopted the declaratory theory of recognition by stating that the political existence of a state was independent of recognition by other States. Yet as the treaty made all the rights of a state dependent on its legal personhood and remained silent as to how such personhood could be

80 For example, Georges Scelle, 'La reconnaissance des insurgés et la guerre espagnole' 37 *Die Friedens-Warte* (1937) 68–69.

81 Rafael Erich, 'La naissance et la reconnaissance des états' 13 *Collected Courses of Hague Academy of International Law* (1926) 461.

82 Habana Convention on the rights and duties of states in civil strife, 20 February 1928, 134 LNTS (1932–1933) 45, arts 1–3. According to Article 1(3), war material might be trafficked for the government 'while the belligerency of the rebels has not been recognized, in which latter case the rules of neutrality shall be applied'.

established other than through recognition, it pragmatically left the final say on the legitimacy of revolutionaries to foreign (i.e. US) governments, which could accord them partial de facto or full de jure legal treatment as they saw fit.[83]

Finally, the Spanish Civil War took place after the social revolutions during the second wave of decolonisation had profoundly altered the political stakes, transforming civil wars from local disturbances into ideological confrontations. Since 1917 the Bolshevik regime, with its unprecedented abolition of private property and the nationalisation of foreign assets and industries, had been challenging not only the individual foreign investors but the liberal international legal worldview as a whole.[84] While the West sought to make recognition of the Soviets conditional on their assuming Russia's old foreign debts and acknowledging the international legal protection due to future foreign investments,[85] the Bolsheviks kept responding with anti-imperialist policies and initiatives that predicted an international world revolution in all countries. In the domain of international law, this ideological confrontation gradually gave rise to two competing understandings of the right of peoples to self-determination – one class-based and revolutionary, the other conservative and legalistic.[86] While liberal visions of tutelage over peripheral peoples perpetuated European colonialism under the umbrella of the League of Nations mandate system, the USSR sought to present itself as the champion of independence and sovereign equality for non-Europeans. But the principle of self-determination was fundamentally indeterminate and vulnerable to controversy. During the Spanish Civil War it was adopted also by the Nationalist cause against what it saw as a radicalised, foreign-controlled Left; together with the cynical invocation of self-determination by Germany in its *Anschluss* policies, this

83 Montevideo Convention, 26 December 1933, 164 LNTS (1936) 19.

84 Andrea Leiter, 'Contestations over Legal Authority: The Lena Goldfields Arbitration 1930' in Greenman and others (eds), *Revolutions in International Law: The Legacies of 1917* (Cambridge University Press 2021) 315–338; Kate Miles, '1917: Property, Revolution and Rejection' in Greenman and others (eds), *Revolutions in International Law*, 280–284. Compare also John Hughes-Wilson, *A Brief History of the Cold War* (Robinson 2006) 4–12.

85 Leiter, 'Contestations', 317–321.

86 Lauri Mälksoo, 'The Soviet Approach to the Right of Peoples to Self-Determination: Russia's Farewell to *jus publicum europaeum*' 19 *Journal of the History of International Law* (2017) 200–218. Compare Robert Knox and Ntina Tzouvala, 'Looking Eastwards: The Bolshevik Theory of Imperialism and International Law' in Greenman and others (eds), *Revolutions in International Law*, 40–42.

highlighted the unpredictable dark sides latent in an international law that promoted the challenging of established governments in the name of popular movements.[87]

6.4.1 *The Last Civil War*

The Spanish Civil War bore all the hallmarks of a public, total war. It was fought on land, sea, and air by both regular and irregular troops between organised and internationally represented governments. When, in July 1936, the Spanish garrisons in North Africa mutinied against the elected socialist government in Madrid, most of the armies positioned in mainland Spain joined their cause, while the desperate Republican government responded by distributing arms to the workers and students who joined the loyalist remnants of the armed forces. The result was a bitter conflict characterised by a great deal of lawlessness, summary violence, and radicalism. From the start, the Spanish Civil War was carried out with foreign assistance, as Italian and German planes and armaments supported the insurgents both in combat and logistics.

Within a month of the outbreak of the Spanish Civil War, international diplomacy around it took a dramatic turn. Fearing international escalation and seeking appeasement, the United Kingdom and France negotiated a so-called Non-intervention Agreement in August 1936, in which both declared that they would prohibit all exportation of weapons and other war materials to either side in Spain and called for other states to join their coordinated response. They agreed to establish international controls on Spanish land borders and to organise naval patrols on the high seas, flying the flag of the North Sea Fisheries Convention.[88] Twenty-five parties joined them, including Germany, Italy, Portugal and the USSR, all suspected of interference; the USSR nevertheless refused to join the naval patrol system.[89] To facilitate and coordinate

[87] See Erich Hula, 'National Self-Determination Reconsidered' 10 *Social Research* (1943) 1–21; Edward J. Kolla, *Sovereignty, International Law, and the French Revolution* (Cambridge University Press 2017) 280–282.

[88] Resolution on the observation scheme, 8 March 1937 in 31(S4) *American Journal of International Law* (1937) 163–178; The patrol system is described in Hans Wehberg, 'Civil War and International Law' in William E. Rappard and others (eds), *The World Crisis* (Graduate Institute/Longmans, Green 1938) 184–185; Stephen Neff, *The Rights and Duties of Neutrals* (Juris Publishing/Manchester University Press 2000) 181.

[89] The declarations are in Norman J. Padelford, *International Law and Diplomacy in the Spanish Civil Strife* (Macmillan 1939) 205–230. See also Francis Hemming, *International Committee for the Application of the Agreement Regarding Non-intervention in Spain*

these non-intervention activities, the parties established a dedicated International Non-intervention Committee in London. This was thus an attempt to coordinate a collective security response to an internal conflict through something resembling an international organisation.

Classical legal indicators of a civil war began to appear soon after the outbreak of hostilities. The Republican government declared several insurgent-held ports under blockade in late 1936, and in 1937 Franco's Nationalists declared their own blockade on Bilbao and the Basque ports.[90] Perhaps owing to the experiences of the First World War, these 'blockades' do not seem to have been instituted in due form: they were aimed primarily at the seizure of contraband goods instead of all vessels, though there appear to have been no published lists of contraband.[91] Throughout the war foreign vessels were subjected to visits, searches, seizures, and later even to mines, attacks, and bombardments in the coastal waters and on the high seas. A notable element in these encounters was the question of the use of force in territorial waters, where many jurists conceded that the government had a sovereign right to take forcible measures but doubted whether the insurgents had the same.[92] The support for collective non-intervention partially emerged from these concerns, in particular from the repeated aerial bombardments and strafings that targeted neutral shipping without an established procedure or precaution.[93]

Foreign governments refused to acquiesce to the blockades. Britain informed Madrid that it refused to regard either party as belligerent and that it would not tolerate any interference with British vessels; it also ordered British warships in the area to protect its merchantmen.[94] When the Spanish Republican navy seized the German freighter *Palos* and

(HMSO 1936). Hugh Thomas estimates that over 150,000 foreign troops supported the Nationalists and 50,000 the Republic (this includes international brigades and volunteers), with thousands of planes, tanks, and artillery pieces. See Thomas, *The Spanish Civil War* (3rd edn, Penguin 1977) 974–985.

90 Padelford, *Spanish Civil Strife*, 9–10.

91 Arnold McNair 'The Law Relating to the Civil War in Spain' 53 *Law Quarterly Review* (1937) 488; H. A. Smith, 'Some Problems of the Spanish Civil War' 18 *British Yearbook of International Law* (1937) 29.

92 Padelford, *Spanish Civil Strife*, 25–52, 663–674; Arnold J. Toynbee and V. M. Boulter, *Survey of International Affairs 1937*, vol II: *Spain* (Oxford University Press 1938) 305–307.

93 Padelford, *Spanish Civil Strife*, 31–35.

94 Ann Van Wynen Thomas and A. J. Thomas Jr, 'International Legal Aspects of the Civil War in Spain, 1936–39' in Richard A. Falk (ed), *The International Law of Civil War* (Johns Hopkins Press/ASIL, 1971) 152–153; Padelford, *Spanish Civil Strife*, 10.

confiscated the goods it was carrying, Germany called the seizure an act of 'red piracy' and used it as a pretext to retaliate by seizing two Spanish government merchant vessels, which it then turned over to Franco's insurgents.[95] The instructions of the French navy also designated insurgent activities at sea as piracy, whereas the United States refused to recognise any of the blockades in the conflict and complained that none of them were effectively maintained.[96]

The Nationalist blockades – and their claim to belligerent status – remained on an insecure footing, as no foreign powers were willing to acknowledge a Nationalist prize jurisdiction. As Franco's navy and air force executed their commands as though they were lawful belligerents, their actions raised foreign protests and pecuniary claims against Spain. The blockade of Bilbao, in particular, became a point of tension, as British warships faced off against Nationalist cruisers. Under pressure from Franco's insurgent government, the British government finally announced that even though it could not recognise or concede belligerent rights, given the conditions British vessels 'should not, for practical reasons, and in view of risks against which it is at present impossible to protect them, go into that area so long as these conditions prevail'.[97] The matter caused something of an uproar in Britain and in the United States, but when a British freighter successfully ran the blockade to Bilbao, the government took this as a demonstration of the lack of its effectiveness and discontinued its cautions, permitting Royal Navy destroyers to resume their protection of British shipping.[98]

The Madrid government never recognised Franco's forces as belligerents, and the relations between the two warring factions in the Spanish Civil War took place in the legally uncertain domain of unrecognised insurgencies. Consequently, the applicability of the laws of war at the time was for the most part unclear or doubtful. Although by 1936 an impressive array of conventions on the laws of war were in force – including the Hague Conventions of 1907, the Geneva Conventions of 1929, and even a tentative draft code of 1923 relating to aerial warfare – it was not clear to what extent these instruments were meant to bind states

95 Thomas and Thomas, 'International Legal Aspects', 153; Padelford, *Spanish Civil Strife*, 10–11; Vernon O'Rourke, 'Recognition of Belligerency and the Spanish War' 31 *American Journal of International Law* (1937) 398–413.

96 Padelford, *Spanish Civil Strife*, 12.

97 Toynbee and Boulter, *Survey*, 308.

98 Ibid 306–309; 'Another British Ship Runs the Blockade' *The New York Times* (29 April 1937).

in internal conflicts. In the absence of belligerent recognition, all that was left was the lonely Martens Clause and the domains of international custom, general principles of law, and the teachings of publicists in various nations calling for minimum considerations of humanity.[99] Their reach was limited, for brutalities occurred on both sides of the conflict, be it summary executions, the destruction of property, the taking and execution of hostages, or the aerial bombing of civilians. Both sides at times gave assurances that prisoners of war would be treated with respect, while the government denied that this had any impact on the status of the insurgents. Despite these assurances, conditions varied for prisoners of war, and although small ad hoc exchanges of prisoners took place through the mediation of the Red Cross, cartels were not established systematically.[100]

The most significant – and perhaps the most controversial – legacy of the Spanish Civil War for international law was the collective response of the international community. The Non-intervention Agreement proved deeply problematic from the outset. Scholars immediately claimed that the agreement amounted to tacit recognition of an insurgency, perhaps even of belligerency, although the governments dismissed this claim. Even more troubling was the fact that the foreign powers sought to apply non-intervention equally towards both sides, without pointing to a clear legal basis for preventing all lawful peacetime interaction with the lawfully constituted government of Spain. Accordingly, the Republican government protested that the agreement amounted in practice to 'a blockade of the legitimate Government' as it impeded Spain's lawful arms purchases while arms continued to be supplied to the insurgents clandestinely by some of the signatories of the agreement. The embargo was 'creating a very grave precedent in the international order' and fostering ideological rebellions.[101] The cooperation on which implementation of the Non-intervention Agreement depended ran continually into practical difficulties as the two warring sides were reluctant to post guarantees and bonds in relation to their behaviour and challenged the credibility of the guarantees of mutual assistance between the supposedly cooperating powers. A testing point came when the German cruiser *Leipzig* was torpedoed off Valencia. The British and French were

99 The Martens Clause is in the preambles to the Hague II Convention (1899) and the Hague IV Convention (1907).

100 Thomas and Thomas, 'International Legal Aspects', 121–140.

101 The note is in Padelford, *Spanish Civil Strife*, 231–232.

reluctant to heed to Germany's call for joint action against both sides in response; as a result, Germany discontinued its cooperation.[102]

The continuing torpedo attacks, aerial bombings, and the sightings of unidentified submarines in the Mediterranean convinced the remaining parties to the Non-intervention Agreement to step up their measures. Meeting in the Swiss town of Nyon, they upgraded their naval observation scheme into an organised international naval patrol system, under which British and French warships were instructed to engage against naval threats and to treat unidentified submarines and airplanes as pirates 'in what became, in effect, the first armed-neutrality effort since the Napoleonic wars'.[103] While the Nyon agreement may have proved somewhat more effective than the first draft of the Non-intervention Agreement, its measures were limited to protecting foreign shipping rather than preventing international interventions. The outcome was that clandestine shipments of arms and personnel to Spain continued by blockade runners, through land border crossings, under neutral flags (the non-intervention system applied only to its members' flags), or simply by airplane.

***

Behind the facade of joint non-intervention, the international community fragmented completely, and even disagreed on which side represented the lawful government. In November 1936, Germany and Italy had already recognised Franco's government as the lawful government of Spain and withdrawn their chargés d'affaires from Madrid.[104] Though the measure was strongly criticised and denounced as a violation of international law,[105] from their perspective it allowed them to respond to accusations of foreign intervention by maintaining that they were, in fact, supporting what they considered the lawful government. Throughout the war there was no serious doubt that both countries were supplying the insurgents with considerable material assistance (while, on the other side, the USSR tried to do the same for the socialists).

[102] Padelford, *Spanish Civil Strife*, 29.

[103] The Nyon agreement and supplementary agreement, 14 and 17 September 1937, in Padelford, *Spanish Civil Strife*, 603. Citation from Neff, *Rights and Duties of Neutrals*, 181.

[104] Thomas and Thomas, 'International Legal Aspects', 160–161; German recognition, 18 November 1936, in *Documents on German Foreign Policy 1918–1945*, vol 3: *Germany and the Spanish War* (US Department of State 1950) 134, doc no 125. See also 'Germany and Italy Recognise Rebel Government' *The Guardian* (19 November 1936).

[105] For example, McNair, 'Law Relating to the Civil War in Spain', 497.

This left Britain, France, and their closest allies hovering in the middle with the threat of a major international war limiting what their statesmen thought was their room for manoeuvre. Variations of de jure and de facto recognition of the insurgents came from Portugal, Guatemala, Albania, Nicaragua, the Holy See, Yugoslavia, Japan, Manchukuo, Uruguay, Austria–Hungary, Turkey, Greece, Romania, Czechoslovakia, and the Netherlands,[106] before Britain itself, in 1937, entered into a de facto consular relationship with the Franco regime. It exchanged agents with both warring factions, who were to function as consuls on questions of 'trade' in their territories but without formal diplomatic status – an arrangement that sought to pragmatically depoliticise commercial matters and to separate them from uncomfortable questions of sovereignty, war, peace, and the life and death of innocent people.[107]

The lack of clarity surrounding de facto and de jure recognitions in the Spanish War – 'a confusing, nebulous, and unsettled area of international law'[108] – caused incessant problems for the courts and administrations charged with giving them effect. When courts of law aligned themselves with the government's views in accordance with the *Gazette* principle, they found it increasingly difficult to understand what exactly the government's position was in the first place. In the British cases of *Banco de Bilbao* v. *Sancha* and *Rey*,[109] the question was whether authority over the bank's London branch should be governed by the laws and decrees of the Republicans or of the insurgents once Franco's forces had taken over Bilbao. The court approached the Foreign Office for a certificate on the status of British recognition of the insurgents and was informed that Britain recognised Franco's government as 'the government which exercised de facto administrative control over the Basque country, including Bilbao', but at the same time the crown recognised the Republican government 'as the de iure government over the whole of Spain', including Bilbao.[110] As the

[106] Padelford, *Spanish Civil Strife*, 6 fn 18; 'Aperçus des rapports diplomatiques' 34 *Bulletin de l'Institut juridique international* (Bulletin IJI) (1936) 137; 36 Bulletin IJI (1937) 126; 37 Bulletin IJI (1937) 158; 38 Bulletin IJI (1938) 105–108; 39 Bulletin IJI (1938) 167–169, 473–475.

[107] The agreement is in 38 Bulletin IJI (1938) 105–106. See also Lauterpacht, *Recognition*, 273.

[108] Thomas and Thomas, 'International Legal Aspects', 159; Herbert W. Briggs: 'De Facto and De Jure Recognition: The Arantzazu Mendi' 33 *American Journal of International Law* (1939) 689–690. See also Lauterpacht, *Recognition*, 329–348.

[109] *Banco de Bilbao* v. *Sancha* and *Rey* (1938) 2 KB 176; see also Matthias Herdegen, 'Banco de Bilbao v Sancha and Rey Case' *Max Planck Encyclopedia of Public International Law* (updated 2024).

[110] *Banco de Bilbao* v. *Sancha* and *Rey* (1938) 177.

matter concerned the applicable law in the territory under the control of the de facto government, the court ruled in favour of the Nationalists and dismissed the Republic's appeal. However, things became more complicated when another bench had to decide whether Franco's influence should extend beyond his own territory. A case in point was the affair of the *Arantzazu Mendi*, a Spanish merchantman from Bilbao that had been requisitioned by the Republican government. While docked in Britain, the vessel was libelled for restitution by her owners, with the Nationalists filing their own requisition and demanding that the British officials hand the ship over to them instead. Again, the court turned to the Foreign Office for a statement concerning the status of Franco's government. The response it received was similar to the previous one, once more referring to the Republic as the de jure government and the Nationalists as the de facto government but it ended with a rather remarkable conclusion: 'The question whether the Nationalist Government is to be regarded as that of a foreign sovereign state appears to be a question of law to be answered in the light of the preceding statements and having regard to the particular issue with respect to which the question is raised.'[111] In other words, the government put the matter back in the hands of the court.

Acting on these directions, Judge Bucknill decided the case in favour of Franco, asserting that 'that the Nationalist Government of Spain in law is for the purposes of this case a foreign sovereign state'.[112] The court of appeals and the House of Lords upheld the decision.[113] With this, British courts had gone so far as to treat Franco's de facto government as internationally indistinguishable from one recognised de jure. It therefore begged the question why the government had not recognised the Nationalists as an independent state or a lawful government in the first place. In reaction, Hersch Lauterpacht wrote a review of the doctrine of the recognition of insurgency, in which he recalled that limited recognition of insurgents amounted only to the sum total of what had been granted, not more; treating a de facto government as a sovereign state outside its immediate territory would indeed be excessive. He concluded that considering the Spanish insurgent government as a lawful government even of a part of Spain would have violated an established principle of international law.[114]

[111] *The Arantzazu Mendi* (1938) P 233 at 242–243; 9 *International Law Reports* (ILR) 60, at 61–62.

[112] *The Arantzazu Mendi* (1938) P 233 at 248.

[113] *The Arantzazu Mendi* (1939) AC 256; 9 ILR 60.

[114] Hersch Lauterpacht, 'Recognition of Insurgents as a *De Facto* Government' 3 *Modern Law Review* (1939) 7. Lauterpacht was not alone with his critique. As Herbert Briggs

The *Arantzazu Mendi* was not unique, as the issue of recognition between the de jure Republican government and the de facto Nationalists arose in the courts of several states in both property law and, later, insurance cases. By the time the war ended, contradictory interpretations had been advanced and adjudicated in different jurisdictions.[115]

The Republican government appealed directly to the League of Nations in Geneva on four separate occasions in the hope of assistance, support, cooperation, and reconsideration of the non-intervention arrangement. In response, it received little more than non-binding reiterations of the principle of non-intervention,[116] condemnation of the bombing of civilians,[117] and calls for peaceful shipping to be respected.[118] Before the Assembly of the League of Nations, the Spanish representative requested arms and troops for his lawful government and insisted that any system of collective security 'must, before all, protect States against the risk of internal rebellions which are supported and fomented from outside'.[119] But the majority of members timidly defended the Non-intervention Agreement, which they referred to as their substitute for taking action.[120] A lonely exception was Mexico, which continued to support the Republic at the League throughout the war and hosted the Republican government-in-exile after its defeat. Mexico refused ever to recognise Franco's regime and argued that the war had not been a civil war but rather an international aggression, whereby foreign powers had helped an armed minority faction overturn a lawful government in violation of the nation's right to self-determination and non-interference – not to mention Article 10 of the

commented, 'If it was truly the policy of Lord Halifax to support the German-Italian policy of premature recognition of the Franco insurgents as a means of destroying a friendly recognized government, it would obviously not be a proper judicial role for British courts to interfere. By tradition they must follow the political branch of the government on matters of this kind. However, in this particular case the Foreign Office letter was sufficiently ambiguous to warrant a decision in conformity with juristic logic and common sense, pending a more clear declaration by the Foreign Office that it intended to embark on a policy of unfriendly and illegal intervention in the affairs of a recognized state.' Briggs, 'De Facto and De Jure Recognition', 699.

115 Padelford, *Spanish Civil Strife*, 20–23.

116 Council resolution, 12 December 1936, 18 *League of Nations Official Journal* (LNOJ) (January 1937) 18–21, 35.

117 Council resolution, 29 May 1937, 18 LNOJ (May–June 1937), 333–334, 572; 165 LNOJ Spec Supp (1937) 1–86.

118 18 LNOJ (December 1937) 914–919, 944–946, 1161–1166.

119 155 LNOJ Spec Supp (1936) 47–50. See also Richard Veatch, 'The League of Nations and the Spanish Civil War, 1936–9' 20 *European History Quarterly* (1990) 183.

120 For example, Council resolution, 12 December 1936, 18 LNOJ (January 1937) 18–19.

League Covenant, which required all members of the League to respect and preserve each other's territorial integrity and existing political independence in the face of external aggression.[121] Very little came out of these discussions for the Spanish government, however. The Assembly failed to agree to condemn Germany and Italy as aggressors,[122] and a draft resolution brought before the Council of the League calling for an end to the non-intervention policy was defeated by four votes to two, with nine abstentions.[123] Diplomatically, Spain's fate was sealed not in the League's debates on the Spanish Civil War but elsewhere. After the Republican government's withdrawal from Spain in early 1939, the Nationalists rapidly received full international recognition.[124] A month after the end of the war, the Franco government filed a notice of Spain's withdrawal from the League of Nations.[125] Four months later, Germany and the Soviet Union marched into Poland, igniting the Second World War.

6.4.2 *The Spanish War in Legal Scholarship*

The Spanish war sent international lawyers scuffling after the legal principles applicable to internal conflicts, causing the classical law of civil war to experience a final resurgence. Never before (nor thereafter) had the doctrines of belligerent recognition and de facto recognition been so widely written about, as scholars took the opportunity to reintroduce them in contemporary literature. Despite its evident shortcomings and old age – in 1936, Dana's *Wheaton* was 70 years old and Vattel's *Droit des gens* almost 180 – the classical language of civil war was still part of the professional vernacular of international law. Echoing the French *doctorants* who had synthesised the doctrine at the beginning of the century, lawyers observed that '[f]ew branches of international law have received as little attention in the past quarter of a century from publicists as that

[121] 155 LNOJ Spec Supp (1936) 100–101; 1937 FRUS vol V, 274–275; Thomas and Thomas, 'International Legal Aspects', 161–162, 173; Padelford, *Spanish Civil Strife*, 625–626; Fabia Fernandes Carvalho Veçoso, 'Mexican Post-Revolutionary Foreign Policy and the Spanish Civil War' in Kathryn Greenman, Anne Orford, Anna Saunders, and Ntina Tzouvala (eds), *Revolutions in International Law: The Legacies of 1917* (Cambridge University Press 2021) 242–267.

[122] Assembly minutes, 18 September and 2 October 1937, 169 LNOJ Spec Supp (1937) 55–60, 99–108.

[123] 19 LNOJ (May–June 1938) 325–332, 354–359, 533–534.

[124] Padelford, *Spanish Civil Strife*, 191 fn 8.

[125] Notification of 8 May 1939, 20 LNOJ (July–August 1939) 344.

relating to insurgency and civil war', and that 'progress might well be made through conventionalization of the means of admission of insurgency and recognition of belligerency', its effects, and the questions of state responsibility.[126] At the same time, experts writing with their governments in mind invoked the classical principles for quite the opposite reason: to help them avoid any universally binding effects. Even though recognition of belligerency might be justified on the basis of facts, governments could insist they were under no legal obligation to take this step.[127]

The legal principles and doctrines the scholars found themselves dealing with were mostly the same as at the beginning of the century. Meanwhile, governments paid little attention to their normative details, as amply demonstrated by international political reaction and counter-reaction to the war. Under these circumstances, publicists sought one last time to bridge the enormous gap between law as they understood it and reality as they witnessed it. Many wrote from a position of detached expertise and settled on stating the classical law of civil war as they saw it, explaining the purposes and consequences of belligerent recognition or proposing that the conditions for formal neutrality might be present; they explored the distinction between de facto and de jure recognitions of governments, explained the legal effects of partial de jure recognitions, and rejected the legality of de jure recognition of the Nationalists by Germany and Italy.[128] But many authors – typically with moderately liberal leanings – found themselves faced with an insurmountable political and moral problem: asking foreign states to follow the classical doctrine would likely favour the Nationalists in the war to the detriment of the lawful Republican government. This civil war was not a story of neglected colonies seeking freedom from their empires; it was a reactionary mutiny, stirred up internationally, against an elected government that

[126] Norman Padelford, 'International Law and Insurgency' 37 *Die Friedens-Warte* (1937) 191–193. Similarly, Hans Wehberg, 'Civil War and International Law' in William E. Rappard and others, *The World Crisis* (Graduate Institute/Longmans, Green 1938) 160–162.

[127] For example, Arnold McNair 'The Law Relating to the Civil War in Spain' 53 *Law Quarterly Review* (1937) 491–492.

[128] Vernon O'Rourke, 'Recognition of Belligerency'; Philip C. Jessup, 'The Spanish Rebellion and International Law' 15 *Foreign Affairs* (1937) 260–279; H. A. Smith, 'Some Problems of the Spanish Civil War' 18 *British Yearbook of International Law* (1937) 17–31; Arnold Ræstad, 'Guerre civile et droit international', pt I, 19 RDI (1938) 601–637; pt II, 19 RDI (1938) 809–826; Frede Castberg, 'Folkrettslige spörsmål omkring den spanske borgerkrig' 8 *Nordisk Tidsskrift for International Ret* (1937) 160–170.

was fragmenting and drifting ever further to the extreme left, 'a war of class against class'.[129] On the one hand, the war was an uprising by Spain's traditionalist masses against the spectre of communism; on the other hand, it represented a lawful government's effort to put down a fascist rebellion supported by foreign authoritarians.[130] It was not at all obvious to international lawyers whether they could or should embrace either cause. Although legal doctrine held that belligerent recognition entailed no partiality in the contest, in practice that was precisely what it meant if states opted for it. As a result, the Spanish Civil War condemned most European lawyers to oscillate between two politically opposed positions, neither of which they could fully support.

Louis Le Fur exploited this predicament with his lengthy, two-part article on the Spanish war. His perspective was decidedly anti-communist: he saw the war as 'a running race between Bolshevism and Christian civilisation' and portrayed the Republican government as an oppressive proxy regime dependent on Stalin's military aid,[131] whereas Franco's rebels represented authentic European civilisational values, their movement legitimised by their alleged local support in Spain.[132] For him, the Spanish Civil War was a clash between a static state order and the 'dynamism' of a nation, similar to the Holy Alliance in the nineteenth century and the revolution before it.[133] Le Fur pointed to Franco's overwhelming control over Spanish territory and population and argued that the rebel cause was both just and factually successful.[134] Le Fur found no valid reason to withhold from the Nationalists the status due to them and dismissed the non-intervention policy as a betrayal of the distinction between the laws of peace and the laws of war; it was therefore incumbent on all states to recognise the clear facts and accord Franco 'double recognition' as both a government and a belligerent, as in fact they had already done tacitly on several occasions.[135]

129 Charles Fenwick, 'Can Civil Wars Be Brought under the Control of International Law?' 32 *American Journal of International Law* (1938) 540.

130 Martti Koskenniemi, *The Gentle Civilizer of Nations* (Cambridge University Press 2001) 338–342.

131 Louis Le Fur, 'La guerre d'Espagne et le droit' 11(20) *Revue de droit international* (1937) 352–364 (pt I). On Le Fur, see also Koskenniemi, ibid.

132 Louis Le Fur, 'La guerre d'Espagne et le droit' 12(21) *Revue de droit international* (1938) 98–99 (pt II).

133 Le Fur, 'La guerre d'Espagne', pt II, 58–59.

134 Le Fur, 'La Guerre d'Espagne', pt I, 348–352.

135 Le Fur, 'La Guerre d'Espagne', pt II, 78–79.

Le Fur was not alone in leaning towards the Nationalist perspective; German and Italian international lawyers knew how to argue along these lines too, asserting, for example, that the question should not be whether the insurgents had been expressly recognised as belligerents but rather whether they were being treated as such, and that the international non-intervention policy could itself amount to unanimous tacit recognition of the Nationalists as having standing under international law.[136] Spanish lawyers seem to have been more focused on domestic and constitutional questions (as well as on individual survival, exile, collaboration, or worse).[137] When a commission of jurists appointed by Franco delivered a legal report on the legal basis of the Republican government, it unsurprisingly asserted that the Republic itself had been established through radical coercion and that the left's electoral victory in 1936 had been fraudulent and unlawful.[138] Their list of arguments for the Republic's illegitimacy was remarkably similar to Le Fur's.

Then there was the political left, reflected in the views of Georges Scelle. As a committed internationalist and expert on the Covenant of the League of Nations, Scelle believed in a progressive and monistic theory of international law, where a universal, objective, or even natural law was destined to federate the community of states; for him, state sovereignty was a logical impossibility serving an outdated social order.[139] But in the case of Spain, this worldview did not prevent Scelle from defending the Republican government in the name of governmental immunity and state sovereignty: acknowledging his own utopianism, Scelle admitted that in its current rudimentary form the positive customary law of nations still continued to protect the competence of de jure governments whenever they engaged in law enforcement action against insurgents.[140] That Scelle's heart was with the Republic was never in doubt, even if he claimed to be writing from a neutral position: he sternly condemned the German and Italian military aid to Franco and their de jure recognition of the Nationalist government, arguing that they

136 P. Balladore Pallieri, 'Quelques aspects juridiques de la non-intervention en Espagne' 18 RDI (1937) 288, 291, 300–307.

137 Ignacio de la Rasilla del Moral, *In the Shadow of Vitoria: A History of International Law in Spain (1770–1953)* (Brill 2017) 258–267.

138 *Dictamen de la Comisión sobre ilegitimidad de poderes actuantes en 18 de julio de 1936* (Editora Nacional 1939).

139 Koskenniemi, *Gentle Civilizer*, 327–338; Georges Scelle, *Précis de droit des gens*, vol I, 13–14.

140 Georges Scelle, 'La guerre civile espagnole et le droit des gens', pt I, 12 RGDIP (1938) 269–273, 279.

constituted blatant and notorious acts of international aggression that demanded sanctions and counter-measures.[141] But looking ahead to the 'organic evolution of international society', Scelle suggested that the emerging legal principles of solidarity now favoured popular sovereignty, such as that of the Republic, against any other basis for government: 'one must conclude that the spirit of the current institution [i.e. the League of Nations] bears a profound analogy to that of the Holy Alliance, with the significant difference that the new principle of legitimacy is exactly the opposite of the old one.'[142] The privileged status of an elected government derived not merely from its sovereignty but from a sensibility common to the civilised world. From this universalist position, Scelle sharply critiqued the non-intervention system and condemned the entire classical law of civil war as outdated and anchored in a state-centred law of nations that no longer existed.[143] In its place he called for a functional collective security system and suggested that it might be a means of putting into effect the Covenant's promises allowing the international community to intervene in wars.[144]

Moderates and liberals therefore had to wrestle with how to confront the Phalangist sensibilities meaningfully, without sliding too close towards the opposite political extremes. One way forward was to simply defend the international response and the Non-intervention Agreement against their critics, as did Arnold McNair when he examined the legal basis of the British position and defended that position as a valid, if imperfect, course of action.[145] Another option was to focus on the reluctance of states to recognise a clear state of civil war and to defy such reluctance by considering that tacit recognition could be derived from the Non-intervention Agreement or that some of the maritime disputes could be referred to an international forum such as the Permanent Court of International Justice.[146] A third pathway was criticism, directed on the one hand at the outdated doctrine of civil war but particularly at the politically intervening nature of the non-intervention arrangement.[147] Calls for a future reform

[141] Scelle, 'La reconnaissance des insurgés', 69. Compare Wehberg, 'Civil War and International Law', 181.
[142] Georges Scelle, 'La guerre civile espagnole et le droit des gens', pt II, 13 RGDIP (1939) 225.
[143] Scelle, 'La guerre civile espagnole', pt II, 201–206, 222–228.
[144] Scelle, 'La guerre civile espagnole', pt I, 269, 301; pt II, 226.
[145] McNair, 'The Law Relating to the Civil War in Spain', 498–499. See also Lauterpacht, 'Recognition of Insurgents', 1–2; Wehberg, 'Civil War and International Law', 183–187.
[146] O'Rourke, 'Recognition of Belligerency', 412–413.
[147] Edwin Borchard, '"Neutrality" and Civil Wars' 31 *American Journal of International Law* (1937) 304–306; Georges Scelle, 'La reconnaissance des insurgés', 65–70.

were frequent, sparked both by frustration over the shortcomings of the international response and by the utter irrelevance of the classical legal concepts of civil war. Norman Padelford, however, saw the urgency created by events as a cause for optimism: despite the many defects of the non-intervention system, 'the net result in both law and diplomacy appear[ed] to have been a gain'.[148] Lessons learned in international organisation and collective security pointed a way forward; joint action for the localisation of warfare and for the admission of insurgency and the recognition of belligerency appeared as advantageous moves towards a law-abiding and peaceful commonwealth of nations.[149]

Hans Wehberg, editor of *Die Friedens-Warte* and a pacifist heavyweight, focused on calling for broader institutional reforms in his Hague lectures of 1938. While he still acknowledged the classical doctrine of civil war as a valid legal system – he saw Rougier's classic work as the last synthesis on the subject[150] – his objective was to bring civil wars within the ambit of international collective security, where the question of belligerent recognition could be resolved by or within an impartial international institution.[151] Warning his audience of the impending threat fascist and communist ideologies posed to the internal stability of states, he proposed that international law should be brought to bear upon the scourge of civil wars through interstate collaboration and by improving the functioning of the League of Nations: 'Civil war would thus cease to be a *res interna*, and would instead in certain conditions become a problem concerning the international community as a whole.'[152] Like Rougier before him, Wehberg formulated a doctrine of humanitarian intervention, where intervention could be lawful under the League Covenant when a civil war gravely violated 'the laws of humanity', when the war would not otherwise end, or if the civil war jeopardised general peace.[153] Wehberg's faith in collective recognition implied that the international community should also abandon the view of belligerent recognition as a discretionary act by states and accept that a 'system of international

148 Padelford, *Spanish Civil Strife*, 201.
149 Ibid 120.
150 Hans Wehberg, 'La guerre civile et le droit international' 63 *Collected Courses of Hague Academy of International Law* (1938) 10.
151 For example, Hans Wehberg, *The Problem of an International Court of Justice* ([1912] Charles G. Fenwick tr, Clarendon Press 1918) 53–69, 123–128 *et passim*; Wehberg, *The Outlawry of War*, 117–122.
152 Wehberg. 'La guerre civile', 122.
153 Ibid 114–117; Wehberg, 'Civil War and International Law', 190.

law based on natural justice' might grant the insurgents a right of recognition as belligerents on 'the basis of the general interests of mankind'.[154] The 'Spanish revolution' provided an opportunity for the international community to achieve a new step in the advancement of the law of civil war by embracing the idea of 'an automatic genesis of the rights of belligerence'.[155] All the roads led – and had to lead – to increased international organisation:

> The more fully the true nature of civil war is recognized in the future, the more rapidly will the idea be accepted that insurgents in certain definite circumstances automatically deserve to be considered as belligerents, and that some *international body* is necessary *which would be sufficiently impartial to give a just decision, binding on all, as to the exact moment when the so-called insurgents become belligerents.*[156]

By the end of the Spanish Civil War the classical doctrine of civil war had been thoroughly discredited among legal scholars and long since abandoned in state practice. But it still represented the only vocabulary of international law available to interwar jurists for dealing with intra-state conflicts: while they often diverged in their interpretations of the law during the war, their debates were still imprisoned within the narrow classical framework, despite all its deficiencies. In the absence of alternative languages, lawyers continued to debate the war from the perspective of their sensibilities as regards how the world *should* or *could* have operated under the concepts and principles inherited from Rougier and his contemporaries. Even if this did not offer clear solutions in the case at hand, there seemed to be no other choice than to further develop the inherited law of civil war through legal commentary and advocacy for new international organisations. The hopes and fears of the interwar generations were injected into the classical doctrine as future aspirations, such as calls for a reform of the League of Nations or the mandatory pacific settlement of disputes threatening international peace.

Some of these concerns were taken up in one form or another in the United Nations and other international institutions that came to exist after the Second World War. But that post-war international law was a product of a very different world, in which the classical doctrine and its

[154] Wehberg, 'Civil War and International Law', 170, 173.
[155] Wehberg, 'La guerre civile', 108–111.
[156] Wehberg, 'Civil War and International Law', 177–178.

key principles no longer had a place. As we will see, the interwar calls for a codification or restatement of the law of civil war never materialised. Instead, a competing legal framework came into being at the Geneva Conference of 1949, and as new generations of lawyers adopted it, the old principles of belligerency and neutrality fell by the wayside almost without anyone noticing.

7

The End of Civil War

7.1 The Geneva Conference of 1949 and the New Language of Armed Conflicts

The Spanish Civil War was the last major conflict over which international lawyers debated using the vocabulary of the classical doctrine of civil war. Once it was clear that the old law had fallen into desuetude, many international lawyers called for the establishment of new, impartial international institutions capable of authoritatively determining the status of insurgents and belligerents in the world and deciding whenever there were grounds for collective intervention. Other rising ideas included the drafting of a new general convention concerning the application of international law in civil wars, as the laws of war at the time remained largely silent on that particular question.

The unprecedented devastation of the Second World War transformed the rejection of armed conflict from a lofty ideal into a necessity for humanity's survival. At the same time, the waning era of empires gave way to a surging third wave of decolonisation. The post-war years saw the emergence of new legal institutions that would soon take precedence in legal responses to intra-state conflicts in the world. The new United Nations Organization was to be entrusted with the collective security of the world, and its Charter conferred authority on the Security Council to respond to any threats to international peace, without excluding internal conflicts within states. The war crimes tribunals in Nuremberg and Tokyo, the international declaration of human rights by the UN General Assembly, and the international Genocide Convention of 1948 challenged the classical state-centrism of international law and brought individuals and groups undeniably within its ambit.

The Geneva Conference of 1949 was held under the auspices of the International Committee of the Red Cross (ICRC) and was attended by delegations from over sixty nations. International lawyers had high hopes for the conference, seeing it as an opportunity to advance the laws of war from where the international community had left them in the heyday of the international legal profession in 1907. In particular, it opened the prospect of their drafting new, binding international rules to govern the questions of civil war and belligerent recognition. The final outcome turned out to be quite different from what the pre-war jurists might have imagined: far from creating a definitive set of rules on the recognition of belligerency, the conference embraced new, forward-looking treaty language that mostly erased the entire concept of belligerent recognition from its outcomes. Instead of answering the problems of the classical doctrine of civil war in the familiar professional vernacular, the conference circumvented the issue by creating a new framework of its own, rephrasing the problem of civil war as one of 'armed conflicts not of an international character' – an expression taken from the preparatory meetings at the Red Cross and which was intended to be understood as a factual situation evaluated with reference to the conventions. Aligning itself with the renunciation of war enacted in the 1928 Pact of Paris, the Geneva Conference distanced itself from formal distinctions of war, peace, and neutrality, replacing them with a new vernacular of armed conflicts and minimum humanitarian standards. This ushered in an era characterised by a deliberate 'non-definition approach' to internal wars, which would last until the 1990s, when the new International Criminal Tribunal for the former Yugoslavia (ICTY) began to define the factual criteria for the presence of non-international armed conflicts.[1]

Although the 1949 Geneva Conference did not have as part of its outcome a provision affirming the general applicability of all humanitarian law in intra-state conflicts, it did produce the famous Common Article 3, a 'mini-convention' within the conventions,[2] which advanced the purposes of the old Martens clause by further grounding civil wars in the domain of international law. Significantly, Common Article 3 ended with the following sentence, the primary purpose of which was precisely to decouple the new conventions from the classical doctrine: 'The application of the preceding provisions shall not affect the legal status of the Parties to the conflict.' This, in effect, marked the renunciation of the classical law of civil war in modern international humanitarian law.

[1] Sandesh Sivakumaran, *The Law of Non-International Armed Conflict* (Oxford University Press 2012) 156, 164.

[2] Jan Klabbers, *International Law* (Cambridge University Press 2013) 208.

7.1.1 On the Origins of Common Article 3

Legal scholars today have developed a nuanced understanding of the drafting of Common Article 3 and the genesis of its legal language of armed conflicts not of an international character.[3] This study will follow that understanding but will highlight the other side of the coin: how the Geneva Conference considered, and then rejected, the possibility of formulating Common Article 3 using the classical vocabulary of the law of civil war. We are interested here not so much in what was created but in what was left out, for this approach can perhaps best answer the question of what ultimately happened to the classical doctrine of civil war. It reveals that the doctrine did not just sink silently into desuetude in the nineteenth century but was in fact consciously (though unceremoniously) abolished at this major conference revising the principles of the laws of war.

Common Article 3 was the fruit of long labours on the part of the ICRC. Ever since the inclusion of the Martens Clause in the Hague Regulations of 1899 and 1907, members of the ICRC had wanted to extend the protection of the laws of war to intra-state conflicts. In 1912, the Ninth International Conference of the Red Cross examined two draft reports on the role of the ICRC in civil wars prepared by the US and Cuban delegations.[4] The Cuban proposal consisted of seven short rules in the nature of internal guidelines for the organisation, generally emphasising its duty of impartiality.[5] The American draft was more ambitious, proposing that the Red Cross should actively seek permission to lawfully

[3] Most recently, Boyd van Dijk 's excellent *Preparing for War: The Making of the 1949 Geneva Conventions* (Oxford University Press 2022) 99–144. I warmly thank Dr van Dijk for his research, especially on the work of the ICRC prior to the 1949 conference. On the conference records themselves I have mostly retained my own reading, but I highly recommend to the reader van Dijk's rich analysis and archival findings. For other valuable readings of the conference, see Sivakumaran, *The Law of Non-International Armed Conflict*, 156–160; David A. Elder, 'The Historical Background of Common Article 3 of the Geneva Convention of 1949' *11 Case Western Reserve Journal of International Law* (1979) 37–54; Anthony Cullen, *The Concept of Non-International Armed Conflict in International Humanitarian Law* (Cambridge University Press 2010) 27–51; Lindsay Moir, *The Law of Internal Armed Conflict* (Cambridge University Press 2002) 22–31. See also Lindsey Cameron and others, 'Article 3: Conflicts Not of an International Character' in Knut Dörmann and others (eds), *ICRC Commentary on the First Geneva Convention* (Cambridge University Press 2016) 132–140. Thanks also to Rotem Giladi for his useful advice and discussion regarding the *travaux préparatoires*.

[4] *Compte-rendu de la neuvième conférence internationale de la Croix-Rouge* (American Red Cross 1912) 23, 39–40.

[5] Report of the Red Cross of Cuba, *Compte-rendu de la neuvième conférence*, 49.

access battlefields from the governments of countries experiencing insurrections, preferably in exchange for pledges by both parties involved to adhere to the laws of war. If and when granted access, all Red Cross organisations would operate in accordance with the principles of the Geneva and Hague rules of war, adhere to strict and unconditional impartiality, and waive any state responsibility for damage caused to them by the acts of insurgents.[6]

From the US draft arose the question of belligerent recognition. As that draft urged for the international laws of war to be recognised as applicable to internal conflicts, should it be possible to infer from this a tacit recognition of the insurgents as belligerents? Few governments would be willing to take such a risk. To address this concern, two separate paragraphs in the draft sought to stress that neither the offers of the Red Cross nor any potential pledges by the warring parties could constitute belligerent recognition. No offers or acceptances could have 'any political reach'; they could not be understood as anything other than dealings with a 'private', 'philanthropic institution without an official character', and they expressly could not be considered constitutive of a state of war or belligerency.[7]

This was not enough to convince the members at the meeting, and both drafts were roundly shot down. General Yermolow of the Russian delegation, whose government in 1912 was faced with internal turmoil, declared that the Russian Empire would 'in no case and in no form be a contracting or even discussing party to any agreement or *voeu* on this subject' due to its political character and gravity, and that any assistance given to insurgents by foreign Red Cross organisations should be understood as an unfriendly act, fomenting sedition and rebellion in a foreign state.[8] Given the strength of the opposition, the meeting saw no way forward and dropped the subject. Although it achieved very little, the meeting of 1912 has been noted as the first debate over the application of autonomous international 'humanitarian law' to non-international armed conflicts.[9]

The topic of civil wars returned in subsequent ICRC meetings. By the time of the Tenth International Conference in 1921, the involvement of the Red Cross in internal warzones was an established fact. Its national

6 Report of the American Red Cross, *Compte-rendu de la neuvième conférence*, 45–48, paras 1–3, 6, 9, 16.

7 Ibid, paras 4–5.

8 *Compte-rendu de la neuvième conférence*, 45.

9 A. Schlögel, 'La guerre civile' 52 *Revue internationale de la Croix-Rouge* (1970) 138.

branches had engaged in aid operations in various parts of the collapsed Russian Empire, as well as in other parts of Europe where internal struggles had erupted in the wake of the Great War.[10] This time, the conference agreed to adopt a resolution in which the Red Cross affirmed its 'right and duty' to engage in relief work in the event of civil war and social and revolutionary unrest, demanded that the principles of the Hague and Geneva Conventions be generally respected in civil wars by 'analogy', and affirmed that all victims of civil war, without any exception whatsoever, were entitled to relief.[11] At its Tokyo meeting of 1934, the ICRC adopted a resolution in which the members expressed the wish that the Geneva Conventions 'should also be applied by analogy in cases of armed conflicts between States without a formal declaration of war', having in mind the Japanese colonial occupation of Manchuria but also the mounting dissatisfaction over the formal concept of a state of war.[12]

The International Conference of 1938, acknowledging the impasse resulting from the Spanish Civil War, reaffirmed the 1921 resolution and passed a complementary resolution requesting the ICRC 'to continue the general study of the problems raised by civil war as regards the Red Cross'.[13] Accordingly, a committee of legal experts returned to the subject after the Second World War in 1946. In the course of that year, they accepted an ambitious view put forward by Frede Castberg and Jean Pictet advocating the direct application of humanitarian law in internal conflicts, and thus the 'internationalisation' of civil wars.[14] Consequently, between 1946 and 1948 the ICRC worked on a series of templates for a common article that would extend the coverage of future humanitarian law conventions to non-international armed conflicts. The tenor of those templates shifted from the application of convention principles by analogy to the direct applicability of future conventions in civil wars.[15] At the end of its preparatory meeting in Stockholm in August 1948, the ICRC

[10] François Bugnion, 'The International Conference of the Red Cross and Red Crescent: Challenges, Key Issues and Achievements' 91 *International Review of the Red Cross* (2009) 694.

[11] Res XIV, *Dixième conference internationale de la Croix-Rouge tenue à Genève du 30 mars au 7 avril 1921: Compte-rendu* (ICRC 1921) 217–218. See also Bugnion, 'International Conference', 694; Cameron and others, 'Article 3', 135.

[12] Van Dijk, *Preparing for War*, 107; Res XXXVIII, *Quinzieme conférence internationale de la Croix-Rouge, tenue a Tokio du 20 au 29 octobre 1934: Compte-rendu* (Red Cross Society of Japan 1934) 261–262.

[13] Cameron and others, 'Article 3', 135; Elder, 'Historical Background', 41–42.

[14] Van Dijk, *Preparing for War*, 111–112.

[15] Cameron and others, 'Article 3', 135–137; Elder, 'Historical Background', 42–43.

adopted the draft language that it would present to the Diplomatic Conference for the Establishment of International Conventions for the Protection of Victims of War in Geneva in 1949. It proposed that adversaries 'in all cases of armed conflict not of an international character' would be bound by the conventions, 'whatever the legal status of the Parties to the conflict and without prejudice thereto'.[16]

Of all the common articles discussed at the Geneva Conference of 1949, the one on non international armed conflicts turned out to be the most controversial. Its drafting history shows that debates continued throughout the entire summer. At the heart of these debates was the question of whether a distinction between purely internal rebellions and true civil wars should be based on a set of factual criteria to be laid down in the convention, or whether the convention should follow the international legal tradition of formal distinction through the recognition of the insurgents as belligerents. By this time, as van Dijk explains, the context and tone of the debate was thoroughly colonial; the question at issue was not merely the conduct of hostilities in conflicts internal to sovereign states, but above all the legitimacy of the repressive means deployed by Europeans to sustain their fragmenting overseas empires. During preparations for the conference, a loose coalition of shared imperial concerns began to develop around France and Britain.[17] Opposite them were the interests of the decolonising world, supported in part by the Soviet Union, which, seeing this as an opportune moment for ending its boycott of the ICRC, appeared in Geneva to once again champion international law's protection of the revolutionary right of peoples to self-determination.[18]

At the end of the conference, the deliberately ambiguous language of non-international armed conflicts prevailed (and to this day remains in Common Article 3), whereas the classical principles of civil war were erased from the conventions. But the old concept of belligerent recognition did not go down without a fight: its final line of defence was led by Lieutenant-Colonel William Roy Hodgson, a distinguished, cane-wielding Australian diplomat, who at the time served as a Commonwealth representative in post-war East Asia. A former artillery officer, Hodgson had fought, been

[16] *Final Record of the Diplomatic Conference of Geneva of 1949* (Federal Political Dept 1949) (*Final Record*) vol I, 47.

[17] Van Dijk, *Preparing for War*, 113–117, 120–126.

[18] Ibid 127; Boyd van Dijk, '"The Great Humanitarian": The Soviet Union, the International Committee of the Red Cross, and the Geneva Conventions of 1949' 37 *Law and History Review* (2019) 223–234.

shot, and been declared dead at Gallipoli while still in his youth, which had afforded him the privilege of reading his own obituary. After the war, he had served at the army headquarters of the Australian general staff and later in the prime minister's external affairs department, while at the same time finishing a law degree at the University of Melbourne. He had also distinguished himself as a delegate to the United Nations and prominent figure in its early development.[19]

7.1.2 Hodgson's Last Stand: Drafting Common Article 3

The legal positions on the applicability of the Geneva Conventions to civil wars became apparent from the very outset of discussions on the common articles. The joint committee tasked with drafting the articles soon turned to what was then known as 'paragraph four'.

On the one hand were the perspectives of the European powers (and dwindling empires), which invoked sovereignty and the principle of non-intervention. The French representative Albert Lamarle stressed that, notwithstanding the Stockholm conference's insistence on the protection of individual rights, it was simply 'impossible to carry the protection of individuals to the point of sacrificing the rights of States'. The French delegation proposed amending the article to 'mak[e] it impossible, for forms of disorder, anarchy or brigandage to claim the protection of the Convention under a mask of politics or on any other pretext'. Essentially, this amendment would introduce a set of factual conditions requiring the insurgents to possess organised (regular) military forces under a responsible authority that was capable of properly enforcing the conventions.[20] Concurring with his French colleague, the British representative Sir Robert Craigie also opposed the Stockholm draft 'because the application of the Conventions would appear to give the status of belligerents to insurgents, whose right to wage war could not be recognized'. In this sense, 'their application to civil war would strike at the root of national sovereignty and endanger national security'.[21] The logic here was that of the classical doctrine, whereby the application of international

[19] 'Hodgson, William Roy (1892–1958)', *Australian Dictionary of Biography*, vol 9 (Melbourne University Press 1983), http://adb.anu.edu.au/; UN, 'Universal Declaration of Human Rights: Drafters of the Declaration', www.un.org/en/about-us/udhr/drafters-of-the-declaration.

[20] First meeting of the joint committee, 26 April 1949, *Final Record*, vol II-B, 10.

[21] Ibid.

law in a civil war went hand in hand with the acknowledgement of a state of war and, by extension, recognition of the insurgents as belligerents.

The opposite position was expressed by the smaller and newly independent states, whose delegates supported the Stockholm draft as it stood or with minor adjustments. 'The rights of the State should not be placed above all humanitarian considerations', noted Don Pedro de Alba of Mexico, and the Danish representative Georg Cohn 'fully supported' the draft. For Frede Castberg, one of the drafters of the Stockholm proposal, it was a long overdue 'step forward in international law to say explicitly that, even if war was not recognized, the rules concerning the conduct of war should be applied'. Not only did he agree that the language of the convention should be kept distinct from the classical concepts; he saw that very distinction as a way out of the impasse: 'when belligerency was recognized in an internal conflict, serious legal consequences were entailed; but it was to be hoped that the Conference would agree that purely humanitarian rules should be applied in armed conflicts independently of any recognition of belligerency.' To this end, Castberg welcomed the last sentence of Article 2 – 'whatever the legal status of the Parties to the conflict and without prejudice thereto' – as 'a sound innovation' precisely because it prevented the convention from being interpreted as entailing consequences in the sense of the classical doctrine.[22]

Gradually, opposition mounted against the progressive language of the Stockholm proposal. The United States 'did not consider that it could bind itself to observe the provisions of the convention except in the case of war as understood in international law', which harked back to the classical concepts of civil war and belligerency. The United States conceded that in recognised, full-scale civil wars some of the convention's provisions might apply, but this raised the familiar question of who was to decide when a conflict became a full-scale civil war and when recognition was due or could be considered to have been accorded.[23] Canada joined in the critique: to extend the convention to small rebel groups 'would be absurd', and to accord them the status of protected persons would go against the very essence of civil war. Instead, 'the test should be: recognition of belligerency of the rebels by the lawful Government'.[24] Lastly, the head of the Australian delegation, William Hodgson, took the

[22] Ibid 11.
[23] Second meeting, 27 April 1949, *Final Record*, vol II-B, 12.
[24] Ibid 13.

floor. In a speech very briefly recorded, Hodgson sided with the view that the conventions should apply 'when an armed conflict became a full-scale war' but not in minor uprisings. To distinguish between the two, he proposed that the convention should be applied to a civil war when:

> 1) the *de jure* government had recognized the insurgents as belligerents, or; 2) the *de jure* government had claimed for itself the right of belligerent, and; 3) the *de jure* government had accorded the insurgents recognition as belligerents for the purposes only of the present Conventions; 4) that the dispute had been admitted to the Agenda of the Security Council or the General Assembly of the United Nations as being a threat to international peace, a breach of the peace, or an act of aggression.[25]

This was a concrete call to frame the common article in the language of belligerent recognition and the classical law of civil war.

A special sub-committee was constituted to work on a draft of Article 2(4).[26] Amendments were at once presented by Australia, Canada, France, Greece, and Hungary.[27] Of these, the most important were the French and Australian proposals, both of which sought to rephrase the Stockholm draft so as to clarify the limits of the application of the drafted conventions in non-international armed conflicts. The French proposal sought to maintain the spirit of the Stockholm draft – that the conventions would apply to civil wars in full – while addressing states' concerns by introducing a set of familiar threshold criteria: the conventions would apply to internal conflicts 'if the adverse Party possesses an organized military force, an authority responsible for its acts acting within a defined territory and having the means of observing and enforcing the Convention'.[28] The Australian proposal, on the other hand, sought to maintain the central mechanism of belligerent recognition; accordingly, the conventions (or alternatively 'the principles' of the conventions) would apply 'in the case of civil war' if the de jure government had granted the insurgents belligerent recognition in full or to the extent foreseen in the conventions, or if it had exercised its belligerent rights (such as blockade or visit and search), or if the matter had been admitted

25 Ibid 15.

26 Third meeting, 29 April 1949, *Final Record*, vol II-B, 16. It was composed of the members of Australia, France, Greece, Italy, Monaco, Norway, Switzerland, the United Kingdom, the United States, and the USSR. The representatives of Burma and Uruguay were later added in the name of diversity. See Seventh meeting, 17 May 1949, *Final Record*, vol II-B, 26.

27 First meeting of the special committee, 3 May 1949, *Final Record*, vol II-B, 40.

28 French amendment, 26 April 1949, *Final Record*, vol III, 27.

to the UN General Assembly or Security Council as a threat or breach of peace or as an aggression.[29]

The two proposals were soon enough confronted one with the other. Many favoured the Stockholm draft or the French amendment, or both. But Hodgson, in the minority, chose not to stay on the defence any longer. Instead, he explained that he found the Stockholm draft language 'in all cases of armed conflict' too comprehensive for the obvious reason that it 'would presuppose the inclusion of all cases of minor rebellion', whereas the Australian proposal was 'in conformity with international law and permitted the automatic application of the conventions'.[30] The deputy head of the US delegation, Raymond Yingling, noted that as the Australian criteria were subject to the decision of either the de jure government or the Security Council, there was a risk they could be applied subjectively or to selfish ends. Hodgson retorted that their formality was precisely the point: the Australian amendment was 'rigid and precise', while the other proposals might in certain circumstances prevent lawful governments from even applying their own criminal laws against local rioters or rebels.[31]

The Geneva Conference's grapples with the common article became a long procedural odyssey involving two special working groups, compromises, and five parallel proposals put before the joint committee. Throughout the debates, the French and Australians stuck to their original positions. Lapradelle stressed how indispensable it was for the convention to distinguish between civil war and rebellion, while Hodgson maintained that international law already contained well-defined principles for determining the meaning of civil war and its recognition. Yingling recalled that the United States was 'not willing to give a free hand to any organism' to decide whether the conventions would come to effect or not. Ultimately, the committee voted to abandon the Stockholm text and charged Hodgson, Lamarle, Yingling, and Castberg to form a working party to craft a new solution.[32] The working party's draft was a compromise between the Australian and French proposals: the conventions would apply to an armed conflict not of an international character provided that either the government had recognised the belligerency of the insurgents (in full or to the extent foreseen in the conventions) or the adverse party presented sufficient factual

[29] Australian amendment, 4 April 1949, *Final Record*, vol III, 27.
[30] Second meeting of the special committee, 6 May 1949, *Final Record*, vol II-B, 41–42.
[31] Ibid 42.
[32] Ibid 45–46.

'characteristics of a State'.[33] The question of belligerent recognition continued to cause a split in opinions.[34]

Eighteen meetings later, the new draft Article 2A was finally presented to the special committee while Hodgson was momentarily absent from Geneva.[35] After some discussion, the committee chose to lay aside the compromise and to instead resume work on the French and Stockholm drafts.[36] The Frenchman Lamarle quickly pressed his government's amendment. A second working party was then constituted, this time under a French chair.[37] About a week later it presented its draft, which a reader familiar with the ultimate outcome of the process will instantly recognise: this was, in essence, the first draft that looked like Common Article 3 as we know it today.[38] The second working party had now discovered that even if it could not fully resolve the question of when the conventions should apply and when not, it could instead water down the article's substance for easier acceptance. Instead of proposing an article that would make the conventions as a whole apply to internal conflicts in given situations, they included in the article itself a list of principles that had to be followed as a minimum requirement in non-international armed conflicts. The draft's appeal lay in the fact that it would seek maximum applicability while its ultimate impact would remain thoroughly ambiguous.[39]

Upon his return, Hodgson announced that Australia could support only the first compromise.[40] In the meantime, the Soviet delegation intervened with a new, verbose draft, having finally received its overdue instructions from Moscow.[41] Towards the end of the special committee's work it became obvious that it would not be able to agree on a single recommendation. In the end, therefore, it submitted to the joint committee all five of the alternative proposals drafted during its travails.[42]

[33] First draft article of the first working party of the special subcommittee, 16 May 1949, *Final Record*, vol II-B, 46–47.

[34] Fifth meeting of the special committee, 16 May 1949, *Final Record*, vol II-B, 47–48; Seventh meeting of the special committee, 19 May 1949, *Final Record*, vol II-B, 49–50

[35] His absence is noted in *Final Record*, vol II-B, 87.

[36] Twenty-third meeting, 14 June 1949, *Final Record*, vol II-B, 77.

[37] Ibid 79.

[38] Draft article of the second working party of the special sub-committee, 24 June 1949, *Final Record*, vol II-B, 83.

[39] Twenty-eighth meeting of the special committee, 24 June 1949, *Final Record*, vol II-B, 82.

[40] Thirty-fifth meeting of the special committee, 4 July 1949, *Final Record*, vol II-B, 93.

[41] Thirty-seventh meeting of the special committee, 8 July 1949, *Final Record*, vol II-B, 97–98.

[42] Seventh report of the special committee, 16 July 1949, *Final Record*, vol II-B, 120–127.

Lieutenant-Colonel Hodgson, who had led the defence of the classical concepts of civil war and belligerency at the meeting, met his Waterloo in the joint committee with civility and little protest. After the five documents from the special committee had been brought up one last time, the joint committee voted five in favour of Hodgson's proposal, nine for the Soviet text, and twenty-two for the proposal by Lamarle's second working party.[43] In a second vote, the French compromise text was then adopted by a majority of twenty one to six, with fourteen abstentions.[44] Hence, on 20 July 1949 the delegates gathered at the Geneva Conference abandoned both the concept of the recognition of belligerency and the classical distinction between insurgencies, in which international laws of war did not apply, and civil wars, in which they applied in full. In so doing, they brought to an end the classical doctrine of civil war in their relations.

7.2 The Final Decades of the Law of Civil War

7.2.1 A New Law of Non-International Armed Conflicts

The records of the Geneva Conference reveal two things about the fate of the classical doctrine of civil war. First, its language was abandoned openly and consciously at that conference. Second, it was abandoned by a group of diplomats and jurists who were nevertheless well versed in the classical doctrine. Indeed, it had previously served them as a valid law of civil war; but now they agreed to inaugurate a new vocabulary of humanitarian law that was based on less formal standards and might apply to internal conflicts as well. After the conference, a new generation of lawyers soon adopted the view that a fundamental restatement of the laws of war and peace had taken place. Within a decade, the transition from the legal language of civil war to that of humanitarian law and non-international armed conflicts was clearly pronounced by two of Hans Wehberg's students at the Geneva Graduate Institute, Lothar Kotzsch and Jean Siotis. The work of both scholars shows a familiarity with the archetypal examination of the law of civil war in the manner of Rougier, Wehberg, and others, but both reached conclusions that pointed towards the desuetude of the previous tradition of civil war.

The international relations scholar Lothar Kotzsch focused on foregrounding the transition from the formal concept of war towards a new functionalist framework that sought to derive legal consequences directly

43 Eleventh meeting of the joint committee, 19 July 1949, *Final Record*, vol II-B, 34–35.

44 Report of the joint committee, *Final Record*, vol II-B, 129.

from facts on the ground.[45] In his dense thesis, Kotzsch argued that jurists should now learn to understand and accept the phenomenon of war as a sociological concept. As 'the classical notion of *the* legal war ha[d] been developed by modern international law into the broader one of *war in the material and formal senses*', the significance of de facto war had overtaken that of the de jure concept of war.[46] The same applied to identifying non-international wars: in light of the new Common Article 3, the presence of war in the material sense should compel the application of laws of war derived from the principles of humanity and military necessity.[47] The problems of modern international law on the use of force could be solved by openly acknowledging the sociological 'facts' of internal war and peace irrespective of whether states admitted to their existence. This merger of legal scholarship with the social scientific domain was necessary, not merely because states had ceased to adhere to the formalities of declaring and ending wars, but also because of the rise of international communist and decolonial movements that argued for the legitimacy of an ultimate class war and therefore a never-ending struggle that no longer followed the formal patterns of war and peace.[48] That the facts on the ground, just as much as the applicable principles of humanity and military necessity, were a cause of continual disagreement in Cold War diplomacy and the Security Council, did not seem to deter Kotzsch from his materialist rationalism where social scientists could access the truths necessary to overcome the legal problem of subjectivity.

Wehberg's other *doctorant*, the legal scholar Jean Siotis,[49] put his faith less in universal sociology and instead focused on the treaty regime of humanitarian law as a new branch of law that had come to exist separately from the old canon. His thesis *Le droit de la guerre et les conflits armés d'un caractère non-international* (1958) began as a historically anchored study of the international law of civil war in the manner previously established by Rougier and Wehberg, but then proceeded to distinguish between what he called the 'classical doctrine' and the

[45] Lothar Kotzsch, *The Concept of War in Contemporary History and International Law* (Droz 1956).

[46] Ibid 17–18. On differentiating between formal war, material war, armed force short of war, *jus ad bellum*, *jus in bello*, and *jus contra bellum*, see ibid 54–58, 83–105, 175.

[47] Ibid 220–240.

[48] Ibid 18–24, 54–82.

[49] On Siotis as a scholar, see John Goormaghtigh, 'Jean Siotis, éléments pour un portrait' in Victor-Yves Ghebali and Dietrich Kappeler (eds), *Les multiples aspects des relations internationales: Études à la mémoire du professeur Jean Siotis* (Bruylant 1995) 11–19.

modern law of non-international armed conflicts.[50] This timely distinction was warmly received by both the thesis jury and by the corps of humanitarian law professionals.[51]

Charting the development of the classical doctrine from the American Revolution to French Indochina and beyond, Siotis maintained that the old cases could no longer have much relevance for his own period. He examined the classical doctrine of civil war retrospectively, paying attention to what he saw as the rise of *jus in bello* and *jus contra bellum* during the late nineteenth century, and the attendant development of indeterminate doctrines such as the recognition of insurgency.[52] Although he did not go so far as to say that the old law had fallen definitively into desuetude, he made it clear novelty and progress was in his day to come from the new international humanitarian law. The classical doctrine had collapsed in the Spanish Civil War and was unlikely to be resurrected. 'The duty of neutrality in a "recognised" civil war, which underlies all the obligations incumbent on third states in the context of the classical law, now appears unrealisable', he wrote. 'As the non-intervention policy of 1936 to 1938 supported by the great majority of states delivered a *coup de grâce* to the very principle of recognition of belligerency, it is doubtful that a third state or an established government would ever contemplate granting such recognition in the future.' It was now 'impossible to define which rules of the general laws of war still apply to internal conflicts'. The result was that 'the general laws of war have lost the great value which they had at the end of the last century, and we may legitimately ask whether they still belong to the positive law in force'.[53]

Accordingly, Siotis turned his attention away from those timeworn general laws of war to the new and progressive rules of international humanitarian law, which he illustrated through documents and experiences of the Red Cross first in the field (in Spain, Greece, and French Vietnam) and then at the Geneva Conference.[54] Now that Common Article 3 had provided the missing piece that would allow the

[50] Jean Siotis, *Le droit de la guerre et les conflits armés d'un caractère non-international* (LGDJ 1958) 11–14.

[51] Hans Wehberg, 'Jean Siotis: Le droit de la guerre et les conflits armés d'un caractère non-international' 54 *Die Friedens-Warte* (1958) 368–369; 'Bibliographie' 42 *Revue internationale de la Croix-Rouge* (1960) 158–162; Georg Schwarzenberger 's book review in George W. Keeton and Georg Schwarzenberger (eds), *The Year Book of World Affairs 1960* (Stevens & Sons 1960) 375.

[52] Siotis, *Le droit de la guerre*, 97–131.

[53] Ibid 223.

[54] Ibid 133–145, 185–218.

international community to internationalise individual civil wars, the 'evolution' of humanitarian law could proceed on its new-found path free of the recalcitrance of individual states. It was becoming a self-referential legal regime independent of the vocabulary, concepts, and principles of the classical doctrine of civil war:

> We thus arrive at the conclusion that the new humanitarian law constitutes a coherent body of rules the application of which does not depend on denominations given to various actors under the general laws of war, and which has no effect on their legal status outside the sphere of humanitarian law itself. Under these circumstances, it can be regarded as a new body of law and its evolution must not be subordinated to that of the general laws of war.[55]

7.2.2 *The Third Wave of Decolonisation*

The two *doctorants* in Geneva were working at a time when international law and politics were entering a new era of revolution and internal conflicts. In the 1950s and 1960s, the third wave of decolonisation remade the map of the world, while the stalemate of the Cold War fuelled popular movements and intra-national fractures on a global scale. In international law, new multilateral approaches to global ordering began to develop under the umbrella of the United Nations and its subsidiary economic, human rights, and development organs. Following the Bandung Conference, the movement of non-aligned developing countries, conscious of their increasing influence in the UN General Assembly, demanded sovereign and material equality in the world and threw their efforts into realising permanent sovereignty over natural resources and the New International Economic Order.[56] It was a time of decolonial self-determination and world-making:[57] the coexistence that had informed international law in the past was challenged by a new spirit of co-operation, causing international law to move on from being a matter of state-centred diplomacy and diversify into a plethora of functional regimes addressing substantive issues of global development

55 Ibid 227.

56 Nico Schrijver, *Sovereignty over Natural Resources: Balancing Rights and Duties* (Cambridge University Press 1997); Sundhya Pahuja, *Decolonising International Law: Development, Economic Growth and the Politics of Universality* (Cambridge University Press 2011) 103–171.

57 Adom Getachew, *Worldmaking after Empire: The Rise and Fall of Self-determination* (Princeton University Press 2019).

and conditions in individual countries.[58] Yet this new era also saw imperial violence continue in the decolonial world, in response to which the collective security provisions in the UN Charter served as the basis for creating a new international authority to manage the decolonised world, peopled by men and women in blue helmets or tasked with missions of development and governance. The legal language of collective security developed in such a way as to save states and international bodies from having to address the formal legal status of involved actors. Likewise, the deliberately ambiguous legal concepts related to non-international armed conflicts enabled them to articulate their legal positions in relation to the de facto conditions and pragmatic needs of the particular situation without committing to binding determinations about war and peace or belligerency and neutrality.[59]

During these events there was hardly any mention of the classical doctrine of civil war, or at best only scattered references and then to its non-applicability. Of the numerous wars brought about by the third wave of decolonisation, the Algerian War of Independence (1954–1962) offers an illustrative example of the way the new humanitarian law took the place of the classical law of civil war in the world arena. In theory, the classical law could have applied. A major colonial revolution and a landmark case in the law of self-determination, the Algerian war was nevertheless also a civil war in France, as French constitutions since 1848 had considered Algeria and its three *départements* as integral parts of the mother country (though its indigenous population as not equal to the population of metropolitan France). The Algerian war thus had an internal French dimension, in relation to which the classical law of civil war might have been invoked by the parties and international actors had it still had sufficient purchase and relevance. This did not happen; instead, whenever international law was invoked with regard to the conflict, this took place in the context of the new Geneva Convention or the principles of non-intervention and collective security in the Charter of the United Nations.

Throughout the Algerian conflict, the French government refused to characterise it as a civil war. In practice, France allowed humanitarian relief access to rebel-held areas and allowed the ICRC to inspect its prison and detention facilities. The systematic prosecution of the FLN militants

[58] Wolfgang Friedmann, *The Changing Structure of International Law* (Stevens & Sons 1964).

[59] Anne Orford, *International Authority and the Responsibility to Protect* (Cambridge University Press 2011) 69–90 *et passim*.

as criminals in French courts ended in 1958, but the French authorities did not grant them formal prisoner-of-war status and kept referring to them as 'rebels' or 'outlaws'.[60] The significance of the question was not lost on contemporary observers; the head of one French inspection commission even stated that Algerian internment facilities were 'in fact POWs camps that were not given this name in order to avoid acknowledging de facto the FLN as a belligerent'.[61] The situation was not affected by the fact that the conflict also spread to the high seas, where the French navy intercepted ships outside Algeria and inspected them for contraband, while the French government continued to refute all allegations of a state of belligerency. Several flag states raised public protests before the United Nations against seizures of their vessels, and in at least one notable case France issued an apology to West Germany for a capture.[62] Nevertheless, foreign powers mostly acquiesced to the indeterminate nature of the French interdictions, either because they supported France, and thus consented to them, or because their reactions did not go beyond verbal protests. No foreign recognitions of belligerence seem to have been issued or even seriously discussed.

While denying any existence of civil war and belligerency, France did not formally acknowledge the applicability of the Geneva Conventions either. The insurgents, for their part, repeatedly expressed a desire to follow the conventions in their entirety, but the French never reciprocated, and to the very end never admitted to the conflict having an international dimension.[63] The international community did not agree with France's insistence that legally this was a domestic conflict. From the outside, the ICRC characterised the Algerian war as 'an internal conflict in which one of the parties does not recognize the opposing party' and hence sought to act on the basis of Common Article 3.[64] A provisional

[60] Erik Castrén, *Civil War* (Suomalainen Tiedeakatemia 1966) 75; Siotis, *Le droit de la guerre*, 211; Arnold Fraleigh, 'The Algerian Revolution' in Richard A. Falk (ed), *The International Law of Civil War* (Johns Hopkins Press/ASIL 1971) 196.

[61] Raphaëlle Branche, 'The French Army and the Geneva Conventions during the Algerian War of Independence and After' in Matthew Evangelista and Nina Tannenwald (eds) *Do the Geneva Conventions Matter?* (Oxford University Press 2017) 167.

[62] Fraleigh, 'The Algerian Revolution', 203–204; France to UN Secretary-General, 25 October 1956, UN Doc S/3689 and Corr 1; UNSC Report to the UNGA 1956–1957, General Assembly Official Records XII Session Supp 2 (A/3648) 72. See also Conseil d'État – Assemblée – Société Ignazio Messina (30 March 1966) *Recueil Lebon* 1966, 258.

[63] Fraleigh, 'The Algerian Revolution', 194–196.

[64] Ibid 195.

Algerian government, the Gouvernement provisoire de la République algérienne or GPRA, was constituted in Egypt in 1958, and it began to attract cautious acknowledgements of its existence from abroad. This international recognition did not come in clear terms of statehood or belligerency, as would have been expected under the classical doctrine of civil war. Rather, it was made using ambiguous nomenclature such as 'the legal government of the fighting Algerian people', 'the legitimate representative of the Algerian people', or 'the only authority qualified to speak in the name of the Algerian people'.[65] Such language reflected uncertainty not only about the facts on the ground but also about the contemporaneous law of recognition. (An exception was Lebanon, which in 1959 proceeded straightforwardly to 'recognise de jure the provisional government of Algeria'.[66])

The Algerian war took on a multilateral dimension within the UN General Assembly, where it became a *cause célèbre* and trigger for the 1960 Decolonisation Declaration. The aim of the declaration was to establish, as a principle, the legitimacy of popular governments struggling against foreign domination and to bring about the cessation of foreign colonial domination.[67] Five days after the declaration, the General Assembly applied its principles to Algeria in Resolution 1573 (XV)/1960, which recognised the right of the Algerian people to self-determination and independence.[68]

The resolution of the Algerian war was legitimised through popular referendums on both sides of the conflict. In a referendum in 1961, the French people recognised the right of the Algerians to choose their political destiny, and in 1962 the French government and the FLN negotiated for peace at Évian-les-Bains. In accordance with the accords signed there, two more referendums were held in Algeria, confirming self-determination and independence by majorities that approached unanimity.[69] Sovereign equality notwithstanding, separation under the accords involved a familiar pattern of transitional property questions, including the matter of the Saharan petroleum resources whereby Algeria

[65] Charles Zorgbibe, *La guerre civile* (Presses universitaires de France 1975) 136–137.

[66] Ibid.

[67] UNGA Res 1514 (XV) Declaration on the Granting of Independence to Colonial Countries and Peoples (14 December 1960). See also UNGA Res 1541 (XV) (15 December 1960) and UNGA Res 1654 (XVI) (27 November 1961).

[68] UNGA Res 1573 (XV) Question of Algeria (19 December 1960).

[69] 'Agreements Relating to Algerian Independence' 1 *International Legal Materials* (ILM) (1962) 214–230; 'Proclamation des résultats du referendum' *Journal officiel de L'État algérien*, 6 July 1962, 3.

would 'guarantee French interests and the vested rights of individuals and legal entities', such as 'the rights attached to mining or transport titles granted by the French Republic for the exploration, exploitation or transport of liquid or gaseous hydrocarbons'. Despite being free to 'exercise its full and complete sovereignty both internally and externally' and 'freely establish its own institutions',[70] Algeria would still belong to the franc area, and 'French interests' would be 'assured in particular by . . . [p]reference being given, in the case of equal offers, in the granting of new mining titles, to French companies'.[71]

Overall, the Algerian war raised a number of familiar legal questions, such as the status of prisoners of war and the problem of recognition, which might have been addressed in terms of the doctrine of civil war. Yet the principles that the various actors sought to apply when addressing them had little to do with the classical law. Throughout the decades of decolonisation, legal developments continued to abide by concepts and arguments that built on the anti-formalism and creative ambiguity of the law of non-international armed conflicts, the principle of self-determination, and the end of empire. The concept of the 'war of national liberation', for example, sought to address contentious problems of state recognition by reinforcing an international presumption of the legitimacy of armed struggles that aimed to overthrow colonial rule. Conversely, it placed the onus on colonial authorities to justify their continued presence. Thus, in 1970 the UN General Assembly reaffirmed 'the inherent right of colonial peoples to struggle by all necessary means at their disposal against colonial Powers' and adopted a programme of action urging states to 'render all necessary moral and material assistance to the peoples of colonial Territories in their struggle to attain freedom and independence'. Consequently, all 'freedom fighters under detention' were to be treated in accordance with the relevant provisions of the Geneva Conventions.[72] Similarly, in its 1974 definition of aggression the General Assembly excepted wars of national liberation from the definition.[73] The culmination of these General Assembly resolutions

[70] Evian Accords, 18 March 1962, 1 ILM (1962) ch II-A-1, 216.
[71] Evian Accords, General Declaration, ch II-B-2(b), and Declaration of Principles, preamble, IV, art 14. A separate declaration of principles was signed for the exploitation of the wealth of the Saharan subsoil (1 ILM (1962) 226ff) and an arbitral agreement was signed in 1963 for the arbitration of the hydrocarbons in the Saharan subsoil (26 June 1963, *Journal officiel de la République française* 7964).
[72] UNGA Res 2621 (XXV) (12 October 1970) paras 2, 3(2), 6(a).
[73] UNGA Res 3314 (XXIX) (14 December 1974) annex, art 7.

was the legally binding and widely adopted Article 1(4) of the 1977 Additional Protocol I to the Geneva Conventions, which stated that international conflicts 'include armed conflicts in which peoples are fighting against colonial domination and alien occupation and against racist régimes in the exercise of their right of self-determination'.[74] While these legal principles of course continued to raise questions of interpretation and authority, for present purposes the point is that the applicability of international law in decolonial conflicts was no longer determined in terms of the classical concepts of belligerent and insurgent recognition.

7.2.3 *The Last Scholars of the Law of Civil War*

In 1948, Max Planck observed: 'A new scientific truth does not triumph by convincing its opponents and making them see the light, but rather because its opponents eventually die and a new generation grows up that is familiar with it.'[75] Planck's observation helps to explain the slow transition in international legal scholarship from the formal conceptual language of the classical doctrine of civil war to the anti-formal language of the modern law of armed conflicts not of an international character. While new generations of scholars, like Jean Siotis, embraced the outcome of the Geneva Conference with relative ease, remnants of the classical vocabulary were still haunting the teachings and writings of law professors as late as the early 1970s. Authors of general legal treatises, including many who elsewhere had closely observed and even personally influenced post-war transformations in the structure of international law, were loath to discard the classical principles outright. The normative contours of belligerent and insurgent recognition were still much to the fore in Hersch Lauterpacht's *Recognition in International Law* of 1947, and Hans Kelsen's *Principles of International Law* of 1952 likewise mentioned them as valid legal principles with continuing importance.[76]

Besides, monographs devoted to the law of civil war continued to appear, and retained the classical structure at their core. This was particularly the case in continental Europe, where legal scholarship remained faithful to the tradition of cautious and systematic black-letter treatises, in which the question of the desuetude of legal rules and

74 Additional Protocol I (1977), 1125 UNTS 3, art 1(4).

75 Max Planck, *Scientific Autobiography and Other Papers* ([1948] Philosophical Library 1949) 33–34.

76 Hersch Lauterpacht, *Recognition in International law* (Cambridge University Press 1947) 175–328; Hans Kelsen, *Principles of International Law* (Rinehart 1952) 291–292.

principles posed a distinct problem. For the authors of such treatises, it was still possible at the time to avoid pondering whether they 'believed' in the old system of law or the new. Indeed, in their writings they might well treat old principles side by side with the most recent legal sources; arguably, studying both might even be necessary, as their interrelationship might be relevant to interpreting the law. In this light, the abandonment of the classical doctrine of civil war appeared not to be conclusive, but rather to be a question or a possibility that warranted further examination.

As late as 1975, the Parisian professor Charles Zorgbibe could not bring himself to simply sweep aside the past in his monograph *La guerre civile*.[77] The question of belligerent recognition played a central role in his study, and although he sought to be in tune with his contemporaries on modern internationalised civil wars, he did not forsake the classical principles as obsolete. He proposed that the distinction between the 'classical' and 'modern' doctrines of civil war had mainly to do with their international dimension, and that while most 'modern' civil wars were characterised by their international character, purely domestic civil wars could still occasionally be 'classical'.[78] Thus, classical internal wars between domestic factions like the Nigerian war of secession in 1967 could still occur even though 'modern' civil wars like the Carlist wars in Spain and the actual civil war of 1936–1939 had already taken place.[79] This retention of all possible avenues suggests that in Zorgbibe's view the classical debates about belligerent recognition still counted as valid law alongside the more modern law of armed conflicts.[80] In this, he was an outlier, but not alone. A decade earlier, Roger Pinto had lectured on the subject of civil wars at the Hague Academy of International Law and had likewise envisaged the classical doctrine continuing in relation to contemporary questions and problems.[81] Although his focus was above all on foreign intervention and its permissibility, he still anchored his analysis on classical sources such as Wiesse and Vattel.[82] But Pinto was more eager to reject the nineteenth-century concept of belligerent recognition as 'today no longer necessary', given the abolition of war and the

[77] Zorgbibe, *La guerre civile*.
[78] Ibid 99, 104.
[79] Ibid 8.
[80] Ibid 36–56, 71–97.
[81] Roger Pinto, 'Les règles du droit international concernant la guerre civile' 114 *Collected Courses of Hague Academy of International Law* (1965) 455–548.
[82] Ibid 455–469.

confusion this had caused in scholarship.[83] He offered his audience instead a commentary mainly on modern *jus ad bellum*, with particular attention to international organisations, and on *jus in bello* under Common Article 3 of the Geneva Conventions.

Perhaps the most faithful attempt to find a modern role for the seemingly obsolete classical doctrine was Erik Castrén's *Civil War* (1966). Castrén had studied during the interwar years, submitting his thesis on aerial warfare in 1938 and later publishing the monograph *On the Present Laws of War and Neutrality* in 1954.[84] His education and academic background were firmly rooted in the formalist visions of the early twentieth century and the civilising project of the international legal profession. For him, the jurist's task was to formulate new, realistic, and acceptable legal rules and to patiently hope they would one day be followed, because 'even weak rules are better than a complete lack of rules'.[85] Although the rules of war and neutrality had 'been unable to keep pace with time', there was 'no justification for [a pessimistic] attitude, since the international law continues to be necessary, and the task of bringing it up to date continues to be of the utmost importance'.[86] This aspiration was still very much present in Castrén's *Civil War*. He readily admitted that the problems of civil war in international law had caused general confusion and maintained that 'efforts to solve them must rely on logic alone or on finding support in some general principles of law'.[87]

Castrén structured *Civil War* around the questions and principles of the classical doctrine and portrayed the more modern institutions such as the collective security provisions of the UN Charter and the Geneva Conventions as new and important, but still unsettled, law. The book's content was for the most part divided between sections that dealt with law in recognised belligerencies and those that dealt with law in insurgencies where belligerency had not been recognised. Rather than identifying a difference between the past law and the present, Castrén approached the present from the perspective of the classical system. He retained belligerent recognition not only as a theoretical possibility for states but as a key criterion on which the applicable law would depend. Castrén's substantive rules on civil war were a mixture of old principles

83 Ibid, 465–466, 474–475.

84 Erik Castrén, *Ilmasota I–II* (Suomalainen Lakimiesyhdistys 1938–1939); Erik Castrén, *The Present Law of War and Neutrality* (Suomalainen Tiedeakatemia 1954).

85 Castrén, *Ilmasota I*, v.

86 Castrén, *Present Law*, 3.

87 Castrén, *Civil War*, 78–79.

inherited from the nineteenth century (such as the law of neutrality and state responsibility for rebels[88]) and contemporary humanitarian concerns. For Castrén, the applicability of the 1949 Geneva Conventions in civil wars was a matter 'of crucial importance',[89] and he repeatedly explored Common Article 3 and its implications.[90] Reflecting the situation prevailing in the UN Security Council during the Cold War era, Castrén acknowledged the international authority of the Security Council under the UN Charter, especially 'should a civil war acquire characteristics of an international dispute',[91] even if he considered the possibility of collective recognition of civil wars within the UN as 'unrealistic'.[92]

At the end of the day, Castrén's attempts to remain loyal to all available positive norms and practices led him to conclusions that began to contradict each other. His black-letter formalism often came down to simply counting those authors who interpreted a contentious legal question in a such-and-such a way and those who did not, leading to an exposition that portrayed the law at the same time as both fully systematic and thoroughly indeterminate. His understanding of the nature of the recognition of belligerency – motivated by a desire to see facts and 'truth' limit arbitrary uses of power – was so riddled with exceptions and conditions that the resultant mechanism could be bent for almost any purpose. For example, he stated that foreign states were prohibited from assisting insurgents and had 'certain obligations towards the lawful Government which prevent them from deciding at will on their relations with the insurgents', while elsewhere stating they could still recognise the revolutionary government 'as the Government of the State for the duration of the civil war', in which case 'the former lawful Government is now in the position of a revolutionary Government'.[93] When discussing the closing of ports and the establishment of blockades, he recited the classical positions about tacit recognition, the requirement of effectiveness, and the prohibition of blockades in the absence of belligerency – only to recall in a footnote that '[t]o-day the UN Charter censures blockades because they imply force or the threat of force'.[94] Inevitably,

[88] Ibid 200–206.
[89] Ibid 79–80.
[90] Ibid 30, 33, 70, 74–75, 78, 84–89, 91, 97–99, 115, 117, 132, 138–139, 144, 148, 153–154, 157, 211, 225.
[91] Ibid 20–21, 80–91.
[92] Ibid 192–193.
[93] Ibid 23–24, 32, 105, 117–118.
[94] Ibid 102.

the outcome was not so much a fusion between the old and the new as an eclectic catalogue of principles gathered from a number of sources and presented side by side as though they were a single coherent system. *Civil War* was a brave attempt at a synthesis, but ultimately it became as much a monument to the incoherence of the law of civil war as it was an instrument of clarification.

What, apart from Planck's principle, made Castrén and his contemporaries preserve the classical language of civil war until 1975? Part of the answer may lie in their ultimate faith in classical international law. Their scholarship sought to preserve systemic cohesion in international law at a time of rapid change and normative entropy increased by new anti-formal institutions. It did not oppose the change in modern law; it sought rather to maintain a diligent fidelity to as broad a field of legal norms as possible. As such, it was not 'mere' positivism; Castrén's commitments to both belligerency and humanitarian law, for example, aimed to expand the application of international law in civil wars and reflected the old juristic ethos of speaking truth to power, however timidly.[95] Such sensibilities had a dose of faith in universal justice in them. Although textbooks produced by continental lawyers around this time often read more like telephone directories than bold visions of natural justice, they still relied on a possibility of persuasive legal wisdom and dialogue among bona fide international experts that could mitigate the risks and brutal tendencies of modernity. In short, they continued to echo the faith the nineteenth century had placed in a legal conscience of the civilised world.

***

Even if the classical doctrine continued to resound in legal scholarship after 1949, its significance was marginal. Especially in the Anglo-American world, the discipline was now busy debating various new international challenges on matters such as decolonisation and the end of empire, proxy wars in the newly independent world, the emerging nuclear standoff, and international access to the natural resources of the world. In the political climate of the Cold War, various forms of political realism flourished, building on past international relations scholarship that had rejected the possibility of universal moral principles in the international sphere.[96] For Myres McDougal, the state of the current 'world order' was often a confrontation between opposite and

95 Ibid 89, 91, 146.

96 Martti Koskenniemi, *The Gentle Civilizer of Nations* (Cambridge University Press 2001) 438.

incommensurable ideologies of democracy and totalitarianism, in which the latter's use of legal terms and principles was necessarily adversarial and abusive, and thus served to justify international lawfare in defence of the 'free world'.[97] In response, Wolfgang Friedmann warned against subjecting international law to ideological divisions, which would happen if the decisions of one country (such as the US) were elevated to the status of impartial truths.[98] In these debates, the classical doctrine of civil war in international law played a peripheral or anecdotal role at best. The discussions were strongly coloured by the realpolitik of the time and therefore tended to slide towards issues of intervention, the prohibition of aggression, the territorial integrity of sovereign states, and sovereign equality. On these, the relevant legal concepts and principles were derived from the UN Charter and other post-war legal sources and institutions rather than from classics of the law of nations.

The seemingly endless war in Vietnam, in particular, fuelled protracted debates among American international lawyers about the legality of the US involvement and the legal characterisation of the conflict.[99] At its 1967 annual meeting, the American Society of International Law (ASIL) hosted two sessions on 'International Law and Civil Wars', during which members reflected on experiences of past civil wars that had accumulated to their day.[100] The following year, a panel discussion on the theme 'Aggression, War, and Neutrality under the United Nations Charter' opened with Elihu Lauterpacht's talk on 'The Legal Irrelevance of the "State of War"',[101] which intimated that, due to the UN Charter's prohibition of aggression and unilateral use of force, war 'as a technical legal condition' was no longer compatible with

97 For example, Myres S. McDougal and others, *Studies in World Public Order* ([1960] New Haven Press 1987); Myres S. McDougal, 'The Hydrogen Bomb Tests and the International Law of the Sea' 49 *American Journal of International Law* (1955) 356–361.

98 Wolfgang Friedmann, 'Intervention, Civil War and the Rôle of International Law' 59 *Proceedings of the ASIL Annual Meeting* (ASIL Proceedings) (1965) 67–81; Friedmann, *Changing Structures*, 262–272.

99 For example, James N. Rosenau (ed), *International Aspects of Civil Strife* (Princeton University Press 1964); Richard A. Falk (ed), *The International Law of Civil War* (Johns Hopkins Press/ASIL 1971); Richard A. Falk (ed), *The Vietnam War and International Law* (4 vols, Princeton University Press 1968–1976); John Norton Moore (ed), *Law and Civil War in the Modern World* (Johns Hopkins University Press 1974). See also several entries in ASIL Proceedings 1967–1968. For a retrospect, see Richard Falk and Stefan Andersson (eds) *Revisiting the Vietnam War and International Law* (Cambridge University Press 2018).

100 61 ASIL Proceedings (1967) 1–23, 50–81.

101 62 ASIL Proceedings (1968) 58–83.

international law. Commenting on the presentation, Richard Falk responded that while Lauterpacht had been persuasive juridically, it was still not obvious that sovereign states no longer had the legal competence to maintain a state of war. The underlying question was whether such irrelevance simply meant 'an exclusion from vocabulary' or whether it was also necessary for states to actually stop waging war as a result.[102]

Falk's comments reflected his own recent work on the law of civil war, in which he levelled criticisms at the classical system but concluded that 'the rhetoric and doctrine of traditional international law remain useful, especially if they can be adapted to the new roles of supranational actors and responsive to the realities of the cold war'.[103] Like his European counterparts, Falk still had some interest in understanding the classical doctrine on its own traditional terms and had been reluctant to rule out its utility without a proper examination.[104] Observing the non-use of belligerent recognition by third parties and the problem of their almost unrestricted discretion,[105] he made a number of criticisms of the classical doctrine, which generally related to the changing international conditions of the Cold War era.[106] Under international law during the Cold War, what was at stake had to be measured in terms of the advantages and utility it had in confronting the tactics of the political adversaries in the Sino-Soviet bloc.[107] If empire had once depended primarily on the extent of colonial occupation, 'it now increasingly depend[ed] upon the capacity to influence the outcome of important internal wars'.[108] The law of civil war that was emerging in the 1960s was therefore not the classical law concerned with states experiencing civil wars; it was rather a new law to enable the great powers to deal with local insurrections within their spheres of interest.[109]

As the Vietnam War continued to intensify, even the mild interest in classical concepts evaporated in the ASIL debates. By 1971, the general theme of the annual meeting was 'Strategies for World Order', and it comprised a wide array of strategic geopolitical questions ranging from the laws of war to conflict management to the control and exploitation of

102 Ibid 77.
103 Richard Falk, 'Janus Tormented: The International Law of Internal War', in Rosenau (ed), *International Aspects*, 248.
104 Ibid 197.
105 Ibid 203–208.
106 Ibid 222–227.
107 Ibid 238.
108 Ibid 189.
109 Ibid 185.

the oceans to the possibilities of international investment protection.[110] The traditional doctrine at this time received minimal attention, if any.

Standing apart from the American context, one of the finest syntheses of the classical law of civil war was nonetheless written in the 1970s by Roscoe Oglesby.[111] Oglesby was a local member of the ASIL and at least once had participated in person in ASIL discussions on the law of internal war. It seems that what in part catalysed his book project was a personal remark from Friedmann to the effect that there was at the time no norm of international law governing conditions of civil strife.[112] Accordingly, *Internal War and the Search for Normative Order* became a retrospective on the classical doctrine and its demise, and to this day it stands as one of the best histories of the subject. It had the hallmarks and structure of a classical civil war work, beginning with a historical overview of case studies from the American Revolution to the American Civil War, and then separate chapters on the recognition of insurgency, de facto recognitions, and the succession of responsibilities after civil wars. Though its perspective on the classical law was clearly historical, Oglesby suggested his book might serve as 'normative in the sense . . . of seeking clarification of the legal standards which the international community imposed on contestants in a civil conflict in one given era – in an era when the classical balance of power system was the dominant modality of the international system'.[113] He saw the decline of the classical law as something caused by the end of that classical balance of power and its replacement with the Cold War, and he linked the demise of the recognition of belligerency to the end of the practice of classical neutrality. In the end, Oglesby arrived at the conclusion that the classical doctrines of belligerency and neutrality had indeed fallen into desuetude – he meant this in the strong sense, invoking, among other things, the definition of desuetude in the *Digest* of Justinian[114] – and that the Cold War principles of intervention seemed to be emerging as dominant rules for the time being.[115] The conclusion was clear and timely.

Together with Jean Siotis' *La guerre civile*, Oglesby's book remains probably the most complete study on the rise and fall of the classical

[110] 65 ASIL Proceedings (1971).

[111] Roscoe Oglesby, *Internal War and the Search for Normative Order* (Martinus Nijhoff 1971).

[112] Ibid 119; 61 ASIL Proceedings (1967) 19.

[113] Oglesby, *Internal War*, v.

[114] Ibid 110; *Dig* 1.3.32.

[115] Oglesby, *Internal War*, 131–138.

doctrine of civil war in international law. If Siotis distinguished between the 'classical doctrine' of civil war and the modern laws of non-international armed conflict at the time of his writing, Oglesby's historical review made clear the connection between the demise of the classical doctrine and the renunciation of war. He identified the early beginning of the decline of the classical law of civil war after the American Civil War and readily admitted that the doctrine had now lost its normative force. Oglesby's fondness for the classical doctrine is clearly visible throughout the book, but he was not sentimental or unrealistic about the current status of the classical principles. His work, like that of Siotis, was above all an account of a language of civil war that his generation had inherited but no longer found of any real use. When the international lawyers of the world gathered in Rome in 1973 to debate the role of the classical law for one last time, there was no doubt that they already understood how fundamentally different their contemporary legal vocabulary had become from that of the nineteenth century.

7.3 Wiesbaden 1975: A Farewell to Words

Earlier in this chapter we saw how at the Geneva Conference of 1949 the participants introduced several alternative models for drafting Common Article 3 governing the application of the conventions in civil wars. After an extended debate, the conference set aside the draft language based on the classical doctrine of civil war and adopted a novel language of non-international armed conflicts in its place. That decision marked a watershed between the law of civil war and the modern humanitarian law in the modern sources of international law. We then observed that even though legal scholars were quick to understand the significance of these developments, they in fact retained the classical doctrine of civil war in their writings for another two decades, wary of abandoning it prematurely and uncertain whether its old concepts might yet play a role in future encounters. Now, we will recount how the Institut de droit international met in in Rome in 1973 to discuss the relevance of the law of civil war one last time.

Work on the last resolution to deal with the classical law of civil war began four years earlier, when the Institut initiated a study on the question of non-intervention in civil wars.[116] At the time, proxy wars and intervention by invitation were hot topics for scholars. Whereas the

[116] 53 *Annuaire de l'Institut de droit international* (Annuaire IDI) (1969) vol II, 43, 506.

classical scholars had considered a government's right to invite foreign assistance as an inherent part of state sovereignty, there was an increasing feeling among jurists from the interwar years onwards that such a stance might also be contrary to the right of nations to freely choose their political institutions. Experiences throughout the period of decolonisation had brought the international community repeatedly into situations where there was no consensus over which government was the lawful one, or whether a particular conflict was one of liberation or plain rebellion. On setting up a study commission to investigate and report back on the question the Institut soon learned that the debate would take it back to some of the most elementary questions concerning the status of non-international conflicts in international law.

Addressing participants at the Rome meeting in 1973, the commission's president, Dietrich Schindler, explained that 'the objective of the report is not to find a median line between the traditional and progressive concepts, but rather to research those traditional rules that have remained in force, those that have fallen into desuetude or that have been abolished, and new rules that have been created'.[117] If, as Erik Castrén had written, efforts to solve the new legal questions concerning civil war must rely on logic alone or on finding support in some general principles of law, the Institut study was aimed at doing just that. The commission did not seek to propose rules *de lege ferenda*, but 'to crystallise the rules of international law in force on the basis of doctrine and the practice of States while taking into account the recent developments in this domain'.[118] In a classical positivist vein, the study group hoped to fulfil its task by distilling a revised systematisation and interpretation of the law from all the past rules, and, through analysis and open discussion, restore cohesion in the law.

A debate about the fate of the classical doctrine of civil war proved unavoidable in the commission's work.[119] Schindler had begun the study by disseminating a questionnaire asking how broadly the commission should understand the concept of 'civil war' and whether the study should cover the question of insurgents as belligerents and the legal

[117] Final report of the Eighth Commission (Schindler's report), 55 Annuaire IDI (1973) 546. Work on the resolution began at the Edinburgh session in 1969, followed by a provisional report at Zagreb in 1971, the final report and draft resolution in Rome in 1973, and finally a small supplementary report and the full resolution at the session in Wiesbaden in 1975.

[118] 55 Annuaire IDI (1973) 545.

[119] Ibid 517.

consequences flowing therefrom.[120] He observed in his exposé how the recognition of belligerency seemed to have fallen out of use in the preceding decades to such an extent 'that we may ask whether it has not fallen into desuetude'.[121] Castrén responded that the commission should without a doubt study the recognition of belligerency. 'The institution of the said recognition has not fallen into desuetude,' he opined, since 'in recent practice there have been at least some cases of implicit recognition.'[122] Other contributors were more ambivalent, doubting the usefulness of belligerent recognition,[123] suspecting that it might be in the *domaine réservé* of states,[124] or believing that even if civil war could be of relevance to the law of neutrality, it had likely lost its significance with respect to interventions.[125]

Despite the interest in exploring the recognition of belligerency initially expressed within the commission, the subject did not arouse much enthusiasm in the end. There was a ring of dead letters in the exchange. One by one, references to belligerent recognition were removed from the final draft of 1973,[126] 'given that the recognition of belligerency no longer has practical importance today'.[127] By the time the commission presented its final report, the pastness of the classical doctrine had become something of a consensus. Speaking before the plenary in Rome, Schindler openly admitted that in the commission's view 'the recognition of insurgents as belligerents generally has no longer any practical utility' because once the UN Charter had prohibited the use of force, 'the state of war or of belligerency is not, in general, any longer considered to be a state in accordance with international law'.[128] Recognition's decline in practice could also be attributed to the transformation of maritime warfare, states no longer having an interest in exercising belligerent and neutral rights.[129] Furthermore, since the minimum standards enshrined in the Geneva Conventions now bound states in civil wars, the application of

[120] Ibid 526.
[121] Ibid 522.
[122] Castrén's observations, 1969, 55 Annuaire IDI (1973) 528–529.
[123] Chaumont's observations, 1969, 55 Annuaire IDI (1973) 531.
[124] Miaja de Muela's observations, 1969, 55 Annuaire IDI (1973) 533.
[125] Röling's observations, 1970, 55 Annuaire IDI (1973) 540.
[126] Draft of 1973, 55 Annuaire IDI (1973) 568–573; preliminary draft of 1971, 55 Annuaire IDI (1973) 506–510.
[127] Final report, 55 Annuaire IDI (1973) 558.
[128] 55 Annuaire IDI (1973) 748.
[129] Ibid.

humanitarian law in civil wars no longer depended on recognition.[130] In consequence, the Institut omitted the mechanism of belligerent recognition from the final resolution altogether.

When the Institut passed the final resolution in Wiesbaden in 1975, it retained only one element of the classical doctrine. This was the term 'civil war' itself, which nevertheless was emptied of its classical content and given a new definition. The commission had at first considered replacing the old term with one of the more contemporary alternatives, but many shared Oscar Schachter's view that merely changing the term would not overcome the indeterminacy in characterising internal conflicts.[131] The problem was not the term 'civil war' but rather its content in the classical doctrine of civil war, whereas Common Article 3 more usefully invoked 'a notion broader than the civil war in the classical sense'.[132] Somewhat predictably, the commission eventually combined the two. It retained the term 'civil war' but rebranded it to mimic the Geneva Conventions,[133] so that in the final resolution Article 1 read: 'For the purposes of this Resolution, the term "civil war" shall apply to any armed conflict, not of an international character, which breaks out in the territory of a State.'[134] This rebranding of the term 'civil war' had the effect of narrowing the legacy of the classical doctrine. By giving an open-ended definition of 'civil war', the Institut acknowledged the indeterminacy of the concept, abandoning the traditional assumption that the classical concepts had precise formal and substantive meanings deriving directly from customary international law. Moreover, a definition that used the words of Common Article 3 rendered the classical concept of civil war hollow, recasting it in the shape of modern humanitarian law. The classical doctrine of civil war was now decidedly a matter of the past.

What about the issue of intervention itself? Perhaps the most telling aspect of the Wiesbaden resolution on non-intervention was the fact that its drafters chose to omit a definition of 'intervention' altogether. Amidst all the discussion on the desuetude of belligerency and the redefining of 'civil war', the commission could not reach agreement on how to define the question with which it had primarily been tasked. Schindler had originally proposed that the term 'intervention' be understood as 'all

130 Ibid.
131 Schachter's observations, 1972, 55 Annuaire IDI (1973) 601.
132 55 Annuaire IDI (1973) 552–553.
133 Draft of 1973, art 1, 55 Annuaire IDI (1973) 568. See also 55 Annuaire IDI (1973) 549.
134 Resolution on the Principle of Non-Intervention in Civil Wars, 14 August 1975, 56 Annuaire IDI (1975) 545.

actions by a State or an international organisation likely to influence the outcome of a civil war', but the members felt that the definition might be both over- and under-inclusive. 'On the one hand, it may be too broad, because a great many things may influence the outcomes of civil wars', commented Castrén. 'On the other hand, I do not understand why we would eliminate interventions of a humanitarian character or those conducted by States to protect their own nationals abroad.'[135] In the end, intervention was deliberately left undefined so that it could be understood as a 'technical and neutral' concept, not related to questions of legitimacy or lawfulness.[136] Similarly, there were several exceptions to the rule prohibiting intervention. It would not cover disorders or riots, armed conflicts between de facto states, or conflicts arising from decolonisation.[137] The ban on the provision of aid did not extend to humanitarian aid or 'technical or economic aid which is not likely to have any substantial impact' on the war, or aid permitted by the United Nations.[138] And, of particular note, the resolution permitted collective counter-intervention by states 'whenever it appears that intervention has taken place during civil war in violation of the preceding provisions'.[139] All of these points begged the question of who decides whether the conditions stated are fulfilled and on what bases. Such questions have continued to dominate the politics of interventions and civil wars in the international realm ever since.

7.4 Conclusion: After Civil War

In 2019, Alonso Gurmendi reported having found in Peruvian archives a declaration of belligerent recognition from as late as 1979.[140] In the document in question, the Andean states jointly declared that the 'military situation, objectively considered, forces the recognition as belligerents of the popular forces that are currently fighting against the Nicaraguan Government'. According to Gurmendi, this recognition of belligerency had formed part of a toolbox used to intervene in Nicaragua and bring about the end of the dictatorship of Anastasio Somoza. There

135 Castrén's observations, 1969, 55 Annuaire IDI (1973) 527.
136 56 Annuaire IDI (1975) 139, 413.
137 Art 2(2).
138 Art 3.
139 Art 5.
140 Alonso Gurmendi, 'The Last Recognition of Belligerency (and Some Thoughts on Why You May Not Have Heard of It)', *Opinio Juris* (10 December 2019).

seems to be no doubt that the document is intended as a formal recognition of belligerency, but it is less clear what its legal consequences were, or were intended to be. While Gurmendi suggested that the reason for the declaration's obscurity was the language in which it was drafted and its location, the present research encourages us to think there were also more deep-rooted reasons. Although the non-Anglophone context surely did play a major role in the absence of any reference to the case in the literature, and belligerent recognition indeed may still belong in the political vocabulary in Latin America,[141] there are good reasons for maintaining that the Andean recognition of belligerency in 1979 was passed over in jurisprudence primarily because the world around it had ceased to recognise its normative significance.

By the time the Institut de droit international passed its resolution at Wiesbaden in 1975, it was evident that the classical doctrine of civil war had ceased to have any practical relevance in international law. The Wiesbaden resolution became the international legal profession's final farewell to the classical principles. By the time of the 1977 Geneva Conference, they had indeed been abandoned: one would be hard pressed to find a single mention of the recognition of belligerency in that meeting's protocols. The deliberate 'non-definition' approach to the question of non-international armed conflicts persisted until the 1990s, when ICTY returned to the topic and attempted a definition of armed conflicts in its *Tadić* judgment.[142] In the same decision, the tribunal also briefly referenced the classical doctrines of insurgency and belligerency, but framed them as historical concepts from a bygone era.[143]

The long history of the classical doctrine of civil war ultimately leads to the conclusion that it has ceased to hold legal relevance in the present. To be sure, many basic legal questions of civil wars, such as the recognition of the parties and the characterisation of conflicts, which are prerequisites for the identification of the laws that apply to a conflict and its actors, effects, and captives, continue to arise in the present age;[144] but ultimately this persistence relates to the enduring nature of the problem of civil

141 Sivakumaran, *The Law of Non-International Armed Conflict*, 195–196.

142 ICTY, *Prosecutor* v. *Duško Tadić*, Decision on Jurisdiction, 2 October 1995, esp para 70.

143 Ibid, paras 96, 97.

144 For example, Alexander Wentker, *Party Status to Armed Conflict in International Law* (Oxford University Press 2024) 95–148; René Provost, *Rebel Courts: The Administration of Justice by Armed Insurgents* (Oxford University Press 2021); Anthony Cullen, *The Concept of Non-International Armed Conflict*, 117–158; Sivakumaran, *The Law of Non-International Armed Conflict*, 196–211. Compare UNGA, Report of Philip Alston (28 May 2010) UN Doc A/HRC/14/24/Add. 6, paras 46–69.

wars itself, which remains present in no matter what system of international law. The classical law of civil war *stricto sensu* was a product of, and genuinely belonged to, a world in which war, peace, and neutrality were valid and regularly applied legal concepts – a world of sovereign states that sought to manage their ambitions and their coexistence through a mixture of bilateral relations and intuitions about a balance of power and the long-term nature of the diplomatic interactions they participated in. It was conceived to address a world of empires and of sail and steam, at a time when international law was a language more about settling disputes over property and dominion rather than about humanity and intervention. Though the fundamental concepts of the classical law of civil war remain available for modern-day lawyers to invoke and to discuss in their writings, their normative meaning has been exhausted and replaced. In a nutshell, so long as the prerogative of war remains abolished in international law, also the classical concept of civil war will remain without legal foundation. Present-day legal actors and international institutions in the present would probably respond to attempts to invoke classical prize jurisdictions, privateer commissions, close blockades, cartel ships or belligerent recognitions not with legal acknowledgement but with puzzlement, asking what they might mean in current circumstances – or what on earth had happened to the fundamentals of international law to make them suddenly relevant again.

Conclusion

The Rise and Fall of the Classical Doctrine of Civil War

This book has sought to bring together the story of the classical doctrine of civil war in international law, from the early modern revolutions until the twentieth century. It has argued that the doctrine had in fact two lives during that period, one in the practice of states in the age of sail and steam, and another in the writings of academic publicists in the late nineteenth and early twentieth centuries. In the former, the principles of the doctrine were unclear but implicitly accepted, as they emerged out of the needs of states to articulate their legal positions in situations where the formal legal distinction between war and peace became compromised by internal conflicts. The doctrine declined in state practice along with the classical laws of war and neutrality. In the doctrine's second coming, the liberal internationalists of the legal profession sought to make its rules explicit and to create a coherent legal system that states could follow in a spirit of reciprocity, so as to properly and humanely manage international tensions and disputes arising from intestine warfare. While this project created a small scholarly tradition of its own, it had little impact on the behaviour of states faced with the international repercussions of civil wars. The scholarly doctrine came to an end in the 1970s when the Institut de droit international unceremoniously concluded that the classical principles no longer had any practical relevance.

The classical law of civil war had its origin in the erstwhile distinction of lawful enemies from pirates and brigands, whom the law of nations would not protect.[1] In light of experiences like the Dutch Revolt and the execution of Charles I in England, the luminaries of Europe began to acknowledge that revolutionary facts might under certain circumstances triumph over a formal sovereign title. In a sufficiently extensive conflict, rebel mariners and statesmen could be recognised as having valid (even if provisional) standing before the law of nations. Gentili wrote: 'When in

[1] *Dig* 50.16.118; *Dig* 49.14.24; Grotius, *De jure belli ac pacis*, II.18.3.

the strife each faction lays claim by word and deed to the whole organization of the state or to half of it, the right of embassy will certainly hold between the combatants.'[2] In a true civil war, wrote Grotius, 'a single people is considered for the time being as two peoples'.[3] These were the essential principles from which Enlightenment scholars like Christian Wolff and Emer de Vattel extrapolated the classical law of civil war. According to Vattel's famous synthesis, a sufficiently violent and persistent internal conflict should, of necessity, be regarded as a civil war under the law of nations; when this happened, it gave rise within the nation to two independent parties, and the established laws of war should be observed on both sides.[4]

In practice, insurgents had a chance of being recognised under the law of nations if they managed to wage their war at sea. In the age of sail, this was not uncommon. When a rebellion reached so great a scale that insurgents were able to furnish their own privateers and claim their own prize jurisdiction – their power to adjudicate title to captured goods and vessels in a lawful and binding way – their struggle ceased to be a merely domestic concern. Before the eyes of the world, a new Rex took up position, claiming to rely on valid legal rules and decisions, albeit not deriving from traditional succession, or a new authority decreed a new, ultimate rule of recognition or *Grundnorm* over an entire state or part of it.[5] Consequently, foreign governments were obliged to react to revolutionary claims and clarify which rule of recognition they acknowledged. If the rebels, their commissions, and their courts were not recognised, then they were pirates and possibly to be dismissed en bloc as *hostes humani generis*. But if they were recognised, then the law of nations would apply between the parties to the conflict and whoever recognised them. 'A civil war', explained Justice Grier in 1863, 'becomes such by its accidents – the number, power, and organization of the persons who originate and carry it on', until 'the world acknowledges them as belligerents, and the contest a war'.[6]

The high period of the classical doctrine of civil war began during the transatlantic revolutions of the late eighteenth and early nineteenth

[2] Gentili, *De Legationibus*, II.9.82.

[3] *DJBP*, II.18.3.

[4] Vattel, *Droit des gens*, III.18.

[5] See H. L. A. Hart, *The Concept of Law* ([1961] 2nd edn, Clarendon Press 1994) 51–61, 100–123; Hans Kelsen, *General Theory of Law and State* ([1945] Harvard University Press 1949) 117–119.

[6] *The Prize Cases* (1863) 67 US 635, 666–667.

centuries, when the North American and Spanish American colonial revolutionaries declared insurgent prize jurisdictions and claimed belligerent rights on the high seas. From these transatlantic encounters emerged an abundance of state practice in prize cases and diplomatic confrontations, which served as a foundation for later iterations of the classical law of civil war. When foreign powers declared themselves neutrals with respect to a colonial insurrection, they undertook to treat both belligerents equally and acquiesced to their use of belligerent rights at sea; as such, the civil war was understood to have acquired a fully international status. From this practice of neutrality developed the concept of the recognition of belligerency, which in later scholarship would be the structural centrepiece of the classical doctrine of civil war. These components were then digested into the compilations of the law of nations throughout the nineteenth century, such as the later editions of Wheaton's *Elements* by William Lawrence and Richard Dana in the United States, and Johann Caspar Bluntschli's *Moderne Völkerrecht* in Europe.[7]

The classical doctrine of civil war was not applied universally. It was mainly restricted to the transatlantic theatre and there often dominated by anglophone jurisprudence. In the rest of the world – not only Africa and the Orient, but continental Europe as well – the question of belligerent status for insurgents was overshadowed by other, more predominant hierarchies of legal legitimacy. In Africa and the Orient, European lawyers typically resorted to colonial legal principles or inter-imperial rights and arguments. Insurgencies, especially native rebellions, were considered internal affairs of the respective empires, and local people were denied independent standing under international law due to what was understood at the time as their lack of 'civilisation'. Where there were indigenous insurgencies in Oriental empires, these were accepted as indigenous disturbances in which the Orientals might be held responsible for any damage caused to foreign interests. The one insurgency in Asia to come close to legal recognition was the Republic of Ezo during the Meiji Restoration, when the emperor's forces confronted the remnants of the Tokugawa shogunate both on land and at sea. But even then Western governments stopped short of recognising Japanese prize jurisdiction over their flags.

[7] Henry Wheaton, *Elements of International Law* ([1866] Richard Henry, Dana Jr and George Grafton Wilson eds, Clarendon Press 1936) § 23, fn 15; Lawrence's edition of *Wheaton*, same place; Johann Caspar Bluntschli, *Das moderne Völkerrecht der civilisirten Staten* (C. H. Beck 1868) §§ 511–514; Bluntschli, 'Opinion impartiale sur la question de l'Alabama et sur la manière de la résoudre' 2 *Revue de droit international et de législation comparée* (1870) 432–485.

In post-Napoleonic mainland Europe, governments viewed the question of civil wars from the standpoint of their need to contain threats of revolution, constitutionalism, and popular sovereignty. This legitimist movement reached a peak with the unwavering conservatism of Prince Metternich and his allies, who saw in the rise of popular opinion nothing but the coming of anarchy and the end of European civilisation. Application of this ideology proved inconsistent, however. In 1821, the Neapolitan revolt was crushed through an intervention by the Holy Alliance, whereas the Greek revolt against the Ottoman Empire ended in secession after an international naval intervention in 1827. A different kind of legitimism emerged in the Western hemisphere with the proclamation of the Monroe Doctrine in 1823, which began modestly as a policy seeking neutrality and sovereign equality with Europe, but later developed into a principle of legitimacy based on hemispheric power relations. Legitimism in the Western hemisphere was not exempt from discriminatory bias. A notorious example was the Haitian Revolution: France's long-delayed recognition came coupled with an obligation for the Haitians to compensate the financial losses suffered by their former overlords, while recognition by the US was similarly delayed and had to await until after the Civil War.

The case of the American Civil War, marked by the Union blockade and the broad international recognition of the Confederacy as a belligerent, was the great *cause célèbre* of the classical law of civil war. But it was also the last occasion on which several maritime powers of the world formally declared neutrality in a civil war. The long decline of the classical doctrine of civil war in state practice began immediately after the war, at a time when in academic literature the concept of belligerent recognition had barely been coined. The reasons for the decline were many, but this study has identified some of the most significant ones.

First, with the abolition of privateers in the 1856 Declaration of Paris, the maritime powers had effectively deprived future insurgents of their primary weapon at sea, the privateer.[8] The experience of the Confederate privateers during the American Civil War showed that the pronouncement had become a reality; from this point on, insurgencies were to become increasingly fought on land, often in the form of guerrilla warfare. Technological developments, too, caused popular insurgencies

[8] See Eyal Benvenisti and Doreen Lustig, 'Monopolizing War: Codifying the Laws of War to Reassert Governmental Authority, 1856–1874' 31 *European Journal of International Law* (EJIL) (2020) 138–139; Jan Martin Lemnitzer, *Power, Law and the End of Privateering* (Palgrave Macmillan 2014).

to be confined to land; merchant vessels from the age of steam onwards lent themselves less well to being converted into privateers, while iron-clad warships were often much harder to obtain as well as being prohibitively expensive for insurgents. A small number of naval revolts took place in Latin America at the end of the century, leading to a brief revival of the classical doctrine of civil war in diplomatic exchanges. However, they had no decisive impact on the doctrine's overall decline.

Second, developments in the law of neutrality raised the prospect of state responsibility for neutral states towards belligerents. The three Rules of Washington, drafted by Britain and the United States for the Geneva arbitration of 1871–1872, were broadly welcomed by international lawyers as a future model for the international law of neutral duties. The Institut de droit international embraced them and began to promote them as indicators of international legal opinion.[9] As the duties and obligations of neutrals came increasingly to be seen as enforceable international law and not a matter of domestic consent, governments began to lose their appetite for belligerent recognition. The practice of neutrality, which had begun as a way of expressing impartiality in relation to a conflict that involved actors frequenting foreign ports and sailing with international crews, had now turned into the adoption of strict international standards of due diligence, from which the neutrals had less to gain.

Third – and as a consequence of the second reason – new, deliberately ambiguous approaches to recognition emerged, in particular 'recognition of insurgency' as practised by the United States.[10] In the name of considerations of humanity and as a matter of practical expediency, the US began to recognise foreign insurgencies as factual events but precisely without considering itself bound by the international legal duties attendant upon formal neutrality. Domestically, it would still enact neutrality laws in respect of foreign civil wars, but it refused to see this as having international status and capable of imposing international legal obligations. The European powers developed similar models of de facto recognition of their own, focusing on the protection of international shipping but withholding any recognition of the parties that might have binding effects. The net consequence in terms of the international legal status of internal strife was that the law of peace increasingly prevailed over the laws of war and neutrality. When such pragmatism became the norm,

[9] 1 *Annuaire de l'Institut de droit international* (Annuaire IDI) (1877) 139.

[10] Francis Wharton, 'Insurgents as Belligerents' 33 *Albany Law Journal* (1886) 125–131.

new legal vocabularies began to develop that were seemingly distinct from a state of war and questions of belligerent recognition. One such language was that pertaining to the law of state responsibility, which emerged to address the protection of foreign interests during and after civil wars.[11] During the great revolutions of the long nineteenth century disputes over damages and private property were rife and frequently occasioned recourse to gunboat diplomacy. As belligerent recognition declined, practices of diplomatic protection emerged to manage risk for private international actors, and the legal resolution of conflicts would often not be achieved until long after the end of a state of war, when various claims commissions and arbitral tribunals had carried out their work.[12]

The classical doctrine of civil war had its second coming in the scholarly writings of international lawyers. This began in the 1890s around the time of the Chilean and Brazilian naval revolts and the Cuban insurrections that escalated into the Spanish-American War of 1898. Antoine Rougier situated the starting point of this new scholarship in Carlos Wiesse's *Reglas de derecho internactional aplicable a las guerras civiles* (1893) and in two fin-de-siècle studies on the laws of civil war published by the Institut de droit international, one on the duties of foreign powers and the other on state responsibility.[13] To this we might add the work of the Marquis d'Olivart, who wrote in defence of Spanish sovereignty in Cuba during its final years, as well as the summaries in French of the general law of civil law by Rougier himself and his contemporaries.[14] Together, these works sought to establish a branch of international law around the phenomenon and legal concept of civil war, combining the elements of belligerent recognition, the recognition of insurgency, the laws of war, intervention, and the law of state responsibility. In so doing, they produced a francophone synthesis of the

[11] See Kathryn Greenman, *State Responsibility and Rebels: The History and Legacy of Protecting Investment Against Revolution* (Cambridge University Press 2021); Alan Tzvika Nissel, *Merchants of Legalism: A History of State Responsibility (1870–1960)* (Cambridge University Press 2024).

[12] Compare Edwin Borchard, 'Private Pecuniary Claims Arising Out of War' 9 *American Journal of International Law* (1915) 113–146.

[13] Antoine Rougier, *Les guerres civiles et le droit des gens* (Larose 1903) 2; 20 Annuaire IDI (1904) 312–319.

[14] Marquis Ramón de Dalmau y de Olivart, *Del reconocimiento de beligerancia y sus efectos inmediatos* (L. Péant é Hijos 1895); Paul Sadoul, *De la guerre civile en droit des gens: Reconnaissance de belligérance* (Paul Scheffer 1905); L. N. Stéfanesco, *La guerre civile et les rapports des belligérants* (LNDJ 1903).

classical doctrine of civil war at the turn of the century. This was still the form in which the classical doctrine was known and taught when the general laws of war and neutrality began to transform during the era of the two world wars.

With the rise of the League of Nations and the United Nations, the international legal profession embarked on a comprehensive reform of the laws of war and peace that ultimately redefined the deep structure of international law. A fundamental change in the laws of war and neutrality was brought about by the renunciation of war in the Pact of Paris in 1928, the prohibition of the use of force in the UN Charter, and the onset of the Cold War. The laws of belligerency and civil war were irresistibly subsumed into these reconfigurations. The Spanish Civil War provided a notorious moment of anagnorisis for all international lawyers, as the decline and outright obsolescence of the classical doctrine in state practice became incontrovertible. But despite the shortcomings of the concepts of belligerency and insurgency, during the Spanish war they still constituted the common legal vocabulary with which international lawyers could address the events.[15]

The Geneva Conventions of 1949 introduced the concept of 'armed conflicts not of an international character', enshrined in their Common Article 3, which also specified that the application of its provisions would not affect the legal status of the parties to a conflict. In so doing, the Conventions created a new legal vocabulary international lawyers could use to discuss civil wars, disconnecting it from the classical doctrine. The outcome was no accident. Before adopting the final wording, the conference deliberately rejected alternative drafts written in the language and terms of the classical doctrine. The significance of this innovation did not escape later generations of jurists, including Jean Siotis, who was quick to perceive the watershed between the classical laws of civil war and the new humanitarian law of non-international armed conflicts.[16]

Although an older generation of international lawyers still maintained the classical doctrine of civil war as a possibility in their writings for

[15] For example, H. A. Smith, 'Some Problems of the Spanish Civil War' 18 *British Yearbook of International Law* (1937) 17–31; Arnold McNair, 'The Law Relating to the Civil War in Spain' 53 *Law Quarterly Review* (1937) 471–500; Georges Scelle, 'La reconnaissance des insurgés et la guerre espagnole' 37 *Die Friedens-Warte* (1937) 65–70; Hans Wehberg, 'La guerre civile et le droit international' 63 *Collected Courses of Hague Academy of International Law* (1938) 1–127; Louis Le Fur, *La guerre d'Espagne et le droit* (Les Éditions Internationales 1938).

[16] Jean Siotis, *Le droit de la guerre et les conflits armés d'un caractère non-international* (LGDJ 1958).

a while,[17] in 1973 a commission established by the Institut de droit international concluded that the recognition of belligerency no longer had any practical utility. Its final resolution, adopted at Wiesbaden in 1975, defined 'civil war' as 'any armed conflict, not of an international character, which breaks out in the territory of a State'.[18] The concept of civil war had lost its classical meaning, and it could now be read as a reference to modern humanitarian law. By this time, the desuetude of the classical doctrine of civil war had also been finally acknowledged in academic literature.[19]

This book has sought to piece together the story of the classical doctrine of civil war for the most part on the basis of the same cases and examples as were referred in legal scholarship at the time. The story leaves us with two yawning gaps that deserve to be mentioned here. The first concerns the question of the classical law of civil war in the late seventeenth and early eighteenth centuries. It is hardly satisfactory that our picture of the classical law situates its birth in the early modern revolutions and then jumps forward to its systematisation in the Enlightenment days of Wolff and Vattel and the American Revolution. What happened between 1648 and 1758? The academic canon on the doctrine was often silent about this period – a silence that contrasts with the idealisation of *ius publicum europaeum* and its monarchical, 'bracketed' wars manifested in the writings of Schmitt.[20] Further study on the law of civil wars in the period, both in Europe and beyond, might help to complement, challenge, or nuance that portrayal.

The second gap concerns, precisely, the continuing need for a more global or non-Western dimension to the story. The standard history of the classical doctrine of civil war is overwhelmingly dominated by Anglo-American transatlantic encounters and documents, as well as by the Eurocentrism pervading diplomatic and legal traditions at the time. The relationship of the classical law of civil war to the mandates system of the League of Nations and colonial insurgencies in the interwar years

[17] Erik Castrén, *Civil War* (Suomalainen Tiedeakatemia 1966).

[18] Resolution on the Principle of Non-Intervention in Civil Wars, 14 August 1975, 56 Annuaire IDI (1975) 545, art 1.

[19] Roscoe R. Oglesby, *Internal War and the Search for Normative Order* (Martinus Nijhoff 1971).

[20] Carl Schmitt, *The Nomos of the Earth* ([1950] Telos 2006) 140–151; James Q. Whitman, *The Verdict of Battle: The Law of Victory and the Making of Modern War* (Harvard University Press 2012) 12–19. Compare Martti Koskenniemi, 'Carl Schmitt and International Law' in Jens Meierhenrich and Oliver Simons (eds), *The Oxford Handbook of Carl Schmitt* (Oxford University Press 2013) 600–608.

deserves further examination.[21] In particular, studies that broaden out this narrative by exploring the role of the classical law of civil war in the colonial peripheries of the world would be of great value. They could both provincialise the European story and refine our understanding of how the classical law of civil war was adopted in the non-Western world through the legal languages of revolution, sovereignty, responsibility, and statehood.[22]

Civil War and the Law of Nations: Between Rebellion and Revolution

What should we think of the classical doctrine of civil war? The purpose of this book has been to reintroduce its story to the modern reader and to show that it would be mistaken to think the law of nations could ever have been indifferent about internal conflicts. The classical law of civil war followed implicitly from the basic principles of war, peace, and neutrality. Its essential features came ultimately from the *ius gentium* of antiquity, but it assumed its more recognisable form during the early modern period and the age of sail, at the time a body of jurisprudence on the principles of sovereignty, neutrality, and recognition was building up. For modern readers, it is important to insist on the maritime dimension of the doctrine, and of the classical laws of war and neutrality more generally. Eighteenth and nineteenth century international lawyers did not emphasise this dimension in their writings because it was self-evident at that time. In our days, however, international law, especially on the use of force, is more concerned with land and the air, so the law of the sea tends to be regarded as a more marginal concern, a specialty field within international law. Happily, the ubiquity of the maritime dimension in the age of sail and steam is easy to see once one starts to delve into contemporary state practice and legal scholarship. Once you see it, you see it.

The story of the classical doctrine of civil war is therefore a story about a relatively simple set of legal rules and principles that were repeatedly debated and argued about for four hundred years. It was anchored in the simple distinction between proper civil wars, to which the laws of war applied, and domestic rebellions, to which they did not – or, in legal

[21] See e.g. Susan Pedersen, *The Guardians: The League of Nations and the Crisis of Empire* (Oxford University Press 2015) 142–168; Thomas Hippler, *Governing from the Skies: A Global History of Aerial Bombing* (Verso 2017) 56–117.

[22] See Arnulf Becker Lorca, *Mestizo International Law: A Global Intellectual History 1842–1933* (Cambridge University Press 2014).

language, between belligerencies, from which belligerent and neutral rights accrued, and insurgencies, from which they did not.[23] The classical doctrine offered a fairly concise set of rules and concepts for all parties involved to invoke in order in articulating their positions. On the one hand, there was the old legitimist presumption of states' territorial sovereignty, meaning that there was no such thing as civil war, but only rebellion, and therefore 'pirates and brigands, who do not constitute a state, cannot avail themselves of the law of nations'.[24] And on the other hand, there was the revolutionary exception, borne out by experience, that in *some* cases, where the facts were abundantly clear and justice so demanded, 'there exists a *civil war* [in which the] two parties must be regarded as forming thenceforth, for a time at least, two separate bodies politic, two distinct Nations, [and things] being so, it is perfectly clear that the established laws of war . . . should be observed on both sides'.[25]

Over time, the manner and exact object of recognition became subject to variation. It could be a question of recognition of belligerency – a full civil war where the international laws of war applied – or of more nuanced problems of recognition of insurgencies, governments (whether de facto or de jure), or new states. The question might be put before the government at war, or a foreign government, or later an alliance or gathering of nations. Still, any such rules of recognition encountered the problems of under- and over-inclusivity; there was always the danger that true pirates and latrons called themselves insurgents, and there was always the possibility of absolute legitimism being invoked to shield manifest tyranny. And yet, throughout this period, one is hard put to find examples of the law having functioned clearly and predictably between all actors, let alone constrained or guided state behaviour through its persuasive force. At no point was clarity or agreement achieved on what the applicable law of civil war was or how it ought to be interpreted. The classical doctrine of civil war never 'worked' – whatever we take that to mean – any better than our present international law in providing objective legal solutions to civil wars.

At the root of this indeterminacy is its intimate connection with the question of recognition, arguably one of the most controversial and intractable problems in international law, and one which cannot be understood in purely legal terms. Although jurists might in principle

[23] Dana's *Wheaton*, § 23.
[24] *DJBP*, II.18.2.
[25] Vattel, III.18.292–294.

agree that there was a legal difference between a riot, an insurgency, and a civil war, the problem was that someone would have to identify the relevant facts and determine which legal rules applied to them. In structural terms, recognition tends to revolve around oppositions between questions of law and fact and between whether something actually exists, or may and should exist, in international law. In the case of revolutions, the *sein* and the *sollen* are constantly at odds with one another.[26] In the classical doctrine, a dispute over the insurgents' status would typically pit the claim of revolutionary fact against the government's constitutional counter-claim that it was nevertheless the lawful government and the rebels had no standing against it. The insurgents could then claim further that they had not only the might but also a right to revolt against a tyrant; while the ruler could retort that the insurgents were not only illegitimate but also in fact harbingers of chaos and anarchy. At the core of the dispute was a contest between two legitimacies both demanding recognition. We arrive at Victor Hugo's remark that every revolution bears its own legitimacy, that in revolutions the rebel is not the people but rather the king.[27]

Although for centuries scholars have debated the nature and preconditions of recognition, the matter has never been completely settled.[28] Hans Kelsen famously conceded that the rules of a legal order are valid only on condition that the total order is efficacious. Since 'the principle of legitimacy is restricted by the principle of effectiveness', it followed that the principle of legitimacy 'fails to hold in case of a revolution'.[29] From Kelsen's juristic point of view, 'the decisive criterion of a revolution is that the order in force is overthrown and replaced by a new order in a way which the former had not itself anticipated'. But who should determine whether, and when, a revolution is successful? And what are jurists – especially foreign jurists – to say in the meantime, while an insurrection is in progress and its outcome not yet decided? In that situation, 'the problem of the basic norm shifts from the national to the international legal order. Then the only true basic norm, a norm which is not created

[26] Kelsen, *General Theory*, 120–122; Hans Kelsen, *Pure Theory of Law* ([1960] University of California Press 1967) 3–15.

[27] Victor Hugo, *Les Misérables* ([1862] Bibliothèque de la Pléiade, Gallimard 2018) IV.I. IV, 816.

[28] Jan Klabbers, 'Rebel with a Cause? Terrorists and Humanitarian Law' 14 EJIL (2003) 299–312; Jan Klabbers, '(I Can't Get No) Recognition: Subjects Doctrine' in Andrea Bianchi (ed), *Non-State Actors and International Law* (Ashgate 2009) 351–369.

[29] Kelsen, *General Theory*, 117–119.

by a legal procedure but presupposed by juristic thinking, is the basic norm of international law'.[30] The long history of the classical doctrine of civil war bears testament to this common presupposition about the validity of some international law over the problem of revolution. However, attempts to articulate the substance of that law were for the most part unable to transcend the inherently political nature of the problem. Instead, scholarship on recognition and revolution tended to produce and reproduce analyses of precedents and historical examples rather than normative solutions. Hersch Lauterpacht famously attempted to show that recognition was essentially a part of international law, 'as distinguished from international politics', both in its function and consequences, and considered that granting recognition might be a legal duty of states under proper circumstances.[31] But as he himself then observed, 'what was originally intended as a monograph of modest dimensions' grew into a remarkably detailed textbook charting and exploring a wide range of diplomatic practice and judicial decisions.[32] Ultimately, the life of the law of civil war has tended to be that of experience, not logic.[33]

Even if the classical doctrine of civil war was irreconcilably indeterminate, it was nevertheless profoundly useful as a language of legal argumentation. It afforded jurists on all sides a common vocabulary with which to articulate the aims and demands of those whom they represented or whose sensibilities they shared or were won over by. The ambiguities of the law did not prevent international lawyers from debating the problem to the fullest. The realities of the age of sail and steam helped here, as they produced tangible circumstances where the problem of recognition was repeatedly brought before courts of law. To mention a few examples, neutral vessels could be seized by insurgent privateers or a governmental blockading squadron; privateers and merchantmen from countries undergoing civil strife might appear in foreign ports flying insurgent colours; or foreign investors and traders might find themselves dealing with local authorities in insurgent-held areas and then end up in trouble with those on the government side. Judges understood the fundamentality of the question they were facing and usually turned to the official positions of their governments for guidance.

30 Ibid 121–122.
31 Hersch Lauterpacht, *Recognition in International Law* (Cambridge University Press 1947) v.
32 Ibid vi.
33 See Oliver Wendell Holmes, *The Common Law* (Little, Brown 1881) 1.

Here, the doctrine of civil war, including its indeterminacies and grey areas, offered room for creative argument. Few governments were willing to tolerate foreign recognitions of their domestic insurgents; therefore, they would interpret any recognition as an unfriendly act and interference in their sovereignty. Few foreign governments were willing to risk a breakdown in trade or even a war merely for the sake of foreign insurgents. As a result, all sides sought creative solutions, and most insurgencies were dealt with within the legal grey zones of recognitions and their legal implications.

Explaining the second coming of the classical doctrine is less straightforward. What should we think of the successive generations of scholars who sought to create explicit rules on civil war several decades after the doctrine had fallen out of state practice? Part of this may have to do with the fact that the classical doctrine declined in state practice quietly and unofficially, while its formal principles were not abolished or replaced until the twentieth century. Yet there is also good reason to consider that the international lawyers of the late nineteenth and early twentieth centuries did, to an extent, believe in their work for the betterment of international law. The rise of the scholarly doctrine of civil war was part of a broader movement that believed civilised rules and principles of international law could promote peaceful coexistence between states by coordinating and limiting their conduct in exceptional circumstances. In this thinking, despite all the adversities and ill luck over the years, the only sustainable way forward was through faith in law. In this spirit, Georges Scelle championed progressive international law in the hope of seeing a return of more enlightened thinking in the world,[34] and Erik Castrén maintained that '[w]eak rules are better than a complete lack of rules'.[35] The long history of both state practice and scholarly debates on civil war illustrates how very difficult that task always was. By the time these scholars abandoned the classical principles, the new generations of lawyers entering the profession had already become familiar with the language and principles of modern humanitarian law and the law on the use of force.

The gradual decline of the classical doctrine was driven not merely by states distancing themselves from its legal rules, but also by legal creativity and innovation. As the old propositions fell into disuse, novelties appeared. The doctrine of recognition of insurgency emerged to enable

[34] Georges Scelle, *Précis du droit des gens*, vol II (Sirey 1934) 15.
[35] Erik Castrén, *Ilmasota*, pt I (Suomalainen Lakimiesyhdistys 1938) v.

governments to circumvent the consequences and responsibilities attendant upon the condition of belligerency. Making states responsible for insurgents was an attempt to address foreign revolutions without resorting to the legal principles of war and neutrality. In the 1890s, the Institut de droit international had hopes of developing the doctrine of civil war in new ways so as to make it appealing and useful for states and courts, but little more than academic textbooks came out of this intention. In the mid twentieth century, when the project of the 'gentle civiliser' generations had run its course,[36] states finally abandoned the classical doctrine and in its place conceived a new framework of collective security and minimum standards of humanity in internal conflicts.

The net result was that throughout its lifespan the classical doctrine of civil war was always in motion, always changing. At the same time, generation after generation of scholars continued to write about the law of civil war as though it were a coherent system firmly grounded in Vattel's distinction between internal insurgencies and civil wars proper. The retention and veneration of these concepts was not meaningless, even if they did not correspond to state practice. Indeed, this may have been a part of its usefulness. The recognition of belligerency, for example, continued to play a role well into the twentieth century, not because it was in frequent use but precisely because it was not being used at all. The *possibility* of belligerent recognition, of a 'true' civil war, enabled states and their jurists to argue, on the contrary, that this or that situation was *not* a civil war but belonged instead in a legal grey zone where such situations could be understood variously in terms of semi-recognised insurgencies, internal colonial wars, neutral interventions, state responsibility over riots, or some other framework. It is often precisely the job of diplomats to save their governments from being bound by unforeseen consequences while allowing sufficient leeway for their own manoeuvring. Indeterminacy in the law brings boundless potential for deliberate ambiguity. Somewhat paradoxically, the most useful aspect of the classical doctrine of civil war may have been precisely the dysfunctionality of its core concepts and rules.

[36] Martti Koskenniemi, *The Gentle Civilizer of Nations* (Cambridge University Press 2001) 510–517.

BIBLIOGRAPHY

Collections of Primary Sources, Documents, and State Papers

Acts and Ordinances of the Interregnum 1624–1660 (C. H. Firth and R. S. Rait eds, 3 vols, HMSO 1911)

Acts and Resolutions of the First Session of the Provisional Congress of the Confederate States, Held at Montgomery, Ala. (Enquirer Book and Job Press 1861)

Acts of the Privy Council of England, Colonial series, vol IV (1745–1766) (James Munro ed, HMSO 1911)

American Archives. Peter Force ed. *Fourth Series* (6 vols, M. St Clair Clarke and P. Force 1837–1846). *Fifth Series* (3 vols, M. St Clair Clarke and P. Force 1848–1853)

American State Papers: Foreign Relations (6 vols, Gales and Seaton 1832–1861)

Authentic Rebel Papers Seized at St Eustatius, 1781 (L. Lambert 1781)

Britain and the Independence of Latin America (C. K. Webster ed, 2 vols, Oxford University Press 1938)

British and Foreign State Papers (170 vols, Public Records Office/Ridgway and Sons 1814–1977)

Calendar of State Papers (Public Records Office 1856–1969)

Cobbett's Complete Collection of State Trials (Thomas Bayly Howell ed, 34 vols, Hansard 1809–1826)

A Collection of Neutrality Laws, Regulations and Treaties of Various Countries (Philip C. Jessup and Francis Deák eds, 2 vols, Carnegie Endowment for International Peace 1939)

A Compilation of the Messages and Papers of the Presidents (James Richardson ed, 8 vols, US Congress 1898)

Compte-rendu de la neuvième conférence internationale de la Croix-Rouge (American Red Cross 1912)

Consolidated Treaty Series (Clive Parry ed, 231 vols, Oxford University Press c. 1969–1981)

Correspondance de Napoléon Ier (Imprimerie impériale 1861).

Correspondence of the Department of State in Relation to the Seizure of American Vessels and Injuries to American Citizens during the Hostilities in Cuba (US Government Printing Office 1870)

Dictamen de la Comisión sobre ilegitimidad de poderes actuantes en 18 de julio de 1936 (Editora Nacional 1939)

Digest of International Law (Green Haywood Hackworth ed, 8 vols, US Government Printing Office 1940–1944)

Digest of International Law (John Bassett Moore ed, 8 vols US Government Printing Office 1906)

Digest of Justinian ([c. 530–533] Alan Watson ed, 4 vols, University of Pennsylvania Press 1985)

Diplomatic Correspondence of the United States Concerning the Independence of the Latin-American Nations (William Manning ed, 3 vols, Oxford University Press 1925)

Documents on German Foreign Policy, 1918–1945, from the Archives of the German Foreign Ministry (59 vols, US Government Printing Office 1949–1983)

Documents Relating to Law and Custom of the Sea (Reginald G. Marsden ed, 2 vols, Navy Records Society 1915–1916)

Doniol, Henri: *Histoire de la participation de la France à l'établissement des États-Unis d'Amérique* (5 vols, Imprimerie nationale 1886)

European Treaties Bearing on the History of the United States and Its Dependencies (Frances Gardiner Davenport ed, 4 vols, Carnegie Institution of Washington 1917–1937)

Final Record of the Diplomatic Conference of Geneva of 1949 (Federal Political Department 1949)

Rymer, Thomas: *Fœdera, conventiones, litterae, et cujuscunque generis acta publica, inter reges Angliæ et alios quosvis impeatores, reges, pontifices, principes, vel communitates* (20 vols, 2nd edn, J. Tonson 1727–)

Foreign Relations of the United States (c. 450 vols, US Government Printing Office 1861–)

A General Collection of Treatys of Peace and Commerce, Renunciations, Manifestos, and Other Publick Papers, from the Year 1642, to the End of the Reign of Queen Anne (Samuel Whatley ed, 4 vols, Knapp 1732)

Great Britain and the Law of Nations (Herbert A. Smith ed, 2 vols, P. S. King & Son 1932, 1935)

History and Digest of the International Arbitrations to Which the United States Has Been a Party (John Bassett Moore ed, 6 vols, US Government Printing Office 1898)

Informes de la comisión mixta de relaciones exteriores sobre el reconocimiento de beligerancia de la junta gubernativa de Iquique hecho por el Gobierno de Bolivia (Tipografia de La Nueva Era 1891)

International Adjudications, Ancient and Modern, History and Documents (John Bassett Moore ed, 6 vols, US Government Printing Office 1933)

International Law Opinions (Arnold McNair ed, 3 vols, Cambridge University Press 1956)

Journals of the Continental Congress, 1774–1789 (34 vols, US Government Printing Office 1904–1937)

Judgments of the High Prize Court of the Republic of China (F. T. Cheng ed, Peking High Prize Court 1919)

Martens, Charles de: *Causes célèbres du droit des gens* (5 vols, 2nd edn, F. A. Brockhaus 1858–1861)

Naval Documents of the American Revolution (William Bell Clark ed, 13 vols, US Government Printing Office 1964–2019)

Nouveau recueil de traités (G. F. Martens ed, 16 vols, Dieterich 1817–1842)

Official Records of the Union and Confederate Navies in the War of the Rebellion (US Government Printing Office 1894–1922)

Papers Relating to the Treaty of Washington (6 vols, US Government Printing Office 1872)

The Parliamentary History of England, from the Earliest Period to the Year 1803 (William Cobbett ed, 36 vols, Hansard 1806–1820)

Quinzieme conférence internationale de la Croix-Rouge, tenue a Tokio du 20 au 29 octobre 1934, Compte-rendu (Red Cross Society of Japan 1934)

Recueil van alle de Placaten, Ordonnantion, Resolutien, Instriuctien, Lysten en Waarschouwingen, betreffende de Admiraliteyten, Convoyen, Licenten, en verdere Zee-Saaken. Het eerste Deel (Jacobus Scheltus 1730)

The Revolutionary Diplomatic Correspondence of the United States (Francis Wharton ed, 6 vols, US Government Printing Office 1889)

Sources of Our Liberties: Documentary Origins of Individual Liberties in the United States Constitution and Bill of Rights (Richard Perry ed, American Bar Foundation 1952)

The Statutes at Large from the Magna Charta, to the End of the Eleventh Parliament of Great Britain, Anno 1761 [Continued to 1806] (Danby Pickering ed, 46 vols, J. Bentham 1762–1807)

The Statutes at Large of South Carolina, vol I (Thomas Cooper ed, A. S. Johnston 1836)

The Statutes at Large of the United States, (Little, Brown 1845–1874, US Government Printing Office 1874–1950, National Archives and Records Administration 1950–)

Treaties and Other International Acts of the United States of America, vol III (David Hunter Miller ed, US Government Printing Office 1933)

Treaties and Other International Agreements of the United States of America 1776–1949, vol 11 (Charles I. Bevans ed, US Department of State 1974)

The War of the Rebellion: A Compilation of the Official Records of the Union and Confederate Armies (128 vols, US Government Printing Office 1880–1902).

Literary Sources

Abbenhuis, Maartje: *An Age of Neutrals: Great Power Politics, 1815–1914* (Cambridge University Press 2014)

Adams, Charles Francis (ed): *The Works of John Adams*, vol 3 (Little, Brown 1851)

Adams, Henry: *The History of the United States of America*, vol IV (Scribner's Sons 1889)

Ador, Gustave and Moynier, Gustave: 'Les destinées de la convention de Genève pendant la guerre de Serbie' 7 *Bulletin international des sociétés de la Croix-Rouge* (1876) 164–176

Alvarez, Alejandro: 'The Monroe Doctrine from the Latin-American Point of View' 3 *St. Louis Law Review* (1917) 135–146

Ammon, Harry: *The Genet Mission* (Norton 1973)

Anderson, R. C.: 'Royalists at Sea', pts 1–4, *Mariner's Mirror* 9(2) (1923), 14(4) (1928), 17(2) (1931), 21(1) (1935)

Andersson, Stefan (ed): *Revisiting the Vietnam War and International Law: Views and Interpretations of Richard Falk* (Cambridge University Press 2018)

Anghie, Antony: *Imperialism, Sovereignty and the Making of International Law* (Cambridge University Press 2005)

Aquinas, St Thomas: *The 'Summa Theologica' of Thomas Aquinas* ([c. 1274] R. & T. Washbourne 1917)

Armitage, David: *Civil Wars: A History in Ideas* (Yale University Press 2017)

Ascham, Anthony: *Of the Confusions and Revolutions of Governments* (W. Wilson 1649)

Augustine of Hippo: *The City of God* ([426 CE] Catholic University of America Press 1949)

Austin, James: *The Life of Elbridge Gerry* (Wells and Lilly 1828)

Australian Dictionary of Biography, vol 9 (Melbourne University Press 1983)

Auxier, George W.: 'The Propaganda Activities of the Cuban Junta in Precipitating the Spanish-American War, 1895–1898' 19 *Hispanic American Historical Review* (1939) 286–305

Ayala, Balthazar: *De jure et officiis bellicis et disciplina militari libri III* ([1582] John Westlake tr, Carnegie Institution 1912)

Balladore Pallieri, P.: 'Quelques aspects juridiques de la non-intervention en Espagne' 18 *Revue de droit international et de législation comparée* (1937) 285–309

Ballard, G. A.: *The Influence of the Sea on the Political History of Japan* (John Murray 1921)

Bancroft Davis, J. C.: *The Committees of the Continental Congress Chosen to Hear and Determine Appeals from Courts of Admiralty and the Court of Appeals in Cases of Capture Established by That Body* (Banks & Brothers 1888)

Becker Lorca, Arnulf: *Mestizo International Law: A Global Intellectual History 1842–1933* (Cambridge University Press 2014)

Bederman, David J.: 'The Feigned Demise of Prize' 9 *Emory International Law Review* (1995) 31–69

Bederman, David J.: *International Law in Antiquity* (Cambridge University Press 2001)

Bell, Christine: *On the Law of Peace: Peace Agreements and the Lex Pacificatoria* (Oxford University Press 2008)

Bemis, George: *Hasty Recognition of Rebel Belligerency and Our Right to Complain of It*

Bemis, George: *Precedents of American Neutrality in Reply to the Speech of Sir Roundell Palmer* (Little, Brown 1864)

Bemis, Samuel Flagg, *The Diplomacy of the American Revolution* (Indiana University Press, 1957)

Bemis, Samuel Flagg: *Jay's Treaty: A Study in Commerce and Diplomacy* (Macmillan 1923)

Benrath, Stuart: *Squall across the Atlantic: American Civil War Prize Cases and Diplomacy* (University of California Press 1970)

Benvenisti, Eyal and Lustig, Doreen: 'Monopolizing War: Codifying the Laws of War to Reassert Governmental Authority, 1856–1874' 31 *European Journal of International Law* (2020) 127–169

Bernard, Mountague: *A Historical Account of the Neutrality of Great Britain during the American Civil War* (Longmans, Green, Reader, and Dyer 1870)

Bingham, Tom: 'The Alabama Claims Arbitration' 54 *International & Comparative Law Quarterly* (2005) 1–25

Birdal, Murat: *The Political Economy of Ottoman Public Debt: Insolvency and European Financial Control in the Late Nineteenth Century* (I. B. Tauris 2010)

Black, J. B.: 'Queen Elizabeth, the Sea Beggars, and the Capture of Brille, 1572' 46 *English Historical Review* (1931) 30–47

Black, Jeremiah S.: 'Power of the President in Executing the Laws', 9 Official Opinions of the Attorneys General of the United States 516 (1866)

Blakemore, Harold: 'Chile from the War of the Pacific to the World Depression, 1880–1930'in Leslie Bethell (ed), *The Cambridge History of Latin America*, vol V (Cambridge University Press 1986)

Blancpain, François: *Un siècle de relations financières entre Haïti et la France, 1825–1922* (L'Harmattan 2001)

Blaufarb, Rafe: 'Arms for Revolutions: Military Demobilization after the Napoleonic Wars and Latin American Independence' in Alan Forrest, Karen Hagemann, and Michael Rowe (eds), *War, Demobilization and*

Memory: The Legacy of War in the Era of Atlantic Revolutions (Palgrave Macmillan 2016) 100–116

Bluntschli, Johann Caspar: *An Impartial Opinion on the Alabama Question and the Manner of Settling It* (Government Printing Office 1871)

Bluntschli, Johann Caspar: *Das moderne Kriegsrecht der civilisirten Staaten als Rechtsbuch dargestellt* (C. H. Beck, 1866)

Bluntschli, Johann Caspar: *Das moderne Völkerrecht der civilisirten Staaten als Rechtsbuch dargestellt* (C. H. Beck 1868)

Bluntschli, Johann Caspar: 'Opinion impartiale sur la question de l'Alabama et sur la manière de la résoudre' 2 *Revue de droit international et de législation comparée* (1870) 432–485

Bodin, Jean: *On Sovereignty* ([1576] Julian H. Franklin ed, Cambridge University Press 1992)

Bodin, Jean: *The Six Bookes of a Commonweale* ([1576] R. Knolles tr, G. Bishop 1606)

Bolívar, Simón: *El Libertador: Writings of Simón Bolívar* (David Bushnell ed, Oxford University Press 2003)

Borchard, Edwin: *The Diplomatic Protection of Citizens Abroad or the Law of International Claims* (Banks Law Publishing 1919)

Borchard, Edwin: '"Neutrality" and Civil Wars' 31 *American Journal of International Law* (1937) 304–306

Borchard, Edwin: 'Private Pecuniary Claims Arising Out of War' 9 *American Journal of International Law* (1915) 113–146

Borschberg, Peter: *Hugo Grotius 'Commentarius in Theses XI': An Early Treatise on Sovereignty, the Just War, and the Legitimacy of the Dutch Revolt* (Peter Lang 1994)

Bourguignon, Henry J.: *The First Federal Court* (American Philosophical Society 1977)

Branche, Raphaëlle: 'The French Army and the Geneva Conventions during the Algerian War of Independence and After' in Matthew Evangelista and Nina Tannenwald (eds), *Do the Geneva Conventions Matter?* (Oxford University Press 2017) 161–173

Brett, Annabel: *Liberty, Right and Nature: Individual Rights in Later Scholastic Thought* (Cambridge University Press 1997)

Brett, Annabel: 'Protection as a Political Concept in English Political Thought, 1603–51' in Lauren Benton, Adam Clulow, and Bain Attwood (eds), *Protection and Empire: A Global History* (Cambridge University Press 2017) 93–113

Briggs, Herbert W.: 'De Facto and De Jure Recognition: The Arantzazu Mendi' 33 *American Journal of International Law* (1939) 689–699

Brutus, Stefanos Junius (pseud): *Vindiciae contra tyrannos* ([1579] George Garnett tr, Cambridge University Press 1994)

Bugnion, François: 'The International Conference of the Red Cross and Red Crescent: Challenges, Key Issues and Achievements' 91 *International Review of the Red Cross* (2009) 675–712

Burke, Edmund: *The Works of the Right Honourable Edmund Burke, Collected in Three Volumes* (J. Dodsley 1792)

Burman, John: *Britain's Relations with the Ottoman Empire during the Embassy of Sir Nicholas O'Conor to the Porte, 1898–1908* (Isis Press 2010)

Bynkershoek, Cornelius van: *Quaestionum juris publici libri duo* ([1737] T. Frank tr, Carnegie Endowment 1930)

Calvo, Carlos: 'De la non-responsabilité des États à raison des pertes et dommages éprouvés par des étrangers en temps de troubles intérieurs ou de guerres civiles' 1 *Revue de droit international et de législation comparée* (1st series 1869) 417–427

Cameron, Lindsey and others: 'Article 3: Conflicts Not of an International Character' in Knut Dörmann and others (eds), *ICRC Commentary on the First Geneva Convention* (Cambridge University Press 2016) 132–140

Campbell, Robert Granville: *Neutral Rights and Obligations in the Anglo-Boer War* (Johns Hopkins Press 1908)

Carpenter, William S: 'United States and the League of Neutrals of 1780' 15 *American Journal of International Law* (1921) 511–522

Carson, Hampton L.: 'The Case of the Sloop "Active"' 7 *Green Bag* (1895) 17–26

Case, Lynn M. and Spencer, Warren F.: *The United States and France: Civil War Diplomacy* (University of Pennsylvania Press 1970)

Cassese, Antonio: 'The Martens Clause: Half a Loaf or Simply Pie in the Sky?' 11 *European Journal of International Law* (2000) 187–216.

Castberg, Frede: 'Folkrettslige spörsmål omkring den spanske borgerkrig' 8 *Nordisk Tidsskrift for International Ret* (1937) 160–170.

Castrén, Erik: *Civil War* (Helsinki: Suomalainen Tiedeakatemia 1966)

Castrén, Erik: *Ilmasota I–II* (Suomalainen Lakimiesyhdistys 1938–1939)

Castrén, Erik: *The Present Law of War and Neutrality* (Suomalainen Tiedeakatemia 1954)

Chasteen, John Charles: *Americanos: Latin America's Struggle for Independence* (Oxford University Press 2008)

Chen Daley, Mercedes: 'The Watermelon Riot: Cultural Encounters in Panama City, April 15, 1856' 70 *Hispanic American Historical Review* (1990) 85–108

Cicero, Marcus Tullius: 'De res publica' in *The Political Works of Marcus Tullius Cicero*, vol I ([c. 51 BCE] Francis Barham ed, Edmund Spettigue 1841)

Clark, William Bell: *Ben Franklin's Privateers: A Naval Epic of the American Revolution* (Greenwood Press 1956)

Coke, Edward: *Institutes of the Lawes of England* (4 vols, Societie of Stationers 1628)

Coogan, John W.: *The End of Neutrality: The United States, Britain, and Maritime Rights 1899–1915* (Cornell University Press 1981)

Crawford, James: *The Creation of States in International Law* (2nd edn, Oxford University Press 2007)

Crawley, C. W.: *The Question of Greek Independence: A Study of British Policy in the Near East 1821–1833* (Cambridge University Press 1930)

Crawley, C. W. (ed): *The New Cambridge Modern History*, vol IX (Cambridge University Press 1965)

Crossland, James: *War, Law and Humanity: The Campaign to Control Warfare, 1853–1914* (Bloomsbury 2018)

Crump, Helen J.: *Colonial Admiralty Jurisdiction in the Seventeenth Century* (Longmans, Green 1931)

Cullen, Anthony: *The Concept of Non-international Armed Conflict in International Humanitarian Law* (Cambridge University Press 2010)

Daly, Charles P.: *Are the Southern Privateersmen Pirates? Letter to the Hon. Ira Harris, United States Senator* (New York 1862)

Dana, Richard Henry: 'The Trent Affair: An Aftermath' 45 *Proceedings of the Massachusetts Historical Society* (1911–1912) 3–20

Davis, Lance E. and Engerman, Stanley L.: *Naval Blockades in Peace and War: An Economic History Since 1750* (Cambridge University Press 2006)

Desjardins, Arthur: 'L'insurrection cubaine et le droit des gens' 3 *Revue de Paris* (1896) 354–366

Despagnet, Frantz: *La guerre sud-africaine au point de vue du droit international* (A. Pedone 1902)

Dijk, Boyd van: '"The Great Humanitarian": The Soviet Union, the International Committee of the Red Cross, and the Geneva Conventions of 1949' 37 *Law and History Review* (2019) 209–235

Dijk, Boyd van: *Preparing for War: The Making of the 1949 Geneva Conventions* (Oxford University Press 2022)

Domenech, Roberto: *Las guerras civiles americanas ante el derecho internacional* LLD (thesis, University of Buenos Aires 1915)

Dow, George F.: *American Vessels Captured by the British during the Revolution and War of 1812: The Records of the Vice-Admiralty Court at Halifax, Nova Scotia* (Essex Institute 1911)

Dowdeswell, Tracey Leigh: 'The Brussels Peace Conference of 1874 and the Modern Laws of Belligerent Qualification' 54 *Osgoode Hall Law Journal* (2017) 805–850

Dubois, Joseph: 'La France à Madagascar' 28 *Revue de droit international et de législation comparée* (1895) 477–501

Dubois, Laurent: *Avengers of the New World: The Story of the Haitian Revolution* (Laurent Dubois 2004)

Dubois, Laurent and Garrigus, John D.: *Slave Revolution in the Caribbean, 1789–1804: A Brief History with Documents* (2nd edn, Bedford 2017)

Dubois, Laurent and others: *Documents constitutionnels d'Haïti 1790–1860* (De Gruyter 2013)

Elder, David A.: 'The Historical Background of Common Article 3 of the Geneva Convention of 1949' 11 *Case Western Reserve Journal of International Law* (1979) 37–54

Erich, Rafael: 'La naissance et la reconnaissance des États' 13 *Collected Courses of Hague Academy of International Law* (1926) 431–507

Falk, Richard: 'Janus Tormented: The International Law of Internal War' in James N. Rosenau (ed), *International Aspects of Civil Strife* (Princeton University Press 1964) 185–248

Falk, Richard A. (ed): *The International Law of Civil War* (Johns Hopkins Press/ASIL 1971)

Falk, Richard A. (ed): *The Vietnam War and International Law* (4 vols, Princeton University Press 1968–1976)

Fenwick, Charles: 'Can Civil Wars Be brought under the control of international law?' 32 *American Journal of International Law* (1938), 538–542

Feron, Georges: *Des tribunaux de prises (organisation – compétence – procédure)* (Pedone 1896)

Ferrer, Ada: *Insurgent Cuba: Race, Nation, and Revolution, 1868–1898* (University of North Carolina Press 1999)

Fitzpatrick, John C. (ed): *The Writings of George Washington from the Original Manuscript Sources*, vol 4 (Government printing Office 1931)

Foster, John: *A Century of American Diplomacy: Being a Brief Review of the Foreign Relations of the United States, 1776–1876* (Houghton Mifflin 1901)

Foucault, Michel: *'Society Must Be Defended': Lectures at the Collège de France, 1975–76* (David Macey tr, Picador 2023)

Fowler, William M. Jr: *Rebels under Sail: The American Navy during the Revolution* (Charles Scribner's Sons 1976)

Fraleigh, Arnold: 'The Algerian Revolution' in Richard A. Falk (ed), *The International Law of Civil War* (Johns Hopkins Press/ASIL, 1971) 179–243

Franklin, Benjamin: *Works of Benjamin Franklin*, vol V (William Duane 1809)

Friedmann, Wolfgang: *The Changing Structure of International Law* (Stevens & Sons 1964)

Friedmann, Wolfgang: 'Intervention, Civil War and the Rôle of International Law' 59 *Proceedings of the ASIL Annual Meeting* (1965) 67–81

Frowein, Jochen A.: 'Recognition' in *Max Planck Encyclopedia of Public International Law* (Oxford Public International Law 2010)

Gardina Pestana, Carla: *The English Atlantic in an Age of Revolution, 1640–1661* (Harvard University Press 2004)

Geffcken, M. H.: 'Incidents de droit international dans la guerre civile du Chili' 23 *Revue de droit international et de législation comparée* (1891) 577–589.

Gentili, Alberico: *De iure belli libri tres* ([1612] John C. Rolfe tr, Clarendon Press 1933)

Gentili, Alberico: *De legationibus libri tres* ([1585] G. J. Laing tr, Oxford University Press 1924)

Getachew, Adom: *Worldmaking after Empire: The Rise and Fall of Self-determination* (Princeton University Press 2019)

Giladi, Rotem: 'The Enactment of Irony: Reflections on the Origins of the Martens Clause' 25 *European Journal of International Law* (2014) 847–869

Giladi, Rotem: 'Francis Lieber on Public War' 4 *Göttingen Journal of International law* (2012) 447–477

Girard, Philippe: 'The Leclerc Expedition to Saint-Domingue and the Independence of Haiti, 1802–1804' (Oxford Research Encyclopedia of Latin American History, 23 May 2019) https://oxfordre.com/latinamericanhistory

Goebel, Dorothy Burne: 'British Trade to the Spanish Colonies, 1796-1823' 43 *American Historical Review* (1938) 288–320

Goebel, Julius: *The Recognition Policy of the United States* (Columbia University 1915)

Goormaghtigh, John: 'Jean Siotis, éléments pour un portrait' in Victor-Yves Ghebali and Dietrich Kappeler (eds), *Les multiples aspects des relations internationales: Études à la mémoire du Professeur Jean Siotis* (Bruylant 1995) 11–19

Grafton Wilson, George: 'Insurgency and International Maritime Law' 1 *American Journal of International Law* (1907) 46–60

Green, Philip James: *Sketches of the War in Greece* (London 1827)

Greenman, Kathryn: *State Responsibility and Rebels: The History and Legacy of Protecting Investment against Revolution* (Cambridge University Press 2021)

Griffin, Charles Carroll: *The United States and the Disruption of the Spanish Empire 1810–1822* (Octagon Books 1968)

Grotius, Hugo: *The Antiquity of the Batavian Republic* ([1610] Jan Waszink tr, Van Gorcum 2000)

Grotius, Hugo: *Commentary on the Law of Prize and Booty* [*De iure praedae commentaries*] ([1604] Gwladys L. Williams tr, Clarendon Press 1950)

Grotius, Hugo: *Commentary on the Law of Prize and Booty* (M. J. van Ittersum ed, Liberty Fund 2006)

Grotius, Hugo: *De jure belli ac pacis libri tres* ([1625] Francis Kelsey tr, Carnegie Institution 1913)

Grotius, Hugo: *De rebus belgicis, Or, The Annals and History of the Low-Countrey-Warrs* ([1657] Middle Temple 1665)

Gurmendi, Alonso: 'The Last Recognition of Belligerency (and Some Thoughts on Why You May Not Have Heard of It)' *Opinio Juris* (10 December 2019) https://opiniojuris.org/

Halleck, Henry W.: *Elements of International Law and Laws of War* (Lippincott 1866)

Halleck, Henry W.: *International Law; Or, Rules Regulating the Intercourse of States in Peace and War* (D. van Nostrand 1861)

Halstead, Murat: *The Story of the Philippines and Our New Possessions, Including the Ladrones, Hawaii, Cuba and Porto Rico* (Our Possessions 1898)

Hanke, Lewis: 'Baptis Irvine's Reports on Simón Bolívar' 16 *Hispanic American Historical Review* (1936) 360–373

Hanke, Lewis: 'Simón Bolívar and Neutral Rights' 21 *Hispanic American Historical Review* (1941) 258–291

Harcourt, Vernon ('Historicus'): *Letters by Historicus on Some Questions of International Law* (Macmillan 1863)

Harrington, Matthew P.: *Jay and Ellsworth, The First Courts: Justices, Rulings, and Legacy* (ABC-CLIO 2008)

Hart, H. L. A.: *The Concept of Law* ([1961] 2nd edn, Clarendon Press 1994)

Hart, Marjolein 't: *The Dutch Wars of Independence: Warfare and Commerce in the Netherlands 1570–1680* (Routledge 2014)

Hathaway, Oona A. and Shapiro, Scott J.: *The Internationalists: How a Radical Plan to Outlaw War Remade the World* (Allen Lane 2017)

Haworth, Paul Leland: 'Frederick the Great and the American Revolution' 9 *American Historical Review* (1904) 460–478

Head, David: *Privateers of the Americas: Spanish American Privateering from the United States in the Early Republic* (University of Georgia Press 2015)

Heffter, August Wilhelm: *Das europäische Völkerrecht der Gegenwart* (G. H. Schroeder 1867)

Hegel, G. W. F.: *Philosophy of Right* ([1820] Batoche 2001)

Hemming, Francis: *International Committee for the Application of the Agreement Regarding Non-intervention in Spain* (HMSO 1936)

Herdegen, Matthias: 'Banco de Bilbao v Sancha and Rey Case' *Max Planck Encyclopedia of Public International Law* (Oxford Public International Law 2013)

Hershey, Amos: 'The Recognition of Cuban Belligerency' 7 *Annals of the American Academy of Political and Social Sciences* (1896) 74–85

Hippler, Thomas: *Governing from the Skies: A Global History of Aerial Bombing* (Verso 2017)

Hobbes, Thomas: *Leviathan* (Andrew Crooke 1651)

Hobsbawm, Eric: *The Age of Capital 1848–1875* ([1975] Vintage 1996)

Hobsbawm, Eric: *The Age of Empire 1875–1914* (Vintage 1989)

Hobsbawm, Eric: *The Age of Revolution: Europe 1789–1848* (Weidenfeld & Nicolson 1962)

Holmes, Stephen: 'Two Concepts of Legitimacy: France after the Revolution' 10 *Political Theory* (1982) 165–183

Holsti, Kalevi J.: *Peace and War: Armed Conflicts and International Order 1648–1989* (Cambridge University Press 1991)
Howe, Samuel: *An Historical Sketch of the Greek Revolution* (New York 1828)
Hübner, Martin: *De la saisie des batimens neutres, ou Du droit qu'ont les nations belligérantes d'arrêter les navires des peuples* (2 vols, The Hague 1759)
Hughes-Wilson, John: *A Brief History of the Cold War* (Robinson 2006)
Hugo, Victor: *Les Misérables* ([1862] Bibliothèque de la Pléiade, Gallimard 2018)
Hula, Erich: 'National Self-determination Reconsidered' 10 *Social Research* (1943) 1–21
Hunter, Mark C.: *Policing the Seas: Anglo-American Relations and the Equatorial Atlantic* (Liverpool University Press 2008)
Immerwahr, Daniel: *How to Hide an Empire: A History of the Greater United States* ([2019] Vintage 2020)
Israel, Jonathan I.: *The Dutch Republic: Its Rise, Greatness and Fall, 1477–1806* (Oxford University Press 1995)
Ittersum, Martine Julia van: *Profit and Principle: Hugo Grotius, Natural Rights Theories and the Rise of Dutch Power in the East Indies (1595–1615)* (Brill 2006)
Jakjimovska, Viktorija: 'Uneasy Neutrality: Britain and the Greek War of Independence (1821–1832)' in Inge Van Hulle and Randall Lesaffer (eds), *International Law in the Long Nineteenth Century (1776–1914): From the Public Law of Europe to Global International Law?* (Brill Nijhoff 2019) 45–72
Jameson, J Franklin: 'St. Eustatius in the American Revolution' 8 *American Historical Review* (1903) 683–708
Jessup, Philip C.: 'The Spanish Rebellion and International Law' 15 *Foreign Affairs* (1937) 260–279
Jessup, Philip C. and Deák, Francis: *Neutrality, Its History, Economics and Law* (4 vols, Columbia University Press 1935)
Joachim, Benoît: 'La reconnaissance d'Haïti par la France (1825): Naissance d'un nouveau type de rapports internationaux' 22 *Revue d'histoire moderne et contemporaine* (1975) 369–396
Kari, Ville: 'Hugo Grotius and the Classical Law of Civil War' 41 *Grotiana* (2020) 412–427
Kari, Ville: 'A Less Elevated Cosmopolitanism: Victor Hugo, Francis Lieber, and the Franco-Prussian War of 1870' in Jan Klabbers, Maria Varaki, and Guilherme Vasconcelos Vilaca (eds), *Towards Responsible Global Governance* University of Helsinki 2018) 31–52
Kaufmann, William W.: *British Policy and the Independence of Latin America, 1804–1828* (Yale University Press 1951)
Kelsen, Hans: *General Theory of Law and State* (Harvard University Press 1949 [1945])
Kelsen, Hans: *Law and Peace in International Relations* (Harvard University Press 1942)

Kelsen, Hans: *Principles of International Law* (Rinehart 1952)
Kennedy, David and Koskenniemi, Martti: *Of Law and the World* (Harvard University Press 2023)
Kent, Andrew: 'The Constitution and the Laws of War during the Civil War' 85 *Notre Dame Law Review* (2010) 1839–1930
Kestell J. D. and van Velden, D. E.: *The Peace Negotiations between the Governments of the South African Republic and the Orange Free State, and the Representatives of the British Government* (Clay & Sons 1912)
Kiraly, Bela L. and Stokes, Gale (eds): *Insurrections, Wars, and the Eastern Crisis in the 1870s* (Columbia University Press 1985)
Klabbers, Jan: '(I Can't Get No) Recognition: Subjects Doctrine' in Andrea Bianchi (ed), *Non-state Actors and International Law* (Ashgate 2009) 351–369
Klabbers, Jan: *International Law* (Cambridge University Press 2013)
Klabbers, Jan: 'Intervention, Armed Intervention, Armed Attack, Threat to Peace, Act of Aggression, and Threat or Use of Force: What's the Difference?' in Marc Weller (ed), *The Oxford Handbook of the Use of Force in International Law* (Oxford University Press 2015) 488–506
Klabbers, Jan: 'Rebel with a Cause? Terrorists and Humanitarian Law' 14 *European Journal of International Law* (2003) 299–312
Klingberg, Frank W.: 'The Southern Claims Commission: A Postwar Agency in Operations' 32 *Mississippi Valley Historical review* (1945) 195–214
Knight, Betsy: 'Prisoner Exchange and Parole in the American Revolution' 48 *William and Mary Quarterly* (1991) 201–222
Knox, Robert and Tzouvala, Ntina: 'Looking Eastwards: The Bolshevik Theory of Imperialism and International Law' in Kathryn Greenman, Anne Orford, Anna Saunders, and Ntina Tzouvala (eds), *Revolutions in International Law: The Legacies of 1917* (Cambridge University Press 2021) 27–55
Kolla, Edward J.: *Sovereignty, International Law, and the French Revolution* (Cambridge University Press 2017)
Koskenniemi, Martti: 'Carl Schmitt and International Law' in Jens Meierhenrich and Oliver Simons (eds), *The Oxford Handbook of Carl Schmitt* (Oxford University Press 2013) 592–611
Koskenniemi, Martti: *From Apology to Utopia: The Structure of International Legal Argument* ([1989] Cambridge University Press 2005)
Koskenniemi, Martti: *The Gentle Civilizer of Nations* (Cambridge University Press 2001)
Koskenniemi, Martti: 'International Law and Imperialism' in David Freestone (ed), *Contemporary Issues in International Law: A Collection of the Josephine Onoh Memorial Lectures* (Brill 2002) 197–218
Koskenniemi, Martti: 'The Lady Doth Protest Too Much: Kosovo, and the Turn to Ethics in International Law' 65 *Modern Law Review* (2002) 159–175

Koskenniemi, Martti: *To the Uttermost Parts of the Earth* (Cambridge University Press 2021)

Koskenniemi, Martti: 'A Trap for the Innocent …' in Claus Kreß and Stefan Barriga (eds), *The Crime of Aggression: A Commentary* (Cambridge University Press 2016) 1359–1385

Koskenniemi, Martti and Kari, Ville: 'A More Elevated Patriotism: The Emergence of International and Comparative Law (Nineteenth Century)' in H. Pihlajamäki, M. Dubber, and D. Godfrey (eds), *The Oxford Handbook of European Legal History* (Oxford University Press 2018) 974–999

Kotzsch, Lothar: *The Concept of War in Contemporary History and International Law* (E. Droz 1956)

Kunz, Hugo: *Der Bürgerkrieg in Chile* (Brockhaus 1892)

Lauterpacht, Hersch: *The Function of Law in the International Community* ([1933] Oxford University Press 2011)

Lauterpacht, Hersch: *Recognition in International Law* (Oxford University Press 1947)

Lauterpacht, Hersch: 'Recognition of Insurgents as a De Facto Government' 3 *Modern Law Review* (1939) 1–20

Le Fur, Louis: 'Chronique des faits internationaux: Espagne et États-Unis' 6 *Revue générale de droit international public* (1899) 196–229

Le Fur, Louis: *La guerre d'Espagne et le droit* (Les Éditions Internationales 1938)

Le Fur, Louis: 'La guerre d'Espagne et le droit' 11(20) *Revue de droit international* (1937) 347–369 (pt I), 12(21) *Revue de droit international* (1938) 53–100 (pt II)

Le Normand, René: *La reconnaissance internationale et ses diverses applications* (Imprimerie Camis 1899)

Lehr, Ernest: 'Question de la reconnaissance des insurgés comme belligérants, suivant un mémoire récent de M. le Marquis d'Olivart' 28 *Revue de droit international et de législation comparée* (1896) 100–103

Leiter, Andrea: 'Contestations over Legal Authority: The Lena Goldfields Arbitration 1930' in Kathryn Greenman, Anne Orford, Anna Saunders, and Ntina Tzouvala (eds), *Revolutions in International Law: The Legacies of 1917* (Cambridge University Press 2021) 315–338

Leiter, Andrea: *Making the World Safe for Investment: The Protection of Foreign Property 1922–1959* (Cambridge University Press 2023)

Lemnitzer, Jan Martin: *Power, Law and the End of Privateering* (Palgrave MacMillan 2014)

Lesaffer, Randall: 'The Classical Law of Nations' in Alexander Orakhelashvili (ed), *Research Handbook on the Theory and History of International Law* (2nd edn, Edward Elgar 2020) 326–358

Lesaffer, Randall: 'Peace Treaties and the Formation of International Law' in Bardo Fassbender and Anne Peters (eds) *The Oxford Handbook of the History of International Law* (Oxford University Press 2012) 71–94

Lieber, Francis: *Guerrilla Parties Considered with Reference to the Laws and Usages of War* (D. Van Dostrand 1862)

Lieber, Francis: 'Lecture by Dr. Francis Lieber on the Laws and Usages of War – No. 1' *New York Times* (27 October 1861)

Lieblich, Eliav: *International Law and Civil Wars: Intervention and Consent* (Routledge 2013)

Lillich, Richard B.: 'The Jay Treaty Commissions' 37 *St. John's Law Review* (1963) 260–283

Locke, John: *Two Treatises of Government* ([1690] Yale University Press 2003)

Lokke, Carl Ludwig: 'The Leclerc Instructions' in 10 *Journal of Negro History* (1925) 80–98

Lorimer, James: 'La doctrine de la reconnaissance, fondement du droit international' 16 *Revue de droit international et de législation comparée* (1884) 333–359

Lorimer, James: *The Institutes of the Law of Nations: A Treatise of the Jural Relations of Separate Political Communities* (Blackwood and Sons 1883)

Loveman, Brian: *No Higher Law: American Foreign Policy and the Western Hemisphere since 1776* (University of North Carolina Press 2010)

Mälksoo, Lauri: 'The Soviet Approach to the Right of Peoples to Self-determination: Russia's Farewell to *jus publicum europaeum*' 19 *Journal of the History of International Law* (2017) 200–218

Maloy Anderson, Frank: *The Constitutions and Other Select Documents Illustrative of the History of France 1789–1907* (2nd edn, Wilson 1908)

Marriott, James: *The Case of the Dutch Ships, Considered* (R. and J. Dodsley 1758)

Marriott, James: *Mémoire justificatif de la conduite de la Grande Bretagne en arrêtant les navires étrangers et les munitions de guerre destinées aux insurgens de l'Amérique* ([1778] B. Rickerstaff 1801)

Marx, Karl and Engels, Friedrich: *The Manifesto of the Communist Party* ([1848, *Manifest der Kommunistischen Partei*]; Samuel Moore tr (1888), Progress (Moscow) 1971, revised edn 1977)

McCarthy, Matthew: *Privateering, Piracy and British Policy in Spanish America 1810–1830* (Boydell Press 2013)

McCullough, Stephen: *The Caribbean Policy of the Ulysses S. Grant Administration: Foreshadowing an Informal Empire* (Lexington Books 2017)

McDougal, Myres S.: 'The Hydrogen Bomb Tests and the International Law of the Sea' 49 *American Journal of International Law* (1955) 356–361

McDougal, Myres S. and others: *Studies in World Public Order* ([1960] New Haven Press 1987)

McNair, Arnold: 'The Law Relating to the Civil War in Spain' 53 *Law Quarterly Review* (1937) 471–500

McPherson, James: *War on the Waters: The Union and Confederate Navies, 1861–1865* (University of North Carolina Press 2012)

Merkin, Rob: *Marine Insurance: A Legal History* (Edward Elgar 2014)

Metternich, Prince Klemens Lothar Wenzel von: *Memoirs of Prince Metternich* (Mrs Alexander Napier tr, Richard Bentley & Son)

Miles, Kate: '1917: Property, Revolution and Rejection' in Kathryn Greenman, Anne Orford, Anna Saunders, and Ntina Tzouvala (eds), *Revolutions in International Law: The Legacies of 1917* (Cambridge University Press 2021) 271–290

Mill, John Stuart: *The Contest in America* (Little, Brown 1862)

Moir, Lindsay: *The Law of Internal Armed Conflict* (Cambridge University Press 2002)

Moore, John Norton (ed): *Law and Civil War in the Modern World* (Johns Hopkins University Press 1974)

Morgan, J. T.: *Belligerent Rights for Cuba* (Washington 1897)

Morison, Samuel Eliot: *Sources and Documents Illustrating the American Revolution 1764–1788* (2nd edn, Oxford University Press 1965)

Mulder, Nicholas and van Dijk, Boyd: 'Why Did Starvation Not Become the Paradigmatic War Crime in International Law?' in Ingo Venzke and Kevin Jon Heller (eds), *Contingency in International Law* (Oxford University Press 2021)

Murphy, D. F.: *The Jeff Davis Piracy Cases: Full Report of the Trial of William Smith for Piracy as One of the Crew of the Confederate Privateer the Jeff Davis* (King & Baird, 1861)

Neff, Stephen C.: *Justice in Blue and Gray: A Legal History of the Civil War* (Harvard University Press 2010)

Neff, Stephen C.: *Rights and Duties of Neutrals* (Manchester University Press, 2000)

Neff, Stephen C.: *War and the Law of Nations: A General History* (Cambridge University Press 2005)

Nettles, H. Edward: 'The Drago Doctrine in International Law and Politics' 8 *Hispanic American Historical Review* (1928) 204–223

Nicoletti, Cynthia: *Secession on Trial: The Treason Prosecution of Jefferson Davis* (Cambridge University Press 2017)

Nissel, Tzvika Alan: 'A History of State Responsibility: The Struggle for International Standards (1870–1960)' (LLD thesis, University of Helsinki 2016)

Nissel, Tzvika Alan: *Merchants of Legalism: A History of State Responsibility (1870–1960)* (Cambridge University Press 2024)

Offner, John L: An Unwanted War: The Diplomacy of the United States and Spain over Cuba, 1895–1898 (University of North Carolina Press, 1992)

Oglesby, Roscoe R.: *Internal War and the Search for Normative Order* (Martinus Nijhoff 1971)

Olivart, Marquis Ramón de Dalmau y de: *Del reconocimiento de beligerancia y sus efectos inmediatos* (Tipolitografía de L. Péant é Hijos 1895)

Olivart, Marquis Ramón de Dalmau y de: 'Le différend entre l'Espagne et les États-Unis au sujet de la question cubaine' (7 parts): 4 *Revue générale de droit international public* (1897) 577; 5 RGDIP (1898) 358; 5 RGDIP (1898) 499; 7 RGDIP (1900) 541; 9 RGDIP (1902) 161; 10 RGDIP (1903) 577; 12 RGDIP (1905) 469

Oppenheim, Lassa: *International Law* (2 vols, 2nd edn, Longmans, Green 1912)

Orford, Anne: *International Authority and the Responsibility to Protect* (Cambridge University Press 2011)

Orford, Anne: *International Law and the Politics of History* (Cambridge University Press 2021)

O'Rourke, Vernon: 'Recognition of Belligerency and the Spanish War' 31 *American Journal of International Law* (1937) 398–413

Orr, Alan: 'The Juristic Foundation of Regicide' in Jason Peacey (ed), *The Regicides and the Execution of Charles I* (Palgrave 2001) 117–137

Otis, James: *The Rights of the British Colonies Asserted and Proved* (Boston, New England 1764)

Padelford, Norman J.: *International Law and Diplomacy in the Spanish Civil Strife* (Macmillan 1939)

Padelford, Norman: 'International Law and Insurgency' 37 *Die Friedens-Warte* (1937) 191–193

Pahuja, Sundhya: *Decolonising International Law: Development, Economic Growth and the Politics of Universality* (Cambridge University Press 2011)

Pares, Richard: *Colonial Blockade and Neutral Rights, 1739–1763* (Clarendon Press 1938)

Pares, Richard: *War and Trade in the West Indies, 1739–1763* ([1936] Frank Cass 1963)

Pedersen, Susan: *The Guardians: The League of Nations and the Crisis of Empire* (Oxford University Press 2015)

Perl-Rosenthal, Nathan: *Citizen Sailors: Becoming American in the Age of Revolution* (Harvard University Press 2015)

Perry, Thomas (ed): *The Life and Letters of Francis Lieber* (Osgood 1882)

Piggott, Francis: *The Freedom of the Seas Historically Treated* (HMSO 1920)

Piggott, Francis and Omond, G. W. T.: *Documentary History of the Armed Neutralities 1780 and 1800* (University of London Press 1919)

Pinto, Roger: 'Les règles du droit international concernant la guerre civile' 114 *Collected Courses of Hague Academy of International Law* (1965) 455–548

Planck, Max: *Scientific Autobiography and Other Papers* ([1948] Philosophical Library 1949)

Podestá Costa, Luis A.: *El extranjero en la guerra civil* (De Coni 1913)

Podestá Costa, Luis A.: *Ensayo sobre las luchas civiles y el derecho internacional* (Rezzónico 1926)

Politis, Nicolas: *Neutrality and Peace* (Francis C. Macken tr, Carnegie Endowment for International Peace 1935)

Popkin, Jeremy D.: *A Concise History of the Haitian Revolution* (Wiley-Blackwell 2012)

Powell, J. R. (ed): *The Letters of Robert Blake together with Supplementary Documents* (Navy Records Society 1937)

Pradier-Fodéré, Paul: *Traité de droit international public européen et américain* (8 vols, Durand et Pedone 1885–1906)

Prelinger, Catherine M.: 'Benjamin Franklin and the American Prisoners of War in England during the American Revolution' 32 *William and Mary Quarterly* (1975) 261–294

Provost, René: *Rebel Courts: The Administration of Justice by Armed Insurgents* (Oxford University Press 2021)

Pufendorf, Samuel: *De jure naturae et gentium libri octo* ([1688] C. H. Oldfather tr, Clarendon Press 1934)

Quisenberry, A. C.: 'Kentucky's "Neutrality" in 1861' 15 *Register of Kentucky State Historical Society* (1917) 9–21

Ræstad, Arnold: 'Guerre civile et droit international' 19 *Revue de droit international et de législation comparée* (1938) 601–637 (pt I), 19 *Revue de droit international et de législation comparée* (1938) 809–826 (pt II)

Ralston, Jackson H. and Doyle, W. T. Sherman (eds): *Venezuelan Arbitrations of 1903, Including Protocols, Personnel and Rules of Commissions, Opinions, and Summary of Awards, With Appendix, &c.* (US Government Printing Office 1904)

Randall, James G.: *Constitutional Problems under Lincoln* (2nd edn, University of Illinois Press 1951)

Rasilla del Moral, Ignacio de la: *In the Shadow of Vitoria: A History of International Law in Spain (1770–1953)* (Brill 2017)

Ravina, Mark: *To Stand with the Nations of the World: Japan's Meiji Restoration in World History* (Oxford University Press 2017)

Rech, Walter: *Enemies of Mankind: Vattel's Theory of Collective Security* (Martinus Nijhoff 2013)

Reuter, Paul: *Étude de la règle: 'Toute prise doit être jugée'* (Les Éditions Internationales 1933)

Ritsema, Alex: *Pirates and Privateers from the Low Countries, c. 1500–c. 1810* (Alex Ritsema 2008)

Robertson, William S.: 'Metternich's Attitude toward Revolutions in Latin America' 21 *Hispanic American Historical Review* (1941) 538–558

Robertson, William S.: 'The Recognition of the Spanish Colonies by the Motherland' 1 *Hispanic American Historical Review* (1918) 70–91

Robertson, William S.: 'The United States and Spain in 1822' 20 *American Historical Review* (1915) 781–800

Robinson, William Morrison Jr: *The Confederate Privateers* (Yale University Press 1928)

Rodríguez, Jaime E.: *The Independence of Spanish America* (Cambridge University Press 1998)

Rolin-Jaequemyns, Gustave: 'Moyens pacifiques de régler les difficultés pendantes' 1 *Revue de droit international et de législation comparée* (1869) 153–154

Rolin-Jaequemyns, Gustave: 'Rejet par le Sénat Américain du traité Clarendon-Johnson pour le règlement des réclamations Anglo-Américaines' 1 *Revue de droit international et de législation comparée* (1869) 449–456

Rosenau, James N. (ed): *International Aspects of Civil Strife* (Princeton University Press 1964)

Rougier, Antoine: 'La théorie de l'intervention d'humanité' 17 *Revue générale de droit international public* (1910) 468–526

Rougier, Antoine: *Les guerres civiles et le droit des gens* (Larose 1903)

Rutherford, Thomas: *Institutes of Natural Law; Being the Substance of a Course of Lectures on Grotius de Jure Belli et Pacis* ([J. Bentham 1756] 2nd American edn, William and Joseph Neal 1832)

Sadoul, Paul: *De la guerre civile en droit des gens: Reconnaissance de belligérance* (Imprimerie Paul Scheffer 1905)

Sainlaude, Stève: *France and the American Civil War: A Diplomatic History* (University of North Carolina Press 2019)

Sarkees, Meredith Reid and Wayman, Frank Wheylon: *Resort to War: A Data Guide to Inter-State, Extra-State, Intra-State, and Non-state Wars, 1816–2007* (CQ Press 2010)

Scarfi, Juan Pablo: *The Hidden History of International Law in the Americas: Empire and Legal Networks* (Oxford University Press 2017)

Scelle, Georges: 'La guerre civile espagnole et le droit des gens' 45 *Revue générale de droit international public* (1938) 265–301 (pt I), 46 RGDIP (1939) 197–228 (pt II)

Scelle, Georges: 'La reconnaissance des insurgés et la guerre espagnole' 37 *Die Friedens-Warte* (1937) 65–70

Scelle, Georges: *Précis de droit des gens*, vol I: *Principes et systématique* ([Sirey 1932] Dalloz 2008)

Scelle, Georges: *Précis du droit des gens*, vol II (Sirey 1934)

Scharf, J. Thomas: *History of the Confederate States Navy from Its Organization to the Surrender of Its Last Vessel* (Rogers & Sherwood 1887)

Schindler, Dietrich: 'J. C. Bluntschli's Contribution to the Law of War' in Marcelo G. Kohen (ed), *Promoting Justice, Human Rights and Conflict Resolution through International Law: Liber Amicorum Lucius Caflisch* (Martinus Nijhoff 2007) 437–454

Schlögel, A.: 'La guerre civile' 52 *Revue internationale de la Croix-Rouge* (1970) 137–148

Schlüter, Ferdinand: *De-facto Anerkennung im Völkerrecht* (Verlag Konrad Triltsch 1936)

Schmitt, Carl: *The Nomos of the Earth* ([1950] G. K. Ulmen tr, Telos Press 2006)

Schmitt, Carl: 'The Turn to the Discriminating Concept of War (1937)' in *Writings on War* (T. Nunan ed, Polity Press 2011) 30–74

Schrijver, Nico: *Sovereignty over Natural Resources: Balancing Rights and Duties* (Cambridge University Press 1997)

Scott, Eva: *Rupert, Prince Palatine* (Putnam's Sons 1899)

Scott, James Brown: *The Controversy over Neutral Rights between the United States and France 1797–1800* (Oxford University Press 1917)

Scott, James Brown: 'The Sixth Pan-American Conference' 22 *American Journal of International Law* (1928) 351–362

Scott, James Brown (ed): *The Armed Neutralities of 1780 and 1800* (Oxford University Press 1918)

Scott, James Brown (ed): *The International Conferences of American States 1889–1928* (Oxford University Press 1931)

Scott, James Brown (ed): *Resolutions of the Institute of International Law* (William S. Hein 1916)

Semmes, Raphael: *The Cruise of the Alabama and the Sumter* (Saunders, Otley 1864)

Sexton, Jay: *The Monroe Doctrine: Empire and Nation in Nineteenth-Century America* (Hill and Wang 2011)

Siotis, Jean: *Le droit de la guerre et les conflits armés d'un caractère non-international* (LGDJ 1958)

Sivakumaran, Sandesh: *The Law of Non-international Armed Conflict* (Oxford University Press 2012)

Skinner, Quentin: 'Conquest and Consent: Hobbes and the Engagement Controversy' in *Visions of Politics*, vol 3: *Hobbes and Civil Science* (Cambridge University Press 2002) 287–307

Smith, H. A.: 'Some Problems of the Spanish Civil War' 18 *British Yearbook of International Law* (1937) 17–31

Smith, Joseph: 'Brazilian Diplomacy and Foreign Intervention in the Brazilian Naval Revolt, 1893–94' 26 *Revista Complutense de Historia de América* (2000) 117–134

Sparks, Jared (ed): *The Writings of George Washington*, vol III (Harper & Brothers 1847)

Stéfanesco, L. N.: *La guerre civile et les rapports des belligérants* (LNDJ 1903)

Stimson, Henry L.: 'The Pact of Paris: Three Years of Development' 11 *Foreign Affairs Special Supplement* (1932) vii–xv

Stråth, Bo: *Europe's Utopias of Peace: 1815, 1919, 1951* (Bloomsbury 2016)

Sumner, Charles: *The Complete Works of Charles Sumner* (Lee and Shepard 1872)

Takahashi, Sakuyé: *Cases on International Law during the Chino-Japanese War* (Cambridge University Press 1899)

Talleyrand-Périgord, Charles Maurice de: *Memoirs of the Prince de Talleyrand*, vol II (G. P. Putnam's Sons 1891)

Thomas, Ann Van Wynen and Thomas, A. J. Jr: 'International Legal Aspects of the Civil War in Spain, 1936–39' in Richard A. Falk (ed), *The International Law of Civil War* (Johns Hopkins Press/ASIL 1971) 111–178

Thomas, Hugh: *The Spanish Civil War* (3rd edn, Penguin 1977)

Toynbee, Arnold J. and Boulter, V. M.: *Survey of International Affairs 1937*, vol II: *Spain* (Oxford University Press 1938)

Tröster, Manuel: 'Roman Hegemony and Non-state Violence: A Fresh Look at Pompey's Campaign against the Pirates' 56 *Greece & Rome* (2009) 14–33

Tuchman, Barbara: *The First Salute: A View of the American Revolution* (Ballantine Books 1988)

Ubbelohde, Carl: *The Vice-Admiralty Courts and the American Revolution* (University of North Carolina Press 1960)

Ulloa, Alberto: 'Wiesse, internacionalista' 1 *Nueva Revista Peruana* (1929) 322–335

Unger, Harlow Giles: *Lafayette* (Wiley 2003)

Vale, Brian: *Cochrane in the Pacific: Future and Freedom in Spanish America* (I. B Tauris 2008)

Valin, René-Josué: *Traité des prises, ou Principes de la jurisprudence françoise concernant les prises qui se font sur mer* (Jérôme Légier 1763)

Vastey, Baron de: *An Essay on the Causes of the Revolution and Civil Wars of Hayti* (Western Luminary Office 1823)

Vattel, Emer de: *The Law of Nations, Or the Principles of Natural Law Applied to the Conduct and to the Affairs of Nations and of Sovereigns* ([1758] Charles G. Fenwick tr, Carnegie Institution of Washington 1916)

Veatch, Richard: 'The League of Nations and the Spanish Civil War, 1936–9' 20 *European History Quarterly* (1990) 181–207

Veçoso, Fabia Fernandes Carvalho: 'Mexican Post-Revolutionary Foreign Policy and the Spanish Civil War' in Kathryn Greenman, Anne Orford, Anna Saunders, and Ntina Tzouvala (eds), *Revolutions in International Law: The Legacies of 1917* (Cambridge University Press 2021) 242–267

Verzijl, J. H. W., Heere, W. P., and Offerhaus, J. P. S.: *International Law in Historical Perspective*, pt IX-C: *The Law of Maritime Prize* (Martinus Nijhoff 1992)

Vitoria, Francisco de: *De indis et de ivre belli relectiones* (Ernest Nys ed, John Pawley Bate tr, Carnegie Institution 1917)

Vivian, James F.: 'The *Paloma* Claim in the United States and Venezuelan-Colombian Relations, 1818–1826' 14 *Caribbean Studies* (1975) 57–72

Waddell, D. A. G.: 'British Neutrality and Spanish-American Independence: The Problem of Foreign Enlistment' 19 *Journal of Latin American Studies* (1987) 1–18

Warburton, A. F.: *Trial of the Officers and Crew of the Privateer Savannah on the Charge of Piracy in the United States Circuit Court for the Southern District of New York* (Baker & Goodwin 1862)

Ward, A. W. and others (eds): *The Cambridge Modern History*, vol IV (Macmillan 1907)

Wehberg, Hans: 'Civil War and International Law' in William E. Rappard and others, *The World Crisis* (Graduate Institute/Longmans, Green 1938) 160–199

Wehberg, Hans: 'La guerre civile et le droit international' 63 *Collected Courses of Hague Academy of International Law* (1938) 1–127

Wehberg, Hans: 'Jean Siotis, Le droit de la guerre et les conflits armés d'un caractère non-international' 54 *Die Friedens-Warte* (1958) 368–369

Wehberg, Hans: *The Outlawry of War* ([1928] Carnegie Endowment for International Peace 1931)

Wehberg, Hans: *The Problem of an International Court of Justice* ([1912] Charles G. Fenwick tr, Clarendon Press 1918)

Weiler, Joseph: 'Cancelling Carl Schmitt?' *EJIL: Talk!* (13 August 2021) https://www.ejiltalk.org/

Wentker, Alexander: *Party Status to Armed Conflict in International Law* (Oxford University Press 2024)

Westlake, John: *The Transvaal War: A Lecture Delivered in the University of Cambridge on 9th November 1899* (C. J. Clay and Sons 1899)

Wharton, Francis: 'Insurgents as Belligerents' 33 *Albany Law Journal* (1886) 125–131

Wheaton, Henry: *Elements of International Law* (1st edn, B. Fellowes 1836)

Wheaton, Henry: *Elements of International Law* (7th edn, William Beach Lawrence ed, Little, Brown 1863)

Wheaton, Henry: *Elements of International Law* ([1866] 8th edn, Richard Dana ed, Clarendon Press 1936)

Whitaker, Arthur Preston: *The United States and the Independence of Latin America, 1800–1830* (Johns Hopkins Press 1941)

Whitman, James Q.: *The Verdict of Battle: The Law of Victory and the Making of Modern War* (Harvard University Press 2012)

Wiesse, Carlos: *El asunto de Tacna y Arica; primera conferencia histórico-geográfica sobre las negociaciones diplomáticas entre el Perú y Chile de 1887 a 1894* (Imprenta Torres Aguirre 1905)

Wiesse, Carlos: *Le droit international appliqué aux guerres civiles* (B. Benda 1898)

Wiesse, Carlos: *Reglas de Derecho Internactional aplicable a las guerras civiles* (Viuda Galland 1893)

Wijffels, Alain: 'Sir Julius Caesar' in *Oxford Dictionary of National Biography* (Oxford University Press 2008)

Wilson, Andrew: *The 'Ever-Victorious Army': A History of the Chinese Campaign under Lt.-Col. C.G. Gordon and of the Suppression of the Tai-ping Rebellion* (Blackwood and Sons 1868)

Witt, John Fabian: *Lincoln's Code: The Laws of War in American History* (Free Press 2013)

Wolff, Christian: *Jus gentium methodo scientifica pertractatum* ([1749] J. H. Drake tr, Clarendon Press 1934)

Wolff, Christian: *Jus naturae methodo scientifica pertractatum, Pars octava, sive ultima* (Magdeburg 1748)

Wood, Gordon S. (ed): *John Adams: Revolutionary Writings 1775–1775* (Library of America 2011)

Zorgbibe, Charles: *La guerre civile* (Presses universitaires de France 1975)

INDEX

CAMBRIDGE STUDIES IN INTERNATIONAL AND COMPARATIVE LAW

Books in the Series

196 *The Classical Doctrine of Civil War in International Law*
Ville Kari

195 *Adjudicating over Anarchy: Judicial Remedies, Compliance, and Enforcement in International Law*
Geraldo Vidigal

194 *Regional Trade Agreements, Prosperity and the Global South: Normative Beliefs and Interests*
Yenkong Ngangjoh Hodu and Collins Chikodili Ajibo

193 *A Theory of International Organizations in Public International Law*
Orfeas Chasapis Tassinis

192 *The Individual in the Law and Practice of the International Court of Justice*
Yusra Suedi

191 *Ghosts of International Law: The Figure of the Foreign Fighter in a Cultural Perspective*
Alberto Rinaldi

190 *Merchants of Legalism: A History of State Responsibility (1870-1960)*
Alan Tzvika Nissel

189 *The Functions of International Adjudication and International Environmental Litigation*
Joshua Paine

188 *Demystifying Treaty Interpretation*
Andrea Bianchi and Fuad Zarbiyev

187 *International Law-Making by the International Court of Justice and International Law Commission: Partnership for Purpose in a Decentralized Legal Order*
Omri Sender

186 *The Rebirth of Territory*
Gail Lythgoe

185 *Reimagining Sustainable Development in International Law: Perspectives from African Legal Cosmologies*
Godwin Eli Kwadzo Dzah

184 *Collective Self-Defence in International Law*
James A. Green

183 *Weaponising Evidence: A History of Tobacco Control in International Law*
Margherita Melillo

182 *The Justice Factory: Management Practices at the International Criminal Court*
Richard Clements

181 *A Communitarian Theory of WTO Law*
Chi Carmody

180 *Drones and International Law: A Techno-Legal Machinery*
Rebecca Mignot-Mahdavi

179 *The Necessity of Nature: God, Science and Money in 17th Century English Law of Nature*
Mónica García-Salmones

178 *Making the World Safe for Investment: The Protection of Foreign Property 1922–1959*
Andrea Leiter

177 *National Governance and Investment Treaties*
Josef Ostřanský and Facundo Pérez Aznar

176 *Who Owns Outer Space? International Law, Astrophysics, and the Sustainable Development of Space*
Michael Byers and Aaron Boley

175 *Intervening in International Justice: Third States before Courts and Tribunals*
Brian McGarry

174 *Reciprocity in Public International Law*
Arianna Whelan

173 *When Environmental Protection and Human Rights Collide*
Marie-Catherine Petersmann

172 *The International Law of Sovereign Debt Dispute Settlement*
Kei Nakajima

171 *The Everyday Makers of International Law: From Great Halls to Back Rooms*
Tommaso Soave

170 *Virtue in Global Governance: Judgment and Discretion*
Jan Klabbers

169 *The Effects of Armed Conflict on Investment Treaties*
Tobias Ackermann

168 *Investment Law's Alibis: Colonialism, Imperialism, Debt and Development*
David Schneiderman

167 *Negative Comparative Law: A Strong Programme for Weak Thought*
Pierre Legrand

166 *Detention by Non-State Armed Groups under International Law*
Ezequiel Heffes

165 *Rebellions and Civil Wars: State Responsibility for the Conduct of Insurgents*
Patrick Dumberry

164 *The International Law of Energy*
Jorge Viñuales

163 *The Three Ages of International Commercial Arbitration*
Mikaël Schinazi

162 *Repetition and International Law*
Wouter Werner

161 *State Responsibility and Rebels: The History and Legacy of Protecting Investment Against Revolution*
Kathryn Greenman

160 *Rewriting Histories of the Use of Force: The Narrative of 'Indifference'*
Agatha Verdebout

159 *The League of Nations and the Protection of the Environment*
Omer Aloni

158 *International Investment Law and Legal Theory: Expropriation and the Fragmentation of Sources*
Jörg Kammerhofer

157 *Legal Barbarians: Identity, Modern Comparative Law and the Global South*
Daniel Bonilla Maldonado

156 *International Human Rights Law Beyond State Territorial Control*
Antal Berkes

155 *The Crime of Aggression under the Rome Statute of the International Criminal Court*
Carrie McDougall

154 *Minorities and the Making of Postcolonial States in International Law*
Mohammad Shahabuddin

153 *Preclassical Conflict of Laws*
Nikitas E. Hatzimihail

152 *International Law and History: Modern Interfaces*
Ignacio de la Rasilla

151 *Marketing Global Justice: The Political Economy of International Criminal Law*
Christine Schwöbel-Patel

150 *International Status in the Shadow of Empire*
Cait Storr

149 *Treaties in Motion: The Evolution of Treaties from Formation to Termination*
Edited by Malgosia Fitzmaurice and Panos Merkouris

148 *Humanitarian Disarmament: An Historical Enquiry*
Treasa Dunworth

147 *Complementarity, Catalysts, Compliance: The International Criminal Court in Uganda, Kenya, and the Democratic Republic of Congo*
Christian M. De Vos

146 *Cyber Operations and International Law*
François Delerue

145 *Comparative Reasoning in International Courts and Tribunals*
Daniel Peat

144 *Maritime Delimitation as a Judicial Process*
Massimo Lando

143 *Prosecuting Sexual and Gender-Based Crimes at the International Criminal Court: Practice, Progress and Potential*
Rosemary Grey

142 *Capitalism As Civilisation: A History of International Law*
Ntina Tzouvala

141 *Sovereignty in China: A Genealogy of a Concept Since 1840*
Adele Carrai

140 *Narratives of Hunger in International Law: Feeding the World in Times of Climate Change*
Anne Saab

139 *Victim Reparation under the Ius Post Bellum: An Historical and Normative Perspective*
Shavana Musa

138 *The Analogy between States and International Organizations*
Fernando Lusa Bordin

137 *The Process of International Legal Reproduction: Inequality, Historiography, Resistance*
Rose Parfitt

136 *State Responsibility for Breaches of Investment Contracts*
Jean Ho

135 *Coalitions of the Willing and International Law: The Interplay between Formality and Informality*
Alejandro Rodiles

134 *Self-Determination in Disputed Colonial Territories*
Jamie Trinidad

133 *International Law as a Belief System*
Jean d'Aspremont

132 *Legal Consequences of Peremptory Norms in International Law*
Daniel Costelloe

131 *Third-Party Countermeasures in International Law*
Martin Dawidowicz

130 *Justification and Excuse in International Law: Concept and Theory of General Defences*
Federica Paddeu

129 *Exclusion from Public Space: A Comparative Constitutional Analysis*
Daniel Moeckli

128 *Provisional Measures before International Courts and Tribunals*
Cameron A. Miles

127 *Humanity at Sea: Maritime Migration and the Foundations of International Law*
Itamar Mann

126 *Beyond Human Rights: The Legal Status of the Individual in International Law*
Anne Peters

125 *The Doctrine of Odious Debt in International Law: A Restatement*
Jeff King

124 *Static and Evolutive Treaty Interpretation: A Functional Reconstruction*
Christian Djeffal

123 *Civil Liability in Europe for Terrorism-Related Risk*
Lucas Bergkamp, Michael Faure, Monika Hinteregger and Niels Philipsen

122 *Proportionality and Deference in Investor-State Arbitration: Balancing Investment Protection and Regulatory Autonomy*
Caroline Henckels

121 *International Law and Governance of Natural Resources in Conflict and Post-Conflict Situations*
Daniëlla Dam-de Jong

120 *Proof of Causation in Tort Law*
Sandy Steel

119 *The Formation and Identification of Rules of Customary International Law in International Investment Law*
Patrick Dumberry

118 *Religious Hatred and International Law: The Prohibition of Incitement to Violence or Discrimination*
Jeroen Temperman

117 *Taking Economic, Social and Cultural Rights Seriously in International Criminal Law*
Evelyne Schmid

116 *Climate Change Litigation: Regulatory Pathways to Cleaner Energy*
Jacqueline Peel and Hari M. Osofsky

115 *Mestizo International Law: A Global Intellectual History 1842–1933*
Arnulf Becker Lorca

114 *Sugar and the Making of International Trade Law*
Michael Fakhri

113 *Strategically Created Treaty Conflicts and the Politics of International Law*
Surabhi Ranganathan

112 *Investment Treaty Arbitration As Public International Law: Procedural Aspects and Implications*
Eric De Brabandere

111 *The New Entrants Problem in International Fisheries Law*
Andrew Serdy

110 *Substantive Protection under Investment Treaties: A Legal and Economic Analysis*
Jonathan Bonnitcha

109 *Popular Governance of Post-Conflict Reconstruction: The Role of International Law*
Matthew Saul

108 *Evolution of International Environmental Regimes: The Case of Climate Change*
Simone Schiele

107 *Judges, Law and War: The Judicial Development of International Humanitarian Law*
Shane Darcy

106 *Religious Offence and Human Rights: The Implications of Defamation of Religions*
Lorenz Langer

105 *Forum Shopping in International Adjudication: The Role of Preliminary Objections*
Luiz Eduardo Salles

104 *Domestic Politics and International Human Rights Tribunals: The Problem of Compliance*
Courtney Hillebrecht

103 *International Law and the Arctic*
Michael Byers

102 *Cooperation in the Law of Transboundary Water Resources*
Christina Leb

101 *Underwater Cultural Heritage and International Law*
Sarah Dromgoole

100 *State Responsibility: The General Part*
James Crawford

99 *The Origins of International Investment Law: Empire, Environment and the Safeguarding of Capital*
Kate Miles

98 *The Crime of Aggression under the Rome Statute of the International Criminal Court*
Carrie McDougall

97 *'Crimes against Peace' and International Law*
Kirsten Sellars

96 *Non-Legality in International Law: Unruly Law*
Fleur Johns

95 *Armed Conflict and Displacement: The Protection of Refugees and Displaced Persons under International Humanitarian Law*
Mélanie Jacques

94 *Foreign Investment and the Environment in International Law*
Jorge E. Viñuales

93 *The Human Rights Treaty Obligations of Peacekeepers*
Kjetil Mujezinović Larsen

92 *Cyber Warfare and the Laws of War*
Heather Harrison Dinniss

91 *The Right to Reparation in International Law for Victims of Armed Conflict*
Christine Evans

90 *Global Public Interest in International Investment Law*
Andreas Kulick

89 *State Immunity in International Law*
Xiaodong Yang

88 *Reparations and Victim Support in the International Criminal Court*
Conor McCarthy

87 *Reducing Genocide to Law: Definition, Meaning, and the Ultimate Crime*
Payam Akhavan

86 *Decolonising International Law: Development, Economic Growth and the Politics of Universality*
Sundhya Pahuja

85 *Complicity and the Law of State Responsibility*
Helmut Philipp Aust

84 *State Control over Private Military and Security Companies in Armed Conflict*
Hannah Tonkin

83 *'Fair and Equitable Treatment' in International Investment Law*
Roland Kläger

82 *The UN and Human Rights: Who Guards the Guardians?*
Guglielmo Verdirame

81 *Sovereign Defaults before International Courts and Tribunals*
Michael Waibel

80 *Making the Law of the Sea: A Study in the Development of International Law*
James Harrison

79 *Science and the Precautionary Principle in International Courts and Tribunals: Expert Evidence, Burden of Proof and Finality*
Caroline E. Foster

78 *Transition from Illegal Regimes under International Law*
Yaël Ronen

77 *Access to Asylum: International Refugee Law and the Globalisation of Migration Control*
Thomas Gammeltoft-Hansen

76 *Trading Fish, Saving Fish: The Interaction between Regimes in International Law*
Margaret A. Young

75 *The Individual in the International Legal System: Continuity and Change in International Law*
Kate Parlett

74 *'Armed Attack' and Article 51 of the UN Charter: Evolutions in Customary Law and Practice*
Tom Ruys

73 *Theatre of the Rule of Law: Transnational Legal Intervention in Theory and Practice*
Stephen Humphreys

72 *Science and Risk Regulation in International Law*
Jacqueline Peel

71 *The Participation of States in International Organisations: The Role of Human Rights and Democracy*
Alison Duxbury

70 *Legal Personality in International Law*
Roland Portmann

69 *Vicarious Liability in Tort: A Comparative Perspective*
Paula Giliker

68 *The Public International Law Theory of Hans Kelsen: Believing in Universal Law*
Jochen von Bernstorff

67 *Legitimacy and Legality in International Law: An Interactional Account*
Jutta Brunnée and Stephen J. Toope

66 *The Concept of Non-International Armed Conflict in International Humanitarian Law*
Anthony Cullen

65 *The Principle of Legality in International and Comparative Criminal Law*
Kenneth S. Gallant

64 *The Challenge of Child Labour in International Law*
Franziska Humbert

63 *Shipping Interdiction and the Law of the Sea*
Douglas Guilfoyle

62 *International Courts and Environmental Protection*
Tim Stephens

61 *Legal Principles in WTO Disputes*
Andrew D. Mitchell

60 *War Crimes in Internal Armed Conflicts*
Eve La Haye

59 *Humanitarian Occupation*
Gregory H. Fox

58 *The International Law of Environmental Impact Assessment: Process, Substance and Integration*
Neil Craik

57 *The Law and Practice of International Territorial Administration: Versailles to Iraq and Beyond*
Carsten Stahn

56 *United Nations Sanctions and the Rule of Law*
Jeremy Matam Farrall

55 *National Law in WTO Law: Effectiveness and Good Governance in the World Trading System*
Sharif Bhuiyan

54 *Cultural Products and the World Trade Organization*
Tania Voon

53 *The Threat of Force in International Law*
Nikolas Stürchler

52 *Indigenous Rights and United Nations Standards: Self-Determination, Culture and Land*
Alexandra Xanthaki

51 *International Refugee Law and Socio-Economic Rights: Refuge from Deprivation*
Michelle Foster

50 *The Protection of Cultural Property in Armed Conflict*
Roger O'Keefe

49 *Interpretation and Revision of International Boundary Decisions*
Kaiyan Homi Kaikobad

48 *Multinationals and Corporate Social Responsibility: Limitations and Opportunities in International Law*
Jennifer A. Zerk

47 *Judiciaries within Europe: A Comparative Review*
John Bell

46 *Law in Times of Crisis: Emergency Powers in Theory and Practice*
Oren Gross and Fionnuala Ní Aoláin

45 *Vessel-Source Marine Pollution: The Law and Politics of International Regulation*
Alan Khee-Jin Tan

44 *Enforcing Obligations Erga Omnes in International Law*
Christian J. Tams

43 *Non-Governmental Organisations in International Law*
Anna-Karin Lindblom

42 *Democracy, Minorities and International Law*
Steven Wheatley

41 *Prosecuting International Crimes: Selectivity and the International Criminal Law Regime*
Robert Cryer

40 *Compensation for Personal Injury in English, German and Italian Law: A Comparative Outline*
Basil Markesinis, Michael Coester, Guido Alpa and Augustus Ullstein

39 *Dispute Settlement in the UN Convention on the Law of the Sea*
Natalie Klein

38 *The International Protection of Internally Displaced Persons*
Catherine Phuong

37 *Imperialism, Sovereignty and the Making of International Law*
Antony Anghie

36 *Principles of the Institutional Law of International Organizations*
C. F. Amerasinghe

35 *Necessity, Proportionality and the Use of Force by States*
Judith Gardam

34 *International Legal Argument in the Permanent Court of International Justice: The Rise of the International Judiciary*
Ole Spiermann

33 –

32 *Great Powers and Outlaw States: Unequal Sovereigns in the International Legal Order*
Gerry Simpson

31 *Local Remedies in International Law (second edition)*
Chittharanjan Felix Amerasinghe

30 *Reading Humanitarian Intervention: Human Rights and the Use of Force in International Law*
Anne Orford

29 *Conflict of Norms in Public International Law: How WTO Law Relates to Other Rules of International Law*
Joost Pauwelyn

28 –

27 *Transboundary Damage in International Law*
Hanqin Xue

26 –

25 *European Criminal Procedures* Edited by Mireille Delmas-Marty and J. R. Spencer

24 *Accountability of Armed Opposition Groups in International Law*
Liesbeth Zegveld

23 *Sharing Transboundary Resources: International Law and Optimal Resource Use*
Eyal Benvenisti

22 *International Human Rights and Humanitarian Law*
René Provost

21 *Remedies against International Organisations*
Karel Wellens

20 *Diversity and Self-Determination in International Law*
Karen Knop

19 *The Law of Internal Armed Conflict*
Lindsay Moir

18 *International Commercial Arbitration and African States: Practice, Participation and Institutional Development*
Amazu A. Asouzu

17 *The Enforceability of Promises in European Contract Law*
James Gordley

16 *International Law in Antiquity*
David J. Bederman

15 *Money Laundering: A New International Law Enforcement Model*
Guy Stessens

14 *Good Faith in European Contract Law*
Reinhard Zimmermann and Simon Whittaker

13 *On Civil Procedure*
J. A. Jolowicz

12 *Trusts: A Comparative Study*
Maurizio Lupoi and Simon Dix

11 *The Right to Property in Commonwealth Constitutions*
Tom Allen

10 *International Organizations before National Courts*
August Reinisch

9 *The Changing International Law of High Seas Fisheries*
Francisco Orrego Vicuña

8 *Trade and the Environment: A Comparative Study of EC and US Law*
Damien Geradin

7 *Unjust Enrichment: A Study of Private Law and Public Values*
Hanoch Dagan

6 *Religious Liberty and International Law in Europe*
Malcolm D. Evans

5 *Ethics and Authority in International Law*
Alfred P. Rubin

4 *Sovereignty over Natural Resources: Balancing Rights and Duties*
Nico Schrijver

3 *The Polar Regions and the Development of International Law*
Donald R. Rothwell

2 *Fragmentation and the International Relations of Micro-States: Self-Determination and Statehood*
Jorri C. Duursma

1 *Principles of the Institutional Law of International Organizations*
C. F. Amerasinghe

Printed in the United Kingdom by TJ Clays Ltd.